# The Politics of

# The Politics of Duplicity

*Controlling Reproduction in Ceausescu's Romania*

Gail Kligman

UNIVERSITY OF CALIFORNIA PRESS

Berkeley   Los Angeles   London

University of California Press
Berkeley and Los Angeles, California

University of California Press, Ltd.
London, England

© 1998 by
The Regents of the University of California

Library of Congress Cataloging-in-Publication Data

Kligman, Gail.
    The politics of duplicity: controlling reproduction in
Ceausescu's Romania / Gail Kligman.
        p.   cm.
    Includes bibliographical references (p.     ) and index.
    ISBN 978-0-520-21075-2 (pbk.: alk. paper)


    1. Romania—Population policy.   2. Birth control—Moral and
ethical aspects—Romania.   3. Romania—Politics and
government—1944–1989.   4. Romania—Social conditions.   I. Title.
HB3631.K58   1998
363.9'09498—dc21                                           97–49421
                                                                CIP

12  11  10  09  08
9  8  7  6  5  4  3  2

*For my mother, Dr. Beatrice Troyan,*
*obstetrician-gynecologist*

# CONTENTS

# ILLUSTRATIONS

## PHOTOGRAPHS

*following page 112*

## FIGURES

# TABLES

# ACKNOWLEDGMENTS

This book has been long in the making. Both the subject matter and its writing have been fraught with anguish. I wish to thank the following persons for their unequivocal support and assistance. My debt to them is much greater than words can possibly convey: Nick Andrews, Rita Bashaw, Jean-Claude Chesnais, Henry David, Eva Fodor, Rodica Radu, Vladimir Tismaneanu, and Katherine Verdery. In addition, I have benefited from the valuable input kindly offered by Georgiana Farnoaga, Michael Heim, Claude Karnoouh, Frances Olsen, Nancy and Al Stepan, and Stelian Tanase. Also to be thanked for their generosity are Dana Romalo Andrews; the late Mihai Botez; Isabel Ellsen; Susan Gal; Ken Jacobson; Ken and Rebecca Jowitt; Albert, Lori, and Michael Kligman; Pat Merloe; Ruth Milkman; Linda Miller; Jason Parker; Anca Oroveanu; the extended Pop family; Nancy Scheper-Hughes; Sydel Silverman; Mary Sladek; and Ivan Szelenyi. Among the others who provided valuable suggestions on the project's conceptualization and on early drafts are Dan Chirot, Murray Feshbach, Paul Rabinow, Dumitru Sandu, Stefana Steriade, and Richard Stites.

Over the years, this project has received recognition and funding from the Rockefeller Foundation; the National Council for Soviet and East European Research; the American Council of Learned Societies; the International Research and Exchanges Board; the Ratiu Chair, Georgetown University; the UCLA Academic Senate and Center for the Study of Women; and the Wenner-Gren Foundation for Anthropological Research, to which I extend special thanks.

I also wish to acknowledge my gratitude to the then Munich-based staff of Radio Free Europe's research section on Romania, and to the Romanian Embassy in Washington, D.C., for assistance at various times during the course of research and writing. I am similarly grateful to the Institute of International Studies at the University of California, Berkeley, for providing me with a stimulating environment in which the framework for this book was developed,[1] and to the University of California Press for sustained encouragement—and patience. I have enjoyed the support of Stan Holwitz and Harry Asforis in the Los Angeles office, and have benefited greatly from the creative insights of Sue Heinemann, Janet Mowery, and Nola Burger in the Berkeley office.

In Romania, more people and institutions contributed to this project than can be mentioned here. I nonetheless wish to acknowledge the assistance in particular of: the Romanian Academy of Sciences, with special thanks to Dan Ghibernea during the initial phase of research; the Institute of Sociology; the Ministry of Health, especially former minister Bogdan Marinescu, and Alin Stanescu, former general director; the Ministry of Health's Center for Statistical Calculation; the National Commission for Statistics, especially former member Vasile Ghetau and professor emeritus Vladimir Trebici; the National Adoption Committee; the Society for Contraceptive and Sex Education (SECS); archival staff at the Ministry of Defense; the Consular Section of the U.S. Embassy in Bucharest; and the U.S. Embassy staff itself, especially Christian Filostrat and Mary Jo Furgal.

Finally, I must note the contributions to this project of Smaranda Mezei, researcher at the Institute of Sociology, Bucharest. In 1990, in the optimistic spirit of the immediate post-1989 events, I engaged in a cooperative endeavor with her. Like myself, she had been working on issues related to women and the demographic policies of the Ceausescu regime, albeit from a different perspective. What started in earnest as a promising collaborative book project in 1992 came to an abrupt end in December 1994 under unfortunate circumstances.[2] Her individual contributions to this book are duly recognized throughout the notes. As I did, she collected empirical data, conducted interviews, and participated in the discussions and writing of the initial drafts of chapters 1 through 6. I made all of the final revisions and did all of the translations. Mezei has had no engagement with this project since 1994. Moreover, I have been careful to ensure, to the best of my ability, that the materials contained in these collaboratively produced chapters either represent new scholarship or have been appropriately referenced.[3] The legacies of the Ceausescu regime are many and often painful, to which this book and the process of its crafting bear witness.

# NOTE ON DIACRITICS

*Please note that the diacritics have been
omitted from all Romanian citations.*

# Introduction
## Politics, Reproduction, and Duplicity

*Freedom Triumphs and Romania Goes Pro-Choice: Romania's Pre-revolution Abortion Laws Should Serve as Warning to U.S.*
J. ROWE, *Christian Science Monitor,* JANUARY 27, 1990

*Shame about the Babies: Why Romania Has to Learn to Care.*
C. SARLER, *London Sunday Times Magazine,* JANUARY 20, 1991

*Irish Supreme Court Allows Teenager to Seek Abortion: Girl Who Had Been Raped Can Go to England for the Procedure*
G. FRANKEL, *Washington Post,* FEBRUARY 27, 1992

*U.S. Rights Group Asserts China Let Thousands of Orphans Die*
P. TYLER, *New York Times,* JANUARY 6, 1996

Headlines such as these appear regularly on the front pages of prominent newspapers around the world. In 1996, six years after dramatic and disturbing pictures of Romania's orphans were publicly circulated, the neglected orphans of China replaced them as objects of the world's sympathy and outrage. The unwanted children in these countries are in part the tangible consequences of coercive pro- and antinatalist state policies as these collide with or collude against family interests and possibilities. In China, where the one-child policy was imposed in 1979 to control population growth, this limitation on family size has prompted a variety of popular resistance strategies, including female infanticide.[1] In Nicolae Ceausescu's Romania, where abortion was banned in 1966, the state demanded that each family produce four or five children as a way of forcing population growth. As a result, illegal abortion became the primary method of fertility regulation.[2]

Illegal abortion and what is known as "abortion tourism" are widely practiced elsewhere, notably in staunchly Catholic countries such as Brazil, Italy, Ireland, and Poland, where the moral authority of the Church permeates everyday life. It is estimated that some 4,000 Irish women travel each year to England for abortions.[3] Abortion tourism became rampant in

Poland after the Catholic Church succeeded in its campaign to have abortion banned in postcommunist Poland.[4] Brazilian women are believed to have one to three abortions during their fertile years; sterilization has become a preferred method of birth control.[5] The Italian birthrate is the lowest in Europe, despite claims by approximately 84 percent of the population that they are practicing Catholics.[6] In each instance, a clear disarticulation exists between what has been preached from the political podium or the pulpit and what has happened in response to the exigencies of real life.

But this book is not about Italy, Poland, Brazil, China, Ireland, or the United States. It is explicitly concerned with the Socialist Republic of Romania under the rule of the dictator Nicolae Ceausescu. During twenty-three of the twenty-four years of Ceausescu's reign (1965–1989), the regime enforced one of the most repressive pronatalist policies known to the world. The legislative centerpiece of these policies was the strict anti-abortion law that was originally passed in 1966. These policies—which affected the lives of every adult man and woman regardless of marital or reproductive status—brought the state into intimate contact with the bodies of its citizens, and its citizens into the social organization of the state.[7] In the end, these policies contributed to what may be characterized as a national tragedy.

This book presents both an ethnography of the state—Ceausescu's Romania—and an ethnography of the politics of reproduction. An analysis of what was highly politicized demographic policy offers a provocative means through which to explore the institutionalization of social practices, such as duplicity and complicity, and of identities that together constituted the Romanian socialist state and everyday life. This critical inquiry enables us to comprehend more fully both the lived processes of social atomization and dehumanization that are legacies of the Ceausescu era, and the means by which reproductive issues become embedded in social-political agendas, both national and international in scope.

A cautionary word is in order: Around the world, the politics of reproduction are burdened with duplicitous rhetoric and practices, as the opening epigraphs attest. When reproductive legislation and policies are formulated according to abstract ideological and religious tenets rather than in consideration of actual socioeconomic factors that affect the quality of human life, the lived consequences are often tragic, particularly for women and children. Romania offers a unique case study. The comparative implications are sobering.

## AN ETHNOGRAPHY OF THE STATE

The interests of states (and nations) in social reproduction often conflict with those of women and families in the determination of biological or individual reproduction. Modern states and their citizens alike claim rights to the regulation of diverse reproductive concerns such as contraception, abortion, and adoption.[8] Hence, reproduction serves as an ideal locus through which to illuminate the complexity of formal and informal relations between states and their citizens, or noncitizens, as the case may be.[9] How are state policies institutionalized in official discourse and in bureaucratic procedures and practices? How are these policies implemented and enforced? How do such policies affect people in their daily lives—that is, how are macro-social issues of state policy and ideological control experienced in everyday life?

As the above questions suggest, the modern state is interventionist; historically, intervention has provoked diverse forms of resistance to varying kinds of constraints. The "arts of resistance" are many; often performed as mechanisms of survival, they represent characteristic reactions to institutional or individual relations of domination, hierarchy, and inequality.[10] "Beating the system," "defying authority," "conning someone," and "getting away with murder" are familiar phrases throughout the world, and likely always have been. These acts enrich people's daily lives by seeming to give them a measure of control over oppressive environments and everyday routines.[11] With respect to fertility regulation, the banning of abortion has always encountered resistance, the consequences of which nonetheless remain historically and comparatively consistent across political and religious systems.

By an ethnography of the state, I refer to an analysis of the rhetorical and institutionalized practices of the state within the public sphere and their integration into daily life. How do the supposedly objective interests of the state acquire legitimacy or become taken for granted as a natural feature of the environment? Anthropologist Derek Sayer suggests that state formation and routinization necessarily entail tacit complicity between states and their citizens, regardless of the latter's actual belief in the political legitimacy of any particular state.[12] To the extent that citizens are able to manage their daily lives in a reasonable fashion, the state will be able to function relatively unchallenged. What techniques of control are utilized to shape and discipline the body politic and public culture in the interests of the state? What are the effects of the state on the lives of its citizens? And how do people "use their local cultural logics and social relations to incorporate, revise, or resist the influence of seemingly distant political and economic forces"?[13]

Citizens are typically incorporated into states under the rubric "we, the people," who together make up nations and populations. Such inclusive social abstractions linguistically homogenize social diversity by presuming certain shared features that identify peoples as Americans, Romanians, or whomever. These shared features may be political, social, or cultural and are treated differently in different political contexts. In the United States, for example, the tolerance of diversity is a revered component of liberalism. At present, diversity is highly politicized: the homogenized rhetorical "we" has been challenged by the heterogeneous "we's," which constitute the whole. By contrast, in Ceausescu's Romania homogenization, or the eradication of social difference, was a formal political goal. Diversity was denied in the official discourse of the state, which celebrated what was termed "original democracy."

States are always given form through the actions of peoples. The objectification of the state as a legitimate entity unto itself masks what all too frequently is "the petty, the personal, the corrupt, the backstabbing, the wheeling and dealing."[14] Yet objectification rhetorically transfers the locus of human subjectivity and agency from persons to the state.[15] In the former socialist states and according to popular understanding, the state, the party, and the secret police were virtually synonymous with respect to their referent: "the power." These rhetorical devices distinguished "them" from "us," and in part legitimated acts of complicity with, and duplicity against, the state. As shall be discussed, duplicity and complicity—viewed as modes of communicative behavior—were crucial to both the endurance and the demise of the Ceausescu regime.

The embodiment of the state was accompanied by the formulation of its imaginary subjectivity. The state claimed needs and desires that had to be satisfied. As such, it represented itself as embodied, corporeal. The socialist state reconstituted itself as what Claude Lefort, the French social and political theorist, termed the "People-As-One."[16] The people's body, so to speak, was the property of the state, to be molded and developed into the socialist body politic. The state as personified being spoke incessantly about itself and exercised power in its own interests, presented as those of its citizens.[17] Through rhetorical, institutionalized, and disciplinary strategies, the state defined the parameters of the permissible, the limits of what could be tolerated.[18] It also constituted a self-serving symbolic order to which interests other than its own were to be fully subjugated. Fertility control was a critical issue around which conflicts of interest between the state and its citizens, especially women, were likely to erupt. Socialist economies were dependent on the availability of labor, or human capital, and "reproduction of the labor force" became a virtual mantra of political rhetoric. To this end, reproduction was consciously politicized, especially in Romania. Political demography, which is addressed later in this introduction, was the strategy by which the state controlled both social and biological reproduction for the "building of socialism."

## THE POLITICS OF REPRODUCTION

As feminist anthropologists Faye Ginsburg and Rayna Rapp have reminded us, "'reproduction' is a slippery concept, connoting parturition, Marxist

notions of household sustenance and constitution of a labor force, and ide-
ologies that support the continuity of social systems."[19] That reproduction
has been politicized in all societies in one way or another is hardly surprising: reproduction provides the means by which individuals and collectivi-
ties ensure their continuity, a point to which I will return momentarily.
First, it is pertinent to clarify what I mean by the politics of reproduction.
I broadly refer to the complex relations among individual, local, national,
and global interests that influence reproductive practices, public policy,
and the exercise of power. Otherwise stated, the politics of reproduction
center attention on the intersection between politics and the life cycle,
whether in terms of abortion, new reproductive technologies, international
family planning programs, eugenics, or welfare.[20]

Reproduction is fundamentally associated with identity: that of "the
nation" as the "imagined community" that the state serves and protects,
and over which it exercises authority;[21] or that of the family and the lineage—in most instances, a patrilineage—in the protection and perpetuation of itself and its name. As mentioned above, social reproduction and
biological reproduction secure the continuity of peoples in social units—
couples, families, ethnic groups, and nations. But discontinuity is also a possibility, and one that is frequently exploited for national(ist) purposes.[22]
The failure to reproduce is instrumentally claimed by political "entrepreneurs" to threaten the very existence of the family or the nation-state.

In view of the multiple interests and values attached to reproduction, it is
understandable that reproduction is highly politicized, frequently at the
expense of the concerns of individuals, especially women. It is equally understandable that individual, familial, and political interests in reproduction
differ so dramatically. The state, as in Ceausescu's Romania, may demand
that women bear children in fulfillment of their patriotic duties; or, as in
Deng's China, the state may restrict the number of children per family in an
effort to curtail population growth. International family planning organizations' fertility regulation efforts have been aimed especially at Third World
countries to bring fertility rates in line with development and economic interests.[23] Indeed, economic issues are always linked to social and biological reproduction. Cost-benefit considerations necessarily enter into individual as well as political calculations, the results of which are often at odds. To
underscore again, reproductive issues constitute a focus for contestation
within societies as well as between them.[24]

The intervention of states or governments into reproductive issues also
blurs the distinctions between public and private prerogatives. In general,
women are the most affected, although not exclusively so, by the transgres-
sion of embodied boundaries. As one Romanian woman poignantly commented, "When the state usurps the private [one's privacy], the body is un-
dressed in public." That which is most intimate—sexuality—is exposed
to public scrutiny, or, as some maintain, to voyeurism in the name of the

public good. The personal becomes political by virtue of the state's penetration into the body politic not as metaphor but as practice.

Questions about the sanctity of the body and what individuals do with their bodies point to issues of individual rights. Here, I wish to emphasize that this book is not about political struggles over reproductive rights, although I hardly mean to dismiss their significance. I strongly believe that states must protect women's right to safe abortions and that the protection of this right is fundamental. Children remain the primary responsibilities of women the world over; hence, women should have the ultimate say about the control of their reproductive lives.[25] To argue otherwise is to engage in rhetorical obfuscation. The "family values" so often invoked by anti-abortionists are an ideal to which many of the world's peoples adhere, including those who support the right to abortion. But the realization of family values is differently managed among different peoples and cultures and is complexly mediated by the variables of race, class, ethnicity, gender, and situation. Beliefs that represent social, moral, and ethical principles are frequently compromised by necessity, as illustrated by the author of a *New York Times* op-ed article who volunteered: "I'm a Republican who always believed that abortion is wrong. Then I had one."[26] By the same token, Catholic women have often resorted to abortion despite deep sentiments that abortion is wrong.

In Ceausescu's Romania, individual rights did not form part of public or private discourse.[27] The state legislated social equality and ideologically supported social rights (e.g., jobs, housing, access to medical care). The banning of abortion and the bearing of children were related to citizens' obligations to the paternalist state that "cared" for them. Individual rights were not at issue. During my extended research on abortion and Romania's pronatalist policies, neither women nor men ever expressed their thoughts or recounted their experiences in terms of rights. Conceptualization about the self is culturally contextualized and conditioned.

## CEAUSESCU'S ROMANIA
## AND THE POLITICS OF REPRODUCTION

Ceausescu's Romania presents an extreme instance of state intrusion into the bodies and lives of its citizens. It also represents "the most striking failure of a coercive public policy designed to influence reproductive behavior."[28] Banning abortion has never eradicated the practice of abortion— neither in repressive, totalizing states such as Ceausescu's Romania or Stalin's Soviet Union, nor in countries where the Catholic Church reigns supreme, such as Brazil, Italy, Ireland, or Poland. Instead, banning abortion renders the practice of abortion invisible in the public sphere and women's lives vulnerable to the physical and psychological risks that accompany illegal abortion.[29] Theological and ideological arguments against abortion promulgate abstract moral imperatives on behalf of the soul or the good of society. Ironically, whether one is discussing the dictates of the Catholic Church or of Ceausescu's regime, the body is instrumentalized as a vehicle through which "greater" goals than those of the individual are intended to be realized.[30] Here, it is worth commenting on organizational parallels between the Catholic Church and the Communist Party, both being hierarchical, male-dominated institutions seeking growth in the number of their adherents, who are to be highly disciplined in comportment.[31] Domination of the public sphere by church or state demands the selfless dedication—or sacrifice—of persons to it, rather than the self-interested practices of individuals in it as typically associated with capitalism.[32] This fundamental contradiction captures the tensions that characterize the conflicts of interest between states, churches, and their populations that pertain to reproductive politics and practices. In each case, the fact of life itself supersedes consideration of its quality, especially with respect to the mother or the child.

An analysis of the politics of reproduction—and more specifically, the banning of abortion—in Ceausescu's Romania offers a dramatic illustration of a tragic reality that is historically and comparatively consistent. At the same time, it presents a detailed excursion into the everyday workings of a totalizing regime. A focus on Ceausescu's political demographic policies serves other purposes as well. The contradictions, traumas, and opportunities that emerge from the banning of abortion are highlighted or made more explicit in nondemocratic contexts, as are international responses to them. In a neo-Stalinist state, the legitimate spaces in which citizens could seek refuge or resist the penetrating gaze of state surveillance were greatly reduced. The state's presence was maximal. To illustrate, abortion tourism was hardly an option for ordinary citizens of Ceausescu's Romania since travel abroad was highly restricted. By contrast, in postcommunist Poland, where abortion has been criminalized, abortion tourism has provided possibilities for women with the means to travel elsewhere.[33] In this respect, the Catholic Church must contend with a political economy that may not support its totalizing view of the body, nature, and sexuality.

In Romania, strict pronatalism served Ceausescu's nationalism and megalomaniacal fantasies under the aegis of the political economy of socialism.[34] Recall that reproduction of the labor force was claimed to be essential to the building of socialism. Socioeconomic hardships were distributed across the majority of the population rather than differentiated by class. By the mid-1980s, daily life had become impoverished in almost all respects. Women's circumstances were especially dire because women also bore the greatest burden of the political demographic policies. Here, it is important to underline the basic invariance of the relationship between poverty, illegal abortion, and their consequences. In hard empirical terms, poor women, regardless of race or geopolitical context, suffer the harshest effects of delegalized abortion. They are generally unable to afford safer illegal procedures performed by medical personnel or midwives, and they cannot afford to travel abroad. Hence, poor women are especially vulnerable to abortion-related complications and as a result are more likely to become maternal mortality statistics. As chapter 7 discusses, in Ceausescu's Romania, where poverty had become a general condition, the maternal mortality rate for 1989 was the highest ever recorded in Europe. Illegal abortion was the primary cause.

To be sure, analysis of Ceausescu's political demographic policies enables us to explore in detail the tragic consequences of banned abortion in Romania and also calls attention to other aspects of the politics of reproduction, notably how international interests come into play, often in unintentionally nefarious ways. In the 1970s, Ceausescu's pronatalist policies were regarded positively in the West. By the late 1980s those same policies were widely condemned.[35] In post-Ceausescu Romania, international adoption has become a highly politicized issue, which will be discussed in chapter 7. The rapid class differentiation accompanying the present postcommunist transition has affected reproductive practices in Romania at individual, local, national, and international levels. Women's reproductive lives are no longer subjected to the political demographic policies that turned women into human machines that reproduced future workers. However, many poor and single women have instead become vulnerable to market pressures to reproduce babies for foreigners. Transnational inequalities have thus emerged in the complex arena of international adoption.

Clearly, biological and social reproduction rarely prove to be as straightforward as political or religious ideals represent them. Life circumstances intervene, complicating the interrelations between what is said, what is believed, and what is done. Reconciling competing interests and pressures often draws individuals into multilayered acts of complicity and duplicity, which this ethnography of the Ceausescu regime's political demographic policies sadly affirms. Before turning to it, a cursory discussion of both demographic policy—referred to as political demography in this book—and the politics of duplicity is in order.

## Political Demography and Population Control

*The Political Executive Committee of the Central Committee of the Romanian Communist Party appeals to the entire population, to urban and village workers, to understand that to ensure normal demographic growth it is a great honor and patriotic obligation for every family and for all of our people . . . to have enduring families with many children, raised with love, and by so doing, to guarantee the vitality, youth, and vigor of the entire nation. Today, more than ever, we have the utmost obli-*

*gation to assure our* patrie *of new generations that will contribute to the flourishing of our socialist nation, to the triumph of socialism and communism in Romania.*

POLITICAL EXECUTIVE COMMITTEE
OF THE ROMANIAN COMMUNIST PARTY[36]

*In this climate of economic stability, we all celebrated the arrival of the child whose birth at the end of last year enabled our country's population to surpass the threshold of 23 million inhabitants. We are a free people and masters of our own destiny. We have a wonderful country, with a strongly developed economy, fully involved in the process of modernization.*

NICOLAE CEAUSESCU[37]

*When social power is exercised through statistics, experience is no longer a moment of awareness but an experimental practice . . . a test of the precise degree to which a given social objective has succeeded.*

T. ASAD, "ETHNOGRAPHIC REPRESENTATION,
STATISTICS, AND MODERN POWER"

During the 1960s and 1970s, international debates about population policies tended to reflect two divergent, if rhetorically reconcilable, geopolitical perspectives: the promotion of family planning (in the interest of regulating what was presented as the population explosion), and the right of each state to determine the population policies most suited to its national interests. The former position was generally endorsed by the developed countries of the West; the latter by the developing countries, especially the Third World.[38] Debates along these geopolitical lines dominated the agenda at the 1974 World Population Conference, held in Bucharest. At this conference, the critical role of women in population policies was officially acknowledged.[39] Romania, acting in accord with the World Population *Plan of Action,* took the significance of women to heart; women and the family were placed on the population pedestal of socialist development.

In Romania, "politica demografica" or "demographic policy" was explicitly politicized for the purpose of building socialism. The control of demographic phenomena was generally considered vital to the success of development strategies in planned economies. The customary connotation of "demographic policy" as understood in the West does not adequately capture the extent to which demography was harnessed for ideological goals by the Ceausescu regime. "Politica demografica" was taken to be an "attribute of state sovereignty" (of all states in the interest of self-determination).[40] Hence, throughout this book, in most instances I refer to "political demography" or "political demographic policies" rather than "demographic policy" or "population policy."

Demography entails the study of factors related to the life cycle of a population: natality, mortality, longevity, morbidity, the structure of the population by age and sex, mobility (social, economic), and migration (internal and international). Political demography focuses on all demographic factors and their interrelations. According to Romanian specialists, political demography referred to "the ensemble of measures and actions in the socioeconomic domain . . . related in one way or another to the population with respect to the conditions of life,"[41] or "the integral aspect of socioeconomic development policies, such that demographic variables are incorporated into the general system of socioeconomic variables."[42] Otherwise stated, the objectives of political demography were "to accord greater attention to strengthening the family—the basic nucleus of society—increasing natality and maintaining a corresponding age structure of the population, ensuring the vigor and youth of our population, caring for and educating children, the young generations who represent the future of our socialist nation."[43]

Political demography legitimated the state's intervention in the "internal affairs" of its citizens' lives: birth, schooling, labor force participation, marriage, sexuality, reproduction, and death. To this end, "demographic investments" in Romania were to cover the "material and financial costs and the services that advance society and the family, and support a growing population."[44] The overall political demographic system consisted by and large of policies aimed at coordinating the economic and social aspects of demographic development.[45] These policies, in turn, were buttressed by all-encompassing legislation designed to facilitate their effective implementation.

Political demography was claimed by the state as its "right" to determine and control the interests of Romania's population. It also served as a mechanism with which the state was able to directly control the population itself. In keeping with the human capital needs of command economies, the state's primary interest was professed to be the creation and maintenance of the labor force to build socialism; steady population growth regulated through political demography was to be the principal means of achieving this end. As elsewhere, "the population" served as a strategic element to be disciplined and manipulated, ostensibly for purposes of maximizing development potential.[46]

This was surely the case in Ceausescu's Romania. There, "family planning" acquired a meaning specific to the context in which it was applied. Crudely put, the state assumed responsibility for family planning on behalf of the population. Family planning was a prerequisite for achieving "the ideal number of children suited to the family and to society,"[47] both of which were to be socialist. As indicated above, in Romania, family planning was designed to maximize human reproduction, not decrease it. Population rights in Romania were ideologically grounded in the "profound humanism" of the Romanian Communist Party; economic incentives were deemed essential components of the state's pronatalist policy in the best interests of "the family." The rights of the population included those of "well-being, the improvement of the quality of life and the human condition in general,"[48] among which figured social rights such as health and environmental protection, education, and work.

Political demography and the interests of the population were inextricably entwined, interrelating the macro-level policies of the state with the micro-level practices of the population. "Population," officially defined as an aggregate of individuals,[49] transformed individuals into collective abstractions. As classificatory terms, "the population" (*populatie*) was synonymous with "the masses" (*maselor*), "the people" (*poporul*), or "the nation" (*natie*). It is important to recognize that objectification works both ways. The facelessness of the masses (or the population) was reinscribed in the facelessness of "the state" (*statul*), of "they" (*ei*), or of "the power" (*puterea*). Dehumanization of the individuals who together constituted the collectivized referents of these terms (whether the state or the population) was discursively reproduced in official as well as everyday language.[50] These disembodied speech acts became standard features of communication and contributed to the rationalization of dissimulation as a social practice.

For the paternalist socialist state, attention to the needs of the population was represented, in Foucault's words, as "the ultimate end of government":

> In contrast to sovereignty, government has as its purpose not the act of government itself, but the welfare of the population, the improvement of its condition, the increase of its wealth, longevity, health, etc.; . . . it is the population itself on which government will act either directly or through large-scale campaigns, or indirectly through techniques that will make possible, without the full awareness of the people, the stimulation of birth rates, the directing of the flow of population into certain regions or activities, etc. . . . the population is the subject of needs, of aspirations, but it is also the object in the hands of the government.[51]

Population superseded the family in ideological prioritization among the government's concerns. Although the family no longer served as the principal model for governance, it nonetheless remained a primary social institution through which the paternalist regime governed. In this respect, the family was "both a subject and an object of government."[52] As shall become clear, Ceausescu's appreciation of the family as ideological construct and political-cultural practice remained ambivalent throughout the long years of his rule.

Indeed, the family and women bore particular responsibilities in the interest of creating the "new socialist person" and communism's radiant future. As secretary general of the party, Nicolae Ceausescu constantly reminded the population: "We are building socialism with and for the people."[53] Control of reproduction—biological and social—was regarded as essential to the achievement of this goal. However, control of reproduction was also of fundamental significance to the interests and well-being of women and their families. As noted previously, childbearing generally provokes consideration of economic possibilities. While cost-benefit analyses are not fully determinate of childbearing decisions, "rational choice" does play a role, and often an important one. As everyday hardships increased in Ceausescu's Romania, the interests of families and those of the state diverged all too frequently. Most women refused to bear the four or five children demanded of them by the state—in spite of the political demographic policies and incessant assertions such as: "All that occurs in our society has no other purpose than the country's development, the improvement of people's lives to a new level of civilization, the securing of conditions such that all members of society will fully enjoy the benefits of socialism."[54]

To "convince" the population of the state's paternalist largesse, the government deployed an arsenal of techniques (in the Foucauldian sense), including the institutionalization of legislation designed to enforce the political demographic policies and to alter fertility behavior, the elaboration of a propaganda apparatus, the implementation of multilevel surveillance practices, and the instrumentalization of both scientific knowledge and human capital in the interests of the state.[55] Marxist-Leninist regimes embraced scientific rationality as a means of legitimizing their modernization strategies; especially in Romania, the body was the favored vehicle through which success would be achieved.

With respect to the focus of this study, statistics, demography, and medicine were of foremost concern to socialism's vanguard. Statistics, or their amassing, were vital to state control of "the population."[56] Indeed, statistics served as powerful weapons wielded on behalf of "the population" in the name of progress. Birthrates, mortality rates, and material production rates were statistically calculated. The relationship between the population and economic indicators was "measured in terms of production outputs, on the one hand, and, on the other, the living standards of the entire population."[57] As reflected in production-oriented data, the fetishization of statistics became a primary tool of disinformation. These dissimulatory processes are discussed at length in the following chapters.[58] As Asad has noted, "Statistics reconfigure peoples into 'commensurable' social arrangements which can be compared." At the same time, he emphasized that "statistical practices can afford to ignore the problem of 'commensurable' culture."[59] Human beings, however, cannot afford to ignore the contexts in which they live. Over time, the disjunction between statistical representations and everyday living conditions in Romania became too great. The credibility of the former was deeply tarnished.

The collection and analysis of statistics became more a political than a scientific practice. In general, the social sciences were also vulnerable to political manipulation and control. Demography, sociology, history, ethnography, and folklore were all, if somewhat differently, required to do the regime's bidding. Data analyses, regardless of the domain, were to yield interpretations consistent with the party line. It was recognized early on that social scientific research could potentially produce results contradictory to those projected by ideological conviction. Hence, the "allegiance" of social scientists was always open to question and subject to surveillance.[60]

Health professionals, crucial to the implementation of the pronatalist policies, were faced with a similar situation. It was doctors who ministered to the needs of the physical body; hence, doctors and their coworkers were held responsible for making certain that the political demographic goals were achieved. The mechanisms by which doctors manipulated laws, statistical categories, medical diagnoses, and patients themselves are examined throughout this ethnography of Ceausescu's state. However, both religion and medicine were practiced at the behest of the Communist Party. Those in power understood well the significance that both priests, and more important, doctors, held as mediating figures between the private lives and life cycles of citizens and the institutionalized interests of what may be viewed as the life cycle of state socialism.[61] Medical professionals armed with scientific knowledge and the hope they offered those in need of their attention were regarded as the ideal masters and servants of political demography. They were the ones who primarily tended to the pre- and postnatal health of mother and child. It was also recognized that medical practitioners were susceptible to the temptations of pecuniary reward for performing safe but illegal abortions. Yet again, diverse laws and policing techniques were instituted to discourage deviation from the socialist norm and to make certain that society's healers were also obedient model citizens.

The "construction of the new socialist person" and of socialist society depended on the careful monitoring and disciplining of the population. Surveillance and control were among the institutionalized mechanisms used to facilitate public compliance with the regime's projects. Political demography provided the ideological framework through which vital population growth was to be monitored and guaranteed. The population, simultaneously the subject and object of social experimentation, was to be molded with or without its consent into the socialist body politic.

## THE POLITICS OF DUPLICITY IN CEAUSESCU'S ROMANIA

*Capul plecat sabia nu-l taie.*
*(The sword does not cut off a bowed head.)*
                    ROMANIAN SAYING

*Although not everyone who lies wants to conceal the truth, not everyone who conceals the truth lies. Generally, we conceal the truth not by lying but by keeping silent.*
                    AUGUSTINE, *Treatises*[62]

In Ceausescu's Romania, the penetration of the state's totalizing power became a "normal" feature of the sociopolitical ordering of life under socialism. The state's domination of the public sphere and usurpation of many of the prerogatives of the private transformed its presence into a familiar aspect of the daily lives of every citizen.[63] Indeed, throughout most of his reign, Ceausescu did not rule by outright terror; Romania's secret police during his rule were not readily comparable to the death squads of El Salvador, Guatemala, or Honduras, or to the terror unleashed by Stalin. Rather, Ceausescu generally kept "his" population in check through the manipulation of diverse forms of symbolic violence, of which fear was a favored form.[64] Domination of the public sphere and penetration of the private were crucial to the successful wielding of symbolic violence and served as effective mechanisms for integrating individuals into the functioning of socialist society. When symbolic violence proved insufficient, physical violence was meted out to coerce compliance. It was not, however, the preferred method of disciplining the body politic. Nor was it necessary; a generalized internalization of the "socialist habitus"—to build upon Bourdieu's term—of the taken-for-granted ways of seeing and being meant that most citizens acted appropriately to fit the context. Self-censorship became a natural reflex; dissimulation, its communicative corollary.

However, the reflexive quality of these modes of acting and understanding simultaneously enabled and disabled the building of socialism. The social dynamics of everyday life were structured by the socialist system itself and contributed importantly to the longevity of the regime.[65] Duplicity and complicity were the hegemonic mechanisms through which social relations came to be organized and by which the organization of socialist society was perpetuated, yet ultimately destroyed. Duplicity is customarily defined as deceitful behavior, as "speaking or acting in two different ways concerning the same matter with the intent to deceive," "double-dealing." Duplicity involves willful, conscious behavior in which social actors are aware of their intentions. Herein enters complicity—often the social ally of duplicity—which refers to "being an accomplice; partnership in an evil action," of participating in the consequences of actions that give rise to certain results—in this case, to the endurance of Ceausescu's rule.[66] Complicity is more nuanced with respect to intentionality. Social actors may, out of fear, indifference, or alienation, actively or passively "aid and abet" that in which they do not believe or with which they do not concur.[67] Complicity, and notably degrees thereof, takes on special significance in a one-party police state in which the public expression of personal opinion is not countenanced. Ceausescu's Romania was such a state.[68]

Nonetheless, it cannot easily be asserted that the relationship between complicity, conformity, and the meaning of one's actions is entirely innocent. A now classic portrayal of the complexity of this relationship is Vaclav Havel's greengrocer, who displayed a "Workers of the World, Unite" sign in his Prague shop window. Whether the greengrocer believed in the message of this slogan remains unknown and, with respect to this discussion, virtually irrelevant. That he displayed this sign as a matter of everyday habit demonstrated his conformity with the system. Or, as Derek Sayer has noted: "The form of power to which this act testifies relies centrally on the *knowledge* of everybody involved that they are 'living a lie.' . . . Had he not displayed that sign, he would be challenging the everyday moral accommodations, grounded in an equally everyday fear, which everyone engages in and which make everyday life livable—even if at the cost of a corrosive derangement of 'private' and 'public' selves."[69]

In Romania, domination of the public sphere functioned through widespread participation in the production of lies; Romania's socialist edifice was constructed on false reports, false statistics, deliberate disinformation, and false selves as well. The doctoring of statistics, which is discussed throughout this study, helped to maintain the fiction of ever greater socialist achievements. Ceausescu's personality cult was fed, in part, by the public display of loyalty in which virtually everyone played a role. Duplicity became a mode of communicative behavior; conscientious lying was customary practice. Each was a characteristic form of *dedublare*, which all together spun the threads of complicity.

*Dedublare*, Romania's version of *ketman*,[70] roughly means division in two, or dual or split personalities. In the context of Ceausescu's Romania, it generally referred to distinctive representations of the self: a public self that engaged in public displays of conformity in speech and behavior, and a private self that may have retreated to the innermost depths of the mind to preserve a kernel of individual thought.[71] *Dedublare* is a descriptively useful term; however, analytically, it masks the resulting psycho-social problem and drama of the double-self or the split between the "true" and "false" self.[72] This distinction, when sharply delineated by analysts or social actors themselves, makes it more possible to skirt the complex issues associated with complicity and the differentiation between degrees of complicitous behavior. Clearly, some people were engaged more actively and avidly than others in "kissing the hand(s) they could not bite." Hence, to argue that *dedublare* as a structurally determined survival mechanism was simply a reflexive rule of the game in which everyone actively participated relinquishes recognition of the self as a legitimate, responsible actor in favor of the self as victim of the arbitrary will of others (i.e., "fate," thereby paradoxically offering existential comfort).[73] People were manipulated by, but also manipulated, "the system." But when duplicity and complicity come to characterize society-wide relations, the system itself is fragile and structurally vulnerable to implosion.

The following chapters explore the dynamics of duplicity and complicity through an analysis of the politics of reproduction—social and biological—in Ceausescu's Romania. Chapters 1 through 5 set out the regime's official vision of socialist reality and the means by which it was to be

engineered into existence. Chapter 1 presents the context in which reproductive politics were shaped, situating them culturally, nationally, and internationally. A brief historical-demographic overview of Romania's population
and of the political significance of human capital for socialist development
serves as the backdrop against which socialist paternalism was constructed.
Paternalism implies certain kinds of relations between the state and its citizens and bears critically on issues of gender equality. The state's attention
to reproduction and the role of women and the family in the building of
socialism rhetorically legitimated policies designed to incorporate women
into the labor force and the political public sphere and to protect the future
of the Romanian nation. However, it simultaneously undermined Ceausescu's ideological insistence on creating equality and "new socialist persons" through a strategy of homogenization. A cursory discussion of the dynamics of official rhetoric is juxtaposed against a parallel discussion of the
social practices of everyday life, underscoring what has been characterized
variously as the contradiction between theory and practice, or representation and reality.

As chapters 2, 3, and 4 make clear, domination over "the masses" or the
population was organized through regulation of the public sphere. Laws,
decrees, and policies objectified the political will of the regime and established a framework for the institutionalization of political interests and
power relations. Institutionalization provided functional structures through
which citizens participated in the actual workings of power and in the trappings of building socialism. It also provided the structures through which discipline and conformity could be monitored. Chapter 2 focuses on the elaboration of anti-abortion legislation throughout 23 years of the Ceausescu
regime. The rationales allegedly motivating legislative actions are discussed
in detail, as are the immediate practical effects of their implementation.
Chapter 3 examines the related social welfare, pronatalist and pro-family
policies that girdled the banning of abortion in political demography writ
large: the anti-abortion legislation was the instrumental centerpiece of a
comprehensive, multidimensional political program to transform reproductive relations in society. Chapter 4 explores the explicit institutionalization
of political demography. The means by which medical practitioners—the
principal mediators between the state and women—were institutionally constrained are contrasted with the means by which medical practitioners circumvented these constraints. The multiplicity of surveillance techniques employed by and against a complex web of institutional workers (from janitor
to director) sheds light on the everyday work-related mechanisms that en-
snared persons to greater or lesser degrees in carrying out the will of the
regime.[74]

The former socialist states of East Central Europe were self-congratula-
tory in their logorrhea. Each state "spoke" incessantly through its mouth-

piece, the propaganda apparatus. In chapter 5, Romania's pronatalist propaganda is analyzed in order to understand how rhetorical forms were used to mobilize the population around issues pertaining to the birthrate, population growth and decline, and the essential roles of women, children, and families in the building of socialism and the future of the nation. Disinformation saturated the public sphere. Ultimately, the gaping disjunction between what was represented as socialist heaven on earth by the propaganda apparatus and what was experienced as widespread impoverishment in all aspects of daily life contributed to the collapse of the regime.

Chapters 6 and 7 scrutinize the political demographic policies, especially the banning of abortion, from the vantage point of their lived consequences. Chapter 6 provides oral commentaries and histories obtained from doctors and women regarding the meaning of delegalized abortion in their professional and personal lives. Doctors and other specialists discuss various aspects of abortion-related practices and how they themselves circumvented the law in what they considered to be their own best interests—which often coincided with those of their female patients. The experiences of two physicians who had been arrested for performing abortions illuminate the Kafkaesque quality of their lives and the manner in which professional and private relations were manipulated. These accounts are followed by a series of personal narratives by and about women's encounters with abortion. Clearly, women's struggles with their bodies, their sexuality, and their reproductive functions reverberated throughout their familial, social, and professional relationships. In these accounts, the family emerges for many as a site of solidarity and resistance, but also of betrayal. Intimate opponents and unexpected allies are revealed to be constant protagonists in the sagas of reproductive politics, underscoring the vulnerability and lack of predictability that were characteristic of everyday life in Ceausescu's Romania.

Chapter 7 turns to the legacies of political demography, specifically those related to the criminalization of abortion, which will continue to haunt Romania's population long after the memories of daily life under the regime have faded. Demographic consequences manifested by disturbingly high maternal and infant mortality rates are reviewed, as is the infant AIDS epidemic, which captured international attention. The reclaiming—however partial—of the public sphere from the clutches of the regime brought to light other social effects that resulted in large part from the state's demand for increased numbers of children. The heart-wrenching circumstances of Romania's orphans and abandoned children contributed to the outpouring of humanitarian aid as well as to an influx of potential adoptive parents wanting to provide homes for these unfortunate children. Trafficking in babies and children flourished until the Romanian government intervened legislatively.

International adoption is but one component of the global politics of re-production, and, as the Romanian case illustrates, there are both positive and negative sides to it. In the context of radical economic change from the penury of Romania's recent past to a market economy, contracting for the purchase and sale of unborn or newborn babies raises difficult questions about the institutionalization and shifting complexity of what has been la-beled "stratified reproduction." Ginsburg and Rapp describe the latter in terms of "the power relations by which some categories of people are em-powered to nurture and reproduce, while others are disempowered."[75]

On December 25, 1989, Nicolae and Elena Ceausescu were executed. The second decree of the provisional government abrogated the anti-abortion laws; indeed, the liberalization of abortion was an essential feature of the liberation of Romania's population. The tragic consequences of the criminalization of abortion serve as a subject for reflection in the conclud-ing chapter. Romania presents us with an explicit and extreme case study of what happens when abortion is banned and equal access to contraceptives and sexual education is not provided to all women. Ceausescu's political de-mographic policies affected the majority of Romania's population.

Elsewhere in the world, the conjoining of duplicity with the politics of reproduction too often results in policies whose effects are disproportion-ately experienced by poor women unable to "buy" a reasonably safe abor-tion, or to acquire the knowledge and means to regulate fertility effectively. Anyone who assumes that the majority of women who resort to abortion do so in their own selfish, immoral interests would be well advised to read on with an open heart and mind. The extended research upon which this book is based does not even minimally support such suppositions. I do not advo-cate abortion as a method of fertility regulation, but neither do I advocate the criminalization of abortion. The empirical consequences of the latter do not vary across cultures, religions, histories, or political systems. Abortion is a fact of everyday life. Its criminalization has never stopped its practice; in-stead, banning abortion has elevated duplicity and hypocrisy to the level of allegedly moral and political imperatives. Women, children, and families are not abstract public goods. Impassioned rhetoric about the sanctity of life as an abstraction divorced from the realities of everyday circumstances does not alter those everyday realities. To this, the following analysis of the poli-tics of reproduction in Ceausescu's Romania stands as tragic witness.

CHAPTER 1

# Building Socialism in Ceausescu's Romania
## Politics as Performance

*At the foundation of totalitarianism lies the representation of the People-as-One.*
CLAUDE LEFORT, *The Political Forms of Modern Society* (1986)[1]

*Society is a very mysterious animal with many faces and hidden potentialities. . . .*
*None of us knows all the potentialities that slumber in the spirit of the population.*
VACLAV HAVEL, MAY 31, 1990

*The story of a family may be the portrait in miniature of a land.*
MILOVAN DJILAS, *Land without Justice* (1958)

Socialist states, driven by command economies, actively pursued their revolutionary goals through massive social engineering projects.[2] Lacking the capital bases of market economies, socialist economies depended on the availability of labor. Thus, mobilization and control of the population were of critical strategic importance for the maximization of development potential, and attention to demographic phenomena was essential to securing long-term national interests. In order to meet the relatively high labor needs of such economies, reproduction of the labor force became a priority planning item. The State Commission for Planning was constituted in July 1948 and charged with detailing a general plan for a nationalized economy.[3] The "plan," understood to be the principal instrument for controlling the economy, became the key element in the political discourse about socialist development.[4] The plan legitimated the scientific nature and veracity of this new and "rational" system.

Planning addressed all aspects of social life, not only the economy. On August 3, 1948, a law about the reorganization of education was adopted. The educational system was commanded to eradicate illiteracy and educate a work force prepared to meet the needs of rapid planned development. Women became the beneficiaries of mass educational efforts. In keeping with the ideology of gender equality and the exigencies of a labor-intensive regime, women were incorporated into the ranks of socialist workers. It is by no means accidental that a state that declared itself a dictatorship of the proletariat had to create a proletariat to whom it could dictate. At the end of World War II, Romania had only an incipient proletariat.

Plans notwithstanding, declining birthrates complicated the labor-needs agenda. In less than two decades, the immediate postwar population problems gave way to those generated by a different set of factors: rapid urbanization, housing shortages, wage labor, and general educational and increased higher educational opportunities, as well as rising expectations about the standard of living—all of which contributed to declining birthrates. Beginning in the mid-1960s as a means of confronting this population trend, pronatalist policies became a general feature of the modernizing strategies of Eastern Europe's socialist states.[5]

Nowhere in the Soviet sphere was the "marriage" between demographic concerns and nationalist interests more extreme than in Ceausescu's Romania. There, women's bodies were increasingly used in the service of the state. The first sign of the instrumentalization of women's bodies appeared with the declaration of Decree 770 in 1966, which banned abortion in almost all circumstances. Ceausescu's decree put an abrupt stop to abortion as a primary and legal method of fertility control—and catapulted Romania into the limelight of the international demographic literature.[6]

Less noticed than the dramatic increase in the birthrate that was provoked by Ceausescu's banning of abortion was his direct policy link between the bearing of children and the social reproduction of the Socialist Republic of Romania. "Political demography," that is, demographic analysis harnessed fully to the interests of the state, and the articulation of a "national ideology under socialism" were essential features of Ceausescu's socialist vision.[7]

For Ceausescu, modernization also entailed the eventual securing of Romania's autonomy, especially in the Soviet bloc.[8] His defiant stand against joining the Warsaw Pact's invasion of Czechoslovakia in 1968 dramatically focused attention on his independent streak, if not on his national and socialist intentions. Facing his nation and the world, Ceausescu momentously announced:

> We know, comrades, that the entry of the forces of the five socialist countries into Czechoslovakia is a great error and a serious danger to peace in Europe and to the fate of socialism in the world. It is inconceivable in today's world, when the peoples are rising to the struggle to defend their national independence and for equality in rights, that . . . socialist states should violate the freedom and the independence of another state . . . there can be no excuse for accepting even for a moment the idea of military intervention in the affairs of a fraternal socialist state. . . . Nobody can set himself up as an adviser and guide for the way in which socialism must be built . . . the Romanian people will not permit anybody to violate the territory of our fatherland.[9]

Yet, armed with the wisdom of analytic hindsight, it is evident that Ceausescu's internal and foreign policies were ideologically consistent. Impassioned rhetoric invoking the "right to self-determination" and the glory of "national pride" (*mindrie nationala*) contributed to the consolidation of Ceausescu's power in Romania as well as his prestige in the West, and also among Third World nations and the nonaligned movement.[10] "Independence" and "national sovereignty" became rallying calls to stimulate enthusiastic support at home and Western approval abroad; the Romanian leader had stood up to the Soviet Union.

In the post-Stalinist period of relative political relaxation in the 1960s, Ceausescu benefited from his growing image as a young and pragmatic "liberal" communist. Various factors contributed to this illusory perception: He had rehabilitated Patrascanu (a victim of Romania's Stalinist-period show trial).[11] He seemed to support economic and intellectual liberalization.[12] He promoted more open relations with the West. And, as part of his consolidation of power, he changed a generation of leaders, thereby offering hope to the population.[13] To most Romanians, Ceausescu represented potential salvation from the harsh grip with which the Soviets held their satellites in check. "Big Brother" signified evil personified: the Soviet army, colonization strategies, invasion, cultural repression. Ceausescu rhetorically reveled in his loyalty to the Romanian nation and was rewarded by widespread popularity among his subjects. In distinct contrast to the internationalist discourse of Soviet-groomed communists, Ceausescu proclaimed the continuing sanctity of "the nation and the State" as the "basis of the development of socialist society. . . . The development and flourishing of each socialist nation, of each socialist state, equal in rights, sovereign and independent, is an essential requirement upon which depend the strengthening of the unity and cohesion of the socialist countries, the growth of their influence upon mankind's advance toward socialism and communism."[14]

To Western leaders, Ceausescu (following more in the footsteps of Yugoslavia's ruler, Tito), was a rising star amidst the darkness of Soviet socialism. "Self-determination" resonated with principles long cherished among the democratic nations of the West. Ceausescu's emphasis on "the family" hailed a respected and familiar form of social organization. His pronatalist initiatives designed to combat declining birthrates, a well-established problem in the West, were favorably recognized at the 1974 World Population Conference held in Bucharest.[15] In similar fashion, his modernization plans for the "systematization" of urban and rural locales were appraised positively as being comprehensive and rational in scope.[16] The West deemed Ceausescu a plausible ally in the Eastern bloc. His position on Israel found approval in the West and made it possible for the United States and others to wink at his open ties with the Libyans and Palestinians, for example. He was a facilitator of talks between the United States and China.[17] Read from afar and through the lens of Western political vision, Ceausescu's policies in part served Western Cold War interests.

When these policies were read from within, however, it became increasingly difficult to assert that they served the interests of the Romanian population. The signs, already there in 1966 as Ceausescu began to consolidate his power, were misread by Romanians and foreigners alike. The fortuitous conjuncture of international political tensions and Ceausescu's positioning of Romania therein, combined with his emphasis on Romanian national self-determination at home, served the Romanian leader well. Indeed, the declaration of the restrictive abortion law 770 in 1966 was, and remained, a key indicator of the intended relationship between the socialist state and its citizens throughout Ceausescu's rule.

The control of societal reproduction was fundamental to the enormous project of socialist transformation. Hence, it is important to understand the critical cultural role played by the politicization of what traditionally had been worked out within the privacy of family relations, specifically sexual relations and the socialization of children.[18] By legislating reproductive behavior, the state intruded into the most intimate realm of social relations. This radical alteration of social relations and the organizing structures of everyday life was a primary objective of the development strategies promulgated by communist planners. Again, socialist or command economies were dependent on the mobilization and utilization of human resources, namely the availability and control of the work force. In such planned economies in which then current and future labor force needs were relatively high (international in-migration of labor was practically nonexistent, and birthrates were declining), attention to demographic phenomena was strategically vital.[19] Hence, "mobilization of the work force" was not an abstract phrase characterizing the breadth of human activity "mobilized" for the purposes of achieving rapid, "multilateral" change.[20] Rather, control of the body, or of socialist workers' bodies to be more explicit, was the means by which the "plan" was translated meaningfully into the practices of everyday life. The resultant relation between state policy and demographic factors bore directly on the family; it changed gender relations and roles and underscored the often contradictory interests of the state and its citizens, especially those of women.

Here it is worthwhile to sketch briefly a historical demographic profile of Romania before Ceausescu's ascent to power. (Reproductive legislation is discussed more fully in chapter 2.) Romania's demographic transition commenced later than in most other European countries.[21] During the interwar years, capitalist expansion progressed slowly in what was predominantly an agricultural country (i.e., 75–80 percent of the population lived in rural areas). Birthrates were partially a reflection of the generally rural composition of the population, the norm being four children per family.[22]

However, the ravages of World War II created uncertainty and fear among the population, as did Soviet troop occupation and the installation of communist power in Romania. The dynamic pace of socioeconomic change during the first period of communist rule, which resulted in improvement of the public health system, urbanization, industrialization, collectivization, and mass education (including that of women), also contributed to declining birthrates. As a corrective, between 1948 and 1957, abortion was restricted except when pregnancy threatened the life of the mother, or when it was likely that the child would be born handicapped.[23] Although interdicted by law, abortion was nonetheless penalized only as a misdemeanor, and its practice was left by and large to the discretion of physicians. Illegal abortions were also common during this period and carried out with the tacit knowledge of the authorities. Abortion had not yet acquired national political demographic significance.

The interest in political control of the body through reproductive legislation changed in 1957. Abortion was fully legalized in keeping with the logic of the new development strategies then begun in earnest.[24] To facilitate the projects aimed at radical social change, the young communist government needed first to destroy the institutions, norms, and values of the preceding system.[25] It thus took aim at traditional family structures. The liberalization of legal abortion and of access to divorce constituted direct assaults on the solidarity of the traditional family, attacking the hierarchical ordering of authority between generations and genders.[26] Again, the intent was to disrupt the familiar social order and create a mobile labor force consisting of individuals unconstrained by family ties or "tradition."[27] In turn, these individuals would form the labor pool necessary to carry out vigorous industrialization plans and the forced collectivization of the countryside. Among these individuals were women whose entrance into the labor force was facilitated by the newly granted access to abortion and divorce.

To be sure, rapid and radical social upheaval contributed greatly to geographic and social mobility. According to the plan, geographic mobility was restricted.[28] Over time, planned social mobility radically changed the demography of Romania. The working class grew in number and size, as did its concentration in urban areas. By 1966 the urban population had grown to 38.2 percent, from 23.4 percent in 1948.[29] Importantly, the workers' state guaranteed minimum wages and minimum living conditions to all who participated in the building of socialism. Among them, peasants and workers regardless of their gender benefited from upward mobility and escape from the shackles imposed by a feudal order.

But social change also contributed to a pronounced decline in the birthrate, which dropped from 25.6 live births per 1,000 inhabitants in 1955 to 14.3 per 1,000 by 1966.[30] The total fertility rate, or average number of children per woman, had fallen from four before World War II to fewer than two in 1966.[31] (In 1966, Romania—like its neighbor Hungary—had one of the lowest total fertility rates in the world: an average of 1.9 children per woman.)[32] Despite the ideological dictate that reproduction of the labor force was a social necessity, the birthrate had declined. This was facilitated, in part, by the accessibility of abortion.

In 1965 Nicolae Ceausescu, who had become the newly designated leader of the Romanian Communist Party after the death of Gheorghe Gheorghiu-Dej, took stock of the contradictory effects produced by the liberalization of abortion. In 1966, and without warning, he issued Decree 770, prohibiting abortion.[33] The banning of abortion went little noted in international circles and, more tellingly, in Romania, where abortion had become the most widely practiced method of fertility control. The issuance of this decree, which preceded Ceausescu's public consolidation of his legitimacy in 1968, affected all sexually active individuals. The lack of effective popular response to this measure may be attributed, at least in part, to a misguided assumption that it would not be strictly enforced, as much as to the lingering fear that had been pervasive throughout the Stalinist-period reign of Gheorghiu-Dej.[34] Fear and uncertainty are effective weapons of control; the Communist Party capitalized on manipulating them.

The nature of the shortage economy helped control the emergence of a society dependent on the state for the bare essentials of daily life long after the state was able to provide them. Social welfare incentives, however meager, served to integrate the population more deeply into the web of a totalizing system. However, as the years passed and the global recession compounded the inherent problems of command economies in general, coercive measures were again added to the incentives meant to cajole consent in Ceausescu's Romania. The rhetoric of socialist achievement unintentionally sparked consumerist desires that the regime could not satisfy. Manipulative strategies kept people hooked into the system. Workers were enticed by bonuses whose granting was often linked to self-interested but compromising acts. "They pretend to pay us and we pretend to work" was but one manifestation of the management-worker complicity that kept the system going, however feebly.[35]

## SOCIALIST PATERNALISM:
### GENDER EQUALITY, THE FAMILY, AND THE STATE

The socialist ideology of work dictated that all citizens were to contribute to the building of socialism "according to [their] abilities." This axiom served as a legitimating basis for the mobilization of the work force and had immediate practical consequences. Most important, all citizens were formally categorized as productive or nonproductive members of society. In this way, the physical bodies of citizens were instrumentalized for the purposes of the

political economy of the state. Persons were to be recognized, or publicly acknowledged, by their performance as workers, not by factors that marked
their distinctive identities. The implications of this, especially for gender,
are discussed throughout this book. For those judged to be physically or
mentally handicapped, the label of nonproductive member of society consigned them to isolation and neglect as nonpersons; they were often abandoned to state institutions that provided only the most minimal conditions
for survival in what may best be described as institutionalized hells.[36] In essence, those who did not or could not labor in the interest of achieving
socialism were deemed "parasites" eating away at the healthy, disciplined
body of "the people."

Among the potentially productive labor resources were women, who
constituted just over half of the national population.[37] As had been true
in the Soviet Union, the "creation of a new political community made the
political mobilization of women a major concern."[38] In the state-controlled
public sphere, women, like minorities, were present in positions of authority; however, their presence was by and large symbolic, reflecting an operative quota system that paid lip service to the participation of women and
minorities in leadership roles.[39] Access to power was stratified. Most persons
in positions of power were not in the "inner circle," but were instead complicitous with it; they were, to draw upon the work of Pierre Bourdieu, the
"dominated fraction of the dominating class." Women did not represent
women's interests, just as the workers' unions did not represent workers'
interests.[40]

Socialist regimes were distinctive in their professed ideological dedication to gender equality, taken to mean that women should have the right to
work. Integrating women into the public sphere of state production would,
it was proclaimed, eliminate the subordination of women characteristic of
their position in the bourgeois, patriarchal family. The legislated emancipation of women under socialism (through employment) serendipitously contributed to the transformation of family relations as well. But women's participation in the national economy, polity, and society as workers and
mothers through forced egalitarianism, as some have labeled it, created
the classic double burdens of work in the state sphere and in the home. In
Romania, the customary double burdens became triple ones when childbearing was declared a patriotic duty.[41] Occupational advances were not
coupled with the production of time-saving household devices or with any
particular stress on changing gender roles within the family. The legacy of
patriarchal relations was not significantly altered, and, it may be argued, was
further exacerbated by the paternalist structure of the socialist state.

During the "building of socialism," unprecedented numbers of women
were educated. For example, girls constituted 41.2 percent of high school
students in 1938–39; 51.5 percent in 1971; 49.8 percent in 1989–90. At

the university level, women's share of enrollment grew from 25.9 percent in 1938–39 to 43.3 percent in 1971 and 48.3 percent in 1989–90. By 1990, 48.5 percent of the total student body (primary school through university) was female.[42] Moreover, women entered the labor force in droves. By 1989, 40.4 percent of employees in state enterprises were women.[43] However, women tended to be employed in occupations less suited to their educational levels than were their male counterparts.[44] Despite official rhetoric about equality, the division of labor was distinctly gendered. The core sectors of socialism—the bureaucracy, the repressive state security apparatus, and heavy industry—were predominantly populated by males, especially at the top. Women were brought in at lower levels, held clerical jobs, worked in light industry and agriculture, or were employed in education, health care, culture, and accounting.[45] Traditional female roles in the family remained largely feminized in the broader state division of labor. In everyday rhetoric, ideological dedication to women's "emancipation" camouflaged a continuing gendered stratification of the division of labor in the workplace and in the family.

In recognition of women's unique "ability"—childbearing—the socialist state intended to help women enter the economy by providing various forms of social assistance: guaranteed maternity leaves, guaranteed job security, childcare facilities. These entitlements were positive incentives and were progressive in intention if not in their realization. Under the ideological banner of supporting gender equality, such measures were designed to facilitate the state's utilization of women's labor power. In turn, the state took upon itself some of the more "traditional" nurturing and care-giving roles that were the responsibility of women in the patriarchal family. But despite the ideological heralding of gender equality in all of the formerly socialist states, the progressive legislation regarding women's rights as workers often conflicted with their obligations as reproducers of the labor force—that is, with their roles as childbearers. The contradictions inherent in women's roles as (re)producers for and of the socialist state, as well as for and of the patriarchal family, necessarily gave rise to a blurring between public and private spheres of daily life.[46] Ironically, contradictions in men's roles also emerged; the nationalization of property and the banning of abortion challenged men's patrilineal "rights" to the sexual and reproductive lives of their wives, which the paternalist state expropriated by fiat.

To be sure, when states attempt to legislate biological reproduction in the interest of social reproduction, public and private concerns become formally entwined.[47] But in the former socialist states of Eastern Europe, the intentional (if formal) eradication of the private sphere had effects on relations between the state and families, between spouses, parents, and children, and social relations in general. The abolition of private property, including the condition of women as private property,[48] was fundamental to the success of transforming the "old order" and destroying the "habitus" of capitalism. With this, the "traditional [bourgeois] family" would eventually cease to exist.[49]

In the interim, the Party/State was forced to reconcile family interests with the political-economic needs of the state. It did so in formal and simplistic terms. In effect, the state usurped the prerogatives of the traditional patriarchal family by claiming them for itself. In the Family Code, the state staked out the parameters of its authority: "In the Socialist Republic of Romania, the state shall protect marriage and the family; it shall support the development and strengthening of family through economic and social measures. The state shall defend the interests of mother and child and shall display a special care for the upbringing and education of the young generation . . . In the relations between a couple, as with the exercise of their rights relative to their children, a man and woman have equal rights" (article 1).[50]

The codification of the state's "rights" over the private lives of its citizens through the protection of marriage and the family points to certain basic ambiguities and contradictions. Regarding the equal rights of women, the Family Code de jure "protected" women's equality in the private sphere. However, the notion of women's equality was foreign to everyday practice, for it violated traditional patriarchal norms. Moreover, once the dynamics of gender equality within the family had been formalized in legal statutes and expounded in official propaganda, the state took little interest in them. For example, women's disproportionate share of housework and their victimization by domestic violence were beyond the purview of the state.

In the public sphere, women's equality with men was similarly "protected" under the constitution (article 23): "In the Socialist Republic of Romania, women shall have equal rights with men. The state shall protect marriage and family and shall defend the interests of mother and child." But equal status for women represented the legal affirmation of communist doctrine more than the state's attempt to redress inequality in any real way. Equality between the sexes in a "dictatorship of the proletariat" meant that proletarians, regardless of gender, were socially and economically defined through their lack of private property.[51] What they had in common was their labor power, which, from a sociological point of view, made them equal under the law. In Ceausescu's words: "If we speak about the creation of conditions of full equality between the sexes, this means that we must treat all people not as men and women, but in their qualities as party members, as citizens, for which they are exclusively judged according to their work contributions."[52] This principle of equality was formalized not only in legitimating documents such as the Constitution of the Socialist Republic but also in state policies. However, the granting of "equality" did not reflect a public attitude about equality or a recognition of inequality, nor did it inspire political activism when the discrepancy between state rhetoric about equality (among other matters) and the conditions of everyday life became blatantly evident. Gender equality was not understood, or lived, in cultural terms; it was simply proclaimed politically.

In theory, gender equality was meant to transform radically the very institution that the state "said" it would protect: the family. Through the Family Code, the state cast itself in the role of arbiter and protector of the family, marriage, and maternity. The state usurped familial patriarchal authority, thereby altering relations between the gendered domestic sphere and the state public sphere. In so doing, the boundaries between public and private spheres were made transparent, enabling the state to exercise control in this domain under the guise of benevolent protection. But as Carole Pateman has pointed out: "Protection is the polite way to refer to subordination."[53] Men's and women's interests alike were subordinated to those of the state.

Socialist paternalism was predicated upon the belief that what was good for the state was good for its citizens.[54] The state's assumption of legal responsibility for the family constituted the state's paternalist authority and the hierarchicalization of state-family relations, while simultaneously emphasizing the social role of the family in the development of the "new socialist person."

Under Ceausescu, "the family" was accorded institutional legitimacy. As a social institution, the family was reified in ideological campaigns as the archetypical metaphor of the social order itself. Over the years, policy toward the family varied; however, its rhetorical significance steadily increased. As the bulwark of socialist society in which the nation's future was nurtured, the state "accorded special attention to the family . . . for its continuing consolidation and strengthening. . . . It is necessary to combat firmly retrograde attitudes and manifestations of laxity with regard to the family which give rise to a growth in the number of divorces, the demise of family units, neglect of children's education, and their socialization for the future."[55]

The regime recognized the abstract use-value of the family in constructing socialism as well as the need to guarantee that families respected their obligations to the nation-state. Despite lip service about the virtues of the family, the preeminence of the state was never left in doubt. Ultimately, it fell to the state to socialize families into new "socialist families." The traditional Romanian peasant family was destined for extinction. The social-emotional solidarities and material practices embedded within its everyday functioning were anathema to the architects of socialism. These were to be replaced by loyalty to the "family of the nation" and selfless labor on behalf of the paternalist state. The mobilization of the family was central to the state's resolution of various infrastructural problems. In addition to reproducing the labor force, extended family relations could partially relieve problems resulting from inadequate childcare facilities and homes for the elderly. For example, grandparents frequently served as childcare providers. Daughters-in-law continued to care for the aged and the incapacitated.

Critically, the family, in the interests of its members but also as a "state institution," was especially vulnerable to the demands of the regime. To cajole or coerce individuals into conformity, the regime issued none-too-subtle threats—for example, that noncompliance (with whatever request) would result in loss of a job (i.e., a father or mother would be denied the means to support his or her family).[56] Job security functioned as an effective disciplinary safeguard. Contrary to popular assumptions, job security was not valued simply because workers were innately lazy. Most workers, despite the fact that salaries were inadequate to meet the costs of living, formally depended on their jobs to have access to social welfare benefits and a sense of relative security in what was thought to be an unpredictable sociopolitical environment.[57] As elsewhere in the Eastern bloc, job security was guaranteed by law—as long as the workers acted according to expectation. Expectation, however, far exceeded concerns strictly related to the workplace. Instead, the workplace constituted an institutionalized microcosm of the socialist society being built.[58]

The ever-present threat of being fired from a job heightened the sense of vulnerability felt by Romanian citizens. In turn, this potential vulnerability made people vulnerable to administrative harassment. (Such harassment was frequently but not exclusively carried out by Securitate personnel.) The arbitrariness of this dynamic played an important role: no one knew whom to trust. Potential dangers lurked in the person of a colleague who might or might not work for the secret police. Moreover, it was common knowledge that obtaining another position was both difficult and costly, and that the "undoing of a contract" automatically was noted in one's personal (qua personnel) file.

The search for a new job was further complicated by official residence permit requirements (obtained from the authorities) and institutionalized restricted mobility, which formally confined most persons to particular locales.[59] Legal residence requirements were rigorously monitored. Every socialist apartment building or "bloc" had an administrator or superintendent, usually someone who lived in the building. The superintendent kept the book containing all data about the building's inhabitants: how many resided there and what their current status was.[60] This individual's role was designed to instrumentalize the multilateral surveillance of Romania's population in yet another facet of daily life. In this manner, an insidious link between state authorities and their citizens was ensured day and night. Suspicion pervaded living environments, further eroding the damaged walls of the private sphere.

Job vulnerability was thus a constant source of psychological blackmail. Reconciling the necessity of meeting the needs of one's family with supporting those of the "family" of the nation often required actions that compromised one's sense of self. In consequence, as the years passed, the builders of socialism became increasingly alienated from themselves and from the nation-state that was purported to serve their interests.

The paternalist state in part expressed its power through the elaboration of a discourse and related set of practices centered on "the family." Official rhetoric concerning the family resonated with familiar cultural patterns. Traditional Romanian family structure is patrilineal and patriarchal; the typically gendered dependency relations that are created through this type of family organization were elevated to the level of the socialist state's "legitimate" rule over its citizens. In consequence thereof, citizens of the socialist state were treated as if they were children who benefited from the care (or neglect) of their parents, and particularly from the wizened guidance of the pater familias.

Ceausescu seems to have taken the kinship-familial metaphor literally, believing that "father knows best."[61] Raised in a peasant family himself, he seemed unable to transcend the imprint of a traditional family upbringing—however much he tried, which, as will be seen, he did with vigor. Ceausescu's "fundamentalist" attitudes about hard work and proper behavior seemed to reflect the ambivalence of his abstract esteem for "the family" and his disdain for his own father and family, whom he left at the age of eleven to seek work in Bucharest. As a teenager, he found a new urban family—the then clandestine Communist Party of Romania. To what degree these early experiences influenced his presumption of the state's "legitimate rule" over the family cannot be known, yet the legacy of his past cannot be dismissed out of hand. The psychodynamics of Ceausescu's childhood within his natal family collided with the psychohistory of his rule over his statal family. "Tradition" was destined to do battle with Ceausescu's version of modernity.

Indeed, Romanian socialism under Ceausescu became known as "socialism in one family." The Romanian Communist Party was characterized in terms of family organization: Jowitt referred to "party familialization"; Tismaneanu and Georgescu to "dynastic socialism."[62] To many among the populace, extended family kinship relations "explained" the functioning of the party: PCR was the acronym for the Partidul Comunist Roman (Romanian Communist Party). These were also the initials of the Petrescu and Ceausescu families. Everyday kinship practices informed a more subtle meaning of PCR: *Petrescu, Ceausescu si Rudele* (Petrescu, Ceausescu, and relatives—that is, extended family relations). Petrescu was Elena Ceausescu's maiden surname. The symbolic equivalence between the formal acronym and its unofficial sibling referred to the holding of important political positions by extended family members. In traditional society, marriage creates relations between corporate families. The PCR operated accordingly.[63] Furthermore, mothers (and mothers-in-law) in the patriarchal family were generally powerful within the household,[64] and their authority increased with age. So it was to be with Elena Ceausescu.[65]

Paradoxically, Ceausescu brought village values to bear upon the organization of the Party/State at the same time that he planned the extinction of the village social organization in which these values were sacrosanct. Crudely put, Ceausescu transposed peasant family organization to the level of state socio-demographic plans. As mentioned above, the number of children Ceausescu decreed mandatory before women were eligible for legal abortion reproduced the peasant norms of four and five children per family characteristic of pre–World War II Romania. Historically, in peasant households, maximizing the number of living children was the customary means by which family subsistence was reproduced. Infant mortality rates during the 1930s were quite high; between 1937 and 1939, for example, for every 1,000 live births, 180 infants under the age of one died. However, after the war infant mortality rates declined steadily.[66]

In effect, the state expropriated the right to determine family size in order to meet its presumed labor needs. By so doing, the state also expropriated male rights to the reproductive labor of women.[67] To underscore, paternalism generalized the dependency relations experienced by women and children in the patriarchal family. Men were similarly subordinated; citizens of Ceausescu's socialist state may be said to have been structurally "feminized" in their positioning within the state.[68] From the perspective of the paternalist state, all citizens, regardless of gender, were its dependent children. Healthy orphans, potential future workers, became actual wards of the state, being "raised" under the supervision of the Ministry of Education, the Ministry of Health, and later, the Ministry of Labor. It was also widely believed that a special secret police corps was made up of orphans selected and raised expressly to loyally serve their "parents," the Ceausescus.

The state's usurpation of basic parental roles transformed the family into an instrument of control. Control of the body, and specifically of sexuality, brought the state directly into the lives of most of its subjects. The public sphere was saturated with social and biological reproduction. Although in proper village society such personal matters were not usually discussed in public, social control over the body was not foreign to village life. There, socio-sexual behavior was controlled by *gura satului*—the mouth of the village. Gossip functioned as an effective weapon against the flouting of local norms. Rarely did misbehavior escape the punishment of public humiliation; in keeping with the patriarchal order, women were more harshly treated than men.

Also, among the community of families that populated a village, highest respect was given to families known to be of a *neam bun*—a good family (an attribution taken to be "in the genes" and inherited by the extended lineage). And that is what Ceausescu wanted to (pro)create: a new *neam bun* for the entire Romanian population, *un popor unic* (a unique people [nation]).[69] To this end, village norms and values were reproduced in the norms and values enshrined in the *Codul principiilor si normelor muncii si vietii comunistilor, ale eticii si echitatii socialiste* (in essence, a code of communist ethics) of the "new socialist state." Children were to be socialized in the family according to these principles. Just as heredity played an important role in knowing from what sort of family a child came (a good, weak, or bad *neam*), so it did in determining the status of socialist citizens. A critical aspect of any person's identity was family background, whether she or he was of an *origine sanatoasa*, a healthy origin—that is, the family history did not contain priests (especially Uniate ones),[70] landowners, relatives abroad, former political prisoners, or divorced members. Such "class" blemishes often created difficulties for young people in their educational and career pursuits. The education of future upstanding party activists was furthered in the communist youth organizations: the *soimii patriei* (fatherland's falcons) for children three to six years of age (set up by Ceausescu in 1976), the *pionieri* (pioneers) for those nine to fourteen years old, and the *Uniunea Tineretului Comunist* (UTC; the Union of Communist Youth) for those over age fourteen. Members of the ideal socialist family-nation were to be hardworking, productive, procreative, and proper.[71] Marriage at a young age, already strongly entrenched as cultural practice in Romania, was extolled. (Women tended to marry around the age of 22; men, 25.) Nonetheless, for good measure, legal and practical impediments to obtaining a divorce further ensured that most families would stay together in spite of the disruptive mobility sparked by rapid industrialization.

The regime's contradictory policies affecting "the family" both in symbolic and in practical terms contributed to the culturally embedded practice of dissimulation. People internalized the norms appropriate to two interrelated worlds and behaved accordingly. The milieu of "them" included all that was linked to centralized power; "us" to all that was outside of this encompassing category. The conceptualized spaces of "us" and "them" implicitly corresponded to the private and public spheres; as social spaces in which people actually lived, the boundaries between them were fluid.[72]

## "HOMOGENIZING"
## THE SOCIALIST BODY POLITIC

Ceausescu manipulated the discourse of the family, interweaving the reproduction of the labor force with the reproduction of the nation, all the while emphasizing women's special roles in these "noble," "patriotic" endeavors. The nation itself was to be "reconstituted" through a neo-Stalinist social engineering project known as *omogenizare* (homogenization), to "homogenize" the populace and create the "new socialist person."[73] At the National Conference of the Communist Party in 1972, Ceausescu proclaimed:

> Under socialism, we are witnessing the formation of unique concepts about the world and life deriving from dialectical and historical materialism. Moreover, there is the formation of a new science and new culture, the crystallization of a new and advanced ethic, which contribute to the formation of a new person—the person of the socialist and communist society. In the socialist society, a process has begun to make the village more like the city, to encourage the gradual disappearance of classes, and [to give rise to] the homogenization of society, gradually erasing the fundamental differences between physical and mental labor.[74]

Homogenization, fully elaborated by the mid-1980s, was meant to produce social equality by rendering social differences insignificant. Race, gender, and ethnicity were all to be homogenized, as were spatial and other distinctions. Each body was to be molded into a productive member of the socialist masses. This masking of difference inadvertently contributed to the image of the "faceless masses." Deviation from the socialist norm was tantamount to treacherous activity directed at the overthrow of the state. "Difference" was considered to be "Other," hence deviant. Among the most obvious others were foreigners, particularly those from the imperialist, capitalist West. ("Fraternal" relations were between those in the communist bloc; note the kinship terminology, which was dictated from the Soviet Union.)[75] The state also took precautions against the dangerous, contaminating effects of its "internal" others, among whom were dissidents, reformers, and those who insisted on the legitimacy of their ethnic identities or human rights, including the right to determine their reproductive interests. Laws existed to protect the body politic and could be invoked arbitrarily to legitimize official actions against particular forms of "deviation."

For example, Decree 153/1970 served as a disciplinary measure against deviation from the norms of socialist citizenship as set out therein.[76] Its contents ranged from defining persons as societal parasites (among whom were individuals who did not work "according to [their] abilities") to forbidding the production of graffiti (and the destruction of socialist property). The terms of this decree were so broad that accusations of its violation could be justified on vague grounds. Parasitism was taken to be a "legitimate" cause for arrest and was generally employed for political purposes.[77] The arbitrariness with which measures such as Decree 153/1970 were applied contributed importantly to an inchoate sense of vulnerability felt by most citizens, including, or perhaps especially, members of the ruling apparatus. The manipulation of human vulnerability was one of the most important psychodynamic weapons perfected by the regime.

Homogenization structured its others; within its stark terms, anything other than sameness was unacceptable. Persons only "existed" legitimately in the public sphere of the state; again, the Romanian state appropriated the private realm of social interaction unto itself.[78] By refusing to acknowledge the legitimacy of private domains of interaction, the state extended its tentacles of control into the bodies and minds of its citizens. Consciousness was to be shaped accordingly. In that a developmental process was entailed, "instruction" about the practices, ethics, and morals of socialism began at a young age through mass participation in the youth organizations mentioned above. Socialist education was similarly an ongoing endeavor; students and workers took part in practical and ideological "work" throughout their lives. Competitions were organized in all realms of professional and amateur activities; these served as the mechanisms through which citizens became recognized as and rewarded for being "heroes of socialist labor." As shall be seen, bearing children was essential (re)productive labor. Hence, mothers who yielded "notable results in (re)production" were awarded heroine mother medals. The final outcome of the homogenizing process would be the socialist body politic, the embodiment of a totalizing image of the state in which the boundary between state and citizen was porous.[79] The blurring of boundaries, if not their eradication, was a fundamental element of socialist transformation. The state's intrusion into private life through reproductive policies blurred the boundaries between public and private spheres of everyday life, changing the relations between citizens and the state. This is a point that warrants stressing in that it emphasizes an ideological dynamic that resulted in myriad practical contradictions.

All domains of life were affected by *omogenizare*. As a strategy for change, homogenization was communicated through homologous discursive practices in diverse areas of political speech and policy formulation such as cultural activities, political demography, education, and so on. *Cintarea Romaniei*, the Singing of Romania, was the national cultural festival that epitomized the breadth of the homogenization process in the cultural domain. "Art" was broadly defined as the creative activity of the masses, thereby blurring the boundary between high art and popular culture. In keeping with the communists' political culture of anti-intellectualism, elite professionalism was displaced by the celebration of mass amateurism. Conformity and standardization were the nuts and bolts of homogenization. This "multilaterally developed" project assumed the production of identical conditions of daily life for all citizens. An ideal form of social organization would be achieved through the advancements that the *sistematizarea* (systematization) of rural and urban settlements would bring. Rural and urban communities would be homogenized, eradicating the glaring differences in living conditions.[80] Urban amenities would be available to all.

Building codes dictated a national public aesthetic. Only minimal variation, usually reflecting local or regional motifs, was permitted. For example, construction along primary roads took place in strict adherence with these codes. "Appearance" marked the spatial materialization of the regime's ideology of homogenization and Ceausescu's fixation on "standardization" (*tipizare*). That appearance seemed to matter more than substance was exemplified in the now infamous case of the apartment complexes lining the major roadway to the national airport. From the outside, viewers cannot guess that these were built without running water. Occupants were required to trek outside to use communal outhouses and to haul water up several flights of stairs. Ironically, rather than bringing urban amenities to village communities, such constructions brought unmodernized village infrastructure to the city.

Ultimately, Ceausescu envisioned that the country would be dotted with apartment complexes, each with communal eating halls. In keeping with these plans to create social equality, conformity, and homogeneity, a plan to standardize what and where Romanians ate was devised. Romanian bodies would be identically nourished. Meals prepared according to "scientific" indicators would eventually be served in the communal eating halls. (The implementation of "scientific nourishment" among the population was unsuccessful, partially because of the difficulties of procuring food in general, let alone foods that were designated "healthful." By the 1980s, much that was produced was exported as a means of repaying the foreign debt.)[81]

From an ideological perspective, the paternalist state viewed itself as beneficent. In actuality, the ethos of homogenization reflected a crude paternalism in which the Party/State claimed for itself the prerogative to define the public good. Again, and tautologically, this public good was to be achieved through homogenization. Policies that were consistent with these ideological goals were formulated. Public discourse was a vehicle through which Ceausescu's ideas were disseminated; yet, contrary to standard assumptions about totalitarian states, there was no one-to-one correspondence between what was dictated at the top and what actually happened.

In the end, the Romanian dictator's "totalitarian" homogenized vision was only partially realized. The regime's policies were implemented by individuals who, despite their party functions, lived their daily lives as members of extended families, communities, and workplaces; they did not live solely in ideological scripts. Enough of them experienced the contradictions between the state's strategies for building socialism and citizens' strategies for living their everyday lives. In consequence of the growing disjunction between official rhetoric and lived experience, these strategies were increasingly at odds.

## THE POWER OF WORDS: OFFICIAL RHETORIC

Modes of public communication were also subjugated to political efficacy. The wooden language of official discourse shaped the discursive strategies of communication in the state-dominated public sphere.[82] For Ceausescu and his regime, official rhetoric became more real than apparent realities (that is, than those conditions that are empirically verifiable). The "word"—official rhetoric—represented and dictated what were to be "objective" realities. This celebration of official rhetoric in the public sphere was meaningful as official "signifying practice"; understanding it enabled individuals to conform publicly, as well as to resist (however passively) through black-market secondary economic activities or personal thought. Hence, the importance of ideological discourse for the functional legitimation of the Ceausescu regime must not be dismissed as "just so many words." These discursive practices were understood in terms of the "magical power of words" and their power to embody what the state should be, if not what it was. In this regard, ideology may be characterized as "that enterprise of fantasy which tends to produce and to fix the ultimate foundations of knowledge in every sphere."[83] The image of the state as a body with an identity and desires is powerful in its potential to appeal to the emotional sensibilities of citizens, as well as to the perception of the state as a being unto itself, a paternalist one at that.

Indeed, the state "spoke" incessantly about its identity, desires, and achievements. Contrary to the predictions of Marxist theory, ideological rhetoric rather than material conditions came to represent social life in Ceausescu's Romania. In accordance with this twist of theoretical fate, the extent to which official rhetoric was reified by and for ideologues helps to clarify how the system represented itself and functioned within the terms of its own rhetoric. Despite increasing scarcity and dramatically deteriorating conditions of everyday life throughout the 1980s, abundance was realized daily—in the formulaic speeches of the leader. The achievements of the socialist state were measured by fulfillment of "the plan." Conscientious manipulation of data enabled reality to conform to the plan's dictates. As shall be seen, statistics were rarely used to signal problems in need of attention: for example, early AIDS data were deliberately suppressed; and in response to the rising incidence of infant mortality, births were not recorded for several weeks. Instead, statistics were generally used as political instruments. Interpreted as objective representations of "reality," they became the tools by which officials were removed or individuals were punished or by which plan targets were formulated. In this regard, official rhetoric functioned as an effective means of control.

It should be noted that interpretation of official text (that is, party platforms, plans, and so on) was predicated on strictly formalist, literal readings of their content. Basically, public meaning was revealed by analysis of the text, not by analysis of the text in relation to the context in which it was embedded. Ultimately, this resulted in a fully disembodied rhetoric in which all played a part. Thus a false "reality" was created and supported in the encompassing public sphere of the state. Adherence to "the word" engaged

all citizens in varying degrees and acts of daily dissimulation, as well as varying degrees and acts of complicity in perpetuating the system, or subvert-
ing it.

Over the years, public representation and personal belief increasingly
diverged, transforming dissimulation and deceit into customary forms of interpersonal exchange. (The long-term deleterious effects of distorted communication patterns are among the internalized practices of the past that
negatively affect the present.) Nonetheless, the magical power of language
to mobilize sentiment was repeatedly used in the service of the nation-
state: Ceausescu's defense of Romania's right to sovereignty against the de-
signs of outside forces, notably from Soviets or Hungarians bordering on
Romania's territory, became a convenient mechanism by which the population's vulnerability as well as national interest was aroused and maintained.
Historical precedent lent rhetorical weight to the manipulation of a political culture long accustomed to victimization by others. In the end, Romania's citizens were victimized by their own leadership and themselves with
the implicit consent of the West.[84]

## THE POLITICS OF DUPLICITY:
### PUBLIC AND PRIVATE LIVES

As the years passed under Ceausescu's grim rule, the regime's representation of socialist achievements in Romania came increasingly into conflict
with the everyday experiences of Romania's citizens. The domination of
the public sphere was coordinated with that of the private. Subjugation of
the private sphere was achieved in large part through the state's penetration
into the intimacy of the body and the sanctity of privacy. Political demography was a critical point of intercourse between the state and its population.
The state's attention to "the family" and to the control of sexuality was
meant to instill patriotic behavior in the interests of "protecting" the future
of the Romanian nation. However, the demand for an increased birthrate,
for "families with many children," was not matched by the provision of a
basic standard of living that facilitated the care and raising of those children.
The birth of a child meant that parents had increased responsibilities to find
milk and food products, which were already scarce. Access to these things,
which was taken for granted by Westerners during this epoch, was the source
of constant anxiety, despair, and frustration to Romanians. No one in Romania could remain indifferent to the consequences of the political demographic policies, to which the effective banning of abortion was central.

Other bodily interventions such as the program for "scientific nourishment," the criminalization of homosexuality, and the deprivation of heat,
electricity, and hot water enabled the regime to control the population's

daily habits. For example, during the freezing winter of 1984–85, the regime ordered that central heating be turned off in apartment buildings throughout the country as an energy-saving measure. The Romanian population was humbled by the will of its paternalist leaders. Sampson commented on this cynical technique of exercising power: "Living for months in a freezing apartment is not just uncomfortable and unhealthy. It is a symbol of one's own powerlessness. The heat crisis differed from the food crisis, for obtaining food is an individual effort . . . in the food struggle there may be small victories; other days there were defeats. . . . When the regime turns the central heating off . . . , it is a centralized act. Everyone in an entire apartment complex—an entire neighborhood—suffers."[85]

All of society, including the privileged, became more and more alienated from the regime. Although the public performance of socialist (sur)realism continued unabated, people's dependence on informal networks and secondary economic activities increased. The public and private were interpenetrated "from below" as well, with the public sphere being pillaged by those who nonetheless ritually recognized "the power" in it.

To develop direct relations between the state and its citizens, the state sought to reconstitute in its own image the mediating institutions that modulate state-society relations in the public sphere and in civil society.[86] Education, religion, the mass media, and, in particular, the family were explicitly targeted for state control of the body politic. These institutions were meant to promote the "process of identification between power and society, the process of homogenizing the social space" (as articulated through *omogenizare*). The boundaries between the public and the private were, at the very least, to be blurred. As noted previously, within a homogenized social order, difference and heterogeneity have no place.[87] Seemingly little was left to chance. Additional measures were instituted to prevent acts disapproved by the regime: typewriter scripts had to be registered so that they could be easily identified,[88] contacts with foreigners were discouraged.[89] The list of taboos was long and detailed.

The state's control of the public sphere and the formal subordination of the private were much more problematic in lived terms than in ideological ones. As the histories of oppression and dependency throughout the world repeatedly reveal, control by the state may nonetheless be resisted. Although the above-noted institutions as well as interpersonal relations within them were radically transformed by state domination, the regime fundamentally misunderstood the significance of informal social relations in everyday life. Citizens' dependence on the "state" for the minimal ministering to their basic needs was simultaneously paralleled by their altered dependencies on— and consequent vulnerabilities to—each other. Ever scarcer resources increased competition between groups and individuals with respect to acquisition of those resources; social atomization in part resulted from such interpersonal competition. Yet, in order to satisfy those same needs, new social networks were spawned that situated interpersonal dependencies in the informal realm of daily activities. Urban-rural kin, friendship, and collegial relations were reshaped in response to resolving those problems. For example, in the 1980s urban dwellers often depended on rural-based kin to supply them with eggs and meat.[90] The latter needed their city relatives in exchange to furnish them with such scarce items as toilet paper. Or a worker who lived in a city and could not "arrange" to buy pork from the local butcher might ask a colleague from work who lived in a nearby village to bring her five kilos of meat. Although this service had to be recompensed, the problem of obtaining pork had been resolved. In this way, the system was also perpetuated. The internal contradictions spiraled.

These types of dependencies also emerged in the reconstituted mediating institutions mentioned above. The organization of informal relations compensated for the structural constraints that affected formal "socialist" relations. The lateral as well as vertical dependency relations created by the system's formal limitations forced almost everyone to use informal opportunities to resolve pressing needs, whether this meant arranging for a job or an abortion, or obtaining milk for one's children. In effect, corruption was systemically created. This intermeshed yet dual system of everyday life (symbiotic dependency, or codependency in today's popular parlance) simultaneously chipped away at the system's formal structure and secured its increasingly fractured continuation. In a redistributive economy, those with resources acquired special clout. Hence, buying off "supporters" became a necessary aspect of maintaining the formal system—as well as its informal counterpart of secondary economic activities. Into the 1980s, workers were periodically placated by pay raises, which were more symbolically than materially significant.[91] Nomenklatura members, secret police, and many physicians, Orthodox priests, and others were kept "in" the system (regardless of their convictions about it) as a result of the privileges from which they benefited.[92] Many of them had been dramatically elevated in class and status (from peasant to party boss, so to speak) and knew what they stood to lose for disobedience. These persons occupied positions that mediated between the formal demands of the system and the private lives of citizens. The loyalty of persons "betwixt and between" the public and private was requisite as well as subject to ongoing scrutiny.

Also of critical importance to the functioning of daily life were those who worked in transport, services (e.g., plumbers, electricians, mechanics), and sales. All of these occupations were well suited to black marketeering. Those working in them formally labored in socialist enterprises whose state-provided materials could also be utilized to personal advantage. Individuals who had the wherewithal to offer "a gift" in the form of money, goods, or services in kind to acknowledge a middleman's attention to their needs often acquired what they wanted. For an additional sum, many unavailable or limited items magically became available.[93] Virtually everyone was involved in some form of informal illegal activity, meaning that this multilaterally developed dual system was functional for and beneficial to many. Living in two interrelated "realities"—a stagnant official public sphere and a dynamic informal private one—defined what had become the habitus of socialism in Ceausescu's Romania.

The Romanian population adapted to and endured the increasing hardships imposed upon them, often with great ingenuity. Moments of respite were provided by jokes, bitter complaints, a few hours of hot water, and the small satisfactions that accompanied the celebration of a family event, such as a wedding or a child's passing the school entrance exams. For many years, a generalized impoverishment was partially offset by the advantages particular sectors of society managed to accrue. The heaven-on-earth extolled by the propaganda apparatus was at best a socialist hallucination. Disinformation was another essential component of maintaining uncertainty and dependency. Nonetheless, most people learned to "muddle through" (to greater or lesser degrees of personal benefit).[94]

Although less commonly noted, Ceausescu's Romania was not consistently perceived to be a living hell by all residing there. At least through the early 1980s, the political strategies of divide and conquer, and of concession combined with repression, created enough space for people to participate in an illusion of exercising a minimal degree of individual autonomy (in certain domains such as the informal sphere). Social action became synonymous with making do or beating the system.[95] Pensioners often painstakingly stood in endless lines; some of them eked out a supplementary "wage" by selling at a profit to their neighbors a portion of what they had obtained.[96] In the evolving context of give and take, people's interpretations of political measures that increased their dependency on the state but simultaneously seemed to reduce the stress of daily life became more and more convoluted. In the 1980s, some people even found the rationing of basic items (flour, eggs, sugar, oil, etc.) to be a relief. The "rationalizing" of the distribution system suggested that people might waste less time and energy trying to procure those necessities.[97] Rationing cynically institutionalized the state's attempt to control its citizens' bodies through "scientific nourishment." Salespeople, like everyone else, complained about increasing shortages, but they also profited substantially from them. Had their stores been filled with goods, they would not have amassed the "small attentions" that supplemented their meager state salaries.[98] Despite the considerable hardships suffered by many, enough of them were able to selectively promote their own interests while also helping those in need. People were recompensed for the risks they took and the trouble they went to on behalf of their fellow citizens. Corruption rhetorically represented as "gifting" was an integral feature of rendering service to others.

The dependencies sketched here compelled almost all citizens, to varying degrees, to be complicitous with the regime. Persons were either integrated into the system or forced to emigrate, other options being less evident and certainly harsher.[99] The regime skillfully manipulated the body politic in literal as well as metaphoric terms. It is not in the least surprising that "the family" was officially regarded as an important site for the transformation and manipulation of personal relations, both by the regime and by family members themselves. The former, through its dictatorship over daily needs, threatened the latter, but family members also relied on culturally rooted sentiments to plead with a vendor to sell them something extra (for an additional sum) because "am copii acasa" (I have children at home).

The tensions generated by the state's expectation of obeisance from its subjects and citizens' attempts to manage their everyday lives gave rise to increasing alienation that finally exploded into what Jowitt has termed a "movement of rage."[100] It is because of this necessary confrontation between public and private interests that reproductive legislation and policies are of such critical significance. The analysis of the interrelations between official discourse, public policies, and the response to them brings to the foreground both convergent and divergent strategies employed by the state and by society. It is here in the struggle over control of the body, and relatedly, of the body politic, that mechanisms which produce conformity and complicity, as well as evasion and resistance, may be understood. The following chapters explore the dramatic tensions between official rhetoric and practices and the experience of everyday life. Ceausescu's socialist ideals and the actual lived realities of Romania's citizens came to be increasingly at odds. The growing chasm between them helped to sow the seeds of the eventual implosion of the system.

CHAPTER 2

# Legislating Reproduction under Socialism

*Romania, for instance, had anticipated Gilead in the eighties by banning all forms of birth control, imposing compulsory pregnancy tests on the female population, and linking promotion and wage increases to fertility.*

MARGARET ATWOOD, *The Handmaid's Tale*

*The practice of abortion is both an antinational and antisocial act, and an impediment to the normal development of our population. . . . It is necessary to introduce the most perfect order and discipline with respect to the application of the existing laws and regulations pertaining to the interruption of pregnancy.*

DECISION OF THE POLITICAL EXECUTIVE COMMITTEE OF THE CENTRAL COMMITTEE OF THE ROMANIAN COMMUNIST PARTY[1]

*The first great socialist industry was the production of personal files. . . . This new industry has an army of workers, informers. Also, ultramodern electronic equipment (microphones, recorders, etc.) plus an army of typists. Without all of this, socialism would not be able to survive. . . . In the socialist world, people and things exist only in personal files. The owner of [these] files is the owner of all existence.*

ANDREI SERBULESCU,
*Monarhia de Drept Dialectic: a doua versiune a memoriilor lui Belu Zilber*

The "political reconstruction of the family" was a fundamental component of socialist transformation.[2] Laws, decrees, and normative regulations were instituted and revised when deemed necessary to achieve this goal. Laws and decrees were functionally identical; the difference between them reflected the institutions from which they were issued.[3] These legislative decisions were vital to the new regime's efforts to restructure social relations to be compatible with the political and economic organization of a communist state.[4] In their scope, these various measures addressed the family, gender and generational relations, attitudes about human reproduction, and the reciprocal relations between the family and the structural process of creating a new socio-political system. Significant among them were the following: In 1948 article 482 of the Penal Code was revised, criminalizing abortion. In 1952 the "proper conduct" of social relations between men and women, between parents and children, between family members, and between the family and other public institutions was inscribed in the newly re-edited constitution. One year later, these normative prescriptions were further elaborated in the Family Code.[5] In 1955 the laws about abortion were revised to specify the conditions under which women were legally permitted to have a pregnancy terminated.[6] In 1956 the state introduced financial assistance for families with children.[7] In 1957 abortion policy was again revisited; this time, abortion was liberalized.

The Communist Party used legislative activity to reshape the relationship between the public and private spheres of daily life such that the latter would become a partner, willing or not, in the radical project of societal change upon which Romania had embarked after World War II. This chapter and the next explore the complex process by which political ideology found expression in legislative initiatives and policies that were then interpreted in everyday life by the Party/State and by Romanian citizens. They focus, in particular, on the mechanisms that transformed a category of the population, women, into persons whose roles in building the new socialist socioeconomic order were construed as predestined. From the introduction of this new order in the late 1940s, the relationship between human reproduction and gender relations in the family, as well as in the public sphere of the state, was treated juridically in the Family Code and in abortion regulations. The rights granted women in the Family Code were often negated in the abortion-related legislation and related social-familial policies. The resultant denial of women's right to determine their reproductive lives came to embody the nature of relations between the public and private spheres, shorthand for relations between the state, the family, and individual interests. At one and the same time, this essential interdiction underscored the tension between the professed principles of the new regime's ideological discourse and the concrete conditions of their practice.

Equality was among the fundamental ideological tenets of socialist states and was an important element in official political discourse. With the publication of the Family Code, women's equality with men in the private sphere—that is, in the family—was officially secured by law. Their equality with men in the public sphere of the state was formalized in the constitution. By so doing, the new political regime created an important break with the past and formally redefined the boundaries between the public and private. The state claimed its paternalist rights to protect the family and to determine reproductive cycles. The resultant conflict of interests between projected plan targets and everyday life circumstances was played out all too frequently in the lives of women who literally bore the consequences. Demographers and sociologists alike recognized that the demographic and social roles of women had to be better reconciled. Research consistently confirmed that the social, economic, and political policies promulgated on behalf of women's equality "reduced fertility."[8]

The emancipation of women through the restructuring of their roles was partial, at best. Women's rights remained conditioned, first and foremost, by the privileging of their reproductive roles. Later, at the end of the 1950s, political and economic priorities were modified, causing a shift in the hierarchy of gender roles. Consistent with the increased labor force needs of socialist industrialization, the salaried female worker became the dominant role envisaged by the state for women, replacing that of motherhood—at least temporarily. Access to legal abortions was liberalized. However, access to contraceptives was not simultaneously promoted. Abortion was the political tool used to manage the change in women's prescribed roles. In part, abortion suited the productionist orientation of communist regimes. In contrast to contraceptives, abortion—already a cultural practice—was not dependent on consumer-based devices or on "distribution" networks.[9]

The political manipulation of abortion and contraceptive practices is, in part, why the politics of reproduction constitutes such an important confrontational site between the state and the interests of its citizens. Reproductive legislation brought the state directly into the private realm of its citizens' bodies and set the stage on which human dramas were enacted. Analysis of reproductive policies and practices thereby illuminates the strategies employed by the state and by individuals to achieve their respective goals and exposes how intrusions of the former led to conformity, or to evasion and distortion by the latter.

This chapter deals with the legislative decisions that pertain more narrowly to the control of demographic (qua reproductive) behavior. Chapter 3 discusses related legislation and policy initiatives directed at the social dimensions of demographic behavior, such as financial incentives to families, childcare benefits, and maternity leave guarantees.[10]

### DEMOGRAPHIC PRACTICES, POLITICAL CONCERNS: POPULAR APPROACHES TO FERTILITY REGULATION

The instrumental efficacy of laws is best understood when the laws are considered in the economic, political, social, cultural, and demographic contexts in which they function. To encourage socialist development, many legislative endeavors focused specifically on demographic factors; therefore, it is instructive to begin with a summary of Romania's demographic profile at the end of World War II. At the time, Romania was fully engaged in what is known as the "demographic transition." Historians and demographers tend to agree that the process generally began in Romania at the end of the nineteenth century. Demographic transition refers to an irreversible structural process during which high levels of births and deaths in a given society decrease. This transition marks the change from "traditional" fertility and mortality patterns to modern ones. In the ideal typical first phase of demographic transition, the characteristically high rates of death and/or birth begin to fall, especially the former. In Romania, as elsewhere, the mortality rate was the first to decline, dropping by one-fifth, from approximately 30 deaths per 1,000 inhabitants at the end of the nineteenth century to 24 deaths per 1,000 by the end of World War I. To illustrate, between 1888 and 1890, the death rate was 28.7 per 1,000 population; the birthrate during these years was approximately 40 per 1,000. Between 1911 and 1915, the death rate declined to 24.4 while the birthrate increased slightly, to 42.1. By then, maintaining the birthrate at a constant level as the death rate fell resulted in the highest natural growth rate in Romania's history. However, at the end of World War I, the birthrate began to decline dramatically, marking the beginning of a new phase of demographic transition. In this period, both birth and death figures fell, albeit at different rates, the drop in the birthrate being more pronounced. The crude birthrate for the period 1920–1924 declined to 37.6 per 1,000, while the death rate stayed approximately the same as it had been before the war (24 deaths per 1,000). In the interwar years, 1935–1940, the crude birthrate plummeted to 29.3; the death rate fell to 19.1 deaths per 1,000 inhabitants.[11] From then on, the decline was more accentuated.

The birthrate decline is also reflected in the total fertility rate representing the average number of children per woman in the population of fertile women age 15 to 49. According to Trebici and Ghinoiu, in 1900 the total fertility rate per woman was 5.26 children.[12] By the middle of the 1950s, it had declined to three.[13] (Recall, nonetheless, that abortion had been criminalized in 1948.) Over a period of 50 years, the number of children per woman had dropped by more than 50 percent.[14]

Infant mortality, the demographic indicator most sensitive to social and economic changes, followed this same pattern. In 1919 the infant mortality rate (children under the age of one) was 205 deaths per 1,000 live births,[15] which was meaningful for the transition with respect to fertility behavior. Among peasant families, the birth of many children generally paralleled a high infant mortality rate. The very survival of the family and society was at stake. When the infant mortality rate dropped, however, the fertility rate began to follow suit.[16] At the same time, it must be recognized that the decision of Romanian couples to have fewer children was also the result of changing attitudes about life and death, society, and history.

Throughout much of the twentieth century, modern contraception was unavailable in urban and rural Romania. Couples relied on abstinence, coitus interruptus, the woman's monthly cycle, douching after sexual intercourse, and a variety of plant and herbal remedies to control the number of children. Women resorted to abortion to correct the failure of traditional contraceptive methods (or "natural contraception"). Peasant women continued to treat births and abortions as they always had. Both were attended to by midwives who had learned their traditional "trade" from their predecessors, often from their own mothers, with the understanding that they too would pass on their skills.[17] Midwives were among the most highly regarded members of village communities. Later, after abortion was banned, midwives (whether "traditionally" or professionally trained) acquired yet more prestige because they could offer women an alternative to reproducing for the state.

In urban environments, there was a clear preference for smaller families. Large segments of the provincial urban population lived in precarious cultural and economic conditions. Among peasant families that had recently migrated to urban centers, male members were the most mobile. However, their success in the new urban setting depended on their being unfettered by large families.[18] These newcomers, both men and women, were members of a hybrid culture, living their daily lives mostly in accordance with the popular peasant practices with which they were familiar.

In addition to the "traditional methods" mentioned above, fertility control was managed by abortion.[19] Self-induced abortions were common and are evidence of the unequal availability of medical services and of the risks women took with their lives. As the Romanian novelist Panait Istrati wrote about such practices in the 1930s: "This was pure barbarism . . . these poor women punctured their uteruses with long crochet needles. One of them had the idea of stuffing boiling polenta into her vagina. Another preferred a bit of caustic soda. Naturally, hemorrhages, sometimes fatal, ensued."[20]

For the sake of context, it is worth noting that in 1938, the year considered to represent Romania's highest level of economic development during the interwar period, there was one doctor per 2,036 inhabitants.[21] Abortions done in private medical offices were confined to the privileged segment of the urban population, the "petite bourgeoisie" constituting the cut-off line of those able to take advantage of private services.[22] In recounting the history of medical practices in Romania, one gynecologist noted that no private doctor in Bucharest during the interwar years performed more than three abortions a day. While this reveals little about the actual number of requests for such services, it suggests that access to abortion was limited to a minority of women with "means." (The image of a doctor in Bucharest performing two or three abortions daily during the interwar years starkly contrasts with the pictures after the fall of Ceausescu of doctors in Bucharest performing abortions nonstop as women waited in endless lines.)

## THE POLITICAL REGULATION
## OF REPRODUCTION

### Banning Abortion, 1948–1957

By the 1940s, the consolidation of capitalist economic and institutional structures further influenced the changes in cultural and demographic behavior that had emerged at the beginning of the twentieth century. Reduced family size became normative; Romanians fell in line with modern European demographic trends. After World War II, other factors contributed to the preference for a reduced birthrate, among which was the uncertainty provoked by the installation of a new regime intent upon radically transforming society. (This uncertainty was presumably heightened by Soviet occupation.) Physical and mental exhaustion from the war's devastation, including the effects of widespread drought and hunger, also affected reproductive practices. Between 1946 and 1955 the birthrate declined steadily, with the exception of brief spurts that may be attributed to couples making up for time lost during the war, and to the fact that those born after World War I had themselves become adults, ready to create their own families.

When in 1948 the newly installed "popular and democratic" regime instituted a law to regulate the legal practice of abortion, it reproduced policies enacted earlier in the Soviet Union, then under the stewardship of Stalin, who had banned abortion there in 1936. As in other critical policy areas, the will of the Kremlin found expression in its satellite countries.[23] Indeed, article 482 of the Romanian Penal Code was revised, making the interruption of a normal pregnancy a criminal act. Since family planning options were limited to traditional methods and illegal abortion, the latter remained common and was performed to greater or lesser degrees with the tacit knowledge of the Romanian authorities. Between 1948 and 1957 the discrepancy between the law and unpunished activities in violation of it became so embedded in daily life that the law itself bordered on the meaningless. Its effects on the birthrate were almost negligible; the decline in births continued, emphasizing the increasing gap between legislative prerogatives designed to ensure that pregnancies were brought to term and the popular practices employed by women to prevent or terminate pregnancies.[24] Especially after 1966, the reasons to break the law often outweighed those demanding accommodation. Minimizing the costs of transgressing the law came to play an especially important role in the sexual and reproductive lives of Romanians.

## The Liberalization of Abortion, 1957–1966

"I recall looking out of my office window in the Palace of Justice, which faced the Hospital Brancovenesc," a jurist who began his career in the mid-1950s recounted.[25] "At its entrance, there was an 'Avortorium.'[26] Every day I watched an impressive number of women waiting in line to get abortions. Many of them seemed to be from the countryside, judging from the things that stuck out of their sacks: the beak of a goose stuffed inside, a hen's head, or even the comb of a turkey. What she had brought depended on each woman's resources and her desire to show gratitude to the doctor."

On September 30, 1957, legislation was passed making abortion legal upon demand. The text of the decree stipulated that "interruption of a normal pregnancy is to be done at the pregnant woman's request."[27] Article 482 of the Penal Code was again modified, this time to read: "Only abortions performed outside of medical or health institutions, or by persons lacking the necessary qualifications, are punishable." Abortion costs were paid by the woman, but the fixed sum was modest. At the time, an abortion cost the equivalent of approximately two dollars.[28] It is worth noting that the text of the decree did not include a preamble giving motives for the passage of the law. Moreover, the press did not pay any attention to this new law.[29] This silence was unusual for a print medium that fully served the interests of the government and did not miss an opportunity to extol and justify any of its decisions.

After almost ten years, the processes of transformation begun at the end of the 1940s acquired a certain degree of consistency. The new political order had been established; the social, economic, and cultural realms were being consolidated. In order to facilitate these radical changes, it was necessary to destroy the institutions, norms, and values of the previous social system. Altering familiar habits and traditional social groups was to provide a means to create social and geographic mobility. In turn, radical change and mobility influenced the population's attitudes about reproduction and sexual behavior.

Among the factors that informed the 1957 decision to liberalize abortion was "international ideological solidarity." Most of the countries in the Soviet sphere began introducing liberal abortion legislation in 1956, moves that were again regarded by some specialists as the satellite countries' mimicry of Soviet initiatives.[30] Abortion had been legalized in the USSR in 1955. In the preamble to that legislation, the principal motive for the decriminalization of abortion was stated to be the need to put an end to the negative consequences to women's health resulting from abortions not done under hospital supervision.[31]

While there is undoubtedly a kernel of truth in this, concern for the health of women was not the primary motive for the adoption of these measures. Political factors seem to have been more important to the Romanian leadership. During this era, the social and familial emancipation of women was omnipresent in the official rhetoric of the Romanian Communist Party's leaders. The liberalization of abortion made it possible for the state to camouflage the fact that it had neither the means nor the interest to support the real economic and social emancipation of women. Underlying the "humane" concern about women's health was the need for their full participation in the "building of socialism."

Other geopolitical factors also seem to have influenced the legalization of abortion. In 1956, Soviet-style communism experienced its first major crisis.

Hungary, Poland, and East Germany revolted against Soviet domination. Many Romanian students and intellectuals in university centers such as Bucharest, Cluj, and Timisoara declared their solidarity with the Hungarian insurrection. Some engaged in demonstrations against the political order. Although the agents of a police state on alert immediately repressed such activities, the wave of arrests and expulsions from universities that followed aggravated the already strained relations between the state and the populace.[32] The liberalization of abortion was among the enticements offered to "the people" to diffuse these tensions and alter the regime's image. This "take and give"—a very little—was a political tactic repeatedly used by those in power.

The coherence of the communists' political project was paradoxically undermined by the structural inconsistencies inherent in "popular and democratic" rule. The conjuncture of the factors discussed above, both international and domestic, conspired to produce a gradual but constant decline in fertility. In the absence of the commercialization and promotion of modern contraceptive alternatives, abortion remained the most highly valued method of fertility control for a population convinced of the need to reduce family size.[33]

## Political Demography and the Body Politic, 1966–1989

During the Ceausescu years, the steadily increasing ideological emphasis on political demography was given material form through legislative and policy initiatives. Over the 23-year period in which the political demographic policies were in force, three phases of legislative activity may be identified: 1966–1973, 1974–1984, and 1984–1989.[34] The banning of abortion in 1966 constituted the centerpiece of the laws and policies that affected the intimate lives of all citizens throughout Ceausescu's rule. The regime's ambivalence to the roles of women in the building of socialism, and to the family itself (whose institutional origins and organization were ideologically suspect), was consistently reflected in the modification of legislative and policy measures. The intensification of measures to restrict abortion occurred despite the popular trend to reduce the number of children per family. The ongoing tensions that resulted from the state's aggressive campaigns against abortion and contraception, and the population's defensive ploys against the state's attempts to control their sexual and reproductive lives, dramatically underscored both the intrusions of the regime into the intimacies of everyday life and the constitution of the body politic.

What today in the United States are known as "family values" were fundamental to Romania's political demography. Ceausescu's personal obsession was, in one form or another, "families with many children" (though the idealized socialist family could be sacrificed as necessary to preserve the discursive integrity of political demography). From the perspective of valorizing the family, the combination of pronatalist and strong anti-abortion measures was ideologically coherent, as was the legislative attention directed at keeping families together. In the interest of the latter, divorce was an important focus of legislative activity. Hence, before turning to a detailed exploration of the central aspects of political demography, a general discussion of the official positions on divorce is in order.

### Divorce Legislation

The state exerted its paternalist authority over the family through varied means, including divorce legislation. As in the Soviet Union, the "legitimacy" of divorce (like that of abortion) fluctuated over time and in keeping with political-propaganda goals. The state's intrusion into the private sphere of family relations grew over the years, and in sync with all facets of the ever more elaborated ideology of the "new" socialist family. Divorce represented the dissolution of this ideal and was to be discouraged.[35] To this end, laws were passed that made the breakup of the family unit increasingly difficult. And like all people who indulged in acts (such as abortion) contrary to the express wishes of the state, those who chose to pursue what they considered to be in their own best interests were usually held hostage by the process that pursuit entailed. In this regard, the secret police served as the arbiters of "conscience." Loyal to the tenets of socialist morality, they tried to help those seeking a divorce to arrive at a "consensual" agreement to remain a family. The line between "mutual consent" and coercion was blurred.

Soon after the installation of the communist government in 1948, the articles of the Romanian Civil Code (nos. 254–276) that referred to the consensual grounds for divorce (and that had been in force since 1864) were eliminated. With Law 18/1948, divorce as a social act became dependent on a legal judgment. Like the abortion-related laws, this one was repeatedly revised, elaborated, and recast in other fundamental texts.[36] Thus, in 1954, article 37 of the Family Code stipulated that a marriage could be undone only through the legal determination of death of one of the parties or through divorce that could be granted only through a "legal decision and if there exist sound motives."[37] By 1966 and in keeping with political demographic initiatives (and a worrisome rise in the number of divorces), divorce became possible only in "exceptional cases."[38] In 1972 the critical role of the family in building socialism was officially stated:

> Everyone must understand that he has responsibilities toward society, including that of leaving progeny. This is not an issue about which we can close our eyes. Youth must be raised in a healthy spiritual environment, to understand its responsibilities toward society and the family. Only then will we create a true socialist society. . . . We cannot be indifferent to what happens to the family, how young people marry or do not marry, believing that this pertains to their per-

sonal lives. Of course, it is their personal lives, but society has always been concerned and must be concerned with the personal lives of people.[39]

Divorce was an option only when the relationship between the husband and wife was deemed irremediably damaged such that the marriage could not go on under any circumstances. The court was instructed to weigh the extenuating circumstances carefully, including the length of the marriage and the interests of any children thereby affected.

Generally, the process of obtaining a divorce involved a waiting period during which attempts were made to reconcile the couple's differences. Certain circumstances were not subject to this condition: for example, if one spouse was diagnosed insane, or if one had abandoned the other through emigration (often illegal). Otherwise, the mandatory period had to be observed. Reconciliation was imposed by law in cases in which the grounds for divorce involved infidelity, battery, degrading behavior, incurable diseases, and the like. These circumstances were not deemed in and of themselves sufficient cause to dissolve a family unit. Reconciliation was even considered a possibility when one of the members had been found guilty of attempted murder of the other or of complicity in such an act, or for inflicting serious physical injuries.[40] Initiating a divorce was further complicated by the financial costs incurred. The cost to begin such a proceeding—that is, for the official request—varied according to monthly wages and ranged between 3,000 and 6,000 lei, not an inconsequential sum.[41]

The divorce measures had an immediate effect, and inversely paralleled reaction to the abortion decree in 1966. For that year, there were 25,804 registered divorces (down from 36,914 in 1965); in 1967 the number of divorces dropped dramatically, to 48.[42] (As was generally characteristic of the reporting of statistics, this dramatic decline reflected the statistical adjustment employed as a political response to the decree.) This abruptly interrupted what had become, after World War II, a general trend throughout the Soviet bloc of increasing numbers of divorces. The introduction of legal strictures to constrain abortion and divorce had the desired effect—but only initially. Mirroring the impact of the abortion law, the spectacular "results" were but ephemeral. After 1968 the number of divorces grew steadily. Ten years after the issuance of Decree 779/1966 the number of divorces had climbed back up to earlier levels: 35,945 divorces were registered in 1976.[43]

Again, the regime had legislated, yet failed to impose, its will. Nonetheless, divorce carried with it more insidious "moral consequences" in the public sphere. The granting of a divorce brought with it the formal mark of social illegitimacy. Such "moral" and civic failings were noted in personal files at the workplace. In this manner, career development—professional and political—was among the prices paid for a divorce. For those unwilling or unable to pay this price, the consequences were costly in other respects.

Living "together" under such circumstances constituted yet another modality through which dissimulation and the internalization of double standards were transformed into the norms of everyday experience.

Keeping "the family" together was considered fundamental to achieving the regime's political demographic goals.[44] Making certain that this family consisted of many children was equally essential.

### Pronatalism and the Nation, 1966–1973

By 1966 the Romanian birthrate had fallen to 14.3 live births per 1,000 population from a 1960 rate of 19.1 per 1,000 (see figure 2.1).[45]

Upon the "authoritative" advice (and consent) of the demographers loyal to the regime, this decline in the birthrate was officially attributed to the liberalization of abortion in 1957. However, the banning of abortion in 1948 did not modify the populace's attitudes about reproduction or the tendency toward a decline in the birthrate. The liberalization of abortion did not cause birthrates to fall but, rather, legalized already existing widespread practice.[46] As Ghetau has noted: "We must admit that the fertility decline in Romania in the 1960s would have occurred even without the easy access to abortion . . . in our opinion, the fertility decline would simply have been less pronounced and of longer duration in the absence of the liberal legislation on abortion."[47]

Those who supported claims that the legalization of abortion caused the birthrate decline argued that by the early 1960s the total fertility rate was lower than the threshold figures for population replacement. By 1966 the number of children per woman had dropped to 1.9 (from the approximate replacement rate of 2.2–2.3 for 1965–66).[48] Romania's crude birthrate during the preceding five years was approximately 94 percent of the average in other Eastern European countries.[49] However, this line of reasoning does not take into consideration the various factors couples weigh in determining the number of children to have, among which are the costs of procuring everyday necessities relative to increased "quality of life" expectations for their own as well as their children's futures. Such calculations included not only greater consumer spending but also better educational and leisure opportunities. The "rationality" of centralized planning increasingly came into conflict with the "rational" choices of families. Those who supported the banning of abortion in 1966 did not seem to understand this.

On October 1, 1966—one decade after abortion had been liberalized—the Council of State issued Decree 770, which forbade the interruption of the course of a pregnancy. The preamble to this decree stated: "The interruption of a pregnancy represents an act with grave consequences for the health of women, and is detrimental to fertility and the natural growth

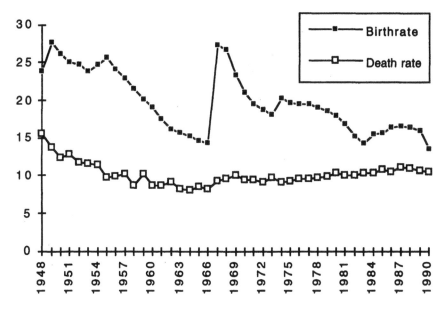

Figure 2.1: Crude Birth and Death Rates, per 1,000, 1948–1989. *Source: Anuaral statistic al Romaniei, 1990*: 67.

of the population." (Recall that the 1957 decree had lacked a preamble justifying the decree's issuance.) Its contents legitimated official reasoning about abortion, or, at the very least, the regime's intentions. The concern expressed for women's health served to presage the special status that the state would increasingly confer on them, namely that of "a nationalized means to increase reproduction." For the first time, population growth was presented as a legitimate political objective, even though the expected goals were not yet specified.[50] These latter would be unveiled over time and increasingly in relation to Ceausescu's obsession with being the leader of a great (that is, populous) country.

The political context in which Decree 770 was issued was relevant to its understanding: After coming to power in 1965, Ceausescu began a campaign to legitimate his rule. He skillfully began distancing himself from the politics of the Dej period. The virtual banning of abortion was among the first "signs" that distinguished Ceausescu from his predecessor. Rather than toeing the Soviet line on reproduction, as Dej had done despite his own national inclinations, Ceausescu publicly initiated his national ideology of Romanian socialism. The Soviets voiced their strong disapproval of Ceausescu's banning of abortion: "While such incentives deserve approval, one can hardly approve of the prohibition of abortion since the experience of many countries, including the USSR, shows that such a measure has never, no matter where, led to any real or prolonged rise in the birthrate. It has merely caused women to put an end to an unwanted pregnancy by having an abortion secretly, the danger of which to a woman's life and health is considerably greater than an abortion performed in a hospital."[51] This ambivalent statement about Ceausescu's political demographic policies provided the Soviets with a means to take public issue with the Romanian leader's politics in general.

While the Soviets expressed their negative reaction, the banning of abortion in Romania went unremarked in the West (see discussion in chapter 4). Because the politics of abortion were used on all sides as a pawn in the dynamics of Cold War animosities, Ceausescu's banning of abortion may have been read erroneously as a "moral" point in common with Western values, suggesting to Western leaders that Ceausescu might prove to be a different sort of communist. That evaluation was, to emphasize, confirmed by his 1968 stance on Czechoslovakia, which earned him the title of a communist "maverick" in search of independence.

The introduction of Decree 770 commanded considerable attention in the Romanian party press, the instrument through which the population was informed of its details. The anti-abortion decree consisted of eight articles, which addressed three basic issues: exceptions to the law, institutionalization of its provisions, and sanctions for their violation. Article 2 listed the following exceptions:

> the pregnancy endangers the woman's life such that no other resolution is possible;
>
> one of the parents suffers from a serious hereditary illness, or from one that will predetermine a serious congenital malformation;
>
> the pregnant woman shows grave physical, psychological, or sensory disabilities;
>
> the woman is over 45 years of age;
>
> the woman has given birth to four children and has them in her care;
>
> the pregnancy is the result of rape or incest.

A woman who wanted an abortion had to prove that at least one of these circumstances applied to her. Approval for a legal abortion was granted by a medical committee, which existed only in clinics and hospitals that had obstetrics-gynecology sections. A complicated administrative ritual had to be officially observed before an abortion was authorized. Details about the decree's implementation were contained in a series of instructions from the Ministry of Health.[52]

A woman requesting an abortion had to have the doctor of the medical institution to which she was assigned complete the proper form, entitled

"Fisa pentru intreruperea cursului sarcinii" (Form for the interruption of the development of a pregnancy). In the event that the woman was already hospitalized, the attending physician had to complete the form, which contained details of the woman's personal history, confirmation of her pregnancy, and the reason why an abortion was recommended. Otherwise, with the form in hand, the woman presented herself to the medical committee, comprising a chairman, who was a primary physician or obstetrician-gynecologist (or, if necessary, a surgeon); a primary physician or internist; and a secretary, who was usually a nurse. The committee was set up by administrators from state institutions at the national level. The committee registered the woman's file in the official "register of requests for interrupting the course of a pregnancy," after which it began its deliberations. In some instances, the committee consulted with other physicians, requested additional tests, or asked for reconfirmation of the diagnosis. The committee's decision was then recorded in her file. If approval was granted, the woman took her file to the appropriate obstetrics-gynecology section, where she was admitted and scheduled for an abortion.

A legal abortion was customarily permitted only in the first trimester of a pregnancy. Article 3 nonetheless allowed that "in an exceptional case, when it is established that a grave condition threatens the life of the woman, an abortion may be performed until the sixth month." If a woman over the age of 45 applied for an abortion, or she had given birth to and had in her care at least four children, or her pregnancy was the result of rape or incest, she had to provide official documents proving her claim(s): identity papers, birth certificates of her children, and, in the case of rape or incest, a certificate from the authorities verifying these causes. Whenever a woman's request for the termination of a pregnancy was denied, her file was returned to her doctor, who was expected to follow the course of her pregnancy closely.[53]

Article 6 of Decree 770 warrants scrutiny. It clarified terminological distinctions and practices associated with abortion. However, the ambiguous style in which it was formulated enabled women and physicians to take advantage of it, within certain limits, in order to justify the legality of terminating a pregnancy. In cases of "extreme medical emergency, when an abortion must be done immediately, the doctor is obliged to inform the prosecutor in writing before beginning, or, if that is impossible, within 24 hours after having done it." With the assistance of a forensic physician, the prosecutor then determined whether the abortion had been necessary (that is, whether it was legal). Any evidence of abortive maneuvers had to be noted on the medical observation chart. Furthermore, this information had to be added to the section on emergencies of the woman's official "form for the interruption of the development of a pregnancy." These data were later statistically compiled at the Ministry of Health.

Medical emergencies of this kind fell under two broad categories: spontaneous abortions—that is, those in which physiological causes, independent of any intervening factors, terminated the pregnancy by miscarriage (for which legitimate conditions were specified in article 2); and illegal abortions—that is, induced abortions or, as stipulated in the instructions about the application of the decree's provisions, those that resulted from an "infraction" of the decree. In the majority of emergency cases, the ambiguity of interpretation arose when an illegally induced abortion could be classified as a legal miscarriage. If the doctor responding to such an emergency found no telling signs of deliberate attempts to terminate a pregnancy (such as lacerations, tears, or erosions of the cervix), then, depending on his or her good will, the abortion could be recorded as "spontaneous," regardless of its actual cause. However, if an anatomical-pathological examination yielded evidence of a deliberate intervention to terminate a pregnancy, then a legal investigation ensued. Punishments were spelled out in the Penal Code.

Illegal abortions consisted of both those that were statistically invisible and those that "counted." The former encompassed successfully completed surgical intervention or curettage, this being the method practiced exclusively then, as well as provoked abortions that did not result in complications. Such abortions were often induced by introducing a sound into the cervix, or by other mechanical or pharmacological means.[54] Since they escaped official detection, they were not recorded. Specialists estimate that only 50 percent of illegal abortions were successful, meaning that no harm came to the women; other women required emergency hospital treatment for infections or other complications, or died.

The second type of illegal abortion included attempts that ended up officially registered in state records. These were "visible abortions" because they fell under the scrutiny of the ever-watchful eyes of the state. When a voluntarily induced abortion remained incomplete, complications endangering the life of the woman often arose. Hemorrhaging was among the most common problems. Women who never arrived at the hospital or who arrived too late were later listed in the mortality statistics under "causes of maternal deaths." Those who made it to the hospital but who had obviously broken the law were subject to punishment according to the dictates of the Penal Code. Statistics from the Ministry of Health indicate that approximately 60 percent of women hospitalized for emergencies related to pregnancy between 1966 and 1989 were diagnosed as suffering from incomplete abortions—that is, abortions that had been provoked at home (or elsewhere in private) and "terminated" in the hospital or morgue. Only 40 percent of emergency cases resulted from miscarriages or other legal causes.[55]

On October 2, 1966, the regime's position on abortion was pronounced on the first page of the party daily, *Scînteia*: "The particular social danger resulting from abortion and from its grave medical, demographic, and social consequences makes it necessary to punish all persons associated with effecting an abortion: the instigators, mediators, and others involved in arranging an abortion as well as the participants themselves." Punishments for the illegal termination of a pregnancy applied to persons who performed illegal abortions, their accomplices, and the women who had sought their services or induced the abortion themselves. In such cases, the woman was to be deprived of her liberty through imprisonment or other forms of punishment.[56]

Imprisonment and loss of certain civil liberties were customary sanctions against criminal activities and were meted out to those guilty of violating the abortion law. For the "abortionist," punishment was spelled out in article 185; for accomplices, article 186, paragraph 2; for the illegal possession of instruments or abortifacients, article 187. The gravity of the sentence depended on the role of the infractors and the records of previous offenses. Punishments ranged from a fine to a sentence carried out at the person's place of work (by definition, a state enterprise) or in prison.[57] (See appendix for sample case summaries.) Terms set out generally in the Penal Code were modified in 1966 to read: "The interruption of a pregnancy performed with the woman's consent is to be punished with a sentence of one to three years' imprisonment and a one- to three-year prohibition against the exercise of specified civil rights."

Punishment in Romania was considered to serve a "correctional" function. Deprivation was presumed to "teach" persons to uphold socialist norms of comportment in their daily lives—that is, to be proper socialist subjects. One important form of deprivation was financial. Hence, violators of the law often received sentences forcing them to work without pay. This simultaneously resolved other infrastructural problems that arose from assigning jail terms, namely, the lack of available space and the cost of maintaining additional prisoners. Even more important, allowing convicted women to remain at home made it feasible for them, in theory, to bear as well as care for children. Presumably, the "correctional" aspect of their sentence would prevent them from seeking abortions.

Another form of deprivation was imposed on physicians if their activities were judged to be particularly grave: gynecologists could be forbidden to practice their specialty for a period of time. They were not removed from the cadre of working medical practitioners, but were shifted into other medical specialties. For example, one gynecologist accused of defying the law eventually received a complex sentence, including eight years' imprisonment and five years' prohibition of civil rights (article 64, paragraphs a, b, and c of the Penal Code), under which was included the interdiction of his right to practice during the five years (article 185, paragraphs 1, 4, and 5, of the Penal Code regarding illegal provocation of abortion). Nongynecologists

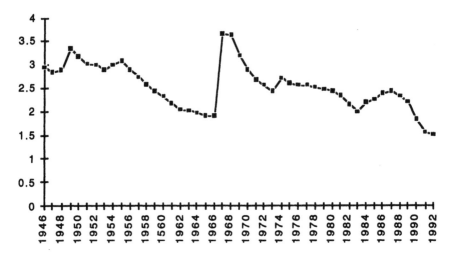

Figure 2.2: Total Fertility Rate, 1946–1991. *Source:* Chesnais 1992: 543, 548 for 1946–82; Muresan 1996 for 1983–1991.

were punished in other ways, such as being sent to village clinics. Doctors were also sanctioned for failing to notify the prosecutor and police organs of infringements. In such cases, they could be imprisoned for one to three months (article 188, Penal Code).

The impact of the "surprise" anti-abortion legislation was to paralyze a population suddenly deprived of its principal means of fertility control. In 1967 the number of live births nearly doubled that of the preceding year; the total fertility rate grew from 1.9 in 1966 to 3.7 in 1967 (see figure 2.2).

The banning of abortion nationalized and centralized this primary method of family planning. The Party/State's full "victory" over private life lasted two years in its most acute form, the time necessary for the populace to find alternative means to prevent and terminate pregnancies, to get around the law, and to form multiple and functional networks of support among themselves. (As shown in figure 2.2, the subjugation of private life nonetheless endured throughout the years of pronatalist politics, from 1966 to 1989.) During these two years, there was a collective effort to reactivate the former "traditional" practices abandoned with the liberalization of abortion back in 1957.

Thus, in spite of Decree 770/1966, fertility began to decline again after 1968. By 1973 the total fertility rate had dropped back to 2.4 children per woman from a high of 3.7 in 1967. Despite all efforts to enforce the law, the population's strategies to thwart the state's interference in their private lives had become more effective. To reverse this negative trend, the instructions for the implementation of Decree 770/1966 were revised and further detailed in 1974. The intent was to see to it that the results of planned and centralized human reproduction matched official representations for them.

### *"The Creation of Ever Better Conditions for Women," 1973–1983*

*It is necessary that our party organs, regional committees, popular councils, and Central Committee accord greater attention to these problems so fundamental to the development of our society, our nation. Given the vital role of women in the development of our society, in maintaining the health and youth of our nation, it is as necessary to raise the level [of women's] consciousness as it is to resolve certain social problems, as well as those related to jobs, consumption, services, and the development of nurseries and kindergartens.[58]*

The next phase of state intervention into reproductive practices began in earnest in 1974, following the signals given at the National Conference of Women in the spring of 1973. Ceausescu's address was replete with subtle warnings of what was to come. In the interest of homogenization, he repudiated gender discrimination, demanding that persons be treated not as men and women but as members of the party and as citizens of the Socialist Republic of Romania.[59] While advocating equality, Ceausescu, in the very same speech, stressed women's distinctiveness: "An obligation of national interest is the protection and consolidation of the family, the development of a corresponding consciousness about the growth of an increased number of children, and the formation of healthy and robust generations profoundly devoted to the cause of socialism; in this realm *women have a distinguished role and a noble mission.*"[60]

The "distinguished role and noble mission" of women in society became the focus of an ongoing and concerted political effort to enable women to realize their "multilaterally developed" abilities. This new campaign, which roughly (and felicitously) coincided with the UN's International Women's Year and Decade of Women, was motivated by strikingly paradoxical concerns: consolidation of Ceausescu's power over the people and enhancement of his reputation in the international arena.[61] In a continuing effort to exert control over the private sphere, ideologues and specialists paid vigilant attention to demographic factors. At the same time, the official discourse on political demography was recast and stylized to promote Ceausescu's positive image abroad, especially in the West. The Romanian leader openly saluted women's significance for development, rhetorically embracing favored Western themes of "self-determination" and the need for "population control." However, his understanding of the relationship between these two cultural-political imperatives was seemingly lost in translation.

With respect to demographic indicators, the government was determined to brake the downward spiral of the birthrate by undermining the strategies used by the population to "plan" their families. Thus began an aggressive propaganda campaign, supplemented by administrative measures. The state-dominated public sphere was discursively and representationally saturated with value-laden talk about the "nation," "population," "independence," "vigor [ of the nation]," "prosperity," and "the future." (This is discussed more fully in chapter 5.) Accompanying this symbolic, rhetorical onslaught were diverse administrative maneuvers ranging from the provision of maternal and familial incentives similar to those found throughout the Eastern bloc, to distinctly repressive measures. To encourage compliance with the political demographic policies, the state offered a series of financial, material, and psychological "incentives." Aimed at lending support—however minimal—to women for bearing children and to families for fulfilling their obligations to raise and educate them for the state, the effect of these initiatives was more symbolic than material. These measures served as a smoke screen, obscuring simultaneously implemented measures to bring the behavior of the populace into line with that desired by the authorities. Various disciplinary steps were also taken to make medical services more "efficient" (that is, to make them conform to the dictates of the state's reproductive politics).

The modifications imposed in 1974 reflected a growing obsession with form and appearance, both of which came to dominate policy decisions of this regime. The seductiveness of symbolic, pseudo-scientific elaboration was striking in the volume of information given and the manner in which details were presented. The eight-page 1966 decree, banally entitled "Instructions for the Implementation of Decree 770/1966 for Regulating the Interruption of Pregnancy," had been defined and explicated in 22 articles. By 1974 the modifications to 770/1966 contained 47 articles in seven sections and totaled 21 pages. To these were added eleven pages of appendices distinguishing the "medical grounds for interrupting a pregnancy," which were grouped into nineteen causal categories. Yet another eleven pages explained the bureaucratic functioning of the medical system. This supplementary document was titled "Instructions for the Implementation of Decree 770/1966 for Regulating the Interruption of Pregnancy, for the Resolution of Incomplete Abortions, and the Improvement of Medical Assistance in Obstetrics-Gynecology."[62]

The principal alterations to Decree 770 affected many of its original articles. The medical commissions empowered to authorize legal abortions were to be appointed by the director of the county Department of Health, the respective prosecutor, and the chief inspector of the county Department of the Ministry of Internal Affairs. This commission was to consist of three primary physicians or specialists (one obstetrician-gynecologist, who was to serve as president of the commission; one internist; and one pediatrician), plus a secretary. During their meetings, a representative from the Ministry of Internal Affairs and one from the prosecutor's office were required to be present. While these modifications may seem insignificant, they created the mechanisms by which control over human reproduction was increased and tightened. Physicians were ever more deeply enmeshed in the tarantula's web of a regime set on having "the people's" will obeyed.

The importance of physicians' roles and decisions often placed them in contradictory positions with respect to those seeking their medical assistance and those politically supervising it. State control was not organized in a simple hierarchical fashion, but rather was managed through a studied combination of vertically and horizontally interwoven sanctions, suspicions, fears, and enticements. As shall be discussed, the presence of members of the state's repressive apparatus at meetings of the medical commissions constituted an evident exercise of state control, and, in and of itself, challenged the scientific authority of physicians. Their presence also demonstrated a literal policing of the female body and intimate acts (through physical examinations), and the politicization of reproduction.

Elaboration of the instructions for the implementation of Decree 770/1966 was predicated on the belief that the body and those who came into contact with it required constant supervision and surveillance. To this end, another commission was constituted in 1974. Its task was to analyze the monthly sale of medicines from pharmacies "in the interest of preventing certain abuses ahead of time."[63] The medicines under such vigilant scrutiny were those "with restricted or contraindicated uses for pregnant women between the ages of 16 and 40." The web of controls became more intricately spun.

The conditions for which an abortion was legally granted remained the same in 1972 as in 1966, with one exception: the age at which women became eligible for this procedure was lowered in 1972 from 45 to 40 (Decree 53 published on February 16, 1972). Although no explanation was given, this concession was perhaps made as a gesture to international demographic convention, thereby precluding objections at the forthcoming World Population Congress about the higher age limit. The fertility of women between the ages of 40 and 45 was markedly lower than that of younger women (see figure 2.3). Analysis of data amassed between 1966 and 1972, when the minimum age for requesting a legal abortion was 45, demonstrates that lowering the legal age of abortion to 40 did not radically alter the total number of live births.[64] The proportion of live births for women in the over-40 category, weighed in terms of the total number of live births, was insignificant. Moreover, a positive correlation between a woman's advanced age and the probability of birth defects in her offspring had been noted in Western medical research. In short, it was clear that lowering the age at which abortion became legal did not affect the overall goal of increasing the birthrate.[65]

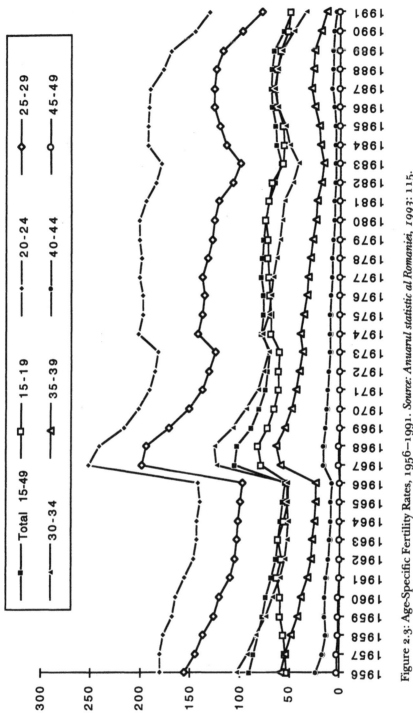

Figure 2.3: Age-Specific Fertility Rates, 1956–1991. *Source: Anuarul statistic al României, 1993*: 115.

An entire section of the revised instructions addressed the problem of incomplete abortions, implicitly acknowledging their role in the birthrate decline after 1968. The attention to technical detail in this section was meant to exhaust the category of "incomplete abortions." To reiterate, incomplete abortions referred euphemistically to illegally induced abortions, whether they resulted in the complete or partial expulsion of the fetus, and which necessitated medical intervention. Emphasis was placed on making the means of surveillance more efficient. The extreme formalization of medical procedures and monitoring protocols was designed to inhibit the practice of abortion. The rationale behind this was that the birthrate would be increased.

This type of bureaucratic control system meant that certain individuals acquired multiple professional responsibilities. To illustrate, a hospital's chief obstetrician-gynecologist also became head "watchman." He or she was held accountable for the medical unit's performance in meeting the plan's reproductive goals. This person had to decide whether intervention was appropriate in the event of an incomplete abortion, see to it that each case was examined on its merits, and perform "unannounced and frequent exams."[66]

One of the most insidious forms of control was managed through what was known as territorialization. With the exception of dire emergencies, incomplete abortions could only be treated in specific hospitals determined according to their "territorial" distribution. Emergencies treated in non-approved hospitals or outside the area to which a woman was assigned had to be reported to the Department of Health within 24 hours. Solid proof of the need for an emergency intervention had to be documented. In addition, access to and use of surgical instruments used in abortions was strictly regulated. By law, such medical instruments were allowed to be used only in medical units, and then only if procedures were scrupulously followed:

> Release of the surgical instruments will be made by the nurse charged with their care upon approval of the head of section or the head doctor on call. The checking out and return of medical instruments will be recorded in the daily report of the attending physician. The (registered) number of instruments given and returned will be mentioned. In the event that these instruments are used while the attending physician is there, the date and hour that they were given must be noted, including the name of the person to whom they were given, the name of the physician who recommended that a curettage be done, and the name of the woman, as well as the number from the registration book in which the intervention for an incomplete abortion was recorded.[67]

It was understood that retention of these instruments or substitution thereof by any individual for the purpose of performing abortions was illegal and would be subject to punishment as spelled out in the Penal Code.

This widespread circuit of surveillance and intra-institutional control was overseen by each county's prosecutor and police who, under normal conditions and during normal working hours, required prior notification by the doctor intending to intervene. Complications resulting from an incomplete abortion could be treated only after representatives from these offices had arrived and confirmed the need for immediate medical aid. Only in very serious cases such as advanced septicemia, renal blockage, or shock due to hemorrhaging would a physician intervene immediately and try to save the woman's life. In some cases, the doctor received permission via telephone. If the woman's condition required emergency intervention, or if she had arrived at the hospital in the middle of the night, then "within 24 hours, [the doctor was required to] present a written report to the prosecutor using the proper form, and specify the police department and rank of the person to whom the previous phone call had been made, as well as the time of this call and its registered number."[68] In this manner, every decision and action could entangle one in different but related strands of the web of organized surveillance. However, the state's totalizing will to power was rarely achieved as intended because of the informal relations that partially humanized these practices. Bribes, connections, and friendships, for example, mediated between legal provisions and actual practices. At the same time, the constitutionally guaranteed "inviolability of the person and his effects" was regularly violated: intimidation, suspicion, denouncement, and blackmail functioned indirectly—and efficiently—to create a pervasive culture of fear.

Directors of the county Departments of Health were obligated by law to inform legal authorities of medical or health personnel suspected of engaging in illegal abortion practices.[69] In turn, appropriate steps were taken to investigate such allegations, as well as the suspect's personal property. Also, members of the medical hierarchy charged with such responsibilities were required every month to analyze the effectiveness of the abortion-related policies. They were also obliged to alert the state administration if examination of the records uncovered a pattern of legal violations.

The need for improved medical assistance in obstetrics and gynecology was also addressed in the revised instructions. While on the surface this reflected the paternalist state's concern for the well-being of its female citizens, these measures served as a pretext to extend the state's means of control over the reproductive lives of women. Calling attention to the importance of preventive medicine in combating malignant diseases affecting women, such as ovarian and breast cancers, the law stipulated that "on a semiannual or annual basis, gynecological exams will be given to all salaried female employees at factories or institutions with a high percentage of female workers." Mechanisms were established to treat sterility, to provide that pregnancies were medically followed from the first months on, and to make certain that women who had had repeated abortions were hospitalized to facilitate the supervision of their pregnancies and the prevention of any mishap. The concern for women's health was espoused through every conceivable propaganda forum. The obsessive "care" manifested in such seemingly benevolent measures as annual gynecological exams distorted the leadership's real interest: maximizing fertility in order to ensure an increased birthrate. All of these actions were designed to compel women to fulfill the demographic plan. It is not accidental that the 1974 program of the Romanian Communist Party contained population projections through the year 1990.[70]

The need to orchestrate these "multilaterally developed" means of control speaks to the recognition by state officials and specialists that the possibilities to evade or violate the prohibition against abortion were numerous.[71] The hierarchization of authority operative in hospitals, combined with control mechanisms that functioned at each level of medical practice, was meant to preclude manipulation of the law's intent. For example, the list of medical conditions considered to be legitimate causes for approval of an abortion defined the parameters of a doctor's legal activities, deviation from which would bring immediate attention to him or her. From a theoretical standpoint, this list of specified causes provided doctors with the leeway to argue in favor of an abortion request before the medical commission that had to approve it. The potential diversity of medical opinions among them opened a window for the eruption of dispute in the commission itself.[72] In consequence, the criteria invoked to decide a case were not always impartial, but rather reflected partisan interests. Nonetheless, professional solidarity often won the day; consensus emerged as a professional response to political domination.

Here, it is worthwhile to touch upon the context in which women sought abortions. Recall that contraceptives were unavailable to most of the population. The use of contraceptives was not forbidden by law—not in the decree of 1966, or in the instructions accompanying it, or in any other normative act related to demographic policy.[73] It had simply become almost impossible to obtain them. Contraceptives were available on the black market, but their cost, combined with the basic difficulties of acquiring them in this way, put them beyond the reach of most women. In the 1970s, condoms were still produced commercially. However, by the 1980s they were nowhere to be found.[74] Yet, despite the lack of contraceptive options and the repressive measures then in force, the birthrate continued to fall. This meant women and families used illegal abortion as the most viable method of "family planning." Traditional methods of birth control were widely used, but these were notoriously unreliable. Abortion, regardless of its legality and the potential risks associated with it, served as a corrective to the mishaps that resulted from the unreliability of the other methods.

Nonetheless, doctors unanimously agreed that women tended to put off the actual decision to arrange an abortion. In view of the laws, abortion was often a high-risk solution. Women were haunted by a permanent fear of legal or medical repercussions in the event that something went wrong. Abortions were expensive, and it became increasingly difficult to gain access to medical practitioners who were willing to perform them. Consequently, many women tried "traditional" methods of interrupting the pregnancy before resorting to an abortion, which offered salvation when all else had failed. Accordingly, many women did not seek an abortion until approximately the tenth week of pregnancy, after they had tried an entire series of alternative procedures and products: lifting heavy items (e.g., rearranging heavy pieces of furniture); jumping from heights; or repeatedly trying both until exhaustion overcame them; preparing and administering various concoctions even though the risk of secondary infection was well known; introducing into the vagina all manner of chemical substances, pharmaceutical products, herbs such as wormwood or lovage, and other items believed to be abortifacients such as concentrated infusions of quinine, oleander, or marigolds as well as saline solutions and aluminum potassium sulfates. Household objects such as hairpins, goose quills, and crochet, knitting, and spinning needles were also customarily introduced to perforate the cervix.[75] If the woman remained pregnant, then she resorted to abortion in despair. Of course, not all women chose this option. The offspring who had clung so obstinately to life were frequently among the growing numbers of children who were physically and psychologically handicapped.

All in all, the new measures adopted at the beginning of 1974 contributed to but a small growth in fertility for that year (2.7 children per woman; the 1973 figure was 2.4). The demographic "success" of 1967 was not repeated; instead, the birthrate again began to fall by the beginning of 1975. The population had become more accustomed to the repetitive nature of the state's tactics and the existence of other means—however precarious—to protect themselves. Comparing age-specific fertility rates for 1967 and 1974 (see figure 2.3)—the years following alterations in abortion legislation—lends supporting evidence. The span of fertile years was divided into standard, five-year age ranges: 15–19, 20–24, 25–29, 30–34, 35–39, 40–44, 45–49. In the first year after the announcement of the 1966 decree there was a noticeable increase in the birthrate among all fertile age groups, meaning that the introduction of this legislation had a real effect on the population. The jump in the birthrate for the two most fertile groups, women 20–24 and 25–29 years of age, was significant, but also predictable, because most Romanians married young and began to have children after one year of married life. Commonly, couples produced two children within the first four years of marriage. The median age of mothers when they gave birth to their second child was 26.[76] The prohibition of abortion prompted young women to become pregnant somewhat earlier than perhaps expected. In this respect, they were better prepared psychologically to tolerate flexibility and adjust their own plans to suit those of the state.

This was not the case, however, for women over the age of 30. By that age, most women had already given birth to the number of children they desired. For them, the banning of abortion in 1966 was particularly stressful. The relative increases in the birthrate for these age groups were notable, especially among those between the ages of 30 and 39 (see figure 2.3). Between 1967 and 1968, the birthrate for women between the ages of 20 and 29 had begun to fall, but not for women between the ages of 30 and 39. In fact, during the first two years of Decree 770's enforcement, this older age cohort was largely responsible for the increase in the birthrate.

This cannot be said for what happened in 1974 following the modification of the accompanying instructions (*Instructiuni*). In contrast to 1967, the effects of the 1974 legislative changes among women over the age of 30 were negligible; the number of children per family decreased slightly. Approximately 80 percent of births were concentrated among women between the ages of 15 and 29. Clearly, women had either modified their family plans or learned to diminish or avoid the brutal effects of these laws. That women had "adjusted" was also evident from the analysis of age-specific fertility rates (see figure 2.3). By 1974 fertility decline had become a stable trend. In spite of strict legislation, the barrage of pronatalist propaganda, and the introduction of symbolic and material measures to stimulate the birthrate, the fertility rate fell steadily.

By 1983 both the birthrate and the total fertility rate approximated those of 1966.[77] However, the context in 1983 was radically different. Unlike in 1966, there had long been no liberal law to which the natality decline could be attributed. The regime had failed to impose new values, norms, and conduct on a society evidently determined to resist the state's intrusions.[78] Recognition of this failure became the basis for the formulation of another set of political demographic initiatives. This third and final phase of political demographic activity was to be the most aggressive—and repressive.

### Policing the Body, 1984–1989

*Joke: The latest slogan: No ovulation without fecundity!*[79]

*Joke: Why does a Romanian hen sing every time she lays an egg? Because she is overjoyed that she is not pregnant!*

The year 1984 ushered in the Orwellian policies that became an inspiration for Margaret Atwood's novel *The Handmaid's Tale*, and foreshadowed a Romanian national tragedy. Having experimented unsuccessfully for almost 20 years with a series of "rational" mechanisms to stimulate the birthrate, those who hoped to maximize the population of childbearing women resorted to the imposition of repressive measures. The decline in the birthrate coincided with a steady deterioration in the material conditions of everyday life. In the interest of national self-determination, Ceausescu had decided that Romania's outstanding foreign debts would be repaid early—at enormous cost to the quality of life. Production was targeted for export. By 1984, winters were endured with little heat or electricity; food staples were rationed. Milk was not regularly available. Demographers and families know that the number of births often declines in times of economic hardship; despite the existence of ample data, the regime did not officially recognize this correlation.[80] The invisible war between state and society escalated with the implementation of a new strategy: outright coercion. In keeping with basic development plans, coercion was applied "multilaterally." On December 26, 1985, Decree 770/1966 was further modified through the publication of Decree 411. The second and most significant article in this decree raised the age at which women became eligible for legal abortions back to the 1966 limit of 45. Theoretically, a woman could become pregnant late into her forties, hence the maximum childbearing age of 49.[81] Furthermore, the modified decree stipulated that interruption of a pregnancy was legal if "the woman has delivered five children and has them under her care." (This increased the number of children from four to five.)

A battle waged to improve the demographic indicators recast the ethical connotations of what it meant to be a mother and the familial contextualization of maternity. The cultural respect accorded motherhood was contingent upon a woman's marital status. The stigma attached to illegitimate children stemmed from the social contempt in which nonmarital sexual relations were held.[82] In socialist Romania, the family continued to be a strong cultural institution in everyday life. Anyone caught transgressing institutionalized norms was considered deviant.

However, the rhetoric of morality invoked to legitimate the official role of the family under socialism was perceived to be nothing more than what it was: ideological veneer. From this standpoint, when rumors began to circulate about the regime's informal support of childbearing regardless of marital status, the general public was scandalized. The deliberate spreading of rumors often functioned as an effective means of disseminating information about official intentions regarding prescriptive behavior and people's reactions. In 1987 it was informally proposed by representatives of the regime that pregnant high school girls not be expelled as stipulated in school rules. They were to be given the opportunity to continue their education by attending night school, or to complete their exams without being present in class. Correspondingly, the state offered to "adopt" the newborn. Especially in the villages, *gura satului* (the village "voice") filled the air with scathing remarks about the state's blessing of the degradation of girls. Yet again, the hypocrisy of socialist discourse about morality stood publicly disrobed. The puritan-like norms about socio-sexual propriety extolled discursively in the "Code of Principles and Norms of Socialist Ethics and Equity" had little bearing upon those meant to be translated into practice. In effect, to encourage a higher birthrate, the state encouraged promiscuity. A joke captured the irony of state-supported pregnancy out of wedlock: "A policeman caught a couple making love behind the bushes. After they were booked, they went on to court. During the trial, the girl was congratulated for her patriotism; the boy for his initiative; the policeman was arrested for the illegal interruption of a pregnancy."[83]

The instrumentalization of these repressive measures by the police and propaganda apparatus led to a slight increase in the birthrate and to a decrease in the number of abortions.[84] However, after 1986 and in spite of a propaganda offensive, the breaking up of illegal abortion networks, and strict surveillance of the activities of medical specialists, the decline in natality was quietly reestablished. It must be noted that the reliability of statistics produced during the latter half of the 1980s was greatly reduced. More than ever before, the manipulation of statistical evidence became second nature to the bureaucratic apparatus. Physicians were compelled to participate in the falsification of data about the numbers of births and deaths. Monthly levels were predetermined in order to guarantee that the demographic plans were fulfilled. To this end, it was stated clearly in Decree 335/1983 issued by the Council of State that all medical personnel were accountable for the realization of these goals.[85] If these goals were not reached, then their wages would automatically be penalized by a fixed percentage. For example, failure to fulfill the birthrate indicators resulted in a fine of 15 percent of a monthly salary; failure to reduce infant mortality rates was also punished by a 15 percent fine; failure to reduce the transmission of illnesses earned a 10 percent penalty. This was another behavioral modification technique designed to "correct" deviance and "stimulate" compliance with the norms dictated by the state.

A recounting of an incident that occurred at a meeting organized by the party committee of the Ministry of Health to discuss the poor performance of Bucharest's medical personnel in fulfilling the demographic goals illustrates the logic of such fines. A dentist asked the presiding party representatives if there was a relation between the number of teeth in a woman's mouth and her fertility potential. This unfortunate, well-meaning dentist simply "didn't get it"—that is, he could not understand why a dentist's salary was penalized monthly because the women of Bucharest, including those with healthy teeth, were unwilling to produce the requisite number of children to fulfill the demographic plan. He had fulfilled his professional obligation as a dentist. What more was there for him to do?[86] There was also a distinct fine against failure to meet the norms associated with political demography. Again, those fines were all set at 15 percent; failure to control other illnesses, as well as financial mismanagement, were also punished, but at the lower rate of 10 percent. Although this ordinance was formally directed to obstetrics-gynecology and pediatric hospitals, a footnote further specified that the reduction of infant mortality, transmission of illnesses, and increase in natality figures had to be met at the county level. Because these indicators had to be met countywide, all doctors—and not only those at particular pediatric and obstetrics-gynecology hospitals—were woven into the web of state control, including dentists. Everyone was held responsible for meeting the plan.

As shall be seen in the following chapters, this was a key mechanism used to ensure complicity with regime politics on a massive scale. At the same time, this very mechanism gave local medical personnel a reason to falsify data as a means of fulfilling their obligations to the plan and protecting their own interests. Although it is difficult to measure or even estimate the actual impact of such administrative practices, the data provided to the authorities were distorted—to greater or lesser degrees. Birth and death figures were manipulated. Given that the creation and internalization of a new demographic behavioral pattern loomed among the political priorities of the state, distorted information on vital statistics may be viewed as the compromised representation of official projections and real practices.

In Ceausescu's Romania, "family values" were politically dictated and legislatively embodied. The banning of abortion was the organizing principle around which political demography was conceptualized and implemented. Pronatalism—introduced in 1966 and modified substantively in the two decades that followed—was an integral feature of Ceausescu's communist nationalism, providing the means through which the Romanian "population" was to be ensured and "secured." Legislation served to legitimate the political will of the regime while simultaneously defining the parameters of "legitimate" intrusion into the practices of everyday life. Yet this formal legislation also offered individuals a blueprint for assessing the windows of opportunity through which they might evade or resist the dictates of the Party/State.

Analyzed in their totality, the pronatalist policies enable us to understand the nature of state-society relations and the means by which individuals both complied with and resisted the state. Beginning in the mid-1970s, the more narrowly focused political demographic legislation discussed thus far was augmented by a series of normative legal measures, pronatalist in intent and designed to have a broader impact on altering social and familial organization. These policy measures are the subject of the next chapter.

CHAPTER 3

# "Protecting" Women, Children,
# and the Family

*The "state allocation for children"... is destined to substantially meet the child rearing expenses which burden the family budget. The allocation is not only an equitable measure, characteristic of the socialist order, but, at the same time, it is one of the measures by which the Romanian state carries out its demographic policy of encouraging childbearing by all means and by constant financial sacrifices and consequently, the continuous growth of the country's population.*

IOAN CETERCHI, V. D. ZLATESCU, I. M. COPIL, AND P. ANCA, EDS.,
*Romanian Legislation on Population Growth and Its Demographic Effects*, 1975

In keeping with the importance of the "rule of law" in Ceausescu's "original democracy," legislation served as the primary form through which the dominant ideology was instrumentalized and officially legitimated. From the 1970s until his execution, Ceausescu unrelentingly stressed the essential roles of the family and of women in the building of socialism and securing the nation's "golden" future. His speeches were filled with exaltations about the glories of bearing and raising children, of which the following rendition is typical:

> The highest patriotic citizens' duty for each family is to have and raise children. It is inconceivable to imagine a family without children. The greatest honor and most important social role for women is to give birth, to give life, and to raise children. There cannot be anything more precious for a woman than to be a mother, except to ensure the realization of nature's laws in her own life, to procreate, to ensure the continuous development of the people, of our nation. There cannot exist for a family and for a woman a greater pride and joy than that of having and raising children.[1]

The social-familial legal provisions were meant to compensate families for fulfilling their patriotic obligation to raise and educate children for the nation. Women's efforts to carry out their socially and culturally "predestined" roles as workers, wives, and mothers were hailed. This legislation symbolically validated the official discourse about equality and social justice and the possibilities created by socialism for every individual to realize his or her human and creative potential; in practical terms, the legislation stipulated the financial resources allocated for families to be invested productively in (re)producing children.[2] In this manner, control by and benefits to the state were guaranteed.

These measures covered the scope of family and maternity benefits. A series of acts meant to protect the interests of salaried women, children, and different categories of minors was also delineated. There were special medical provisions for pregnant women, mothers, and children; social services for preschool children whose mothers worked; assistance for invalids and widowed persons; and financial compensation (mostly symbolic) for mothers with many children.[3] To guarantee that all citizens fulfilled their patriotic social(ist) duty to bear children for the good of the nation, Law 1 of June 30, 1977, took into account that some persons of childbearing age remained childless, thereby eschewing their responsibility to socialist society. Hence, to equalize social contributions, all childless persons 25 years of age or older, regardless of marital status, were taxed on a monthly basis. In this respect, it may be argued that the demographic policies were differentially burdensome for women by virtue of "nature" rather than as a result of deliberate political sexism.[4]

The gist of the content of the pro-family and pro-child measures is presented below. However, it must be emphasized that the following examples reflect formal criteria rather than empirical ones. By the mid-1980s, Romania had become a "hunter-gatherer" industrialized society in which citizens had to scavenge to meet the requirements of daily subsistence. The charts published by the state did not take note of the rationing of staples then in effect, which influenced "rational" cost-benefit decisions made by couples about the size of family they could support under such conditions.

State allocations for children were determined by the number of children living in the family, the order of their birth, and the salary level of the entitled adult.[5] Children living with their families had the right to receive these allowances until the age of sixteen or eighteen (the latter if the child had become disabled before the age of sixteen). The allowances were not taxable. The amount of the allocation was inversely related to the earnings of the beneficiary, usually the head of family, and directly related to the number of children in a family's care (see table 3.1).

In view of the pronatalist goals of the regime, it would be expected that the incentives provided through financial allowances would be greater for higher-birth-order children. Indeed, the average allowance for each child born after the first was higher than for the previous child (see table 3.1). In 1985, the monthly allowances granted to persons living in an urban environment and earning the average monthly salary of 2,827 lei were the following:[6] 250 lei for the first child, 290 for the second, 310 for the third, 400 for the fourth, and 400 for each subsequent child. Otherwise stated, these sums were equivalent to 8.8 percent of the monthly wage of the head of household for the first child, an additional 10.2 percent for the second, another 10.9 percent for the third, and 14.1 percent for each of the others. At

TABLE 3.1    Allocations for Children by Monthly Wage

| Monthly Wage | Child | | | |
|---|---|---|---|---|
| | First | Second | Third | Fourth and Each Additional |
| Under 2,500 lei | | | | |
| urban | 300 | 350 | 430 | 500 |
| rural | 200 | 270 | 300 | 350 |
| 2,501–3350 lei | | | | |
| urban | 250 | 290 | 310 | 400 |
| rural | 150 | 220 | 260 | 290 |
| 3,350–4,450 lei | | | | |
| urban | 220 | 260 | 290 | 340 |
| rural | 130 | 140 | 170 | 230 |

SOURCE:   Decree 410, *Buletin oficial*, no. 76, December 26, 1985.

first glance, these monthly allowances may seem generous. For those in the lowest income category, a salary could be augmented by almost 50 percent; for those in the highest bracket, by 20 percent.[7] (Family incomes were supplemented by the wages of working mothers and other maternity benefits due them; economic and political pressures made it necessary for most women to work.) Although in absolute terms the allowances were not trivial sums, in everyday terms they did not translate into what could be considered a meaningful incentive.

The "incentive" of an approximately 10 percent increase in monthly income per child after the first was inadequate to meet the expense of raising a family, particularly in the difficult conditions in which the majority of Romanians lived during the 1980s. Incomes were low relative to the costs of raising children; moreover, the family allowances in Romania also remained less generous than those of other Eastern bloc countries.[8] Parents who shouldered the responsibility of caring for their children were all too familiar with getting by on inadequate resources, and the conditions of everyday life were deteriorating, not getting better.[9]

Before December 22, 1989, no studies on the costs of raising children with respect to a family's socioeconomic position were accessible; hence, it is difficult to evaluate the effects of the allowances on the quality of family life after the birth of a child.[10] Despite the unavailability of reliable quantitative data, it is nonetheless possible to present a rough picture of monthly costs keyed to family size by comparing the size of the family allowance with estimated actual expenditures (see tables 3.1 and 3.2). Table 3.2 presents estimates for 1989, when the economic crisis was most critical.[11] The Romanian population felt this crisis in terms of decreased purchasing power, rising inflation, and a noticeable degeneration in the conditions of their

TABLE 3.2    Family Expenses According to Family Size

| | Monthly Expenses (lei per family per month) | | | | |
|---|---|---|---|---|---|
| Family Size | Food | Other Goods | Services | Total/Family | Total/Person |
| One | 800 | 525 | 327 | 1,652 | 1,652 |
| Two | 1,530 | 834 | 455 | 2,819 | 1,410 |
| Three | 2,230 | 1,158 | 650 | 4,038 | 1,346 |
| Four | 2,930 | 1,428 | 790 | 5,148 | 1,287 |
| Five | 3,630 | 1,702 | 940 | 6,272 | 1,255 |
| Six | 4,330 | 1,937 | 1,029 | 7,297 | 1,216 |

SOURCE:   World Bank Country Study: Romania, 1990: 70.

daily lives.[12] The information represented in table 3.2 is partial at best, reflecting only formal aspects of the overall economic context. Viewed in these terms, it is evident that family allowances were insufficient to meet family needs and expenses. In Romania, benefits per child covered approximately 20 percent of the direct costs of a child's care.[13]

Using tables 3.1 and 3.2, a general picture of the impact of these social-familial measures may be sketched for a family of three that received an allowance for one child, and for a family of four that received benefits for two children in their care.[14] For each of these hypothetical families, the earnings of the persons entitled to receive the allocation were average (between 2,501 and 3,350 lei; see table 3.1). As above, the sum for a first child was 250 lei per month; for a second, 290. In the case of the family with one child, the monthly expenses per person were 1,346 lei; the allocation thus covered 18.5 percent of their expenses. For the family caring for two children, these costs came to 1,287 lei per person; the allocation covered 22.5 percent of their combined expenses (see table 3.2). The second child's value to the state was but an additional 4 percent of the family's actual cost. This factor may have contributed to the tendency among urban intellectuals to favor one-child families. However, because two-child families are the cultural norm in Romania, even the additional economic burden may not have deterred a couple from having a second child.

The cost of living per family varied, despite overall hardship. The fertility differential between urban and rural families and socioeconomic strata was marked. Intellectuals tended to have one child, whereas the poorest segments of Romanian society tended to have larger families. (Roma, peasants, and rural workers often had four to six children.) Expenses per person were determined by several factors, including educational and cultural "needs." Furthermore, the resources acquired from the exchange of goods between urban and rural family members have not been incorporated into the calculation of the hypothetical family's monthly expenditures. The important role of secondary economic activities in a family's financial profile is also absent. Food supplies that were unobtainable in the state sector could be found in the ever-expanding black market, but at almost five times the official state prices. Hence, the cost of food indicated in table 3.2 is well below the actual amount spent by most families. (Families with two or more children spent at least half of the monthly budget on food; this is double the typical monthly food expenditure for similar-sized families in advanced societies.)

Another factor ignored in the official calculation of family expenses was the cost of educating a child, despite the state's assurance of free education. In a centralized economy, human investment was the key to success—at the family level as well. Particularly in urban areas, families with children about to enter high school were saddled with considerable additional expenses, often well beyond their means. In this type of centralized educational system, the status of a high school was dependent on the degree of competition for places in it. The more prestigious a school, the fiercer the competition to enter it—and, later, the greater the likelihood of continuing on in higher education. Such opportunities were ultimately expected to be translated into important social positions.[15] So, to give their children the best possible chance of succeeding, many parents paid large sums for private tutoring. Access to the upper levels of the Romanian social hierarchy was predicated upon possession of academic titles or political capital; by the mid-1970s, political capital presupposed a certain degree of educational capital. In consequence, educational capital had become a key criterion for achieving upward social mobility.

The effects of the birthrate explosion that followed the banning of abortion in 1966 reverberated throughout the school system as the 1967 and 1968 cohorts entered it in the early 1970s. Figure 3.1 shows that the number of pupils grew significantly. The number in kindergarten began to increase in 1971–72. Similarly, elementary and junior high school enrollments increased substantially in 1974–75 and 1978–79, respectively.

The number of teachers was increased to accommodate the larger enrollments. However, related infrastructural problems and limited budgetary investments further complicated the issue of student:teacher ratios, and, in turn, the quality of instruction suffered.[16] By the mid-1970s, the number of students in urban schools exceeded the capacity of the schools to serve them. The number of school shifts per day was increased from two to three, while the time spent in each class was reduced from 50 to 45 minutes with a five-minute break between classes.

Schools offered educational services that became progressively less rigorous, leading to a widening gap between the level of preparation obtained in junior high school and that expected for admittance to a good

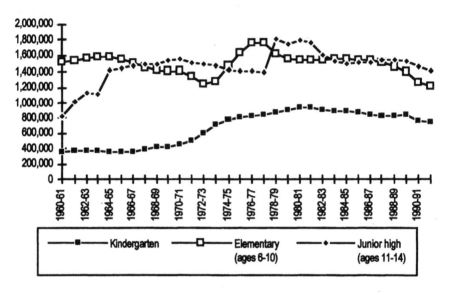

Figure 3.1: Enrollment in Kindergarten and Elementary School, 1960–1991.
*Source: Anuarul statistic al Romaniei, 1992*; and Ruxandra Marincovici, Institute for Educational Sciences, Bucharest.

high school and, later, to university. According to sociological data, the basic functioning of the educational system increasingly became an issue for parents and children alike.[17] Some 68 percent of parents and 70 percent of students believed that their schoolteachers did not teach effectively. To remedy the perceived inadequacies of the formal system and to make sure that their children would be prepared for university, families resorted to "private education," that is, to private lessons. Questionnaire responses suggest that approximately half the population of high school students prepared for university entrance exams in this way. The percentages were similar for students preparing for high school admission tests.[18]

The story of A. and M., who in the early 1990s were middle-aged parents of two children (a boy and a girl), illustrates how an urban family "worked the system" in order to better their children's chances for a brighter future.[19] "Children and the future" were key elements of socialist propaganda, although the strategies of parents and the state differed regarding how best to ensure the futures of "their" children. A., the mother, worked as a printer at one of the largest printing houses in Bucharest. M., the father, was a foreman at the national railway company. Before 1989, A.'s salary was approximately 1,200 lei per month, which was supplemented by about 1,000 lei for additional work done on Saturdays and Sundays. M. earned 2,500 lei per month. They and their two children lived in a modest apartment consisting of a bathroom, kitchen, living room, and one bedroom in a typical socialist high-rise.[20] A. reminisced:

M. and I wanted our children to go to university—to become somebody! It is the most important achievement of our lives. Some people bought cars, others houses. For many years, we barely had enough for clothing, but our kids were good, in school also. With the money we spent on private lessons for them, we could have bought two cars, not one. But Maria, our oldest child, told us before she finished the eighth grade that she wanted to go to N. Balcescu, one of the most prestigious high schools in Bucharest—for that matter, in the country. The entrance exam was very tough. The best children went there; most of them came from families of intellectuals. She needed rigorous private lessons in mathematics, physics, and Romanian. She began one year before she had to take her exams. For that year of private lessons, we had to pay between 22,000 and 24,000 lei. For both children, we had to pay for private lessons for six years. It was hardest in Maria's next-to-last year in high school when she began studying for university entrance exams and her brother, four years younger, began private lessons for his entrance exams at the same high school his sister had gone to. Because our salaries were modest and the cost of lessons was high, not to mention that we had to eat, pay our apartment expenses [telephone, electricity, etc.], and buy clothes for our children, we counted every last coin. We knew that if we didn't, we'd never make it. Even so, many times, we had to borrow money from neighbors, relatives. Our rule was that we'd forgo anything, except we would not touch the money put aside for the children's lessons. Each September, at the beginning of the school year, one of us took a loan . . . for the maximum sum. My salary represented the monthly payment necessary to repay the loan in eleven months. This had to be paid off so that the other could then borrow for the next year. So, we would borrow 20,000 lei, almost ten times my salary, and then we had to pay approximately 22,000–24,000 lei for private lessons, meaning that we still needed to make up two months worth of my salary. In the end, we all lived on three-quarters of M.'s salary each month, the rest going to lessons. So we never took a loan for vacation funds; it would have been impossible. We always went to the mountains for a few days in August. It was really necessary; the kids worked very hard during the school year. Even if the conditions were very modest, it was something. So, for six years of private lessons (three for each child), we paid some 150,000 lei, or the equivalent of our combined salaries for two and one-half years. But our satisfaction is immeasurable. Maria is a mechanical engineer and her brother is a student in metallurgy at the Polytechnic University. I remember when Maria didn't pass the university entrance exam given in the summer. I couldn't believe it, but we didn't give up. To the contrary, we borrowed more money and she began an intensive round of private lessons. She was very depressed, because she knew we had to make this double effort on her behalf. We didn't hassle her. If you haven't been through an entrance exam, it's difficult to understand. I believed in her, knowing she had worked so hard. And this paid off because she was admitted after the fall exams, even though there were 22 students for each available place. When our son entered university also, one of my work mates joked: "Look at that—from you two, two smart kids!" My husband and I denied ourselves many things for many years—I had one warm winter skirt and two summer dresses; when my stockings tore, I had to sew them. When I went to the high school for parental consultations, I was ashamed of the way I was dressed. I knew Maria was also, but this mattered so much less than the children's success. Today, many are envious of us, of the children we have. And they have good reason!

A. and M.'s story is but one variant of a drama lived by many Romanian parents in both urban and rural settings who did their best to educate their children so that they could perhaps get ahead. This informally organized educational system expanded without incurring legal sanctions. In the context of a planned, centralized state, the regulatory role played by this officially unrecognized and uninstitutionalized organization of education paralleled that of black-market activities, which compensated for the lack of goods in the state-controlled sector. The informal economy was, of necessity, also "multilaterally developed." These informal secondary economic phenomena highlight the inherent problem of relying solely on the available statistical information.

The state provided other monetary allocations to families in which at least one parent was employed in a socialist enterprise but without a fixed contract; in which the husband served in the military either as a career or temporarily; or in which the head of household was a student, a teacher assigned for one year, or a pensioner. The rules for granting these sums did not discriminate against children from a previous marriage in a couple's care, or against children born outside of wedlock, adopted, or entrusted to persons other than their parents who were recognized as competent to raise them.[21] Families working in agricultural cooperatives received smaller allocations than those paid to workers in state institutions. The amounts granted to cooperative members were drawn from the same source that covered their pensions and social insurance. (The sums were determined in accordance with the law.)[22] Families engaged in noncollectivized agricultural labor did not benefit from any allocations for children; it was reasoned that they were able to exploit the yields of private agriculture. (There are no statistics covering this productive category of socialist citizens. In consequence of agricultural workers' "self-sufficiency," the state extracted monthly "benefits" from them through the imposition of quotas.)[23]

Additional measures meant to support the family provided financial assistance to mothers with many children and to the wives of men fulfilling their mandatory military service, as well as bonuses for women who had given birth. These sums were allocated in addition to those for children (see table 3.1) and were (supposed to be) granted throughout the mother's life, regardless of other income.[24] Mothers who had given birth to and had in their care three or more children under the age of eighteen were entitled to receive a total of 400 lei per month, or 500 lei for those who had five or more children in their care. Any children who had been put up for adoption, entrusted to someone else to be raised, or placed in a state institution for care (e.g., orphanages for "normal" or handicapped children, or correctional schools) did not count toward determining a woman's eligibility. Allowances for children attending university could be extended until the children reached the age of 25. However, it is again necessary to question the actual "value" of these bonuses granted to mothers who had fulfilled or exceeded the "(re)production plans." Although the sum of 400 or 500 lei was in addition to a mother's salary, this sum did not mean much for a woman who had five children in her care.

Article 22 of Decree 410 stipulated that mothers who were not salaried workers or who had no other means of support, and mothers whose husbands were doing their mandatory military service, had the right to a monthly grant (500 lei in urban and 350 in rural environments), provided that they were in the fifth or later month of pregnancy, caring for a child under the age of eight, or suffering from a serious disability. Single mothers whose "partners" in the military recognized their paternal responsibility were also eligible for this monthly allotment. Last, women who had given birth to one child received a lump-sum "birth bonus" of 1,500 lei at the time of each birth after the first one.[25]

Among these women who produced what the official propaganda had branded as the "country's wealth" and the "nation's future"—children—was another subcategory worthy of mention. Mothers were able to increase their financial resources by donating mother's milk. State Council Decree 100 of April 22, 1977, stipulated: "Women who donate mother's milk will receive as recompense 62 lei per liter of mother's milk donated" (art. 1); moreover, "For the duration of the period during which a woman donates mother's milk, she will be granted medical assistance, medicines, and hospitalization costs, including subsistence, free of charge" (art. 2).[26] Regardless of the initial intent, by the mid-1980s the cynicism behind this measure was taken for granted by a populace unable to find cow's milk for its children. State authorities attempted to acquire milk for children in hospitals by encouraging the patriotic donation of mother's milk; during these years, the Ministry of Health urged mothers—for reasons of health and in an effort to create strong, young bodies—to breastfeed their infants.[27] Recall that most people in Romania were not well nourished, particularly throughout this harsh decade of the dictatorship.

Another set of dispositions pertained to the needs of future mothers: work protection for pregnant women, maternity leave and childcare possibilities, medical services for mother and child, and the like. The Labor Code enumerated a series of protective measures for pregnant working women guaranteed by the paternalist state.[28] Pregnant women were to be spared from heavy physical labor and from working in toxic environments or environments with high temperatures where ionizing radiation or vibration was present or the danger of accidents was high. Pregnant women were also forbidden to work night shifts. The logic behind these provisions was that pregnant women should avoid strenuous physical exertion (to avoid provoking a miscarriage) and that a pregnancy should evolve under "optimal health conditions."

Maternity leave was, moreover, guaranteed by the state. "Maternity wages" were calculated as a fixed percentage of a woman's salary, this percentage varying according to the woman's seniority in the work force.[29] Maternity leaves were divided into pre- and postnatal periods totaling 112 workdays (of a six-day work week): 52 days before birth, 60 afterward. Women were not obliged to respect these intervals strictly; they could take the maximum number of days as they saw fit. The overwhelming majority of women found two months of postnatal leave to be insufficient; in consequence, most took the full 112 days after giving birth. When this period expired and until the infant reached the age of one, mothers had the right to work a reduced schedule of six, rather than eight, hours per day. Whenever a pediatrician certified that a child (up to the age of three) suffered from health problems and required the presence of his or her mother at home, mothers continued to receive paid medical leave at 50 to 80 percent of their salaries, again keyed to their seniority in the labor force.[30] Women whose children did not attend nursery schools or kindergartens had the right to work half-time. During this period, these women's part-time employment was classified as full-time, and they were compensated accordingly.[31] This provision gave women an alternative to dependence on the existing but inadequate social services for children (for example, nursery schools) as well as a way to lessen the material and affective costs of arranging for intra- and extrafamilial childcare. To this end, medical leaves to care for sick children were frequently "prescribed" even when a child was not sick. Here was another opening into the world of informal practices that had emerged illicitly in order to manage the burdens of daily life.[32]

Pregnant women and mothers of young children received special medical attention. Medical institutions were obligated by law to:

> ensure medical attention to pregnant women by clinical and laboratory examinations throughout the entire pregnancy; to carry out a [suitable] medical control and to take appropriate measures for pregnant women whose health is endangered; to ensure qualified medical assistance at birth and to supervise the evolution of a woman's state of health in the postnatal period; to perform periodic medical checkups of newborn children and ensure the [appropriate] medical assistance; to supervise the state of health and to organize the children's living regimen in nursery schools, children's homes, and other collectivities.[33]

Women who had worked for 25 years and who had given birth to at least three children whom they had raised until the age of ten could request early retirement. The legal retirement age for women was 55.[34] Women who had given birth to and raised three children could apply to retire one year earlier; two years for four children; three for five or more. The minimum retirement age was 50.[35]

As was true for other competitions in the sphere of production, mothers who bore many children were honored as "heroes of socialist labor," for which they were awarded decorations and minor privileges. To this end: "Mothers who have delivered and reared several children may be offered the following decorations: the order of 'Heroine Mother,' the order of 'Maternal Glory,' and the 'Maternity Medal.'"[36] These categories were further stratified:

> women who delivered and reared ten children were awarded the title of "Heroine Mother;"
>
> women who had delivered and reared nine children received the first-class "Order of Maternal Glory;" those with eight children, the second-class "Order of Maternal Glory;" those with seven, the third-class award in this category;
>
> women who had delivered and reared six children were awarded the first-class "Maternity Medal"; those with five, the second-class of this category.

The stipulations of this decree must be read carefully. A woman who bore ten children did not automatically qualify for the honor of Heroine Mother. She must also have raised them. The wording of this decree and several others is specific on this point. That a woman was required to "have given birth to and have in her care" *x* number of children was designed to take into consideration the high incidence of infant mortality, especially in rural areas. To illustrate, a peasant woman who had given birth to nine children, five of whom survived infancy and early childhood, only qualified for the second-class Maternity Medal rather than the first-class medal of Maternal Glory.

Mothers, like all citizens upon whom the title Hero of Socialist Labor was conferred, benefited from certain privileges, which included priority invitations to official sociopolitical events, top ranking for credits toward construction or purchase of privately owned dwellings, and additional holidays during the year in which the award was given (see art. 17). Women honored with medals in the categories of seven or more children received a one-time bonus, although the actual distribution of this bonus was haphazard. The financial benefits of these rewards in 1987 were identical with those given in 1977: Heroine Mothers received 2,000 lei; first-class Maternal Glory mothers, 1,500 lei; second-class, 1,000 lei; third-class, 500 lei.

The "mother medals" were by and large symbolic in their significance, as was the case for almost all measures meant to compensate citizens for their contributions to the "building of socialism." The state manipulated them accordingly. Hence, at one "cultural-scientific" event held to popularize the results of the political demographic measures and to laud the quality of the medical services offered to women and children, the organizers "invited" a Heroine Mother to recount her personal experience.[37] A thin woman, looking older than her years and bent over from too many years of hardship, appeared on the stage. Unaccustomed to this milieu, she stood there, uncertain and frightened. Time passed; silence filled the hall. Finally, realizing that she was supposed to say something about herself and her family, this Heroine Mother of ten children plainly stated that they managed as they could but were in desperate need of another bed so that everyone in this large household would have a place to sleep. She had nothing more to say, but her simple plea made a mockery of the state's zealous concern for the well-being of the children it so desired.

Another set of political measures directed at social-familial matters took up the state's socialization of preschool children.[38] The vital need for the services of these institutions, particularly nursery schools and kindergartens, was prompted by the high rate of female employment, the increasing atomization of the family (especially in urban environments), and the dynamics of the "baby boom" stimulated by the aggressive political demographic policies. The preamble to this decree read: "In order to assist parents in rearing and educating children, . . . the state shall organize, in the conditions of workers' self-management and economic-financial self-administration, nursery schools and kindergartens within which medical assistance, instruction, and education of children are provided free of charge." Nursery schools and kindergartens were subordinated to other state enterprises and institutions. Subsidies came from a social fund designated for this purpose by the industrial enterprises and state institutions to which these childcare centers were attached.

Until 1982 childcare services had been completely free. However, the social funds of state institutions were increasingly strained by the general economic recession. To rationalize the consequences of this increasing crisis for a centralized economy, the regime introduced a Romanian version of "self-management" and "self-financing" for all state enterprises. This meant that parents had to support some of the operational costs of the childcare facilities which, in response to necessity, also offered extended daycare and weekly care. Parental costs were graduated according to family earnings.[39] Children between the ages of three months and three years were eligible for nursery school; those between the ages of three and six could attend kindergarten.[40] Given that demand was greater than supply, children were admitted on a priority basis. In the high-priority category were children whose mothers worked or were students; those who were cared for by fathers who

TABLE 3.3    Nursery School Enrollment

| Year | Children Aged 1–3 | Places in Nurseries | Percentage of Children in Nurseries |
|------|-------------------|---------------------|-------------------------------------|
| 1980–81 | 1,217,062 | 92,632 | 7.6 |
| 1985–86 | 992,225 | 86,475 | 8.7 |
| 1988–89 | 1,088,868 | 80,628 | 7.4 |

SOURCE: Data courtesy of Ruxandra Marincovici, Institute for Educational Sciences, Bucharest.

were either employed or retired owing to illness or disability; and those whose mothers were employed and who also had in their care children with physical or mental handicaps.

It is difficult to assess the effectiveness of this legislation because reliable data do not exist.[41] Nonetheless, analysis of statistical data about the nursery school population, the number of openings, and the personnel working in them offers a general picture of the demand for these services and of the quality of service associated with them. Of the total population of one-, two-, and three-year-olds in 1985, 8.7 percent were able to be admitted (see table 3.3). By 1989 the proportion was 7.4 percent as the result of a reduction of approximately 6,000 nursery school slots.

The proportion of children who attended kindergarten (out of the total population of three- [or four-], five-, and six-year-olds) declined steadily between the school years 1982 and 1988. Afterward, the proportion of children in kindergartens declined, but for different reasons. In 1989–90, the cohort of eligible children was larger than in previous years; the number of pupils also grew. However, in 1990–91, although the number of eligible children increased, there was a sizable drop in the number of children enrolled (see table 3.4). Hence, the proportion of enrolled children dropped from 84 percent to 71.8 percent.[42]

The quality of services provided in nursery schools and kindergartens was criticized by those who used them. The number of young children assigned to each teacher was considered to be high, usually 27 children of three, four, and five years of age in a group.[43] After 1985 the quality of care steadily declined, while parental expenses increased. The monthly costs of an urban family with two children, one at nursery school and another at kindergarten, were often considerable.

A significant number of kindergarten-age children lived in rural areas. Their schooling was financed differently from that of their urban counterparts. In consequence of local initiatives, the enrollment of rural preschoolers was financed by community administrations and agricultural cooperatives. As a result of this more direct localized involvement of families and communities, there was considerable variation in the organization and

TABLE 3.4    Enrollment and Teachers in Kindergartens, 1965–1991

| Year | Children 3(4)–5(6) | Children in Kindergarten | Percentage of Children Enrolled | Teachers | Student:Teacher Ratio |
|------|------|------|------|------|------|
| 1965–66 | 1,275,301 | 353,721 | 27.74 | 13,579 | 26:1 |
| 1970–71 | 1,104,198 | 448,244 | 40.59 | 18,887 | 24:1 |
| 1975–76 | 1,188,484 | 812,420 | 68.4 | 33,789 | 24:1 |
| 1980–81 | 1,207,146 | 935,711 | 77.51 | 38,512 | 24:1 |
| 1981–82 | 1,207,804 | 931,217 | 77.1 | 38,977 | 24:1 |
| 1982–83 | 1,212,060 | 902,608 | 74.47 | 34,955 | 26:1 |
| 1983–84 | 1,189,210 | 893,101 | 75.1 | 34,365 | 26:1 |
| 1984–85 | 1,158,332 | 886,199 | 76.51 | 33,955 | 26:1 |
| 1985–86 | 1,113,585 | 864,332 | 77.62 | 33,522 | 26:1 |
| 1986–87 | 1,039,652 | 836,225 | 80.43 | 32,789 | 26:1 |
| 1987–88 | 987,506 | 828,079 | 83.86 | 31,300 | 26:1 |
| 1988–89 | 985,675 | 831,108 | 84.32 | 31,197 | 27:1 |
| 1989–90 | 1,008,856 | 835,890 | 82.86 | n/a | n/a |
| 1990–91 | 1,047,061 | 752,141 | 71.8 | n/a | n/a |

SOURCES: *Anuarul statistic al Romaniei, 1981, 1986, 1990*; Institute for Educational Sciences, Bucharest.

functioning of rural schools. Some children received more personalized attention; others were treated with disdainful neglect by their teachers. What perhaps most distinguished rural kindergartens from urban ones was the comparative overcrowding of the latter. Nonetheless, it would be incorrect to make generalizations about the quantity-quality relation. Differences existed within both urban and rural settings.

The limited number of openings at childcare centers combined with the expense and poor quality of services meant that individuals and families with no other alternatives depended on the state's social services for children. However, the preferred form of care and supervision for children was familial. Grandparents were highly valued in families able to rely on their assistance. The ideal arrangement for a young couple who worked and had small children was to have healthy, retired parents who could raise their grandchildren until the latter were old enough to go to school. Many first-generation urban couples whose parents still lived in rural areas left their children in the countryside under the care of their grandparents during their preschool years; frequently, these children did not move to the city until it was time for them to enter school. In the last years of the Ceausescu regime, retired extended-family members acquired another critical task: procuring the daily necessities for the survival of the young household.

There also existed a relatively small category of persons who nonetheless possessed both the means and the access to an informal network of childcare services. These were usually intellectuals and well-to-do families who were able to hire someone to look after the children during the workday. The lack of data about this type of secondary economic activity makes it impossible to comment meaningfully about how extensively "nannies" were used. But its prohibitive costs placed this solution beyond the means of the majority of the population.

The last "stimulatory" component of the set of legislative measures directed at social and familial matters addressed the needs of certain minors. In particular, these dispositions outlined the conditions for their institutionalization, as well as the responsibilities of the institutions toward their wards.[44] "Protection" was guaranteed legally to the following categories of minors:

> those whose parents are dead, unknown or in any other situation leading to the establishment of guardianship; if they have no goods or other material means and there are no persons who are obliged or who can be obliged to maintain them;
>
> those who, being deficient, need special care that cannot be provided in their family;
>
> those whose physical, moral, or intellectual development or whose health is endangered in the family;
>
> those who have committed [delinquent] acts or whose behavior contributes to dissemination of vices and immoral habits among minors.[45]

With regard to the care, education, and professional training of minors in the first three subcategories, if no other solutions existed, the Commission for the Protection of Minors could send them to one of the following institutions: a nursery for children under the age of one; homes for children age three to seven with minor disabilities; "hospital-dormitories" for children age three to eighteen with serious disabilities; special kindergartens for children age three to six; general schools for children age seven to fourteen with treatable disabilities; special high schools and professional schools for children age fourteen to eighteen with treatable disabilities; and rehabilitation centers for children age ten to eighteen.[46]

The establishment of these surrogate "care" and "educational" institutions was consistent with the state's exercise of its paternalist obligations. If and when families did not fulfill their parental roles, the state took on the "fostering" of these children. (In the late 1980s and in urban areas especially, unwanted children also began to be found abandoned to life on the streets.) Viewed from a strictly formal perspective, this was in keeping with customary practices. Peasant families unable to support another child often asked relatives to raise one of them; others were adopted by childless couples. The material and psychological conditions that enabled parents to give up their children are comprehensible in these terms. During the Ceausescu years, some parents relied upon state institutions as a form of temporary residence for children, meaning that they planned to retrieve them at a later date when they were better able to care for them at home. This "pawn shop" strategy often succeeded; in other cases, parents were unable to relocate their offspring. It was only after the fall of the regime that they—and the rest of the world—learned why. What was hidden behind the walls of state institutions did not figure into the rhetorical representations about the socialist public sphere and the role of the ideal socialist family within it. That role was verbally exalted and materially manipulated. But no matter how "doctored" the statistics were, the results revealed cracks and fissures in the system of demographic policies. The birthrate was not increasing according to plan. In short, the positive and repressive measures discussed thus far were not working.

In centralized socialist states, law was the faithful handmaiden to those in power. Laws were the means by which political intentions were mediated and institutionalized, thereby articulating the normative relation between the state and its citizens. That relation varied considerably among the fraternal states and in Romania was particularly troubled. From a strictly formalist perspective, the paternalist socialist state was a well-intentioned welfare state that cared for its children. Yet discourse is not sufficient to sustain the living body. The abundance promised in official rhetoric was nowhere to be found in daily life.

The legislating of human, familial, and social reproduction highlighted the structural tensions that made dissimulation a "multilaterally developed" feature of this system. The politicization of demographic concerns brought the contradictory interests of the state and its citizens into stark relief. In this respect, the socialist state revealed its Janus-like character: generous in form, punishing in practice. The regime, confronted by the resistance and failures that resulted from the means employed to engineer its utopian social project, resorted increasingly to repressive and coercive strategies to accomplish its ends. Violence—physical and symbolic—was among the strategies most frequently engaged. The means of its institutionalization is the subject of the following chapter.

CHAPTER 4

# Institutionalizing Political Demography
## The Medicalization of Repression

*No central organ, institution or organization may claim not to have an interest in the problems associated with the family or the population.*

V. TREBICI, D. LEMNETE, AND V. SAHLEANU, "LA PLANIFICATION DE LA FAMILLE ET LA CONTRACEPTION EN ROUMANIE," 1977[1]

*The State does not exist in the phenomenal world; it is a fiction of the philosophers. . . . What does exist is an organization, a collection of individual human beings connected to a set of relations. . . . There is no such thing as the power of the State; there are only, in reality, powers of individuals.*

A. R. RADCLIFFE-BROWN, *African Political Systems*, 1940

Among the institutions that played a significant if largely symbolic role in legitimating state power was its "supreme body," the Grand National Assembly. All members were formally elected, making them participants in what was later to be known as Ceausescu's "original democracy." As in any democracy, the Grand National Assembly was meant to serve a legislative function. Indeed, it did; however, the Grand National Assembly served the legislative power of the state rather than that of the people. It fell to this elected political body to approve and apply the legislative decisions of the Party/State, which represented the only real as well as self-proclaimed power. In turn, the Grand National Assembly embodied the "people's will" of the Party/State.[2] (Party and state domains of authority were distinct in their functions before Ceausescu. Under his rule, their distinctions were skillfully consolidated to be used in the service of promoting the personality cult.) In actuality, the Grand National Assembly was dominated by the party, many of whose Central Committee members served in it. As a result, they were able to exert control over the Assembly's activities; moreover, their presence ensured that the Grand National Assembly was complicitous with state power, in the name of the Romanian people. Through its ritualized participation in original democratic politics, the Grand National Assembly legitimated the utopian goals of the Romanian Communist Party.

The rhythm of socioeconomic development in the Socialist Republic of

Romania was metered according to the five-year plan. The five-year plan may be viewed as a centripetally oriented, hierarchically organized framework for controlled socioeconomic change, which targeted all aspects of the organization and functioning of society. The plan operated in two interdependent contexts: that in which political decisions were made, and that in which these political decisions were translated into social and economic practices. Each new five-year cycle was formally authorized at the Party Congress that took place one year before the plan's functional institutionalization. (A Party Congress was held in the fourth year of any five-year cycle; after 1967 interim national party conferences were held to evaluate and adjust the plan's targets.) As shall be seen, the "plan" was implemented at each institutional level and in each state institution. In this manner, the five-year plan provided a blueprint for institutional control and for locating institutional complicity in time and space.

How the state worked on its various bodies—political and physical—to produce institutional consent for and complicity with the political demographic policies is the subject of this chapter. Every year, one of the standing commissions of the Grand National Assembly—the Commission for Health, Work, Social Security, and Environmental Protection—formulated a series of measures pertinent to these domains; upon enactment, they had the authority of law. It then fell to the appropriate ministries and specialized political bodies to flesh out the details of these measures and put them into practice. Concerns related to demography in general and to human reproduction in particular were accorded preferential status in the commission's deliberations. Illustrative of the kinds of directives issued annually were:

— acquisition of thorough knowledge of the evolution of demographic phenomena; periodic analysis of the means by which demographic indicators are realized and the implementation of measures to influence favorably this evolution;

— reduction of the number of interruptions of pregnancy, particularly of self-provoked abortions; discovery and combating of risk factors that endanger the health and lives of women and children;

— supervision and control over the execution of the laws pertaining to labor protection and women's health in socialist enterprises during a worker's pregnancy and maternity leave, especially for those who work in toxic environments or with pollutants;

— intensification of educational efforts about health with regard to the creation of families and the combating of sterility and infertility among couples without children;

—examination of the causes that contribute to the maintenance of a high level of general and infant mortality, and the [introduction] of appropriate measures to ensure the population's health and to combat risk factors;

— increase in the regulation, discipline and responsibility of the medical cadre for the quality and execution of medical practice; elimination of their violation of the laws regarding the interruption of the development of a pregnancy.[3]

At face value, these general prescripts appear to be reasonably straightforward. They were not. The gap between political rhetoric and its translation into everyday practices was in fact a rupture between appearance and experience. Semantic manipulation, especially through the usage of ambiguous formulations, became a regime trademark and functioned as an effective means of symbolic domination.[4] When applied, the above directives roughly meant that all actively employed women between the ages of 16 and 45 were to be examined to determine whether they were pregnant or suffered from any condition that might negatively affect a pregnancy. Those who had had abortions or who in the first two years of marriage had not produced a child were to have their medical histories followed. The state police and attorney general's offices were to coordinate efforts to break up the networks through which illegal abortions were arranged. The medical commissions were to be under permanent surveillance to guarantee adherence to the Ministry of Health's instructions regarding the interruption of pregnancies and the treatment of incomplete abortions.

The pre- and proscriptions designed to control reproductive activities contributed to an Orwellian organization of social reality. Official policy was instrumentalized through a constellation of public institutions and organizations whose administrative and political activities were intercoordinated. (The distinction between administrative and political functions was heuristic, the former being charged with the organizational implementation of policy, by definition political.) Among the diverse institutions and organizations engaged in carrying out demographic dictates were the Ministry of Health, the Red Cross, the National Women's Council, the Union of Communist Youth, the General Union of Romanian Trade Unions, the Interior Ministry, the Attorney General's Office, the School of Medicine, the Institute for Maternal and Child Welfare, the Ministry of Labor, the Ministry of Tourism, the Council for Socialist Culture and Education, the Ministry of Education and Teaching, the Ministry of Justice, the Ministry of the Food Industry, the Ministry of the Chemical Industry, the (regional, municipal, city, and community) Popular Councils, and the journal *The Health Worker.*[5]

To coordinate the activities of all of the institutions directly involved in implementing the policies related to natality, a "supra" organization subordinate to the Grand National Assembly was created in 1971: the National Demographic Commission (NDC). This commission functioned for twelve years after which it was supplanted by the Higher Council on Health (HCH), which had been inaugurated in 1969 to analyze the status of the country's health care and to propose measures to improve it.[6] Despite these institutional efforts, the birthrate continued to decline. Although the number of institutions formally associated with the political demographic policies had grown, their efficacy had not. The eclipsing of the NDC by the HCH did, however, produce a change in the hierarchy of power as well as in the means and modalities of executing institutional responsibilities. Comparison of these two different phases of institutionalizing political demography sheds light on the politics of their respective eras. Moreover, an understanding of the institutions that served the state's interests provides a partial context in which to understand how the intelligentsia participated in their own domination by the state and, in turn, in the reproduction of that domination throughout society.

## THE BIRTH OF INSTITUTIONS:
## CONTEXTS AND SUBTEXTS

One of the primary reasons for creating the National Demographic Commission in 1971 was to have an institutional base from which to legitimate Romania's candidacy to host the World Population Conference in 1974.[7] Seizing a diplomatic opportunity, Romania submitted its name for consideration. In 1973, after two years of negotiations, the UN Economic and Social Council conferred this honor on the Socialist Republic. The Romanians intended to demonstrate to their Western partners that the demographic measures taken in 1966 formed an integral part of Ceausescu's socioeconomic development strategy.

The World Population Conference held in Bucharest in August 1974 offered the Romanians useful tools for consecrating and extending their demographic initiatives. Article 95 of the World Plan for Action in the Domain of Population stipulated: "Population measures and programmes should be integrated into comprehensive social and economic plans and programmes, and this integration should be reflected in the goals, instrumentalities and organizations for planning within the countries. In general, it is suggested that a unit dealing with population aspects be created and placed at a high level of the national administrative structure and that such a unit be staffed with qualified persons from the relevant disciplines."[8]

As noted in the UN regulations, the means by which these recommendations were applied in each country were to be determined by that country, thereby respecting the dictum of noninterference in the internal affairs of a sovereign state. In the case of Romania, the declaration of universal principles served as an umbrella under which diplomatic collusion with Ceausescu's internal practices occurred. Such inadvertent international complicity facilitated the promotion of political, military, and economic interests; it also contributed to the widening distance between what was preached and what was practiced in Romania itself. At that time, the divergence between declarations of intention and the concrete means used to realize them was much less visible than it later became. Between 1966, when the anti-abortion law was introduced, and the beginning of the 1980s, Romania's experience was often cited in the demographic literature. Romania offered demographers an experimental context within which to test hypotheses about demographic factors, state policy, and development. Dispassionate policy assessments were offered:

> The fact that Romania increased its birth rate has been widely cited here and at the Conference as a telling counter-example to so-called Malthusian policy. This is an extremely unperceptive interpretation. The Romanian policy is a classic example of a government's analyzing an existing demographic situation and concluding that a conflict exists between how individuals behave with respect to fertility and individuals' interests in their fellow citizens' behavior. One may disagree with the outcome of the analysis, but that is beside the point. Individual fertility decisions added up to a birth rate of 14 per 1,000 in 1966 in Romania. This was found socially inadequate and inconsistent with an aggregate population target identified as desirable by the end of the century. The government accordingly moved to modify individual behavior and to make it conform to the perceived public interest.[9]

For scientists, theoretical and technical issues apparently overshadowed other concerns, including ethical ones.[10]

Politically, the Western countries' tacit approval of Ceausescu's demographic plans seems to have been as much compensation for his defiance of the Soviet Union as an attempt to gain an ally among adversaries.[11] President Ceausescu publicly unveiled his policies at the opening of the World Population Conference: "To address population problems, we consider it necessary to begin with the fact that man constitutes the determinant factor in social and economic progress. That is why the organization of society and the general politics of states must have as their supreme goal that of the well-being and happiness of [their] people, the safeguarding of human liberty and dignity, the fulfillment of their personalities, the participation of the masses in the creation of their own history."[12]

Those present did not question the principal means to be utilized to secure "the well-being and happiness of people, the safeguarding of human liberty and dignity." Participants from Western industrialized countries, supportive of the objectives of population control, did not inquire whether Ceausescu's goals were to be achieved through relentless control of the private sphere. Participants from developing countries, critical of the West's insistence on curbing population growth as an end in itself, were able to interpret Ceausescu's remarks in terms of their own emerging agenda, which linked population concerns and development issues.

During the days of the international congress, the UN Center for Demography was opened in Bucharest. This teaching and research center,

CEDOR, was devoted to the study of the relation between population and development. For a number of years, its activities were endorsed by the United Nations and the Romanian government.[13] CEDOR provided an institutional context in which specialists, including foreigners, were able to contribute to the training of demographers and social scientists, especially those representing developing countries. The UN's choice of Romania for this endeavor implicitly legitimated Romania's approach to demographic matters and conferred formal recognition of Romania's role in international diplomacy—that is, of Romania's positioning in the Cold War confrontations between the superpowers and their spheres of influence.

In addition to Romania's hosting the World Population Conference and CEDOR, the National Demographic Commission was itself very active in 1974. This institution implemented in Romania the principle embraced by the UN bodies charged with organizing 1974 as the Year of World Population: that demographic phenomena should be incorporated into development planning.[14] The commission organized six national symposia, published the monograph *The Population of Romania,* and prepared numerous radio and television programs and journal articles for specialists.[15] The NDC enabled the Romanians to attach "scientific" and international blessings to what was, in actuality, a political strategy.

## The National Demographic Commission

In the first article of Law 3/1971 constituting the National Demographic Commission, it was stated that the NDC "is an organ of the Council of State whose mission is to study demographic phenomena and to provide appropriate proposals to the Council of State regarding the political demographic problems that are of interest to the party and to the state." The objectives to be pursued by the NDC, especially as related to institutional practices, were:

1. the description and analysis of demographic processes, including the reciprocal influences of economic and social contexts; analysis of the structural and dynamic impact of demographic phenomena on the development of: education, the workplace, health, habitat, the production of consumer goods, living standards, and services; evaluation of the effects of economic and social "progress" on the number, structure, and evolution of the population;

2. the obligatory presentation to the Council of State of a coherent schedule of legislative, economic, financial, health, and cultural measures designed to create efficient mechanisms to promote the political demographic interests of the state;

3. supervision of the means by which political decisions regarding demographic matters are implemented;
4. coordination of national institutions and the establishment of relations with international ones; and coordination of existing scientific and material resources that contribute to the fulfillment of the NDC's mandate.

The ends overwhelmed the means.[16]

Representatives of the following institutions and organizations figured among the 120-person membership of the NDC: the Committee for State Planning; the Ministries of Labor, Finance, Education and Teaching, Interior, Justice, and National Defense; the Council for Socialist Culture and Education; the National Women's Council; the General Confederation of Romanian Trade Unions; the Committee for the Problems of Local Councils; the Central Bureau of Statistics; the Academies of Social and Political Sciences, and of Medical Sciences; the Union of Communist Youth; and the National Union of Agricultural Cooperatives for Production.[17] This institutional web was charged with enacting and enforcing commands from on high. According to highly respected demographers who had themselves been involved as specialists, the National Demographic Commission existed primarily to "legitimate the demographic politics" of the regime.[18] It served as an institutional front that lent scientific veneer to political interests. (As mentioned above, the NDC was particularly useful in the realm of international relations.) The political appointment of a secretary general who was not a demographer but rather a loyal party activist who could be counted on to fulfill his duties corroborated this assessment of the NDC's function.[19]

Seemingly, what motivated the participation in the NDC of the diverse set of specialists was the recognition that effective policies depended on the analysis and circulation of accurate, representative data. However, in a command economy, feedback mechanisms were notoriously unreliable. Central planning required reliable information, but for reasons endemic to "shortage economies," it was not consistently provided.[20] In consequence, decisions at the top of the political hierarchy were often the result of misinformed deliberations. Although the center ultimately called the shots, the localized cynicism and self-interest of the institutions mentioned above contributed to the spiraling out of control of a formally rationalized yet structurally flawed system.[21] The growing formal authority of such institutions made the task of distinguishing what was real from what appeared to be real all the more difficult.

This is not to say that the NDC did little in the years before its "retirement" from public life. Under its auspices, the NDC published a number of theoretical and empirical studies on the dynamics of demographic phenomena.[22] Although these works necessarily supported the party line, the demographic data seem to have been reasonably reliable. Regional and local analyses were often of scientific value to specialists in the capital. As required, the results of the NDC's diverse activities were communicated regularly to the Grand National Assembly and the Political Executive Committee of the party.

The failure of the political demographic strategy for which the NDC had ostensibly been established as the central pillar may be attributed to practical limitations of macroeconomic determinism. Economic development was assumed to be the driving force—or "motor" in the ritualized language of the official propaganda—behind all forms of progress. As time wore on, the stimulatory economic measures that had been designed to increase fertility proved ineffective. This gave rise to the view that such investments were risky, which in turn affected the sums allocated, creating a vicious circle of inadequate investments and yields. In the end, it was deemed more expedient to replace the scientific approach to demographic growth with strong, rigorously enforced political measures. Tightening the screws of repression seemed like the quickest and least financially taxing way to increase the birthrate. Accordingly, the political supervision of demography had to be shifted to another institutional locus—the Higher Council on Health—this time directly controlled by the central nucleus of power.

The Higher Council on Health had remained in the shadows of the National Demographic Commission until the mid-1970s, when it began to gain political weight.[23] In the early years, this council had been incorporated into the structure of the Ministry of Health, including among its members medical researchers, teachers, and practitioners, each of whom served for three years. The Minister of Health acted as president of the Higher Council on Health until 1975, when the council moved up in the institutional hierarchy. Its purpose was transformed, as was its constituency. The Higher Council on Health was ordained "to contribute actively to the realization of party and state policies in this domain." A vice-president of the government replaced the Minister of Health as president of the council.[24] The Ministry of Health came under the purview of the council, which was charged with making sure that the "laws and normative acts pertaining to the continuing improvement of the population's health" were obeyed. The consolidation of institutional power was well under way, as was the monopolization of power in Ceausescu's extended family.

The eclipsing of the NDC by the Higher Council on Health signaled a shift away from pronatalist politics in which positive incentives were used to encourage procreation toward repressive demographic politics in which an obsession with the number of persons comprising "the population" became the raison d'être of demographic policy. The Political Executive Committee of the Central Committee of the Communist Party was meant to gain unmediated control over the human body and its reproduction.

Policing the Body (Politic):
The Higher Council on Health

*In 1983, for every child born there were circa 1.5 abortions. . . . The fact that 742,000 women were registered as pregnant in 1983 . . . invalidates certain attempts to justify reduced natality in terms of the state of health conditions. Unfortunately, of the more than 700,000 pregnant women, more than 420,000 had abortions, which represents approximately 60 percent of them. . . . Data also show that only 9 percent of these abortions, that is, only 37,000 of 420,000, were due to medical reasons, which demonstrates that medical causes did not determine this inadmissible number of abortions. A simple calculation shows that a reduction of 30 per 100 abortions would ensure a natality rate greater than 19–21 live births per 1,000 inhabitants. . . . It is necessary to ensure, each year, a natality rate of at least 19–21 live births per 1,000 inhabitants.*[25]

On August 9, 1983, the Higher Council on Health became, by presidential decree, the repressive apparatus to oversee and rigorously apply the pronatalist policies of the Socialist Republic of Romania.[26] Political demography became synonymous with the politics of abortion, and demography became almost superfluous as a scientific endeavor.[27] The analysis of demographic phenomena became the analytic manipulation of "the population." Statistical data were represented as quintessentially objective; all official rhetoric was laden with numbers. Propaganda spewed forth incontestable "representative" figures. Statistics captured the achievements of socialist progress; they also provided a legitimating discourse for repression. The message was that the "numbers don't lie." But those who supplied them did—out of fear, self-interest, and a complexly organized complicity with a system that structurally produced distortions of what scientists elsewhere refer to as empirical reality.[28] As a result, statistical data, especially that produced during the last decade of the Ceausescu regime, are notoriously unreliable.

Two institutions managed the collection and analysis of vital statistical data: the Central Bureau of Statistics and the Center for the Calculation of Health Statistics. The Central Bureau of Statistics reported directly to the Council of State. Within the bureau, a section devoted to "population and the labor force" coordinated nationwide statistical analyses. Bulletins containing codified data were prepared monthly at the county level and sent to the Central Bureau of Statistics in Bucharest, which then produced synthetic tables and national reports.

The Center for the Calculation of Health Statistics was an institutional appendage of the Ministry of Health. It fell primarily to this unit to analyze the demographic statistics, especially with respect to natality, mortality, abortion, and infant and maternal mortality. The Ministry of Health's reports were then sent over to the Central Bureau of Statistics. The prevailing political climate set the tone for what became either institutional collusion or competition. For example, one prominent statistical analyst from the Central Bureau of Statistics verified that it had been known since 1982 that the abortion statistics had been "worked over." The number of abortions cited in the Ministry of Health's report was lower than that indicated by the data received independently at the Central Bureau of Statistics. However, "it was formally the job of the Ministry of Health to report on abortions; because the 'distortion' was also recognized as socially useful to women, to doctors, and even to the ministerial bureaucracy; we closed our eyes. No one contested the data."[29]

Statistical summaries were sent higher up and served to legitimate regime policies. Those that were "useful" were publicized; others, such as the data on HIV among infants, were deliberately suppressed. By the mid-1980s the *Anuarul Statistic* had become a slim volume, testimony to the politicization of statistics at the expense of scientific integrity.[30] Like history and demography, statistics were valued as instruments of power and were among the political arsenal of the Higher Council on Health which, armed with "evidence," contributed to making the will of the state felt. Through the activities of this council, the intrusion of the state into the intimate lives of women and men alike deepened.

By 1983 the birthrate had declined to the same level to which it had dropped in 1966. The difference between these two seminal years was that before 1966 abortion had been legal, a circumstance to which the decline in the birthrate was incorrectly attributed. Successively restrictive political demographic policies were instituted to alter that situation. Yet by 1983 the demographic picture had not changed. Rather than address the causes for the failure of its political demographic strategy, the regime resorted to a tactic it regularly employed when the customary conspiracy of silence proved insufficient as a response: it found a scapegoat and then designated the Higher Council on Health as arbiter for the resolution of demographic problems. By any stretch of the imagination, this institution did not offer a "kinder and gentler" approach to fertility control.

This council differed importantly from the National Demographic Commission in its composition and in its structural relations to the center of power, thereby affirming the above-noted shift in institutional intention. Although the president of the NDC was a member of the government, the president of the Higher Council on Health was not only a vice–prime minister of the government, but also a member of the Political Executive Committee of the Romanian Communist Party.[31] The president of the NDC figured among the regular members of the Higher Council on Health. In addition to a president, the NDC was directed by three vice-presidents and a secretary; however, the council benefited from the accumulative tendencies characteristic of command economies: nine vice-presidents and a secretary were among those at the council's helm. With the exception of the Higher Council's president, personnel were mostly drawn from the medical system. Each of the council's 125 members had important functions in the bureaucracy of the state and/or party.[32] Of them, 105 were engaged in the public health system.

In part because of a reduction in the scope of its activities, the Higher Council on Health was able to operate more efficiently than its predecessor, the NDC. Even though the official discourse on political demography and the improvement of the population's well-being persisted, the council vigorously directed its institutional energy toward bettering the demographic statistics. In the ritualized wheel of power, the council was but one spoke whose identity derived solely from achieving these "demographic indicators." All writings pertaining to the council's activities contained this formulaic phrase; the titles of the council's periodic reports prepared for the Political Executive Committee of the Central Committee inevitably included "demographic indicators." Of these, birthrates ranked the highest in importance, followed by infant mortality statistics. Herein lies a key to understanding the focus of the council's more limited tasks. Understanding demographic trajectories no longer required factoring in economic, social, or cultural variables. Instead, the production of acceptable demographic statistics was reconceived as dependent primarily on one domain of medical practice: obstetrics and gynecology.

A summary of the measures taken by the Higher Council on Health and the Ministry of Health illuminates the means by which the council exercised its responsibilities to discipline and punish infringements of the political demographic policies. In the "interest of increasing natality, the assurance of women's health, the amelioration of medical assistance for pregnant women, and the tracking of the development of a pregnancy and the curtailment of the interruption of pregnancy," the council through the Ministry of Health undertook the following:

— to ascertain the general state of health of the female population between the ages of 16 and 45 through periodic examinations, especially in enterprises with a significant number of female employees;

— to intensify control [over the situation] through the early detection and recording of pregnancies, and the active surveillance of pregnant women;

— to accord special attention to prenatal consultations in the interest of preventing premature births and malformations;

— to scrutinize the means and efficacy with which health units treat women with risky pregnancies;

— to impose drastic measures against those who are guilty in the case of maternal death;

— to make sure that medical personnel hospitalize any pregnant women who, at the time of her pregnancy, suffers from an illness [that may compromise her pregnancy] so that she brings healthy and vigorous children into the world;

— to see to it that all pregnant women give birth in hospitals;

— to intensify efforts such that all women who have had incomplete abortions are formally registered and periodically examined to avoid abortive phenomena [spontaneous or deliberate];

— to ensure a reduction in the number of abortions due to medical causes through the increased vigilance of the activities of the commissions for the interruption of the development of a pregnancy;[33]

— to accord special attention to newborns and to encourage breast-feeding;

— to organize [spot] examinations of the obstetrical and pediatric sections to determine that hygienic norms are respected and to prevent the circulation of intra-hospital infections;[34]

— to punish medical cadre if the development of a child in the first year is unsatisfactory.

These measures were reaffirmed on August 3, 1987, at the session of the Political Executive Committee of the Central Committee of the Romanian Communist Party. This meeting's agenda addressed the manner in which the decisions regarding public health and demographic trends approved at the Thirteenth Party Congress in 1985 had been enacted. In the report in which the measures listed above were cited, two words appeared repeatedly: control and surveillance. To fine-tune these activities, headquarters were established in each region of the country to "enforce the political demographic measures,"[35] that is, to ferret out those who were somehow engaged in abortion-related activities.

The Political Executive Bureau of the Central Committee, itself at the highest level of party organization, centrally coordinated the activities of local commissions. Such commissions, comprising a broad representation of institutions, were charged with evaluating and deciding upon demographic issues in their area. At the county level, their decisions had the practical force of local laws, even though, formally, they were not made locally. These politically constituted bodies were directed by a president and included for each county: the secretary for social problems of the regional Party Committee, a representative of the Inspector General's Office of the Police, the president of the county Tribunal, the prosecutor, the director of the Department of Health, the director of the Department for Labor Problems and Social Welfare, the head inspector of the Inspector General's Office for Labor Protection, the president of the Organization for Women, the president of the county council of the General Confederation of Trade Unions, the inspector general for schools, and the director of the Department of Statistics. This group met weekly and was required to issue monthly reports on the achievements of the political demographic measures in their respective locales. These reports were presented at a meeting attended by the county Executive Committee of the Consiliul Popular (People's Council) and the county Committee of the Party Secretariat. The former was the local organ of state administration; the latter, an organ of political power. The reports contained information on the discovery and elimination of illegal abortion practices.

Pursuit of this priority objective required time, energy, and organization. A county's population was screened and evaluated using combined information from the hospitals or electoral districts to which persons were assigned. Electoral lists provided biographical sketches of each adult. Health and statistical evidence offered a picture of the principal events of a woman's medical and reproductive life.[36] Given this type of territorial differentiation, data from predesignated institutions could then be evaluated. The number of fertile women, again between the ages of 15 and 49, was compared with the number of pregnancies recorded in the medical dispensary records of the institutions, and with the number of incomplete abortions registered in the statistics of the Department of Health. If during a certain period the number of pregnancies was low but the number of incomplete abortions was high, then that area was considered a "zone at risk." The number of pregnancies and incomplete abortions was evaluated in terms of the area's fertility potential. In other words, it was suspected that abortion-related practices were functioning all too well. An analysis ensued of the zone's professional composition and occupational structure. This was intended to call attention to persons who presumably possessed medical knowledge and those whose standard of living exceeded that made possible by their legal earnings. This sleuthing resulted in a list of persons suspected of abortion activities of one kind or another. Responsibility then fell to the local police and the prosecutor's office to "verify" the list.[37]

## DISCIPLINING AND PUNISHING
## THE MEDICAL BODY

*It is necessary to act firmly to put a stop to the abusive interruption of pregnancy, and to respect uncompromisingly the laws of [our] country. Hospitals, dispensaries, and doctors, and all health personnel must devote themselves to the population's health and the natality figures. Where abortion exceeds 50 percent relative to live births, it will be considered that the activities of the respective institutions and doctors are unsatisfactory, and corresponding conclusions will be drawn.[38]*

The Ministry of Health was responsible for operationalizing the pronatalist directives. To this end, the Ministry of Health and its subordinates devised a plan to secure the compliance of all medical divisions under their purview. By the 1980s, the "health of the population" had come to mean the "reproductive health" of the population, quantified and measured in terms of an increase in fertility statistics and a decrease in infant mortality figures. Accordingly, the "principal objectives and technical-organizational measures for protecting health" referred to "the measures regarding improvement of the protection of mothers, children, and youth."[39]

"Ensuring women's health" presupposed the conformity of doctors and medical personnel with what may be viewed as the medicalization of repression—that is, the means by which the medical profession and medicine were used to "legitimate" repression of the body (politic). Doctors were to be the "principal propagandist[s] in convincing women, [taking care of them throughout their pregnancies], and encouraging them to have children."[40] To (re)produce a natality rate of at least 18 to 20 live births per 1,000 inhabitants, it was determined that women in their fertile years were to have regular gynecological exams.[41] This applied to all women actively engaged in the work force. Particular attention was paid to women who suffered from various illnesses so that appropriate therapeutic measures could be taken to restore their basic health. Moreover, any woman between the ages of 16 and 45 who was hospitalized for any reason was to be given a pregnancy test; if she was pregnant, that fact was recorded. The medical exam was one of the weapons by which the state invaded the physical bodies of its subjects.[42]

The legitimating motivation behind the mandatory performance of gynecological exams was the fact that [reproduction] "isn't only a personal matter, . . . but is of social consequence."[43] Regardless of appearances, the prescribed gynecological examination subjected women of childbearing age to state control of their reproductive lives. Women working in or attending state institutions were given at least annual, and in some areas trimesterly, medical exams to verify that their reproductive health was satisfactory.[44] If, through a routine checkup, a woman was discovered to be pregnant, the development of her pregnancy could then be closely monitored lest any untoward mishap occur. In rural areas, the local medical cadre was expected to follow up on women's pregnancies through home visits, a practice resented by all involved.

The intent of obtaining medical histories on women of childbearing age was to have "in evidence . . . all of the elements that might negatively influence the normal evolution of a pregnancy."[45] While annual medical checkups as well as pre- and postnatal care may be commendable under "normal" circumstances, in the context of a coercive pronatalist policy such prenatal care was tantamount to policing the body, with doctors put in the position of aiding and abetting the interests of the state. Women were not always aware that they were being given pregnancy tests; annual exams were considered routine, simply another obligation. One doctor confided that among his staff, some took pleasure in "finding" a pregnant woman. Others who were more compassionate did not. They found ways to indicate to the woman that she was pregnant and that it was up to her to decide what to do about it. A follow-up session was scheduled so that the doctor could show that proper attention was being accorded her pregnancy. If in the interim she had chosen to abort and no telling signs remained, then, as discussed in chapter 2, the doctor could record the pregnancy as lost to a "spontaneous abortion." One highly esteemed gynecologist emphasized that it was naive at best to think that periodic screenings would contribute to increasing the birthrate: "It is one thing to discover during a gynecological exam that a woman is pregnant and then to record it; that offers no guarantee that the pregnancy will be kept."

Since the medical profession had been made officially responsible for improving the birthrate, the state-employed medical cadre became at one and the same time hostages to the "plan" and to their consciences. From the standpoint of national planners, increasing the birthrate involved a "production plan," as did all aspects of building socialism. Medical activists were required to see that their "medical exam" plans (*plan de controale*) were fulfilled. Toward this end, they were assigned to examine women and to scrutinize all medical records. Again, if the (re)productive norms were not met, physicians were taxed a percentage of their pay. To cover a factory population in a specified period of time, many doctors had to perform 50 to 60 gynecological exams a day. This production-line schedule became the butt of a joke about the gynecological controls: A woman, badly beaten, stood before the court. The accused was a respected gynecologist. In self-defense, he recounted the circumstances that led him to hit her. "One evening, after a long, hard day, I walked into the entry hall of our apartment building to be accosted by this woman. I lost control; I couldn't take it—I had done a full day of [legal] abortions and 60 gynecological exams! Then she appeared and offered to show me her 'little bird' for 100 lei. I couldn't take it! I'd had enough vaginas for one day!"

Reports were circulated internally among the appropriate government institutions, and as mentioned above, many were earmarked for internal use only. To illustrate, one head of an obstetrics-gynecology unit produced an official report titled *Informare asupra modului in care comunistii, toti oamenii muncii din clinica de obstetrica-ginecologie se preocupa de ameliorarea indicatorilor demografici, expresie a eficientei muncii lor* (Information about the means by which communists and all workers in the obstetrics-gynecology clinic strive to better the demographic indicators, an expression of the efficiency of their work). The continuing efforts of the workers in this unit were underscored. Subtly embedded in this official report were veiled criticisms of the political-demographic policies, as well as of general conditions for medical treatment. It was suggested that better-equipped examining rooms be provided at factory clinics in order to increase efficiency. It was noted that health education throughout the country was inadequate and contributed to the high number of illegal abortions as well as to the number of maternal deaths due to them. The report stated forcefully that permanent control was to be exercised by responsible authorities to make certain that the legislation and rules regarding abortions were respected. Data had to be confirmed by the appropriate police authorities and the prosecutor's office.

Official reports from the provinces contained summaries of political-demographic activities in each zone of an administrative region: "Positive and negative aspects, and problems to be resolved in the medical units." These gynecological assessments, for which medical party activists were responsible, were conducted at least annually and contained data on the number of births, infant mortality, abortions, and complications resulting from illegal abortions. The number of females examined was also reported. Typical evaluations read:

> In community *x* . . . in the first trimester of 1986, 500 female students, 1,200 urban women, and 1,500 rural women were examined. Of the urban women, 12 were diagnosed pregnant; 10 amongst rural women. There were no cases of pregnancy among the students, almost all of whom were virgins.

> In community *y* . . . there are 17,000 women between the ages of 16 and 45, of whom 7 percent are unmarried; 10 percent are childless; 13 percent have one child; 20 percent, 2; 13 percent, 3; 19 percent, 4 or more children. The periodic gynecological exams have been conducted thus far on 1,300 students, all of whom are virgins.[46]

The details provided varied from community to community; the style of the report did not. Their contents were popularized for ideological purposes, and disseminated in the press. For example, it was recounted that: "Periodic controls of workers were concluded one month before the end of the year . . . all of the female workers were examined, especially the 6,500 women of childbearing age, of whom 500 were recorded to be in their first trimester of pregnancy. Those with problematic pregnancies were sent to the hospitals that deal with such problems. Sixty sterile couples began treatment."[47]

The director of Bucharest's health department, in reviewing medical performance for 1986, pointed to the inadequacies of health-medical worker performance in the domain of demography:

> We did not succeed in achieving the established demographic indicators [for Bucharest]. . . . This reflects the weak commitment of the health-medical cadre, a higher degree of formalism, aspects that are thoroughly impermissible and that must be thoroughly and seriously analyzed. Although the number of abortions was 23 percent less in 1986 than in 1985, we cannot consider this satisfactory. The incidence of abortion in such high proportions demonstrates that the organizational measures [to control abortions] were not applied resolutely. . . . This year, we are firmly resolved to make all efforts [to fulfill the plan] . . . in

this realm of activity that has deep significance for us, for problems . . . of professional conscience.[48]

Such statements sent shivers throughout the medical community because they indicated that certain heads were likely to roll. The style of wooden language employed by the director was self-servingly protective. Being "firmly resolved" meant that he would take an active role in keeping his eye on the actions of those beneath him in order to save his own position.

Doctors were caught in a web of institutionalized surveillance. Yet, despite the consequences for disobeying the law, many doctors—at all ranks in the party hierarchy—became adept at manipulating both the official rhetoric and statistics. Strikingly, most people offered praise for the attempts doctors made to assist women and families during these harsh years. Many doctors took considerable risks and tried to "hide" a woman's pregnancy if she indicated she, or she and her husband, did not want the child. As one doctor recounted:

> If a woman adamantly was against having a child, there was nothing you could do about it. She would risk dying rather than bear the child. So we tried to help. It wasn't difficult to read a woman's reaction to the news that she was pregnant. We'd ask her how many children she already had and about her living conditions. If she already had two or three children, it often became pretty clear she didn't want the pregnancy. [Under such circumstances], I'd reiterate that I thought she was pregnant but couldn't be absolutely certain, and suggest she come the following month to be sure. I'd tell her that if she was then indeed pregnant, her pregnancy would be officially recorded. Women knew how to decipher such messages. If a woman didn't want the pregnancy, she had been warned that she had one month to do something about it.[49]

When feasible, doctors took advantage of the existence of various ailments such as measles, recurrent fevers, hepatitis, tuberculosis, syphilis, malignant tumors, or diabetes, which qualified a woman for a legal abortion based on legitimate medical cause. Similarly, if a woman was receiving treatment or taking medications that were contraindicated for pregnant women (for example, chemotherapy, antimalarial drugs, anticonvulsants), then her treatment for the preexisting condition would be used as the excuse for an abortion. Given the pronounced lack of available medications in Romania by the mid-1980s, this excuse was not easily manufactured. Nonetheless, whenever possible, many doctors seemed to have done what they could to accommodate a woman's choice.

One prominent obstetrician-gynecologist remarked that he had always acted within the law and tried to save women's lives. But what did acting within the law mean under such circumstances? If a woman died because the prosecutor's office did not respond, the doctor was legally protected. But what about the Hippocratic oath that is professionally self-defining?

Again, this double-bind situation for gynecologists ensured the perpetuation of Ceausescu's political demographic policies and resistance to them as well.

Another institutional mechanism existed to maintain control over medical personnel: the disciplinary board for health workers, which was made up of medical practitioners whose party loyalty was considered unquestionable. In each region, members of the disciplinary board were well positioned in the medical hierarchy. One journalist described the board as "the tribunal of medical ethics [which punishes] medical mistakes, sometimes very grave, that affect pregnant women, mothers, and infants."[50] This same journalist penned an article titled "Discipline as an Expression of Professional Conscience." The disciplinary board provided a context in which professional comportment was held accountable to the norms of socialist medical ethics as dictated by the Higher Council on Health. The board met monthly; each session ended with an existential interrogation of the accused: "Have you understood where, when and how you have erred?" Needless to say, most "understood." These mini-medical show trials were reported in the official publication of the Ministry of Health, *Muncitorul Sanitar* (*The Health Worker*) and illustrate how such a public professional forum was used to cajole conformity among medical personnel and to shore up the dynamics of dissimulation. In 1987, for example, the disciplinary board for health personnel for the region Ialomita heard 89 cases, 34 of which resulted in punishments.[51] (Two of these were later annulled by the central disciplinary board because the doctors in question were judged guilty of more serious crimes.) All but 2 of the 32 who had been reprimanded—including 22 doctors and 10 medical assistants—were disciplined for their improper care of pregnant women and newborns.

Not all doctors learned their lessons. Some refused to "understand." Such cases were also diligently reported in *The Health Worker.* For example, Dr. C.R.,

> a real champion of unfortunate renown of the disciplinary board deliberations. . . . is a regular at these sessions; he appears two to three times per year as the accused. Although he is always harshly criticized, the board has acted with unjustified leniency, not punishing him in the hope that he would straighten up. It is true that he covers a difficult territory. Many of the inhabitants do not show the slightest interest in cooperating with the doctor to ensure their own children's health. Many mothers make a habit of leaving the community with their infants . . . without letting the doctor know.

The doctor in question reappeared before the board at the February meeting because of the death of a child under the age of one. Neither the "objective" situation nor the board's warnings "stimulated" the doctor's desire to be rehabilitated. The board proposed that he be moved to another dispensary, where he would not have to contend with these difficulties and where he would be able to demonstrate his professional abilities. He refused. Nevertheless, the board tried to persuade him to accept a move; Dr. C.R. resigned. What the journalist euphemistically labeled an "objective situation" and the board failed to discuss forthrightly were exactly which means of "professional and efficient intervention" were available to the doctor. In Dr. C.R.'s case, the "difficult territory" and uncooperative population referred to a community inhabited by Roma; the doctor had been sent to "civilize" them.

Missing from such accounts was mention of the professional consequences an appearance before this board entailed. The punishments meted out by this medical ethics tribunal were noted permanently in one's file. Another case from the region of Braila illustrates this process of stigmatization:

> This is about what befell young Valeria I., who worked at the factory for fibers, cellulose, and paper in Braila, and who in her sixth month induced an abortion that ended tragically. No health worker was implicated in the actual performance of this illicit act. Yet, with regard to this drama, three doctors from the dispensary-polyclinic for the chemical factory were called before the board. Why? Because, as was proven through the investigation, they don't examine women properly, especially those between the ages of 16 and 45, and they don't follow the development of those who have had previous abortions.[52]

For the sake of clarification, it is important to underline that none of these three doctors were gynecologists; they were specialists in occupational medicine. Regardless of their specific expertise, all doctors (including dentists, as may be recalled) were required to fulfill the political demographic norms.

## A Case Study in Repression

To guarantee the effectiveness of surveillance and control, the state police and the attorney general's office became increasingly engaged in matters of human reproduction.[53] As discussed in the preceding chapters, legislative decrees legitimated their activities. Pre- and proscriptive comportment for socialist citizens was set forth in these official declarations, which professionals were then required to enforce, or potentially suffer the consequences of negligence. The following entangled case of M.T.—accused of and sentenced for participating as an accomplice to an illegal abortion— illuminates how they carried out their mandate as well as the typical miscarriage of justice in Ceausescu's "original democracy." It also illustrates how the state repressive apparatus perversely manipulated personal relations to its own ends.[54]

One day in January 1975, M.T. received an urgent phone call from Bucharest's prosecutor's office, informing her that Dr. G. was suffering from acute gastritis. Dr. G. and M.T. had been living together for years, even though he was legally still married to G.G. At the time of the call, Dr. G. was being held in jail under suspicion of having performed illegal abortions. M.T. was requested to come that very day and to bring food supplies and other basic necessities for her partner.[55] M.T. claims to have taken whatever she had in her refrigerator: milk, cheese, a turkey breast, lemons. She also packed some sugar, a toothbrush, and toothpaste. The attorney general's office was in the same building as the Militia Inspectorate for the Ilfov region. At the prosecutor's office on Calea Rahovei, an officer greeted her and introduced her to Colonel C., who suggested that she be seated until the public prosecutor arrived. M.T. did not understand why the prosecutor needed to be present for her to hand over the package she had been instructed to bring for Dr. G. Not wanting to create problems, she took a seat. However, after waiting three hours she lost her patience. She sought out the colonel, telling him that it had become late and she had to leave. Without comment, M.T. was then led into a room where she was bodily searched. She protested, but was told that her remonstrations were futile. She was being held under preventive arrest.

M.T. was led into a cell in the militia's headquarters and jailed until April, when she was transferred to the Vacaresti prison. She recalls that she had been arrested on a Friday, yet her first interrogation by a Major R. occurred only that Sunday. M.T. distinctly remembers that her revulsion at this flagrant abuse of power was greater than her fear. She asked her interrogator why she had been detained for three days. He responded that she was presumed guilty of assisting Dr. G.'s criminal activities (i.e., performing illegal abortions). In view of the fact that she was his "concubine," it was likely that she was also his accomplice. Moreover, in December 1974 one of the witnesses against Dr. G. had declared that her own abortion, carried out in the fifth month of pregnancy, took place in an apartment in the same area as M.T.'s.[56] It is important to understand that the "witness" was also one of the accused; she had broken the law by seeking an illegal abortion for which she claimed to have paid to Dr. G. 1,500 lei—almost a month's salary. Her cooperation with the authorities throughout the investigation would presumably result in a more lenient sentence.

M.T. nonetheless explained that she herself was a technical designer who worked at an institute where she was appreciated for her professionalism and honesty. She asked what was inherently incriminating about her living with Dr. G. When they had first met at the end of 1959 or the beginning of 1960, he had been separated from his wife for some five years. She and the doctor had been together ever since then. "The fact that he lives with me without legally being my husband does not automatically make me his accomplice, nor my apartment the place in which he practiced his gynecological profession illegally!"[57] That said, the initial interrogation ended.

M.T. was taken back to her cell after her first interrogation. She went on a hunger strike, demanding an audience with the head of the Militia Directorate. This was refused. After three days without food, she was told that her detention was necessary to verify certain matters pertaining to Dr. G.'s case and that it would not take much longer.[58] The emotional stress seems to have contributed to the deterioration of her physical state. She hemorrhaged. The militia doctor examined her, stating that her condition was not serious and would pass. Nonetheless, they called M.T.'s son, telling him to bring cotton for his mother's use.[59] With this phone call, M.T.'s son learned of his mother's arrest; he supplied her with cotton until her hemorrhaging finally stopped approximately one year later. (After her release from prison, she underwent medical treatment.) M.T. remarked that she wore the same clothes in which she had arrived at the prosecutor's from January until April, when she was incarcerated in the penitentiary. Every night, the guard accompanied her to the washroom, where she managed to clean herself minimally and wash out her underwear.

Until M.T. was transferred to the Vacaresti prison, the mandate for her arrest had to be extended every two weeks. At each fourteen-day interval, she was taken to see the prosecutor responsible for her case, who appeared determined to make sure that M.T. would be found guilty. M.T. was repeatedly asked to "recognize" that she herself had opened the apartment door for the witness mentioned above, G.D., whose formal declaration was used as circumstantial evidence (File 270/1974). M.T. contested this on the grounds that many of the statements in it were contradictory and could not be verified. "The description of the apartment as well as of my person was inexact."[60] At one of these biweekly sessions, the prosecutor showed M.T. the "material evidence" found in the apartment when it was searched: two forceps, a speculum, eleven vials containing morphine and anticholinergic agents, and other medicines necessary for abortions.[61]

On the basis of the indictment prepared by the prosecutor's office for the Ilfov region on April 10, 1975, M.T. was formally charged with having been an accomplice to the "infraction of interrupting the course of a pregnancy" (see art. 185, paras. 1 and 5 of the Penal Code), and with trafficking in narcotics (see art. 312 of the Penal Code), and for the infraction of retaining instruments at home for performing abortions (see art. 26 reported in art. 187 of the Penal Code). "I was sentenced to two years in prison even though not one of their accusations could be substantiated."[62]

M.T. did not stay long at Vacaresti. One day, despite a torrential rain, the inmates were taken out for mandatory labor in the fields. The rain was so heavy that "we were swimming in mud. When we were taken back to the prison, I went to file a complaint; we were not cattle, and I had been assigned to forced labor without my consent." M.T. was then moved to one of the oldest prisons for women, Tirgsor, where she remained until her release on January 7, 1976. The granting of her freedom was due to the fact that the central figure of this convoluted saga, Dr. G., had been set free. If there were no longer compelling grounds to detain Dr. G., then there surely was no reason to detain M.T., his alleged accomplice. State authorities and institutional procedures functioned with striking consistency when their fabrications and/or mistakes became obvious "beyond a doubt." Rather than confess error, they found a polite formulaic expression to cover their guilt. In the case of Dr. G., his failing health proved to be convenient for all involved.

Not long after her release, M.T. went to seek employment at her former place of work. The head of her division told her in confidence that he regretted being unable to help her; her file contained a statement that she was a "social danger" (*pericol social*). He counseled her not to waste time looking for another job in a similar institute.[63] Her only chance would be to be hired as an unskilled worker. "I went to the Bureau of Labor, whence I was sent to work as an unskilled worker in a warehouse, where I lasted only one month. I then took a course in cosmetics at the people's university so that I could earn pocket money. . . . I was unable to find work suitable to my qualifications." M.T. retired at age 57, the upper limit for women. She received a very small pension because she had only thirteen years of salaried service. Dr. G. also retired at age 57, below the normal age for men, because of his health. Although he was released from prison in 1976 at the age of 52 because of failing health, he did not receive the pension benefits due him until the regular minimum retirement age of 60. For a period of time, they had to make do with assistance from M.T.'s mother, son, and other relatives.

After some time had passed, M.T. went to the regional Militia Inspectorate where she had first been detained for preventive arrest. She intended to reclaim her family jewelry and personal belongings, which had been confiscated from her apartment when it was searched. M.T. was eventually able to prove that these possessions had been legally hers. Most, but not all, were returned to her.[64] When M.T. arrived at the Directorate, she tracked down a colonel whom she remembered from her experience there. Having recounted what brought her to him, she reported him as saying: "Madame, what happened to you was really in the realm of the fantastic! I have been involved in the practice of criminal law for better than twenty years, and in all that time I never arrested anyone without having proof that the person was guilty. Your case was handled by the prosecutor's office because we [from the militia] did not agree with the methods."[65]

The colonel's memory had long before fallen victim to the distortions of dissimulation. What he is alleged to have said—which is believable in terms of the logic of the circumstances—was itself in the realm of the fantastic. It was indicative of another structural feature of institutional behavior in Ceausescu's Romania: individuals found it easier to blame matters on someone else than to assume responsibility for actions that were morally reprehensible or predicated on an abuse of power.

In 1977, as part of an amnesty granted certain prisoners (Decree 115/1977), M.T. was pardoned from completing the remainder of her initial two-year sentence for being an accomplice to an illegal abortion, keeping instruments used to perform abortions in her apartment, and trafficking in narcotics. When all was said and done, M.T. was again a free citizen. Nonetheless, her official record continued to show a criminal charge.[66] The official documents contained no admission of judicial impropriety or legal error. The possibility that she was innocent was never raised; any such admission would have served to acknowledge the arbitrariness of institutional justice in Ceausescu's Romania.

### The National Women's Council of Romania: Institutionalizing Women's "Energies"

*The Party has given its full support to [women]; it has created conditions such that they will no longer be considered women . . . but people, just like men.*
COMRADE ELENA LIVEZEANU, EXECUTIVE COMMITTEE, NATIONAL WOMEN'S COUNCIL, 1974[67]

To achieve its demographic goals, the state was most dependent on the willingness of women to comply with its agenda. Homogenization as a governing ideology notwithstanding, women were the bearers of children. Their bodies were ultimately subject to the greatest instrumentalization both in and outside the home. Women had to be brought out of the home and into the labor force and public sphere of the state; they also had to be encouraged to yield increasing numbers of future socialist citizens. Hence, in addition to the tightly interwoven institutional apparatus that was created to compel compliance at all levels, the "woman question" had to be tackled and legitimated.

The National Women's Council provided the institutional framework through which women were formally incorporated into—and disciplined by—party activities. In 1957 the Democratic Women's Organization of Romania, as the women's movement was known, was renamed the National Women's Council and brought directly under the control of the Central Committee.[68] This regime-initiated and regime-controlled change was meant to attract and utilize "women's energy." The National Women's Council was the "only organization in the country" for women, reflecting the fact that Romania's "women's movement" was a state-constituted and state-controlled social movement. Through its activities, the National Women's Council officially demonstrated the "mass participation of women" in the "building of socialism."

The council was formed to foster the political socialization of women and to initiate them into the fold of militant activists. As activists, they would be "liberated" from the individualized patriarchal servitude to which they were subjected and rewarded with equal status before the generic patriarch: the "Romanian Communist Party, beloved leader." Women were called upon to pursue "the cultivation of love and devotion for the fatherland, the Romanian Communist Party, the education of the masses of women to militate with conviction in defense of revolutionary gains, of [our] sovereignty and national independence, for the consolidation of [our] people's moral-political unity and the strengthening of brotherly friendship between all working people. . . . [These] form the bases of the permanent mission of the women's movement."[69]

As stated in the council's statutes: "The women's movement develops its entire activity under the unmediated leadership of the Communist Party. The National Council, and the women's committees and commissions, periodically inform the Central Committee of the Romanian Communist Party and other appropriate party organizations about the unfolding of those activities."[70] An abbreviated summary of those activities, provided in the "Code of Organizational and Operational Norms" of the National Women's Council, included:

1. the mobilization of the masses of women in productive activities: economic, social, public welfare, and political;
2. the unmediated mobilization of urban and rural women to participate patriotically in the beautification and maintenance of their respective localities and the operation of municipal projects related to nurseries, kindergartens, dormitories; the landscaping of parks, green zones, and play areas for children;
3. contribution to the "continuing improvement of conditions at the workplace and at home, and to easing household burdens, which will enable women to combine harmoniously their roles as active participants in the efforts of the entire population . . . with those of wife and mother";[71]
4. contribution to "the carrying out of the political demographic measures promoted by our party and state, in the interest of the continuing evolution and flourishing of our socialist nation, the consolidation of families and strengthening of their responsibility for keeping the youth of our people, for the education and raising of children, of the young generations [socialized] in the spirit of respect for work, unflinching love for our socialist fatherland, devotion and profound appreciation for the party and people, in the spirit of peace, friendship, and understanding between peoples. The National Council, the committees and commissions of women actively support the efforts of the health organizations to strengthen the health of women, mothers, and children, and to guide mothers in the raising and care of children";[72]

5. collaboration with other institutions in the interest of [increasing] the political and cultural-scientific education of the masses of women.

To carry out these activities, the council's division of labor was organized hierarchically according to territorial and professional criteria. Every five years, the supreme body of the National Women's Council—the National Conference for Women—convened. Key functionaries were appointed at this national gathering. The normal responsibilities of the council were undertaken by committees at each territorial level: regional, municipal, city and community. The number of "representatives" per level were as follows: regional, 65 to 75 women; municipal, 35 to 55; city, 25 to 35; community, 15 to 25. Various commissions consisting of 7 to 15 women worked under the aegis of the committees. Participation in them was determined by place of work. Hence, the women's commission of a large textile factory in Bucharest was subordinate to the women's committee for the sector in which the factory was located. The commissions were responsible for organizing, for example, the calendar of events linked to the cultural and political socialization of women, or environmental care of the locales in which they worked and/or lived.

According to Suzana Gadea, president of the council in the early 1960s, intellectuals were recruited into the movement to help "raise the level of women" in the country.[73] By the late 1950s it was recognized that sending women to the party school for one or two years was insufficient; they needed professional training. Illiteracy was tackled and, by and large, obliterated. Women encouraged their "sisters" to attend high school, pursue professional training, and then do political work. They learned by example from each other.[74] Women fought against wage discrimination. They were also encouraged to participate in voluntary public works. Intellectuals conducted seminars after hours on all manner of topics. They instructed other women on the importance of personal hygiene, especially for pregnant women and mothers. Activists were sent into the field to evaluate the conditions at homes for children and for the elderly. Negligence was reprimanded. Unsanitary conditions created by dirt, unwashed clothing, and the spread of lice in state institutions were not tolerated. Ineffective and corrupt personnel were dismissed. To the best of their abilities, these women resolved the problems with which they were confronted.

The institutionalization of women's activities ritually recapitulated the principles of democratic socialism and centralism. The "women's movement" was organized as an open system and operated according to a pyramid structure.[75] Organizationally, this meant access was conditional upon a single criterion: gender. One did not have to be active to be a formal member; instead, the movement claimed to represent *all* women. Accordingly, with an agile semantic flourish, "rights" and especially the duties written into the code of the organization applied to the entire female population without distinction. The pyramidal authority structure served as an effective instrument for mobilization and control of the council's members. Although these two aspects may seem contradictory, in practice, they were not. That every woman was potentially a member without having to be active did not preclude her from being mobilized. Any citizen in a command economy was, by definition, subject to mobilization.

The National Women's Council participated in mobilizing women's potential differently over time. Their emphases at any particular moment were determined by the interests of the party, whether priority was accorded to women in the role of woman-producer, or woman-reproducer/woman-mother.[76] For example, at the beginning of the 1970s, when Romania received financial credits from the West to facilitate the intensification of the industrialization process, the image of woman-producer was highlighted; encouraging women to enter the labor force was deemed essential for meeting the labor needs of a growing economy. In 1974 the president of the organization of women was quoted in the official journal of the National Women's Council, *Femeia (Woman)*:

> The decision at the plenary session of the C.C. P.C.R. on June 18–19, 1973, and the program elaborated by the Secretariat of the C.C. P.C.R. in December 1973 were to mobilize all responsible factors. . . . Analyses demonstrated the [positive] results obtained thus far in raising the proportion of women in the total work force as well as the need to apply more rigorously the measures established about professional orientation, training. . . . The party believes firmly in the work capacity and managerial spirit of the masses of women, in their ability to contribute to an important cause, in their receptivity for [personal] renewal, in their creativity and intelligence. [The party] has fixed as a goal . . . to take the necessary steps to ensure the best conditions for the active and effective participation of women in the management of the entire economic-social life.[77]

Even when the "significance" of women in the nondomestic economy—that is, in the socialist labor force—was emphasized, the role of working woman remained secondary to that of good wife and mother. To help women fulfill their domestic roles, *Femeia* in 1974 also published moralizing articles offering advice as well as warnings concerning women's appropriate behavior. For example, a lengthy article of "medical advice" on pregnancy and psychological health was presented alongside a legal column informing violators of the abortion restrictions that they would be caught and punished, no matter the circumstances. This article called women's attentions to the dangers of as well as punishments for aborting illegally: a 22-year-old mother of a young child died because a medical assistant had botched the abortion, perforating the young mother's uterus. The medical assistant was

Address of the first secretary of the Romanian Workers' Party, Gheorghe Gheorghiu-Dej, at the National Women's Conference, 1958. (Courtesy of the Photo Department, ROMPRES, Bucharest.)

Peasant family roots: the mothers of Nicolae Ceausescu and Elena Petrescu Ceausescu with their children, 1977. (Courtesy of the Photo Department, ROMPRES, Bucharest.)

The 20 millionth inhabitant of the Socialist Republic of Romania presented to
Nicolae Ceausescu and other important political leaders, 1969. (Courtesy of the
Photo Department, ROMPRES, Bucharest.)

The 1985 National Women's Conference with President Ceausescu, Prime Minister Dascalescu, and other leaders presiding. (Courtesy of the Photo Department, ROMPRES, Bucharest.)

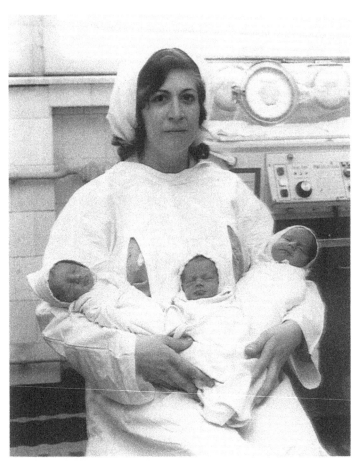

A mother of triplets in a Bucharest maternity hospital, 1984.
(Courtesy of the Photo Department, ROMPRES, Bucharest.)

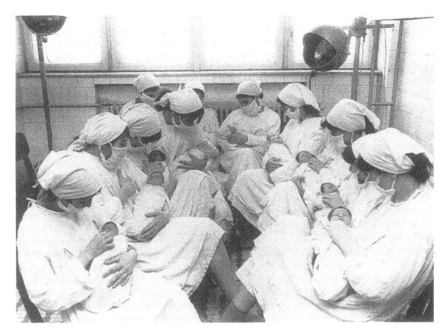

Mothers nursing in a Bucharest maternity hospital, 1987. (Courtesy of the Photo Department, ROMPRES, Bucharest.)

Women on trial for having illegal abortions. (Courtesy of the Photo Department, ROMPRES, Bucharest.)

Honoring the Ceausescus' presence in Hunedoara county. (Courtesy of the Photo Department, ROMPRES, Bucharest.)

Ceausescu uses the occasion of an official holiday celebration to praise "the country's future" and promote his demographic policies. (Courtesy of the Photo Department, ROMPRES, Bucharest.)

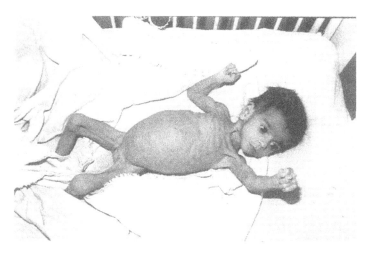

Child with AIDS at a home for children needing medical care, Focsani, 1990. (Photo by Emilian Savescu, courtesy of the photographer, with thanks to Anca and Mihai Oroveanu for their assistance in acquiring it.)

A meal at Gradinari House, about fourteen miles outside Bucharest, 1990. (Photo by Isabel Ellsen, courtesy of the photographer.)

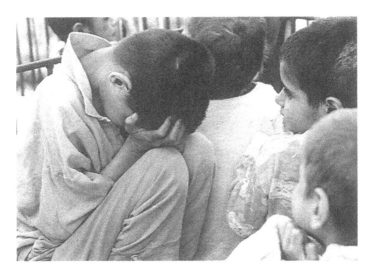

Children left outside in playpen cages at Gradinari House, 1990.
(Photo by Isabel Ellsen, courtesy of the photographer.)

Children of Ceausescu's "Golden Era," at Gradinari House, 1990.
About 150 children aged fifteen months to sixteen years lived
there at the time; some 40 had died there in 1989. (Photo by
Isabel Ellsen, courtesy of the photographer.)

tried and made into a public example. A dentist assisted by two accomplices performed seventeen abortions for monetary gain; all were caught and punished. A young gynecologist was similarly tried and punished for performing 31 abortions that were not medically indicated. Women had to realize the consequences of their actions—for themselves as well as for others, most notably for their other children.[78]

As the regime's concern about demographic statistics increased, women's roles as socially productive workers were overshadowed by their roles as socially *re*productive workers. Women's contributions to the building of socialism were taken to be biologically determined. Thus, in his address to the National Conference for Women in 1966, the year when Decree 770 was proclaimed, Ceausescu introduced what became an all-too-familiar chant: "One of the most important obligations of women as mothers and educators is that of devoting themselves to the raising of new generations and [endowing them] with an ardent spirit of patriotism, with respect and appreciation for the glorious history of our people, with the desire to consecrate their entire life to the flourishing of our socialist homeland and the ideals of communism."[79]

The bearing and raising of children were construed as women's national duties. Through these "nationalized" activities, women were considered essential(ized) workers for achieving Ceausescu's brand of national socialism. The remarkable continuity in Ceausescu's thinking on women's contributions to the building of socialism echoed throughout his innumerable and redundant speeches. On International Women's Day, in 1986, Ceausescu intoned: "There is no obligation more noble, more honorable for families, for women, than that of raising and giving to the country as many children [as possible], to educate and form them in a healthy spirit, as the future citizens, the hope, of our fatherland, [who will be] able to develop and further their parents' efforts [toward the realization] of the socialist and communist causes on Romanian soil."[80]

As chapter 5 makes clear, Ceausescu's preaching on women's most noble missions, childbearing and child rearing, became ever more insistent and passionate. The National Conference for Women and the National Women's Council were favored instruments through which Ceausescu proselytized about the glorious rewards of obeisance. In its final years, the National Women's Council did little more than brazenly cater to the desires of Ceausescu's "original" democratic socialism. The National Women's Council was enjoined by the party to concentrate its activities explicitly on natality. That was in 1983. But women "with their tireless energy"—as then president of the National Women's Council, Ana Muresan, complimented them[81]—did not harken to their leader's call to provide their country with more children. Quite to the contrary, the birthrate dropped to the low point reached in 1966.

Also in 1983, the executive bureau of the National Women's Council developed the idea of organizing clubs named Femina along the lines of other mass organizations especially to engage nonparty members in activities of "political-educational" value. These clubs were controlled by the various women's committees and commissions; club presidents were drawn from the loyal membership of these party institutions. Diverse indoctrinational events were scheduled to "intensify legal and health propaganda, to increase the patriotic accountability of women for raising our people's youth, and for the consolidation of the family."[82] Femina encouraged civic activism by offering edification on practical matters such as women and the family, the young mother, legal education, scientific materialism, health education, and household education. The council had hoped that this addition to the available "consciousness-raising" opportunities would make it possible to focus discussions at these gatherings narrowly on political demographic concerns. Reproducing the logic of the system, these duty-bound activists seemed to believe that giving birth to yet another institution would produce the missing key to the demographic dilemma. They would transform the none-too-conformist attitudes and practices of their "sisters." What the National Women's Council did accomplish, in conjunction with the Higher Council on Health and all the other councils, committees, and commissions, was to contribute to the state's institutionalization and surveillance of everyday life.

Ceausescu's pronatalist policies initially received nodding approval from the West because his policies seemed to mesh well with international interests: for example, Ceausescu stressed the relationship between population control and development strategies, as well as the right to self-determination. To Western ears, the Romanian leader sounded sensible and anti-Soviet. To representatives of the Third World, Ceausescu's words were equally welcome and underscored Romania's anticolonialist (and imperialist) stance. It was only in the mid-1980s that Ceausescu's "enlightened" plans to increase and homogenize the population began to be seen as dictatorial follies. Until then, the world's leaders contributed to Ceausescu's political legitimacy through institutionalized recognition, of which the creation and operation of CEDOR was one instance.

The institutionalization of political demography transformed official discourse into a complex web of material practices by which the interrelated policies discussed in chapters 2 and 3 were implemented. Interlocking institutional dependencies gave rise to the formalization of political consent as well as political duplicity. To secure the allegiance of both doctors and women, the regime engaged them actively in their own subordination to "national interests." This was achieved through what amounted to the medicalization of repression on the one hand, and, on the other, to evasion through illegal abortion-related activities. As a result, professional integrity and personal health suffered. The gap separating public representation from personal belief and behavior widened. Yet propaganda ignored everyday hardships, fervently replacing them with the wonders of socialist utopia. These romanticized versions of daily life are discussed in the next chapter.

## CHAPTER 5

# Spreading the Word—Propaganda

*In the beginning was the Word, and the Word was with God, and the Word was God.*
JOHN 1:1

*You shall serve the Lord your God, and He will bless your bread and your water. And I will remove illness from your midst. No woman in your land shall miscarry or be barren, and I will give you the full count of your days.*
EXODUS 23: 25–27

*A Family with Many Children—A Law of Life and of Human Fulfillment, a Noble Patriotic Duty*
HEADLINE, *Scinteia,*
THE ROMANIAN COMMUNIST PARTY DAILY, MARCH 9, 1984

*Based on the countless proofs that life offers, our propaganda must make emphatically clear the essential superiority of our socialist democracy in comparison with bourgeois democracy.*
NICOLAE CEAUSESCU, 1971[1]

The ruling commandments of the Communist Party were enshrined in five-year plans and laws or other documents with the force of law (i.e., decrees, decisions). These were communicated to the masses through diverse vehicles, including party texts, speeches, mass gatherings, and labor competitions. State institutions at all levels were entrusted with the vanguard task of organizing ideological dissemination. To facilitate their work, each institution had a propaganda section responsible for mobilizational activities ranging from political-educational forums to mass-media pronouncements or institutionally targeted pamphlets and campaigns.

Propaganda in Leninist systems simultaneously served as a means of regime legitimation and mass education. Western commentaries tended to undervalue the significance of the latter, dismissing the revolutionary consciousness-altering intention of socialist propaganda as little more than a brainwashing technique.[2] A vanguard party assumes the "correctness" or immanent truth of its positions as well as its obligation to enlighten the masses.[3] Enlightenment and mobilization drove propaganda forward. The propaganda apparatus resembled the military in its organization; its efforts were organized in campaigns. As in most wars, it employed strategies and a mobilizational language designed to win everyone over to the "war" effort, whatever the current campaign was. All responsible communists were to participate in this all-important "multilaterally developed" undertaking to create the "new man" and build socialist society.[4]

In view of its mission, it is not surprising that propaganda simultaneously constituted one of the most dynamic and conservative of Communist Party structures. In Romania propaganda remained true to its early Stalinist heritage, and in this sense was quite conservative.[5] While rivals were eliminated elsewhere in the system, continuity and "efficiency" were demanded of the propaganda apparatus, whose chiefs dedicated themselves and their units to the causes of mobilization and enlightenment.[6] Organizational stability encouraged "departmental" dynamism, enabling the propaganda apparatus to fulfill its "noble obligations" energetically over the decades. This is not to suggest that propaganda was immune to difficulties. Both ideological content and propaganda were enemies of empirical reality. Nonetheless, the relationship between them was tense: although they often shared the same goal, ideology and propaganda were frequently at odds with each other. For example, the family was attacked in order to destroy its bourgeois basis, and yet consolidation of the family as a unit instrumental to the development of the socialist state was heralded.

As already noted, an important aspect of revolutionary change was the state's expropriation of the private sphere unto itself. The legal formalization of social, cultural, political, and economic principles and the five-year plans as blueprints for their practical translation facilitated this process. Yet the state's intrusion into everyday life required legitimation. Resistance to state interference had to be minimized at the same time that acceptance of and conformity to state control had to be maximized. To these ends, an effective and manipulative technology to engineer psychological and emotional compliance had to be devised.[7] That technology was propaganda; it was used willfully, with a coherence of purpose rarely achieved in other domains of state activity. Propaganda was on the offensive all the time. It assaulted the individual symbolically and constantly in all arenas of life. Symbolic violence was an insidious form of domination employed by the state, and propaganda was one of its principal weapons.[8] The diffuse effectiveness of symbolic violence contributed significantly to the creation of a culture of fear that kept a population trapped for decades in the webs of state domination.

Propaganda was distinctive in the realm of Romanian political economy. It was among the few activities in which supply far exceeded demand. The allocation of intellectual, material, and human resources toward the perfection of propaganda was ensured even as daily living standards declined steadily. Indeed, the relation between the saturation of daily life with propaganda and the deterioration of everyday conditions was an inverse one: there was a dramatic increase in propagandistic capital against an equally dramatic erosion of political and economic capital. This dynamic balancing act was characteristic of state socialism: nothing was lost or gained; everything was compensated for or substituted.[9] Propaganda produced a continual supply of substitutes: the satisfaction of basic subsistence needs was provided through an artificial stimulation of ideological consumption. The precariousness of economic development was counterbalanced by an inflation of propaganda production. Verbal and representational determinism were the dominant threads weaving the state and society together. The regime's belief in the magical power of words as the effective media through which doctrine acquired the trappings of reality implicitly acknowledged the bankruptcy of Ceausescu's "actually existing" socialism. Rich in intention, poor in means, and dilettantish in management, words were not enough to sustain it. Especially in the 1980s the incongruity between the ever-increasing ideological achievement of abundance realized through the discourse of propaganda, and the ever-increasing degeneration of the material conditions of everyday life as experienced by most people, was as striking as it was jarring.

Propaganda was highly fetishized and formulaic in Ceausescu's Romania, and was reproduced homologously throughout the system at all institutional levels. Conceived as a general panacea, its compositional elements varied to fit the specifics of the matter under scrutiny. Propaganda was constructed from a ritualized set of discursive practices; redundancy was a structural feature of its method. Ritual repetition was important as a consciousness-altering technique. By incessantly and repeatedly bombarding the state's public sphere with ideological rhetoric and images, propaganda became a naturalized part of the everyday environment in which people lived; seemingly so familiar, it was also then possible not to pay it much attention. The price for inattention was to be exacted in full over the years, and with interest.

The rhetorical logic of propaganda remained coherent as long as it was understood within its own self-referential system of meanings. However, when considered in relation to empirical evidence, that coherence vanished. The failure of propaganda as a political-educational technique stemmed primarily from the lack of resonance between the official messages about everyday life that it diffused and the bleak realities of daily experience that people lived. The widening credibility gap paralleled the increasing divide between the Party/State and its population.

## PRODUCING REPRODUCTIVE PROPAGANDA

The politics of reproduction provided a central focus for the production and circulation of political propaganda, the dynamics of which varied throughout the years 1966–1989. Shifts in political-economic emphases were signaled discursively, as were shifts in the intensity of symbolic violence inflicted upon the population. Symbolic violence was wielded daily through unrelenting propaganda campaigns, which represented the beneficent paternal intentions of the state at the expense of the "domestic violence" that the paternalist state simultaneously inflicted upon the Romanian households it battered into obedience. The resultant dependency relations were played out in complex struggles between complicity and resistance. Political demography brought the state into intimate contact with its population, with or without the latter's consent.

The pronatalist propaganda of the Ceausescu regime may be explored through a roughly chronological analysis of pronatalist and pro-family campaigns from 1966 through 1989. The written media were used as an assault weapon to disseminate state policies. Not surprisingly, article 1 of the press law stipulated: "In the Socialist Republic of Romania the press fulfills a high socio-political mission. . . . The press's destiny is to militate permanently for the translation of the Romanian Communist Party's policies into life."[10] In 1966 the state made explicit its intention to regulate the private sphere for its own uses and further articulated in subsequent years the ways in which it would do so. The period 1966–1989 may again be divided into three analytically useful time frames, 1966–1973, 1974–1983, and 1984–1989, which conform roughly to political shifts during Ceausescu's reign.

### "Our Children and Our Country's Children," 1966–1973

*We offer this tribute to woman-mother because, in her very being, nature has endowed her with qualities that belong fully to her.*

PROF. DR. C. STANCA, "ELOGIUL MAMEI," *Sanatatea* 11, 1966

*Expanding socialist reproduction cannot be conceived without enlarging the reproduction of the population and of the work force.*

MIRCEA BULGARU, ADJUNCT DIRECTOR OF THE CENTRAL BUREAU OF STATISTICS, QUOTED IN *Scinteia*, NOVEMBER 26, 1966

*Joke: Beginning in the year 1967, rape will be considered productive labor and will not be punished.*

Immediately following the declaration of Decree 770 on October 1, 1966, a high-ranking official of the Ministry of Health remarked that the legislative act was proof of the [Communist Party's] "deep care and responsibility for the human resources of the country."[11] A prominent doctor declared that the decree would at last put an end to the " intrauterine massacre" that had become the "perfidious enemy of the biological future of our people."[12] An economist from the Central Bureau of Statistics expressed his gratitude that the interdiction of abortion would resolve critical issues that otherwise threatened the steady progress of socialism toward communism. He noted that repercussions from the birthrate decline, resulting from the liberalization of abortion during the years 1957–1966, would be felt in future labor force shortages. If this trend were permitted to continue, it would result in dangerous imbalances between the active or productive population and those in their care (children and the elderly). Increases in the production of material and spiritual goods were dependent on a steady population increase. Accordingly, the decline in the number of "hands available for work" had to be stopped, to which the vanguard party in its ever-vigilant wisdom attended.[13]

However, it should be emphasized again that the 1966 introduction of legislation to regulate sexuality and reproduction was primarily linked to political concerns. Reproduction of the labor force, a mantra of party activists and propagandists, was not the primary preoccupation of the regime. One of the interests driving the inauguration of political demographic measures was Ceausescu's obsession with political self-determination and the geopolitical positioning of Romania in the world of international relations. Ceausescu demanded unequivocal recognition of his role in guiding Romania to political greatness. The pronatalist policies constituted an essential means to (t)his end.[14]

Whatever the reasons for its implementation, Decree 770 became a fact of life. Pronatalism abruptly invaded the dominant discursive space of the newly established regime. The very abruptness with which pronatalist politics were introduced into the public sphere of the state served as the basis for a concerted propaganda campaign. To diffuse the effects of the surprise element accompanying this decree's inauguration, consent had to be manufactured.[15] To this end, the press, mobilized into full service, repeated assertions such as the following ad nauseam: "New measures proposed by the party and government in support of families with children, for increasing natality and improving health care for women and children, have provoked a strong echo [of approval] among the masses."[16] Such statements were expressions of desired rather than actual reactions. The "strong echo among the masses" had to be created. This necessity legitimated the feverish propaganda onslaught that ensued.

As already discussed, the proclamation of Decree 770 took the population by surprise; its publication had not been preceded by any form of public discussion during the planning stages, when amendments customarily were "debated."[17] In the months before the decree's unveiling, the official rhetoric that filled the information media contained discreet warning signs about what was to come, but they failed to raise people's suspicions. The ways people decoded, interpreted, and weighed official communications in order to avoid the state's ably disguised "traps" had not yet been fine-tuned. The anti-abortion "trap" was set at the very beginning of Ceausescu's rule and was maintained throughout it. (Years later, the population had learned, however inadvertently, to distrust government representations, or at the very least, to maintain a healthy dose of skepticism.)

The impending announcement of Decree 770 was foreshadowed in a report presented by the president of the women's movement, Suzana Gadea, at the working meeting of the National Women's Council in June 1966. Several lines buried in the section addressing the political and cultural-educational work required to create and develop socialist consciousness among women, as well as to broaden their cultural-scientific knowledge, alluded to what would follow:

> We consider it an appropriate moment to take the time to raise other important social problems, and in particular, the increase in the number of repeated interruptions of pregnancy, which have harmful effects for the health of many women and negative repercussions for normal population growth. This [situation] is encouraged *by certain deficiencies in the current legislation which must be remedied.* In the same vein, we think it necessary to propose new socioeconomic and educational measures that will contribute to fertility growth and improvement in the care provided for mothers and children.[18]

There is nothing especially alarming about these statements. Gadea called attention to the incidence of repeated abortive procedures, which were assumed to have deleterious consequences for women's health. She also noted that it behooved the women's council to propose measures that would improve living and health conditions for women and children. Her raising of these matters did not, on the surface, suggest nefarious state interests; to the contrary.[19]

In her report, the president of the women's movement also reminded her audience that "love and respect for mothers has always been a cultural trait of our people," and that "during times of great suffering, of misery and privation, when it was extremely difficult for parents to provide their children with life's basic necessities, women stoically confronted hardship and raised [families with] many children with love and devotion. . . . They raised hearty generations who guaranteed the evolution of our people and of enduring continuity on the ancestral lands of our country." Despite these moving words, Gadea's nostalgia for tradition was tempered by critical reference to women's limited emancipation from domestic chores. She condemned the fact that "too much of women's free time is spent attending to family matters." Women's liberation from family labor was supposed to be a benefit of their participation in the state wage-labor force. This emancipatory goal still loomed large for those active in the women's movement. During this period of revolutionary romanticism, the family was considered in part to be an impediment to women's emancipation.

The National Conference for Women also provided the recently elected party leader, Nicolae Ceausescu, with a perfect opportunity to accumulate political capital. Even though he condemned the "liberal" legislation that facilitated the termination of marriage and pregnancy, Ceausescu's tone remained moderate. The secretary general was simply vexed; socialism had ·created better conditions for women and children, yet:

> A decline in the birthrate has been recorded; the rate of population growth
> is slow. In this regard, it must be stated that our country's legislation presents
> lacunae that favor a drop in the number of births; in legal proceedings, there is
> a lack of exigency with respect to the dissolution of marriages, and certain legal
> provisions prove to be too lenient in relation to negligent attitudes about family
> and the education of children. I must mention that these matters are not toler
> able and are under scrutiny . . . the party leadership is exploring measures that
> will improve upon existing legislation, that is, in defense of the family as a unit,
> and toward an increase in responsibility for the home and the raising of chil
> dren, and an increase in the birthrate.[20]

This interlude did not detract from the comrade secretary's primary emphasis on women's productive contributions to the "steadfast continuation of the country's industrialization." Women's place in society was determined by a trio of interrelated roles: woman-mother, woman-wife, and woman-producer. These integrally-linked roles did not, however, preclude the weighting of their social(ist) importance. Beyond the propagandistic evocation that "the Romanian people have always accorded profound respect to women-mothers; [in our] literature and art, our folklore, countless pages have been dedicated to them . . . [and their] strong hands";[21] the woman-producer was also held up as an ideal. At the time, it was difficult to imagine that "woman-mother" would soon become the most esteemed occupation for socialist women. In the summer of 1966, the "supreme duty" conferred on women-mothers by the Communist Party was the patriotic education of their children, not the bearing of more and more of them.[22]

As maternity gained in importance as one of the regime's indispensable resources for the "building of socialism and the advancement toward communism," images of mothers, families, and children became ever more prominent in the public sphere. The mass media as well as scientific discourse heralded the Romanian tradition of homes filled with children and of the love for numerous progeny. In 1966 Zaharia Stancu, a well-known writer who for many years had fervently agitated for communist progress, change, and modernization, uncharacteristically reminded his contemporaries of the blessings of village family life at the beginning of the twentieth century. He eulogized traditional Christian values about women and the family as well as the days when each house had more children than the neighbor's.[23] Back then, a typical response to a query about the number of children a woman had borne was "only seven," "only nine," or "only eleven."[24] Peasant families with many children were romanticized; the high infant mortality rates of that bygone era were ignored, as were the customary social and property relations associated with peasants—which the communists otherwise had set about destroying.

"Many children," a secular translation of the Christian moral position on conception, became the sacred chant of the atheist communist regime regarding human reproduction. In popular parlance, the biblical imperative to "be fruitful and multiply" had long been internalized to mean "as many children as God gives us." Church, state, and popular village wisdom conveniently converged. Indeed, the borrowing of theological concepts by the Communist Party was permissible as long as such transmutations could be dialectically resolved.[25]

Maternity was exalted in the media as "the fulfillment of women's destiny," "the wonder of nature," the "wellspring of life."[26] The "miraculous power of the child" and of large families and the unequaled joy that only children can bring became the leitmotifs of propaganda. "Our children and our country's children" were to be the success stories of the building of communism (see *Scinteia*, October 1, 1966). The press was filled with accounts of mothers who had devoted themselves to the bearing and raising of their children and who, in their old age, were finally enjoying the rewards of their selfless efforts. But these moralizing socialist tales differed dramatically from the lived experiences of socialist (sur)realism at the end of the twentieth century in Romania. Those who were obedient were praised by those who chronicled the times; the others were publicly tried. A few examples illustrate the proselytizing style of pronatalist propaganda and why upstanding families with many children were of profound interest to the state:

> Of the 200 families with children ages one to three surveyed concerning the effects of the arrival of a child into a family, 72 percent declared that the presence of a child introduced an important equilibrium into family life. But we must underscore that the presence of only one child makes the parents' educational role much more burdensome.[27]

> He is 57; she is two years younger. Together they have lived a typical life filled with hard work, demanding work—perhaps more so than others in their younger years. . . . but they have climbed the ladder of life with harmonious vitality. What gives the impression of patriarchal authority? They have experienced one of the simple wonders of life: their lives have been extended, multiplied, and relived through each of their children's lives. When they last gathered all of their offspring together at their home, there were nine children between 18 and 37, plus six grandchildren—"for the time being,"—added the head of the family, and eight sons-in-law. All together, they are 25![28]

The basic sermon was that "wholesome character and social responsibility are shaped in the atmosphere of families united by love, respect, understanding, and reciprocity; in the ambiance of a home with brothers and sisters."[29]

These excerpts, which conflate public and private spheres of interest, capture the nature of relations between the communist state, the family, and the population. The priority status of family and fertility for the well-being of society was highlighted both implicitly and explicitly. Society, or the state, had to accord special attention to the family and to its reproduction because the family provided the milieu in which the new socialist person's character could be formed. Again, the state's ambivalence toward the institution of the family emerged. As an abstraction, the family was considered a necessary unit for socialist reproduction. As a form of social organization, the family, especially when of peasant origin, was considered a residue of bourgeois relations that had to be destroyed to facilitate socialist transformation.

A critical element of good socialist character to be cultivated in the family was a deep sense of social obligation, or social indebtedness. This sentiment of social debt served to subordinate socialist citizens to the party and the nation, as well as to a certain kind of centralized social organization and economy and to the symbols representing it. By definition, a debt (or the sentiment of indebtedness) is a "sum of money or other good owed someone else."[30] Social(ist) indebtedness was not predicated on reciprocal equality, but rather on paternalist (therefore hierarchical) gratitude. In this case, the paternalist state would look after family welfare in return for filial gratitude manifest through obedience.[31] As already noted, dependency was a structural feature of such forms of social organization—dependency on a person or the personification of said person's intentions or acts. In totalizing regimes, the personification of the state and the ruler was simultaneous, resulting in their symbolic identification as society itself. Accordingly, Trotsky wrote of Stalin and Stalinism, "La Société, c'est moi."[32] Ceausescu expropriated this identity. The Romanian Communist Party and Ceausescu came to be identified as one and the same: "Ceausescu, PCR."[33]

The paternalist state structure that demanded gratitude from its citizens also fathered the metaphorical inflation of the state as "the people's family." Indeed, after 1966 the public sphere was overwhelmed by familial terminology. Romania was "tara mama" (the mother country) and "plai stramosesc" (the ancestral land); the Communist Party, "partid parinte" (the party as parent); a "santier" (construction site) was "like a family"; the agricultural harvest, "a celebration of the fertility of the Romanian land."[34] State social organization was a larger, encompassing version of family organization. At the same time, the socialization of future communists was to occur in the family. "Social homogenization" was to result from the superimposition of family units simultaneously engaged in interrelated processes of social reproduction.

Another subject that occupied the pages of the press was the health of women and children.[35] Medical knowledge about maternity and health care lent scientific respectability to socialist planning. Combining concern for the health of women and children with the "advances" of medical expertise was particularly expedient for propaganda experts. Recall that propaganda

was used as an instructional medium and was meant to alter consciousness about living in the world. Clearly, health education about "women's
hygiene and that of the newborn," "the health of mother and child," and
"sexual education" helped sensitize the population to the values of "good
health" and sanitary conditions. To a certain degree and in consequence of
the regime's obsession with these matters, propaganda contributed to the
creation of a "medicalized" popular culture sensitized to concerns about
reproduction and the body. However, in the long run, drawing attention
through propaganda to the need for fit bodies and a healthy living environment backfired. The deterioration of healthy living conditions physically undermined the efficacy of these representations.[36] But in the mid-
1960s, the outlook had seemed more promising.

The pedagogical manipulation of medical issues also created a dependency on doctors and their knowledge. In 1966, after biological reproduction was decreed a social responsibility, the state gradually began to exploit
the possibilities for increased surveillance that the medical relationship offered. Indeed, medical practice became an important and insidious locus
for exercising state control. The propaganda media managed to obfuscate
publicly the political subjugation of medical practitioners. The means used
to institute regulatory measures regarding abortion functioned to rationalize the process of subordination.[37] At the meeting where anti-abortion measures were adopted by the State Council in 1966, academician Aurel Moga,
who was then minister of health, elaborated on abortion's detrimental effects for women's health and the new health-related initiatives meant to curtail abortion. He maintained that responsible political and legislative bodies could not ignore the fact that "interrupting a pregnancy is an act with
grave consequences for the state of women's health and for their biological, reproductive functions. From 1957 until the present, there has been a
rise in the number of cases of secondary sterility, extrauterine pregnancy,
spontaneous abortions, infections, hemorrhaging, endocrinological problems, etc. Moreover, medical data show that repeated interruptions of pregnancy are related positively to [the development of] cancer and to uterine
fibroids."[38]

A courtship between medicine and politics based on "scientific reasoning"
ensued. Those responsible for the health of the population were charged
with maintaining the regime's "vigor." Needless to say, not all medical personnel accepted the deliberate subjection of medical practice to the whims
and will of political interests. However, the structural dependency between
medical practice and political power had been established, thereby offering
the state a subtle means to control the body politic through the control of
individual bodies. After 1966, "sickness" (a potential cause of nonproduc-
tivity) also acquired semantic prominence in the increasingly medicalized
rhetoric of state power. Sickness gradually became another modality through

which the state exercised control.[39] The perversion of the physician's creed transformed the guardians of human health into perpetrators of and accomplices to human repression.

Nonetheless, in the 1960s a modicum of professional objectivity still existed in the promotion of public awareness about medical problems. Although the medical advice disseminated through propaganda was geared to the interests of state policy, scientific norms were more or less respected. The vulgarization of obstetrical and gynecological information was still in its infancy in the late 1960s. Propaganda maintained a relative equilibrium between the information diffused through its media and the emotional context in which that knowledge was embedded. In an October 1966 issue of *Femeia,* the opinions of physicians prevailed as authoritative sources.[40] Dr. Gheorghe Theodoru, a specialist at the Polizu hospital-clinic in Bucharest, offered the following:

> I wish to state outright that any termination of a pregnancy through curettage . . . is a brutal act that endangers a woman's health. Unfortunately, at present, certain young women think that the termination of a pregnancy, when done under the best hygienic circumstances and by a specialist, does not present a future risk for their general health or for the possibility of having a child. This is erroneous. Interventions of this kind, performed even by the most skilled hands, can have negative effects on the organism. . . . such as: uterine perforations, which can occur while doing the operation itself, especially for women who have had multiple surgical procedures or who have a lesion that is difficult to detect; hemorrhaging that may endanger a woman's life because of the amount of blood lost; chronic infections such as pelvic inflammatory disease. Another consequence may be uterine adhesions, which can cause amenorrhea, etc.
>
> I also want to remind you that genital ailments have ill effects on women's psyches. The first trauma that leads to demoralization is involuntary sterility. In any woman's life there comes a time when she wants to have a child, and if she is no longer able? The second is the heightened sensitivity of the entire organism. A similar result may derive from the repeated use of anesthetics.[41]

Dr. Theodoru's medically grounded assertions lent legitimacy to pronatalist propaganda. Declaring that abortion gave rise to a "heightened sensitivity of the entire organism" opened the door for the kind of platitudes upon which propaganda thrived, but in view of the generality of the scientific claim did little to contribute to an understanding of the "organism's" physiology.

Abortion affected more than women's physiological states; significantly, genetic studies showed that the biological profile of the entire population could be changed over time if natality trends were altered. It had been theoretically "demonstrated" that "if 97 percent of the population was less fecund while the remaining 3 percent was very fecund, then within ten generations, the latter would become dominant. Another study determined that if 25 percent of families in a given generation produced 50 percent of the total first generation, then in the fourth generation, their descendants would make up 98 percent of the population. This is an expression of the well-known phenomenon of natural selection through fertility and natality."[42]

Prohibiting abortion would preclude a potential biological transformation of the ethnic composition of the Romanian population. Population decline was viewed as synonymous with national decline and was intolerable for the national ideology of Ceausescu's socialism.

It was similarly reported that the results of a socio-psychological study revealed that "the productivity of worker-mothers, with exemplary family lives, is greater than that of unmarried [women] or of those without children."[43] Furthermore, approximately 9 percent of unmarried and childless women were diagnosed as functionally depressed, tired, and bored. It was concluded that "such states—exhaustion and boredom—which affected work efficiency were especially evident among women without children." Combined, the results of this study and Dr. Theodoru's claims suggested that abortion made the entire body more vulnerable and gave rise to socio-psychological pathologies. To avoid these undesirable effects, women were to avoid having abortions. Female psychological equilibrium and increased productivity resulted from bearing and raising many children. Ultimately, the "laws" of socio-biology determined harmony in a woman's life.

Dr. Aneta Danila-Muster, endocrinologist and doctor of medical sciences, similarly insisted:

> A woman must not renounce the role of mother, and must never terminate her first pregnancy because this may produce serious consequences. Pregnancy is a natural female condition that creates systemic changes in a woman's body. Pregnancy causes the digestive system to function differently. Natural modifications occur in the glandular system also, and affect ovarian functioning, etc. . . . The entire organism adapts, naturally, to this new situation, and then, if the pregnancy is interrupted, [there is] a brusque change, unnatural, but which cannot so abruptly alter the functioning of the other organs and glands. Disequilibrium is produced. The more frequently a woman has abortions, the more pronounced the disequilibrium. These women become permanent patients at diverse clinics, without much hope for full recovery.

Dr. Adrian Ciovirnache, another endocrinologist, added: "Secondary sterility is sometimes consciously produced by tying the tubes. From that moment on, a woman who has accepted such an operation becomes incurably afflicted." Continuing in this vein, Dr. Alexandru Pescaru noted the dire consequences of abortion for the "entire organism:" "Typically, repeated abortion leads to gynecological and endocrinological difficulties and disorders. The lack of children has an important and negative influence on the psychological health of a woman and her family. Our research, based on comparative analysis of different groups, demonstrates clearly that married women who do not have children are more neurotic."

· Despite the prominent display of socio-biological argumentation in the propaganda of the 1960s about women's roles, the importance of women to the economic development of the country still received attention. Nonetheless, the woman-worker role was minimized, subordinated to her other roles of woman-mother and woman-wife.[44] The ever-widening circulation of a more socialist connotation of maternity as an occupation served as a semantic marker of the hierarchicalization of women's options and the priority status of one of them: motherhood.[45] Being both a mother and a wife presupposed a harmonious family life, which Ceausescu emphasized during his speech to the National Conference for Women. Presenting socialist moral commandments from on high, he proclaimed: "It is necessary to combat with conviction retrograde attitudes, laxity toward the family, which have real consequences for a rise in the number of divorces, the breakup of homes, negligence about the upbringing of children, about preparing them for their future lives."[46]

Not surprisingly, the stigmatization of divorce and the exaltation of family life became favorite topics for the machinations of state propaganda and would remain so throughout Ceausescu's rule. However, their public relevance varied in accordance with the political agenda of the day. Throughout the 1960s, propaganda focused its finely refracted lenses on "the family with many children—a law of life and of human fulfillment, a noble patriotic duty."

### Woman-Creator, 1973–1983

*Creative woman, bless you!*
*The nation's love envelops you,*
*scholar, and political personage, and mother at the same time,*
*you, strong role model, of charm and wisdom*
*will be always felt and followed*
*Be forever happy, you, eternal symbol*
*of Romanian heroines, which you have become*
*Forge onward at the side of the country's Hero*
*through the great epic of the Romanian people! . . .*
    CORNELIU VADIM TUDOR, "FEMEIA CREATOARE, SLAVA TIE"[47]

*We demonstrate . . . our recognition of the permanent support and precious guidance*
*that Comrade Elena Ceausescu gives the women's movement, for all that she does for*
*the happiness of all our fatherland's women, for the well-being of our entire people.*
    ANA MURESAN, PRESIDENT OF THE NATIONAL WOMEN'S COUNCIL, 1980

Between 1973 and 1983, two issues dominated official representations pertaining to the family, women, and children: women as economic actors and women as political actors. Propaganda tried to direct public attention away from an emphasis on the "profession" of motherhood and toward the productive participation of women in the command economy. Skillfully assisted by propaganda, women emerged into the political spotlight as well. Even though propaganda and policy accents were changed to stress the social participation of women in the public sphere, women were not absolved of their patriotic obligation to reproduce human life. Decree 770 remained in force. Women had to be propelled into the economic and political realms so as not to undermine the pronatalist politics. The productive anonymity of "the family" was brought to the rescue. The disproportionate valorization of woman-mother was tempered, and the image was recast as one of women's vital roles to the family and to the state. The association between family and state served to further blur the distinction between public and private spheres and to instrumentalize women multilaterally.

According to some authors, two needs motivated the propaganda campaigns targeting women's incorporation into the work force and politics after 1973: the need to engage women as a surplus labor resource and the need to legitimate the political and scientific career of Elena Ceausescu. One way or another, the political and economic emancipation of women formed part of the mythic history of socialist women fabricated during the Ceausescu regime. Ceausescu began to clamor for the multilateral promotion of women into the labor force, promising them full equality with men. He militated against gender discrimination, demanding that persons be treated not as men and women but as members of the party and as citizens: "If we speak about the creation of conditions of full equality between the sexes, this means that we must treat all people not as men and women, but in their qualities as party members, as citizens, for which they are exclusively judged according to their work contributions."[48] He also continued to stress that "an obligation of national interest is the protection and consolidation of the family, the development of a corresponding consciousness about the growth of an increased number of children, and the formation of healthy and robust generations profoundly devoted to the cause of socialism; in this realm women have a distinguished role and a noble mission."[49]

Ceausescu superficially recognized the tensions created for women through their roles as mothers and workers. In 1978 he again urged that particular attention be paid to solving these problems through the construction of childcare facilities and the production and distribution of household appliances and semi-prepared foods—so that women could use their time efficiently in their multilateral pursuits.[50] Unfortunately, Ceausescu's verbal expression of concern did little to alleviate the burdens women experienced in their everyday lives.

Indeed, some questioned whether Ceausescu's "goal was not really the promotion of women but of one particular woman."[51] In 1972 at the National Conference of the Romanian Communist Party, Ceausescu's wife, Elena, was elected to full membership in the Central Committee; the next year she became a member of the party's Executive Committee. This same type of suspicion arose when Ceausescu began promoting his son, Nicu, in the early 1980s; at that time, Ceausescu began a public campaign on the importance of the nation's youth. Political-educational campaigns paralleled political moves by the extended ruling family to consolidate power. In part, the public promotion of women (and of youth) served to legitimate a first step in the creation of "socialism in one family"—the Ceausescu family.

Hence, the early 1970s were marked by a barrage of salutary images of Nicolae Ceausescu and his wife, Elena. She did not accompany him merely as a spouse, but rather as his complementary equal in every way: partner in marriage, mother, scientist, and political figure. In short, she embodied the ideal socialist woman. Her public presence, aggrandized through propaganda, served to legitimate the public presence of women in general. Her "coming out" occurred in earnest on Ceausescu's birthday in 1973, when the iconographic feting of the Romanian leader included the symbolic honoring of Elena as well: "We gaze with esteem, with respect, at the harmony of his family life. We attach special ethical significance to the fact that his life—together with that of his life comrade, the former textile worker and a UCY militant, member of the party since the days of illegality, today Hero of Socialist Labor, scientist, member of the Central Committee of the RCP, comrade Elena Ceausescu—offers an exemplary image of the destinies of two communists."[52]

Equality as a constitutive principle was not at the core of this couple's internal relations, but rather the dynamic between them seems to have been (or become) predicated on the notion that even a woman could be first among equals.[53] The public recognition of Elena's abilities signaled the shift in emphasis away from mothering as woman's paramount role to her multiple emancipation and, hence, fulfillment. Simultaneously, the symbolic relation between the state and the family was sanctified; women's diverse capabilities were celebrated; and the "homogenization" of gendered identities was subtly acknowledged. Men and women were equal as communists.

Elena's curriculum vitae read like that of a top achiever who had risen through the ranks and, like her husband, had been rewarded for her efforts. The public sphere was glutted with similar social and political success stories of other women who, nonetheless, respectfully remained in the shadow of their luminous star, Elena Ceausescu.[54] This paragon of communist accomplishment was presented as a "preeminent personality in science and sociopolitical life both in our country and abroad, an illustrious model of what a woman in our contemporary socialist society must be."[55] As director general of the Central Institute for Chemical Research and vice-president of the National Council of Science and Technology, she exemplified the pinnacle of professional achievement; as a scientist, she was honored with membership in the Romanian Academy; as political activist, she was promoted to the rank of member of the Executive Committee of the Central Committee of the Romanian Communist Party; she was also the mother of three children. Elena Ceausescu was omnipresent as propaganda's favorite pin-up girl.[56]

Women's presence in the economic, political, and social life of the country was thus secured by Elena's official debut. Next, the Central Committee issued a series of decisions taken at their plenary meeting, June 18–19, 1973, which elaborated on the "contributions of our women toward the resolution of problems associated with our country's socio-political and economic life." Fundamental among them were:

1. An increase in possible roles for women in economic, scientific, and cultural development, and in political and social life "to demonstrate women's multiple, creative potentials, and to combine harmoniously their role as mother and wife with that of active participant in the efforts of the entire population to achieve the rapid, unceasing progress of our fatherland."[57]
2. The consolidation of the family in the national interest because the existence of healthy families guaranteed an increase in the number of children who would form "healthy, robust generations profoundly dedicated to the socialist cause."
3. The determination of priority professions and functions for women in order to "create new jobs needed to facilitate the incorporation of village inhabitants in industry," and to increase the percentage of women engaged in fields such as electro-technical and chemical engineering, electronics, optics, precision mechanics, food processing, etc., and "in other domains in which new positions [were] suitable for women."[58]
4. The promotion to positions of authority in all party and state institutions of women who had the necessary political and professional training, and who were good organizers and homemakers. "A greater number of women should be chosen as party secretaries of regional, municipal, city, and community party committees, as well as presidents and vice-presidents of regional, municipal, and city people's councils. Similar measures should be taken by union leadership, collective agricultural production units, artisans' cooperatives, and other economic enterprises."[59]
5. The intensification of political-educational work among women "to create and develop socialist consciousness . . . concern for socialist property, respect for work discipline, and for professional and public obligations."

(This point was directed specifically toward propaganda activists, especially in the women's movement.)[60]

These decisions were transformed into measures effective January 1974 and paved the way for the professional training and incorporation of women into the labor force according to "the needs of the national economy."[61]

The reordering of the hierarchy of women's activities was reflected in the semantic structure of official discourse, whether for formal party dissemination or for mass consumption. The role of woman-mother was shrewdly transformed into the more encompassing category of "woman-creator" by the magical power of words. Multiple meanings made it possible for "woman-creator" to signify the role of women in the production of social goods, including children. This semantic artifice homogenized and combined into one fertile symbol the contradictions and tensions inherent in women's productive and reproductive roles.

The arbitrariness of symbols and their meanings was exploited in another featured element of propaganda campaigns: the family. To underscore again, the feminism of "multilaterally developed socialism" did not take issue with the family as a source of female subordination in the relations between men and women. As one noted "feminist" à la Ceausescu wrote in honor of this highly valued social institution:

> The contemporary family is more and more deserving of appreciation as a milieu in which people acquire knowledge, [the family] having at its disposal the media of mass communication: radio, television, local newspapers, centers, journals, etc. Recognizing this as one of the family's roles, a habit should be made, for mothers as well, of listening to TV news, watching live transmissions of major political events. . . . It should be obligatory, just as cleaning potatoes and washing and drying dishes are duties of all family members and should be accepted as such. The socialist family must evolve toward real community spirit of its members, based on reciprocal and equal contributions . . . and in this way, the [family's] educational as well as cultural roles will be fulfilled.[62]

Although the contradictions between party expectations and what were primarily women's burdens tended to be resolved discursively, certain practical measures were instituted to alleviate some of the daily problems faced by a typical family. Pensions for the elderly, more flexible working hours for women with children, and limited improvement of medical assistance and social services were established. Appropriate ministries and production enterprises were charged with bettering the availability and distribution of household appliances, time-saving devices, semi-prepared foods, laundries, public cafeterias, and childcare facilities.[63] In principle, the state was an avid supporter of the family. In fact, the family was one of the most beleaguered sites for the instrumentalization of Ceausescu's political visions.

At the Eleventh Party Congress in 1974, the profeminist political line introduced during the preceding year's party conference was officially embraced. This meant that women's and family interests had to be, and were, adjusted to fit the "actually existing socialism" constructed by the Ceausescus. However, at the end of the decade, the credibility of party policies was wide open to questioning. The discontinuity between political intentions and practical realizations had become too visible. Extending "the benefit of doubt" became an impossible psychological option; official pronouncements were challenged by what was required to manage the simple mundanities of everyday life. That challenge remained relentlessly present in the 1980s.

## "Handsome and Healthy Children
## for the Vigor and Youth of the Fatherland," 1983–1989

*The procreation of children in families must be seen as much from a biological point of view, for the reproduction of the species, as from a social point of view, for the reproduction of the work force.*

AURELIAN CONSTANTINESCU, VALENTINA NEGRITOIU,
AND ECATERINA STATIVA, *Pledoarie pentru maternitate,* 1987

*Joke: The oath of the Fatherland's Falcons: "I swear to grow up big and strong—without eating anything."*

The political priority accorded women's advancement in the public sphere throughout much of the 1970s seemed to have taken its toll on the nation's future. (The toll on the lives of women, children, and families—the focus of propaganda—was of little practical concern.) The 1983 demographic report prepared by the Higher Council on Health was cause for concern at the Political Executive Committee meeting where it was presented. After more than fifteen years of pronatalist politics, the birthrate had declined to the 1966 level of 14.3 live births per 1,000 inhabitants. Moreover, for every one live birth in 1983 there had been 1.3 legal abortions—even with the restrictive abortion legislation. The Ministry of Health and related health providers came under attack for not preventing all unwarranted interruptions of pregnancies. Doctors were scorned for exploiting the population for personal gain—that is, for profiting from the performance of illegal abortions. Such acts were considered to be antinational and would be treated harshly henceforth. Furthermore, infant and maternal mortality statistics were troubling, especially when compared with those of other European countries. Clearly, the state's attempts to control reproduction centrally had not been successful. Romanians had somehow managed to control their own fertility choices in an environment saturated with pronatalist policies and propaganda, and in which contraceptives were unavailable through legal means.[64] These disturbing disclosures presented the regime with a

dilemma. Public admission of the failure of the political demographic policies was out of the question. Party legitimacy rested on the mystique of
enlightenment; as a vanguard party, its policies were, by definition, above
error and reproach.

The regime acted swiftly to save face and to salvage the perceived impending political-demographic disaster. Juridical, administrative, financial,
and propaganda resources were mobilized. Whatever limited institutional
autonomy had been tolerated in the 1970s gave way to centralized coordination in the 1980s. Stimulatory measures were ordered, but this time they
were augmented by repressive ones designed to guarantee positive results.
Repression was the regime's preferred political modus operandi throughout the 1980s. While other Eastern European countries experimented with
limited reforms, Ceausescu emulated the methods of Stalin, whom he
revered.

Western demographers were not thoroughly convinced that Romania's
demographic situation in general and labor force needs in particular lay behind the tightening of the pronatalist measures in the 1980s. Their analyses
of the available data suggested that "these measures were advanced at a
time when the Rumanian population was growing, not declining, in size.
Moreover, the explicit goal is to 'increase the birth rate to 19–20 per thousand population per year,' implying a population growth rate approaching
1% over the indefinite future. The clear implication is that such a growth
rate is what the Rumanian government takes to be 'normal demographic
growth.'"[65]

Here, it is critical to emphasize again that the decline in the birthrate
(despite the growth in population) coincided with a steady deterioration
in the material conditions of daily life. In the interest of national self-
determination, Ceausescu had decided that Romania's outstanding foreign debts had to be repaid, at enormous cost to the quality of life. Production was targeted for export.[66] By 1984, winters were endured with little
heat or electricity; food staples were rationed. Indeed, 1984 ushered in the
Orwellian policies that became the basis for Margaret Atwood's novel *The
Handmaid's Tale,* and for the making of a Romanian national tragedy. In
March the Political Executive Committee of the Central Committee issued
a decision ordering party and state organs as well as medical and health
cadres to take increased responsibility for implementing the political demographic policies and achieving a corresponding population growth.[67]
Medical personnel were to serve as agents of the state, rigorously examining
women's "state of health"—a political euphemism for the determination of
whether a woman was pregnant. In this way, the scope of a gynecological examination was perverted, becoming a venue for political as well as physical
surveillance.

The preamble to this decision provided the reasons for its issuance, all of which pertained to the ritualized "building of multilaterally developed socialism." As noted previously, a "decision" had the force of law but differed from a law or decree in that it marked a transfer from legislative to executive control. In such circumstances, the party wielded power directly, rather than indirectly, through the activities of the Grand National Assembly. In view of the dismal state of demographic affairs, recourse to this ultimate disciplinary mechanism was erroneously considered to be more efficient. Repressive and coercive mechanisms were to be generalized throughout the multilaterally developing socialist society so as to put an end to birthrate problems and strengthen the family as a reproductive unit. Life and death came fully under the exigent control of the party.

This decision, which was to be so consequential in the lives of all adult Romanians, contained a number of articles that spelled out ways to popularize the measures taken to support women and children, and to fortify the seminal role of families in socialist society. Families were considered to be the societal resource par excellence from which children acquired healthy attitudes about marriage; marriage and human reproduction had become building blocks of socialism. The Political Executive Committee appealed to the population, to all "urban and village workers," to understand how essential it was to ensure normal demographic growth, which was "a high honor and patriotic duty for every family and for our entire population, which has always prided itself on the cultural tradition of families with many children raised lovingly, and securing the vitality, youth, and vigor of the whole nation. Even more so today, we have this unparalleled obligation to produce new generations . . . who will contribute to the flourishing of our socialist nation, to the triumph of socialism and communism in Romania."[68]

A few days later, at a meeting of the Superior Health Council, Nicolae Ceausescu declared with impassioned rhetoric (resuscitated and revised for the occasion): "There cannot be anything more precious for a woman than to be a mother, to make certain that the laws of nature themselves are fulfilled in life, to procreate, to secure the continuous development of our people, of our nation. There cannot exist greater satisfaction and joy for a family, for a mother, than to have and raise children. . . . Without a healthy population—physically, intellectually and morally—we cannot speak of constructing communism, or a superior society! Let us do everything for our people . . . so that our people will be dignified, healthy, strong and hearty."[69]

These lines summarized the political demographic propaganda that would dominate the rest of Ceausescu's rule. On International Women's Day, March 8, 1984, Ceausescu saluted women's contributions to the nation by again exhorting them to bear four or more children in order to achieve the national goal of increasing the population from 22.6 to 25 million by

1990. To this end, as little as possible was left to chance; recall that on December 26, 1985, a more stringent anti-abortion law was passed. A woman had to be at least 45 years of age and have delivered five children (who were in her care) before being eligible for a legal abortion.

Demographers, doctors, and women's and youth organizations were solicited to participate in the mass pronatalist propaganda campaign; ideological bombast was cemented by threats of punishment, thereby securing the complicity of most. Active members of the women's club, Femina, swallowed pronouncements such as: "The increase of women's responsibilities with respect to: the realization of our party and our state's demographic politics, to the education of children and youth in the spirit of work, of unlimited love and devotion for the fatherland and the party, for comrade Nicolae Ceausescu . . . for Elena Ceausescu, for the extraordinary conditions of life, work, and education that have been created during the years of socialism."[70]

The propaganda apparatus obediently responded to the regime's urgent political demographic challenge. Themes that had been exploited in the 1970s had to be recast to meet the political demands of the 1980s. The mass media engaged in a general backlash campaign against the economically and politically emancipated woman they had previously heralded. Woman-mother was not only resuscitated as a role model for females; woman-mother became *the* role model for all women. Women as workers and wives became background visions blurred through the lenses of propaganda. Recall that between 1966 and 1973, a woman's role as mother was complemented by her additional roles as wife, worker, and politically active person. By the 1980s, women's "real" role was to reproduce. Of course, this did not excuse her from the work force. Moreover, as another classic study revealed: "Research shows that working mothers are better than housewives. Contact with the social world makes her more receptive to the new . . . and [enables her] to adopt scientific attitudes about the problem of family life and the child."[71] Results of the previously quoted 1967 socio-psychological study of female factory workers were hauled out; it had shown, among other things, that women with children benefited from "superior motivation."[72]

The revival of woman-mother as a key symbol for the 1980s was accompanied by her contextualization in a "family with many children." For the purposes of propaganda, "many children" was an encompassing phrase that accommodated policy changes regarding the requisite number of children per family.[73] This family had two interrelated meanings. The ideal woman-mother belonged simultaneously to the traditional family and to the metaphorical one of the nation-state. Families that did not conform to this romanticized family model were stigmatized in official representations as individualistic, antisocial, and antinational—that is, anticommunist. Propaganda texts created a relationship between parents fulfilling their patriotic duties to reproduce themselves and the labor force, and fulfilling the laws of nature to ensure the evolution of life. The laws of the latter were presented as being synonymous with the laws of state.

The social significance of the romanticized traditional family differed from its socio-biological construction, which in essence was "bio-socialist." For the purposes of propaganda, only the family with many children was sociologically important as an institution. The family was not only a social institution but also a "biological social system . . . for increase of the population and the raising of new generations, thus for human exigencies and historic progress."[74] Moreover, nature had essentialized women, endowing only them with the ability to bear life. Nature lay at the root of the annual toast offered to women as generic species-being: "the honor of the entire country—to [our] country's women."

In this atmosphere, it was not surprising to hear a doctor say:

> "Who is the child's father?"—a hypocritical question from a depraved society (and, I might add, reminiscent of a barbarism perpetuated until so-called modern times)—is, thank God, no longer asked. (In fact, it is no longer asked in any civilized society!) Of the list of questions . . . only the first is valid, that by which the future mother's name and surname is officially registered.
>
> With respect to the horrible question, "who forced you to give birth?," today, this issue is seen completely differently. It is not only that this question is proscribed by our society's laws—by definition, a humane society, or better said, a society of good will—but, today, as you well know, we honor the other side of the coin, that is, the stimulation of natality, viewed as an important responsibility for the destiny of our people. The measures recently established by the Political Executive Bureau of the Central Committee of the PCR, upon the noble initiative of comrade Nicolae Ceausescu, are, in this regard, eloquent.[75]

The efficiency of women's reproductive behavior had become the criterion by which women were recognized socially. This type of social structural reasoning signaled the formal subordination of patriarchal authority to that of the paternalist state. As pater familias of the nation, Ceausescu laid principal claim to women's reproductivity—and not vice-versa. To the degree that familial patriarchal authority did not interfere with Ceausescu's plans, the patriarch of the state did not interfere with men's roles as the heads of traditional families. But, women's reproductive functions were unambiguously to be instrumentalized in the service of the state. "The desire to have children has always been a human imperative. . . . For this reason, the arrival of children . . . must be celebrated . . . the more prolific a woman, the more respected she is."[76] Subsumed in the terms of this naturalized discourse was the state's implicit acceptance of children born out of wedlock.

The propagandized rebirth of woman-mother spawned a series of ritualized phrases, among which were "a home with many children" and "the vigor and youth of the fatherland."[77] The fortuitous convergence between the party's and women-mothers' understanding of the importance of child-bearing and related matters was demonstrated time and again. Articles prominently displayed titles and subtitles such as: "The joy of having children, the satisfaction of raising them [to be] healthy, with respect and dignity"; "Concrete measures, energetic measures for the strict application of political demography"; "Demographic growth—an exalted responsibility of the entire society"; "The joy of being a mother"; "As a mother, I feel and value the party's concern and respect"; "Many and healthy children for the youth of the nation"; "Children—the future of the fatherland, the flowers of life"; "A home with many children: sign of a good citizen [taking responsibility] for the nation's future"; "Strong children—the love and concern of the whole nation"; "The immense care with which the country protects its children."[78]

Propaganda painted pictures of heavenly conditions on earth. But neither urban nor village workers were impressed by these representations of the good life. Propaganda convinced few of their citizenly responsibility to reproduce themselves in these much-trumpeted conditions, or of the high honor and patriotic debt that such behavior entailed. However sophisticated, the most subtle and manipulative propaganda techniques lost their magical power in the face of having to reconcile that which could not be reconciled. The ability to dissimulate notwithstanding, it was impossible to ignore the oppressive reality of daily life. In the prevailing conditions of the mid-1980s it was increasingly difficult for a mother to want to fulfill her patriotic duty when she was uncertain if she could feed, clothe, and provide heat, light, and other basic necessities for the children she was obliged to produce "to ensure normal demographic growth" of the country.[79]

Yet the propaganda apparatus faithfully persisted in efforts to alter people's perceptions of the environment in which they lived. "Scientifically developed" theories pointed to the mutually dependent relation between demographic factors and economic growth. Dr. Vasile Parvu, for example, stated in an economic journal: "The larger the active population, the greater the working potential available . . . and with higher social productivity, the greater the gross national product, from which follows an increased return to the general population, which, in unmediated fashion, influences the living standard. The interrelations between demographic factors and economic growth are similarly interconditioned such that it is difficult to attribute priority at any one moment regarding the general process of development."[80] The message, although expressed in the RCP's highly contorted wooden language, was simple.

The interrelationship between economic conditions and demographic indicators was a favorite workhorse for propaganda treatment. With respect to political demography, data were distorted to underscore only those aspects of reproductive behavior that were compatible with official political demographic norms. Political demographic slogans replaced critical analysis. To illustrate, *Femeia* published an interview of the president of the women's committee representing the county Botosani. This county was highlighted because of its leading position in an interregional contest to attain the highest demographic indicators. The women's committee president stressed: "We, Botosanenii, love families that endure, families with many and healthy children."[81] She affirmed the positive relationship between economic development and increased fertility rates: the greater the economic growth, the higher the demographic indicators: "Our demographic indicators are of seminal importance, reflecting the spectacular progress achieved on the road to economic development, to improvement of the living standard and of the population's health. Industrial development created new jobs, especially for women, who represent a surplus labor force."[82]

It is virtually axiomatic in the comparative demographic literature that fertility behavior is affected by diverse factors. Moreover, the relationship between high fertility rates and the modernization of social and economic structures is customarily considered to be an inverse one. Industrialization and urbanization, as processes of modernization, tend to be accompanied by birthrate declines. In a socialist economy such as Romania's, in which development was synonymous with extensive industrialization and the mandatory incorporation of women into the work force, the negative effects on natality rates were pronounced.[83] In other words, the increased rate of female participation in the state economy correlated negatively with fertility rates, especially urban ones. The number of live births dropped.

Yet this Romanian party activist—like many of her kind—maintained that modernization in her respective region, including women's increased non-domestic wage labor, was positively associated with increased natality rates. The ritualized presentation of regional economic and demographic information revealed the way in which propaganda adjusted material realities to meet ideological requirements. When analyzed, her statements represented a typical manipulation of information for political ends. This region was among those labeled "traditional," and was popularly known for its high fertility rates and the traditional reproductive behavior of its inhabitants. Large families were valued. Moreover, modernization and industrial development there had not progressed rapidly enough to affect the fertility regime.[84] Botosani remained geopolitically peripheral throughout the communist era; it also remained poorer and less developed—an empirical reality ignored by dedicated activists.[85]

In spite of the positive correlation between development and high natality figures claimed by the party activist, birthrates in this region had nonetheless begun to decline. Possible causes were discussed behind closed doors at a meeting of regional party and state officials, who decided on steps to correct the trend; they emphasized that "education has an important role" in rectifying this downward tendency.[86] Activists from the women's movement were instructed to organize political-educational activities that would showcase the virtues of traditional families. Young women were to be made aware of their role in maintaining the vigor and youth of their nation. Women who had given birth to many children were invited to "share their own life stories with others" inasmuch as these mothers were deemed the best teachers to instill in other women the desire to fulfill themselves through childbearing. Yet such consciousness-raising gatherings inevitably were as ritualized as they were ineffective. Propaganda verbally and symbolically obfuscated the contradictory relations between ideological representation and practical experience. "Education," a pseudonym for ideological training, and "political-educational activities," a pseudonym for propaganda, may have offered "spiritual" salvation, but neither concealed the harsh deprivations imposed by increasing shortages.

The socialist press, inured to the disparity between its representations of life under socialism and what the masses experienced, affirmed that no objective circumstances accounted for the existing lack of fulfillment of the demographic targets: "The reality is that the socio-economic development of the country offers a good material basis for the protection of health and for demographic contributions."[87] Socialist planning had taken all of this into account; planners knew that healthy citizens made the best workers. According to the information these skilled technicians projected through their rose-colored lenses, the economic situation of Romania in the mid-1980s provided each citizen adequate nutrition through a monthly allotment of: "3 pounds of processed meat, 1/3 pound of flour, 1 pound of rice, 10 eggs, 2 pounds of cheese and a packet of butter," 3.3 pounds of sugar, and 1.1 quarts of vegetable oil.[88] The bleakness of stores and markets, pharmacies, and other providers of life's basics did not figure into these propaganda pictures.

If foodstuffs were absent from the shelves, they remained present in everyone's minds. Scientific study about "rational alimentation" was strongly supported by the state, and in the early 1980s guidelines based on these studies were made public. "Scientific nutrition" referred to the "quantity of elements introduced into the human organism which qualitatively and quantitatively satisfy the organism's nutritional needs over a period of time, usually over 24 hours."[89] Needless to say, balanced nutrition was especially important for pregnant women, young mothers, infants, and young children. For an adult pregnant woman, a model diet based on three meals and two snacks per day was prescribed, recommending that she eat "bread with cheese and tomatoes, and a cup of coffee with milk" for breakfast, to be followed by a mid-morning snack of a "slice of buttered bread with fresh ham," finished off with a "piece of fruit"; at lunch time, she was supposed to have "chicken soup with homemade noodles, a chicken dish made with white sauce and eaten with polenta, and a fruit jello." A late-afternoon pick-me-up was to consist of "yogurt, bread and butter, cheese, green peppers, and fruit." To complete her nutritional needs for the day, she was to eat a dinner consisting of "fish cooked in parchment paper accompanied by vegetables, a fried pastry filled with white cheese and a heavy sweet cream, and a fruit compote."[90]

Similar Rabelaisian recommendations were devised for women who were breastfeeding, as well as for infants and young children. Menus and charts presenting different sources of nutrition (e.g., milk products, fruits and vegetables, breads and cereals, meats and fish, eggs, fats, sweets, and liquids) were provided. For example, women who were breastfeeding were supposed to consume daily "one liter's worth of milk or milk preparations; one egg; meat at least once; an orange, grapefruit, tangerine or the like twice daily."

A simple comparison between the monthly rations guaranteed each citizen and the scientifically developed list of rations makes it clear why cynicism pervaded the public sphere. The glorified pregnant woman was told by the state's nutritionists to eat approximately 30 eggs per month; at the same time, the "good material basis for the protection of health" provided her with a maximum of ten eggs per month. For a woman to follow the doctor's orders and eat what she was supposed to over the course of one day, she or someone in her family would have had to stand for hours in numerous long lines in different sections of the city. Moreover, this assumed that each item could be purchased somewhere. Under the best of circumstances, procuring only a few of the items on the list required several days of effort, adequate supplies of patience and resources, and good connections. Surrealism was the only prism through which scientific norms could be respected.

By the 1980s, undernourishment had become a chronic condition for almost the entire population in Romania. As noted above, balanced diets were digested by pregnant women through force-feeding of propaganda. The absence of adequate nourishment for pregnant mothers may have contributed to the number of premature births, which in 1989 constituted 7.3 percent of all births.[91] Dystrophy, characterized by inadequate nutrition and muscular development, was among the principal causes of infant death, representing 33.1 deaths per 1,000 live births; its increased incidence has also been linked to maternal malnutrition.

Statistical mystification added to the veritable mystique of socialism's successes, which somehow eluded so many of Romania's citizens. Numbers helped shape reality and a loyal cadre helped shape the numbers. Statistics were published repeatedly to convince the population of the state's benevolent paternalism toward "families with many children," women, and children.[92] Another constantly drilled agenda item was the financial support accorded mothers for raising their many children. More impressive, the increase in family-oriented benefits was made possible by Ceausescu's cutting of the military budget, "a measure that was praised in the four corners of the world," according to Maria Bobu in the 1984 *Women's Almanac.*[93]

Propaganda extolled the virtues of the new socialist morality predicated on family values. Motherhood, children, and families dominated official rhetoric; nonetheless, problems that interfered with the normal unfolding of family life and posed obstacles for "normal demographic development" of the country also received attention in the print media, and from radio and television as well as academia. Divorce, sexual crises, child abandonment, and other forms of social "deviance" were fair play for the moralizers of the masses. The manipulation of feelings was one of the preferred methods used to insinuate the pronatalist package of practices and values into the consciences of the people. Heart-wrenching headlines read: "Siblings separated: divorce is truly a family disaster;" or, "Find me a place in your heart."[94] Morality tales about good and bad mothers abounded. A young, single mother wanting to give her child up for adoption was chastised in the response to her letter of inquiry (of the "Dear Abby" sort): What kind of young woman was she? She had a job, was healthy, and had her whole future ahead of her. She herself had been left motherless at the age of thirteen. The thrust of the argument was that a "single mother is not to be condemned; a mother will always be respected. Perhaps for a while you won't be able to offer your child the maximum, but be certain that no one in this world can offer what you can [mother-love]."[95] The gist of similar responses was that the state provided good care for orphaned children, but nothing was like being in a family.[96]

Medical information about marital relations and the negative effects of abortion and contraception in general was promoted in publications with titles such as: "The secondary effects of modern contraception," "Premarital advice," "The evil effects of abortion."[97] Health and sex education were stepped up, including premarital health counseling and checkups, informational lectures, and films at work locales. Couples were to be instructed on the biological merits of procreation for reproduction of the species, as well as on the social ones for reproduction of the work force. Educators and activists received all manner of booklets on the relationship between health and demography, marital harmony, care of infants and children, and the consequences of abortion. A booklet prepared by the Ministry of Health's Institute for Hygiene and Public Health contained such topics as the methods and contents of health education in problems of demography, and the medical protection of mothers, children, and youth. The latter contained material on reproduction and problems related to it: fecundity, pregnancy, birth, infant and child care, venereal diseases. Discussion groups were organized at which individualized advice was also obtainable. Formal group instruction was offered at schools for mothers, for fathers, and for grandparents. Documentary films were shown for ideological-educational purposes. In addition, health care–related demonstrations were given at club meetings like those held by Femina, or at "young mothers' circles," or "infants' corners."[98]

In view of the evident link between sexual and physical/psychological health, instructions about normal sexual relations were also provided. Sex, like everything else, was subject to regulation, and to achieve a "normal regulated sexual life," relations on an average of three-four times a week were recommended: "Exceptions to this frequency occur in the first months after marriage and are explicable and inoffensive; then there is a gradual decrease, being stabilized at the above-mentioned medium. Excesses in frequency or duration of the sexual act are surely tiring and taxing on health, as are rare sexual contacts, which give rise to nervousness, agitation, and insomnia."[99] It was assumed that non–sexually active adults would fall victim to psychological conditions such as depression and anxiety. Similar psychological states could emerge from other sex-related circumstances; hence, couples were warned that:

> A maneuver with negative consequences when used too frequently is that known as *coitus interruptus,* when the sexual act is interrupted before reaching the culminating point of ejaculation and orgasm. Dysfunctions first arise because partners are afraid they won't interrupt [the act] in time. This leads to the restriction of motor activities during the sexual act and impedes the harmony of intimacy. Furthermore, a man who practices this method often suffers from psychologically generated impotence, as well as urethral irritation and prostate congestion. For women, this method leads to diminished orgasm, and even to frigidity, and may foster pelvic congestion at the same time.[100]

As to homosexuality, socialist puritanism combined with pronatalism and traditional cultural values meant that homosexuality was criminalized as societally deviant behavior (article 200 of the Penal Code).

Another important venue exploited for purposes of sex and health education was that of the socialist competition developed along the lines of those discussed earlier for "heroes of socialist labor." General knowledge about such matters was tested through popular contests sponsored by a magazine. For example, readers were asked to respond to the second quiz in a series appearing in *Sanatatea* (no. 4, 1984), which included questions such as: "What are the necessary annual natality indicators recommended in a recent party document? In what year did the Romanian Red Cross issue a stamp of a girl with a dove in hand, symbol of world peace? How do you resolve $x$ household accident?"

After 1985, other forms of competition, especially between institutions, became prevalent throughout the country. The propagandistic and disciplinary intent of these contests was clear, as was the attribution of responsibility. A typical institutionally directed challenge involved the health department from the region of Suceava, which called upon that of Bucharest to engage in a contest to "better the demographic indicators and increase the natural rate of population growth." Each health department competed in the following categories of activity: "determination of the number of pregnancies in their first trimester; gynecological examination of fertile women; full medical examination of pregnant women considered to be obstetrically at risk; the tracking and testing of all young couples without children . . . and similarly of those with but a few children in order to educate them about their abilities to help realize the political demographic needs of the country; to achieve birthrates of a minimum of 20 per 1,000; the birth of all new-borns in health units; prevention through appropriate medical and educational measures of interruptions of pregnancies such that the number does not exceed 330 abortions per 1,000 live births."[101] Institutional contests of this sort transformed political demographic policies into obligatory propaganda actions with material results. Those extended an invitation to compete did not have the right to refuse. What appeared to be friendly competition between institutions served as yet another mechanism for exerting political control.

The gynecological exams, which gained international notoriety after the fall of the regime, were accorded special attention in such contests, the results of which were popularized through the media. One director of the health department from the region of Buzau boasted, for example, that "with the help of obstetrical-gynecological specialists, we have managed over 34,000 exams of more than 22,000 employed women."[102] In Botosani, they congratulated themselves that:

> Almost 10,000 women between the ages of 20 and 40 have been examined to detect the development of uterine cancer, and the causes of sterility and infertility. At the same time, 7,200 young girls took part in the "pro-family" health education campaign during which they learned about their [national] responsibility as future mothers, . . . prescribed diets for pregnant women, the evil consequences of abortion . . . on women's health. The "mothers' school" enjoys a good audience, offering in 1983 alone more than 600 such courses.[103]

However, in Bucharest, the requisite demographic quotients were never attained. The municipal health department was chastised for the continually poor showing of the nation's capital; criticisms were confined to reproaches of formalism in the implementation of health education and medical controls. The director of the Health Department emphasized for the benefit of those under his supervision—and for his own self-protection—

that the evident deficiencies in professional discipline and practice would have to be rectified, and he was "firmly resolved" to see to it that they would be. His speech, including his self-serving collegial warning, respected the norms of propaganda-speak. The future of the nation was at stake, as was fulfilling the political demographic goals of its leaders.

### POPULAR CRITIQUES OF PROPAGANDA

Propaganda was the quintessential technique used to disseminate official ideology about the demographic policies throughout the state system. Although diverse forms were tailored to fit best the profile of targeted audiences, propaganda content remained constant in the politics of the period. Accordingly, in the 1980s, maternity and large families came to dominate the discursive field, relegating images of politically and economically active women to the back burner. A singular exception was made for Elena Ceausescu, the ideal-typical socialist woman who, paradoxically, was not the ideal-typical mother of a family with many children.

As has become evident, the propaganda apparatus was not perturbed by such inconsistencies. During the years of Ceausescu's rule, women were variously lauded for their participation in the political, economic, and social-cultural life of the nation. However, women could only attain true fulfillment with motherhood. Woman-mother was at times representationally complemented by the other roles open to her gender but never could these compensate for her primary role as childbearer and nurturer. Always, the best option for a woman was motherhood:

> Statistics demonstrate that women who give birth to many children, despite increased demands for their upbringing and care, are more vigorous and live longer than those who do not have children. Childbirth alters women's physiology and hormones in favor of female health. After childbirth, women manifest their mature beauty. The raising and care of children bring invigorating satisfactions for the female psyche, joys that stimulate and ennoble her.[104]

Children were necessary for women to thrive; they were their pride and joy. Children were similarly necessary for the socialist state to thrive; they were the nation's pride and joy as well. In honor of International Children's Day, on June 1, 1989, *Scinteia* published a review of the advantages offered children in Romania. The "untiring care with which Comrades Nicolae and Elena Ceausescu and the party" pampered Romania's children was saluted. This congratulatory article went on to exult in the fact that:

> One hundred percent of the births recorded last year occurred in medical units; 12,169 kindergartens are readying 831,000 children for elementary school; more than 4.6 million children benefit from state allocations, which have been increased by 25 percent in the last years; the sum allocated from

the state budget for maternal assistance for mothers with many children has grown from 488 million lei in 1985 to 3.7 billion. Seven hundred and seventy thousand mothers annually benefit from these sums, compared to 167,000 in 1985; families in which both parents work have 919 nurseries with 89,000 places at their disposal.

By then, all-too-familiar boasts and toasts were ritually dedicated to the benevolence of the paternalist state's ruling family. The repertory of formulaic slogans was accessible on command for ritualized political occasions.

But the relationship between ritualized norms—in this instance, ritualized through propaganda—and everyday practices is never a direct one. In the case of Romania in the 1980s, virtually never did the twain meet. The *"epoca de aur,"* Ceausescu's golden era, glittered for those addicted to their own ideologized imaginings or seduced by the fantasized representations of the propaganda apparatus. Personal privilege shielded them from discontent. Unable to see their shadows reflected in the mirrors of everyday life, they embraced the illusory reality that propaganda supplied on demand.

However, the vast majority of Romania's inhabitants were unable to escape the exigencies of daily necessity. The propagandized discourse that nourished "multilaterally developed socialist society" did not nourish men, women, and children spiritually or materially, especially during the regime's "golden era" that darkened the 1980s. A child's "wish list" to Santa Claus captured the discordant perception of life in Ceausescu's Romania:

Santa Claus, Santa Claus,
Everyone says you're generous and good.
Santa Claus, if you want, bring us some cooking oil.
And if perchance you come by foot, bring us some sugar.
And even if it rains, bring us some eggs.
If you have to go through wind and water, bring us some onions.
And instead of snowflakes, bring us some coffee beans.
Even if it is bitingly cold, bring us some butter.
And if you want us to have good luck, bring us some pork meat.
If you come in a sleigh, bring us toilet paper.
So that at least on New Year's, we can wipe our rears![105]

Indeed, the more difficult life became, the more wicked and biting was the political humor that enabled Romanians to grin and bear it (*a face haz de necaz*). Black humor about pronatalism and the body politic circulated widely, offering a limited venue for the veiled expression of publicly forbidden thoughts: "A man stood in the center of an apartment building complex shouting: menstruation, menstruation . . . (*menstruatie*). A bewildered crowd gathered around him. He kept on shouting. Finally, someone asked him why he was shouting 'menstruation.' In exasperation, he replied: 'Menstruation, demonstration (*menstruatie, demonstratie*)—I don't care . . . only that blood flows!'"[106]

Cultural texts critical of the regime were rarely published. However, in 1984 Ana Blandiana, a respected poet, wrote a poem criticizing the regime's brutal, seemingly senseless, political demographic policies:

*Children's Crusade*

An entire population
as yet unborn
but condemned to birth
lined up in rows, before birth
fetus beside fetus
An entire population
which doesn't see, doesn't hear, doesn't understand
but develops
through the convulsed bodies
through the blood of mothers
Unasked.[107]

Had she foreseen the death sentence unwanted children were later to receive, damned to a life's struggle compressed into days, weeks, or a few years as a consequence of deliberately suppressed infant AIDS statistics? Blandiana's poignant and pained words fell on the deaf ears of the Ceausescu regime. Despite the "extraordinary" quality of life that was fathered by the socialist propaganda apparatus, Romania in 1989 had one of the highest infant mortality rates as well as the highest maternal mortality rate in Europe. The lack of food, heat, and electricity had earned Romania the bitter name of "Ceauswitz."

The discourse characteristic of Ceausescu's personality cult was utopian. Daily quantities of ideological fiber were fed to Romania's citizens, yet most were unable to fully digest the sustenance offered by propaganda. Dissimulation became the aid to digestion that enabled the body politic to continue to function, however poorly.

CHAPTER 6

# Bitter Memories

## The Politics of Reproduction in Everyday Life

*How can you, as a doctor, explain to a woman that the professional assistance she is seeking is against the law? Especially when she presents arguments which, from a humane point of view, you cannot ignore: she has two or three children; salaries are inadequate; she doesn't have enough money to feed and clothe the children she already has; she has many debts; there is no one to take care of the children while she is at work; she is deadly tired from overwork, and so on. What do you do?*

DR. M., INTERVIEW

As is by now amply clear, the socialist state deliberately attempted to destroy the social organization of private, everyday life and to expropriate its most intimate aspects. The socialist state intruded into human sexuality and reproduction, claiming them as and for public state interests. The usurpation of patriarchal authority in the family, notably men's control of women's sexuality, also subordinated men to the desires of state reproduction. The formal system instrumentalized the human body. The socialist body was figured as that of a worker, socially ungendered.[1] The biological rather than the social defined the mode of this body's instrumentalization. Women were endowed by nature to give birth; therefore, the biology of their own bodies determined their most essential role in socialist society. Men, however, through a quirk of nature, contributed to human and social reproduction by fulfilling their marital and sexual obligations (primarily within marriage). Those who did not do so by a certain age were subjected to monthly wage penalties for not doing their share to reproduce the socialist labor force.

Regardless of the state's hold over everyday lives, those lives were lived in the contexts of extended families, friends, school, and work. And life as experienced—rather than as formalized through the ideological construction of the socialist person—*was* gendered as well as cultured. Women in Ceausescu's Romania were, by virtue of their bodies, the direct victims of the pronatalist policies; nonetheless, men were not immune from the exigencies of these state dictates. Heterosexuality as a cultural (and political) norm engaged men and women in the reproduction of the family.[2] The family, a primary object of socialist transformation, ironically became a source of human solidarity against the state's efforts to undermine this venerated

cultural institution. Indeed, the state's intrusion into the private sphere unintentionally strengthened interpersonal relations in some respects while
weakening them in others. For example, as shortages increased and the
content and enforcement of Decree 770 became more repressive, individuals used personal relationships in their efforts to provide for their families or to help women (usually kin or friends) rid themselves of unwanted
pregnancies. Yet, under pressure, these same individuals informed on each
other to the secret police in an effort to protect their own interests.

As a result, the family provided ambivalent refuge from the state.[3] (This
dynamic was similarly true of personal networks established in the second
economy.) This ambivalence arose from the mechanisms instituted by the
state's repressive apparatus to instill fear as the currency through which
personal relations were mediated, and from which the result would be social
atomization. Distrust prevailed in the public sphere. The state's penetration
into intimate family life contributed to the further erosion of private life.
Sexuality was fraught with tension. Its manipulation by the state gnawed at
the bonds of trust between couples, frequently making their sexual lives a
site of intense struggle.[4]

The architects of state repression understood all too well the vulnerabilities of the human body and soul, as well as the function of trust in human
relations. It was not accidental that doctors were targeted to mediate between the state and its citizens' vital health needs.[5] Physicians, in particular, benefited from the trust (and dependency) of their patients. Scientific
knowledge about the body's mysteries gave doctors enormous power over
those in their care. (Many abused that power; others used it as beneficently
as possible.) State authorities recognized that the allegiance of the medical profession had to be secured, and thus early on began to exercise their
will dramatically. Arrests and mini–show trials of doctors who disobeyed the
law accomplished the intended effect of discouraging others from risking
their careers and personal lives. Thereafter, the legal and institutional edi-
fices designed to hold medical practitioners in check managed the complicity of most to greater and lesser degrees.

The official system operated on the presumption that its citizens would,
in their most rational interest, adhere to the dictates of the state. It also presumed literal interpretation of those dictates. Yet everyone who lived in the
hierarchy of everyday relations learned the rules as well as the parameters
of the risks associated with breaking them. The various laws and decrees
provided doctors with a key to just how much they could get away with—that
is, how and when it was possible to declare that a woman had experienced
a "spontaneous abortion" even though she had not. Doctors often manipulated the system successfully. However, they too were human, meaning that
interpersonal and professional power struggles also frequently served as the
basis for denunciations and arrests of colleagues.

Some medical practitioners became overconfident about their ability to get around the law. Whatever their motives—not the least of which was handsome recompense for gambling against the state by breaking the law— they occasionally found themselves trumped by the state's reach, which was far, wide, and deep. The state's henchmen pursued their ends tenaciously and, often, viciously. Intimidation, blackmail, and fear were the methods favored to cajole cooperation and acquire names or networks of persons involved in abortion-related activities. In many cases, women who had resorted to illegal abortions agreed to collaborate with the police in exchange for reducing punishment to a symbolic level.

This chapter presents excerpts from intensive personal interviews with Romanians on the political demographic policies they experienced in their daily lives. The institutionalization of pronatalist legislation was designed to control the reproductive practices of Romania's population; however, individuals struggled against the intrusion of the state into their bodies. Between the official dictates set out in the decrees, laws, institutionalized procedures and propaganda discussed thus far, people muddled along, trying to make the system as livable as possible. The formalized structures and relations through which everyday life was meant to unfold were often subverted by informal, personal interests.

As the voices heard in this chapter make clear, resistance to the pronatalist policies entailed a "myriad of micro-practices, struggles, tactics, and counter-tactics" by medical and other institutional personnel, women, their families, friends, acquaintances and strangers.[6] The reliability of their memories—collective and individual—is subject to the process of reconstructing meaningful, or perhaps just tolerable, life histories. This process is overdetermined for almost all persons in the former socialist states, whose familiar lives more or less vanished with the collapse of communism. In many instances, rationalization and self-delusion have become steadfast friends in the attempt to make sense out of life's experiences. Each of the representations of social reality offered by the narrators carries "many potential meanings, but no definitive answers."[7] Their accounts engage multiple layers of meaning. The stage upon which they lived their individual lives has been described in the preceding chapters. Different people had different and contradictory understandings about the system. Some were overtly complicitous with it; others, implicitly so. Some took risks; yet others were worn down by the oppressiveness of Romanian socialism.

The personal stories in this chapter constitute micro-histories of everyday life during the Ceausescu regime. These tales are replete with continuities and contradictions. Heroes were few in number throughout the years of communist rule in Romania. Most people simply tried to manage their lives in such a way as to minimize the difficulties of daily existence in an openly repressive environment. Complicity with Ceausescu's dictatorship was exhibited both through public silence and withdrawal into whatever privacy of the self remained, and through active, Faustian compromises with the wielders of power.

## DOCTOR'S OPINIONS: SPECIALISTS SPEAK

Because medical practitioners served as intermediaries between the encompassing public sphere of the state and private life, as well as between public and private bodies, I present their comments and opinions about pronatalism first.[8] They have spoken about issues ranging from sex education, doctor-patient relations, and institutional practices to gynecological exams, methods of performing and reporting abortions, and adherence to and evasion of the law. Almost all doctors emphasized that few of them had been willing to risk their livelihoods beyond a certain point. They also uniformly asserted that women usually arrived at the hospital after the fact—that is, as the result of incomplete abortions that had given rise to secondary infections or complications. In many instances, doctors were unable to save these women. That the hospital functioned as women's last resort illuminates the fear and despair that drove them to risk their lives. A certain coherence emerges in these reflections about the methods that physicians used to beat the system at its own game of manipulation. Although medical personnel often succeeded, luck was not always on their side, and they were sometimes arrested and sentenced to prison terms. The cases of two doctors who were imprisoned on abortion-related charges are discussed at length in this chapter.

### About Health and Sexual Education

Dr. D.N.
*(born 1943, male, gynecologist)*
I don't believe many physicians were involved in the anti-contraceptive propaganda campaigns. I even think this applied to those who occupied privileged positions in the power structure. Those of us who went to factories to provide instruction about health education to women workers tried to present specialized information in a manner that served the interests of women's health and dignity. Of course, there were activists who carried out a real crusade against birth control pills and intrauterine devices. The negative effects of modern contraceptives were harped on in the official propaganda. However, a doctor who respected his profession, even though he was required to teach about health and sexuality, found a way to avoid engaging in pronatalist education [as propaganda]. Many gynecologists used this opportunity to provide women with useful information that did not endanger their lives but would enable them to avoid pregnancy. For example, in discussions with patients, especially

with those who admitted to having had many abortions, I advised them to
be careful; another abortion would further traumatize their bodies. Even if
I didn't recommend a particular method, at least I had sensitized them to their
existence. They then began to gather information from friends and coworkers
about how to have sex without consequence.[9]

However intently the party tried to transform sexual education systematically
into pronatalist indoctrination, the results did not correspond with the effort
expended. The reason for this was simple: Official doctrine competed with the
informal contraceptive education that was passed on from one woman to another—resulting in one of the great ironies of historical fate. One of the fundamental roles of Communist Party activists was the diffusion of political ideology
by word of mouth. Diffusion of knowledge by word of mouth was much more
successfully carried out by women regarding contraceptive information than
by activists regarding party philosophy.

### Dr. B.M.
*(born 1944, male, obstetrician-gynecologist)*

When we participated in health education events at socialist enterprises, we
provided women with contraceptive information. Obviously, we couldn't do
this directly and had to manage by means of implicit communication.[10] Doctors were more often than not accompanied on these forced "missionary" endeavors by representatives from the prosecutor's office, the state police force,
or a party secretary, who in the 1980s was frequently a woman responsible for
the district's social problems. The audience, socialized and specialized in de-
coding messages, knew they had to decipher what they needed from what I
said. For example, I would sketch a monthly calendar on the board and explain how a woman could determine which were her most fertile days. I would
add that if a woman wanted to become pregnant, she had to make sure to have
sexual relations during this interval. This could also be interpreted to mean
that in order not to become pregnant it is wise to avoid sexual contact during
these days of maximal hormonal activity.

In similar fashion, I would tell women that if they wanted to have a child,
they should have sexual relations during this recommended period, and, at
the same time, they were not to douche using weak vinegar solutions or use
condoms or spermicidal tablets.[11] They were not to do such things if they
wanted to become pregnant. . . .

Once, while giving a lecture on human reproduction at a large enterprise
in the capital, I had an amusing experience. I presented a list of "precautions"
to be taken into consideration when someone wanted to become pregnant.
When I finished, a very young woman asked me to advise her about what to
do to avoid pregnancy. Before I could respond, one of her colleagues present
in the room told her to sit down and, the next time, to listen attentively to what
the doctor said.

I recall another case, a child—well, she was fifteen but really uninformed
for her age. I was on duty when an assistant announced that we had an emergency. When I examined her, I realized how precarious her condition was.
I operated immediately. Her entire uterus was infected. I saved her but had

to do a hysterectomy. When she was released from the hospital, I told her to come see me if she had any health problems. And, in fact, she did come. She was healthy, but she had a question that she thought only I could answer. She told me she had no idea why, but she no longer had her menstrual cycle. What was the cause? My response was a cursory introduction to the anatomy of the reproductive organs. When I finished my mini-lecture, she promptly and innocently asked another question: "Do you mean that I will not be able to have children?"

Dr. V.C.
*(born 1926, female, obstetrician-gynecologist)*
When we had instructional party meetings for women, I spoke about the male need for sex, but that, at the same time, women should not be their "toilets." I explained to the girls that all men are egoists; they want their wives to be virgins, to be their first sexual experience. Generally, I explained that the sexual organs were reproductive organs.

## About Doctors and Their Female Patients

Dr. G.T.
*(born 1926, male, obstetrician-gynecologist)*
Unquestionably doctors tried to help women. But no one would risk his or her own life. Those who had been previously sentenced for doing abortions were the ones who continued to do so for profit. This should not be confused with humanitarian acts. Those [women] who were unable to pay for medical expertise—that is, working class women or housewives—accounted for the majority of maternal deaths. Intellectuals who died as a result of an abortion were few in number.[12]

N.G.
*(born 1943, female, medical assistant)*
There were doctors who were truly humane. Even when it was dangerous for them, they intervened out of compassion for women. Take Dr. X. from the Municipal Hospital. We were in the operating room when we learned that a medical assistant from another section of the hospital was hemorrhaging badly and that no one would do anything without the permission of the commission or the prosecutor's office. Taking full responsibility, Dr. X. ordered that she be brought into the operating room. Many would have made themselves scarce in this situation. But many more believed that the Hippocratic oath and not the obligation to inform the prosecutor's office defined the qualities of a good doctor.

## About the Gynecological Exams

Dr. B.M.
Periodic preventive examinations or mass screenings should not be confused with an exam to determine pregnancies.[13] A doctor who does such an exam at

the request of anyone other than the individual patient abdicates professional responsibility. It is true that in our country, in the context of a pronatalist state, most women considered [regular] screening as a modality through which a pregnancy rather than cervical cancer was detected. This perception resulted in part from the way in which these screenings were done. Women working at state enterprises were usually subjected to these exams for political or administrative reasons; they were organized and done en masse like the May Day [mass] demonstrations.

### N.G.

T.I.S., or the Immuno-Diagnostic Pregnancy Test, was introduced into hospitals in 1982. Until then, we used the Gagli-Manini test, with a frog. At the Polyclinic, gynecological examinations consisted of vaginal exams. To the best of my knowledge, the T.I.S. was not used at enterprise dispensaries to detect pregnancies because the essential substance used in this test was not produced in sufficient quantities. In hospitals, tests to confirm a pregnancy were performed only at the patient's request. The purpose of the periodic gynecological exams was detection and prevention of cancer.

### V.P.
*(born 1951, male, biologist)*

In the 1980s, at the immuno-chemical laboratory of the Cantacuzino Institute, a diagnostic test was developed to verify a pregnancy early on by immunological means. This method indicated the presence of progesterone in a pregnant woman's urine. Only one milliliter of urine was necessary for this test to be accurate by the third week of pregnancy. It was not a costly procedure and hundreds could be done daily. Also, only indigenous substances were used to produce the testing substance. Between 1984 and 1989, T.I.S. was produced in considerable quantities at the Institute, becoming one of its most profitable revenue sources.

This kit was not produced commercially and could not be found in pharmacies for public sale. It was sold only through a closed network and distributed by large hospitals and regional health departments. In my opinion and as was claimed in the propaganda campaigns, the T.I.S. kit was used primarily for the detection of cervical and uterine cancer and was especially targeted for testing [for pregnancy also] in enterprises with a high percentage of female workers.[14] Women were instructed to bring a urine sample. Many complied, for two reasons. First, the manner in which they were told to bring a sample was authoritative: for example, "Take a small bottle or jar and bring back a urine sample immediately because we don't have time and we have many more to do." Second, there was little information; most women were unaware of the existence of such kits.

### Dr. B.K.
*(born 1957, female, obstetrician-gynecologist)*

The T.I.S. test was, to my knowledge, only used in hospitals. It was not used for the periodic examinations conducted at large enterprises. The quantities used in the hospitals were large because any woman who was hospitalized in the obstetrics-gynecology ward, for whatever medical reason, was tested to make certain that no pregnancy remained undetected (see chapter 2).

Dr. G.T.

Periodic gynecological exams are, in and of themselves, useful—if their purpose is to evaluate women's health. However, if an exam is done to determine if the uterus is enlarged, then this constitutes an abuse. In view of the excessive pronatalist politics, the scope of such exams could indeed have been the latter. Nonetheless, the humanism of many doctors must be underscored. Many did not record a pregnancy discovered during an exam if the woman did not consent. At the same time, these exams did reveal how women's health had been affected by the precarious quality of life. Many women had gynecological problems that were caused by the lack of basic hygiene. I don't mean to refer here only to the already well known conditions: lack of heat, hot water, electricity, soap, detergents, etc. For some reason, perhaps because factories were required to economize on raw materials, and especially metals, douches were no longer produced.[15]

When the West got so excited about these periodic exams, they overlooked one aspect, notably the degree of formalism that was characteristic of such actions. That explains why, in reality, these exams were not perceived as a means by which women were terrorized.[16] Of course, a certain fear existed. But as fear became endemic, we became accustomed to it [as a fact of life]. [Most people] counted on most doctors being medical specialists and not police. The formalism of these exams resulted from the manner in which they were organized and from the nonexistence of the conditions necessary to develop real expertise. If an enterprise's female work force had to be tested in two or three days, it is simply not to be believed that every one of them was examined vaginally. Enterprise dispensaries were modestly equipped and staffed, and the doctors who were required to do these exams were not simultaneously relieved of their other regular medical responsibilities.[17]

Dr. V.C.

It's not true that doctors did trimesterly gynecological exams. That was virtually impossible; we lied and wrote fabricated reports to meet the plan. . . . At a party meeting I protested the proposed three-month intervals for doing these exams. I objected that if these mass screenings had to be organized every three months, that would mean just inserting two fingers, which is not a correct gynecological exam; I would lose my professional honor!

## About Contraceptive Methods

Dr. G.T.

During Ceausescu's time, we gynecologists were blamed for performing abortions. In fact, what we did was curettages on what remained [from the attempts of others].

Dr. B.M.

Customary methods of fertility control used in our country include the calendar method, condoms, and temperature curves.

Dr. G.T.

In our pharmacies, it wasn't very easy to find quinine because pharmacists used it to prepare pills that had an abortive effect. Lemon juice was also used, as well as the stems of geraniums. Coitus interruptus was practiced a lot, provided that the man agreed. But how many men wouldn't agree when they knew what the cost was for women and for their families and, hence, implicitly for themselves?[18] The calendar method isn't sufficient. Reliance on it alone often led to mistakes [unwanted pregnancies]. Combined with the woman's monthly temperature curve, it was more effective. But women had to do so much work and were so exhausted—who among them had the time to take her basal temperature each morning? For whom was this a burning issue first thing in the morning when everything had to be managed against the clock—readying breakfast, making lunches for children going off to school and for the lunch break at work, getting ready for work, taking the children to school—all by 7 A.M. when the work day began; who had time to take her temperature? And when we also think about the cramped quarters in which people lived, and that there was usually but a single bathroom that everyone needed to use, well, it gives us an idea of just how frequently this method was applied.

Before 1989 contraceptives acquired on the black market were of poor quality. Russian birth control pills were accompanied by unpleasant secondary effects. The intrauterine device obtained from Poland was one with a loop, so it was a source of irritation and vaginal bleeding.

Dr. M.
*(born 1927, male, obstetrician-gynecologist)*
Women used all kinds of objects and plants: a spindle, a knitting needle, horseradish, oleander, a finger.[19]

Dr. D.N.

Even without much medical instruction or specialized knowledge, when a woman wanted to avoid pregnancy and to understand how her body functioned, she acquired a "sixth sense." She could estimate when the probability of getting pregnant was greatest. The calendar method was used the most frequently. Some used the basal temperature method. Also, when a woman has regular periods, she has better luck at controlling her fertility by these methods.

After 1989 my students and I did a small study. We asked women who worked at a factory at which we held consultations what contraceptive methods they used during the time of the decree. The calendar was the method most used, followed by coitus interruptus. This latter presupposed that a couple was highly motivated to control fertility, which again demonstrates that people did not want more than two children.

Dr. V.C.

Until 1985 I wrote out prescriptions for the composition of an inserted contraceptive containing quinine. . . . Yes, some women used salt, but that stung
a bit; others, as my husband just mentioned, put *tuica* on some cotton and put
it inside. [Dr. V.C.'s husband noted that the women from Oltenia used this
method: they wet the cotton with distilled plum brandy which, from this region, was fairly weak. It served as a barrier; "the man finished into the tuica-
drenched cotton; it was effective."]

## About Abortion Practices: Induced, Spontaneous, and Therapeutic Abortions

Dr. D.N.

Romanian gynecologists are experts in abortion. Before 1989 the only method
was curettage (dilation and evacuation). Aspiration was not done. We only
knew about this method from the medical literature. Romanian doctors are so
skilled in curetting that they can do them even in the fourth month, when the
fetus has a head of four to five centimeters. It is true, theoretically speaking,
that a curettage by this month in a pregnancy presents risks. But, in general,
abortions did not pose serious problems for our gynecologists. To support this
claim, I can cite the results of a recent study about the complications associated
with abortion and contraceptives; complications from abortion are compared
on the basis of data drawn from the international literature. We are pretty well
off, inasmuch as we have very few cases of post-abortion complications.

Dr. G.T.

Because of the intensity with which abortion was practiced, the Romanian
school of gynecology is extremely competitive with respect to doing "safe" abortions [with minimal risks]. Today, even though we've been equipped with aspirators, I do the abortion through aspiration but, then, to be certain that nothing has remained, I use a small curette to double-check.

There isn't a number after which abortion constitutes a risk to a woman's
health. But with an increasing number of abortions, the risk of an accident also
increases. . . .

Although abortion has been liberalized, we still have cases of women dying
from non–medically induced abortions.[20] For those who are disadvantaged financially, the actual cost of an abortion today [1992] is prohibitive. Abortions
are done in the large hospitals, which have obstetrics-gynecology sections. This
presents particular problems for women living in rural areas. In addition to the
cost of the abortion itself, a woman from the countryside has to travel to a city
to have the procedure done. This requires money and time and creates additional stress. That is one of the reasons why they resort to pre-1989 methods.

Dr. B.M.

Most persons who performed illegal abortions were not doctors. They represented all socio-professional categories. They believed that anyone who knew

how to introduce a thin tube into the uterus was able to interrupt a pregnancy. Most of these dilettantes did so for money. Abortion had become an extremely profitable enterprise.[21] Get the data from the district attorney's office and you will see that in 1987 or 1988—I don't recall which exactly—approximately 1,700 or 1,800 cases were tried throughout the country for the illegal inducement of abortion. Among them, there were only fifteen or twenty medical practitioners, that is, doctors, nurses, midwives, hospital attendants. I know cases in which engineers did illegal abortions.[22]

Over time, the pathology of abortion changed as more and more nonspecialists entered the abortion market. In the early 1970s women came to the hospital with light bleeding; we did a curettage, kept them a day or two in the hospital and then sent them home; by the 1980s, more and more of them arrived with infections and various pathological conditions already in advanced stages.[23]

With regard to therapeutic abortions, in 1985 I was present at a meeting at the Ministry of Health during which the list of medical conditions qualifying a woman for legal, therapeutic abortion was rediscussed. Professor Proca was then the minister. The changes were such that the number of pages on which the acceptable conditions were printed was reduced at the same time that the list itself was increased. It was in this manner that the party's request to limit the possibilities for granting a legal abortion was "respected."

## Dr. G.T.

One of the methods used to induce an abortion was to remove the wire from a conductor line so that only the plastic tube remained. Penicillin or alcohol was then introduced into the uterus through it. The risk was high because alcohol, for example, produces necrosis, which leads to infection and septicemia.

Then there was the category of medical conditions that justified approval for a legal abortion. The list was actually extensive, even after 1985. Unfortunately, young women did not suffer from many such ailments. Doctors found ways to evade the interdictions. But this was only possible for an extremely select population.[24]

## Dr. D.N.

I don't believe there are many women who didn't have an illegal abortion, either self-induced or with the help of someone else. That is why those who arrived at the hospital, with the exception of those who had the right to a legal abortion, were there because of an illegally induced abortion. Of course there were spontaneous abortions, but they were few in number. And then when complications began—bleeding, high fever, infections—they came to the hospital. When they arrived in that kind of condition, they had to be curetted. However, to do so, you had to have the authorization of the commission or inform the prosecutor's office. Even after 1985 when the measures to limit abortion had become draconian, obtaining this authorization was basically a formality. For example, if a patient was bleeding lightly and the commission did not authorize the abortion because it did not consider that the bleeding endangered the pregnancy, then the woman repeated whatever she had done and came back a few days later. Her bleeding was heavier, or by that time her life was endangered.

In the final years before 1989, "socialist competitions" between hospitals were instituted. The hospital with the smallest number of abortions "won" and was recognized accordingly. This did not mean that many abortions were not still done—they were. But, with this in mind, every hospital tried to keep the number of abortions down. How this was done was hardly one of the best kept secrets of the medical community! This was relatively easy: By figuring the population of fertile women and the probability of a woman's becoming pregnant during the course of one year, and then lowering the number of births, one could obtain an estimate of the number of conceptions "lost" through abortion. The result of the calculation was two to three times higher than the number of abortions actually declared. Or, instead of writing that a curettage had been done for an abortion, it was noted that the procedure had been necessary to treat endometriosis or uterine hemorrhaging. Hence, out of 100 abortions, for example, 50 were hidden under the category of "diverse pathologies of the genital organs." Curettage was legal for conditions such as hemorrhaging, endometriosis, uterine bleeding, uterine dysfunctions, uterine fibroids, and extrauterine pregnancy. To prove the existence of such a condition meant that histopathological test results for pregnancy had to be negative. We'd do a curettage and send a sample for histopathological testing to confirm whether an abortion had been done or not. The histopathologist was also subject to the [formal] rules of the hospital competitions. Through deliberate oversight it was confirmed that what had been done was anything other than an abortion. Even the cleaning woman in the hospital knew that an abortion had been done. To avoid sanctions from the party, moral pressure, fines taken out of salaries, and the like, the entire medical corps understood that the number of abortions reported had to be small. The opportunities to tamper with medical procedures, especially under the most oppressive regime, are limited. Even when the number of conditions for which therapeutic abortions were approved had been reduced, if a doctor wanted to help a woman obtain a therapeutic abortion—for humanitarian reasons or reasons that were less humanitarian [such as financial gain]—it was possible to find convincing arguments. For example, it was not so difficult to arrange for a woman to be hospitalized in a nephrology section where some tests would be done on the basis of which the commission could be asked to approve a therapeutic abortion.

Dr. B.K.

The entire process instituted to impede illegal abortions increasingly became a formality. Out of necessity, solutions were found either by women or by doctors. . . . I even encountered cases of women who had introduced blood into their vaginas to simulate a hemorrhage in order to obtain an abortion. Or doctors kept samples from a curettage done to treat a genital condition and then substituted these for histopathological testing to determine if a curettage had been done for an abortion. In this way, the number of abortions was adjusted.[25]

To confirm or invalidate the status of an abortion, especially in emergency cases involving incomplete abortions, histopathological exams were obligatory. But between this obligation and the organizational and operating conditions of medical units, there existed quite a gap. There were not enough specialists in almost 50 percent of the country's counties to perform the histopathological diagnoses of abortion.[26] Overload increased the possibilities for distorting or manipulating the data.

Another means to legitimate an abortion was through a negative T.I.S. result. If a woman came to the hospital bleeding, then a doctor might try to get two negative T.I.S. results to "prove" that she was not pregnant. A negative T.I.S. emerged soon after a pregnancy was no longer viable. Women came to the hospital after they had aborted at home, or when they were suffering secondary complications from having tried to terminate a pregnancy. If, for example, a woman arrived today bleeding and her T.I.S. was positive, there was no way to do a curettage. Instead, she would have had to be treated to maintain the pregnancy. But, if three days later the T.I.S. became negative, then it meant the pregnancy had been "resolved." Another T.I.S. would be ordered. With a second negative result, there was no problem with doing a curettage. It had been "proved" that, in spite of the efforts to save an endangered pregnancy, its course had been stopped and there was nothing more to be done. Irrefutable evidence then existed for anyone who wanted to contest a decision that a curettage had been in order.

Physicians also manipulated the rules regarding birthing practices, namely, cesarean sections.[27] Because the number of cesareans had increased over the years, planning targets were established; the percentage of cesareans out of the total number of births was not to exceed 4–5 percent per year. Otherwise, "objective justifications" had to be provided. One woman recalled that her labor pains had begun in earnest around midnight, and she was taken to the maternity ward to deliver. Her fear of the unknown was instantly transformed into terror as she entered the hospital elevator. A long, pained scream had filled the hallway. When she was taken into the maternity ward, she joined the throng of women already going through the travails of birth. One woman shrieked in agony, imploring them to do a cesarean. The midwife who was taking care of the newly admitted mother-to-be commented that the poor woman had been struggling in pain for 24 hours, but no one heeded her entreaties for someone to do a cesarean. At the time, most persons did not know that cesareans were also the object of centralized planning, and that another cesarean in that ward would probably have resulted in bureaucratic sanctions against the hospital.[28]

## About Doctors, the State Police, Prosecutors, Corruption, and Complicity

Dr. B.M.

The prosecutors were themselves human beings; they had wives, daughters, sisters, lovers. Neither they nor doctors were interested in punitive actions against a woman who had had an illegal abortion but rather against the person who

had induced it. I would have been ruthless [with these abortionists, who] knowingly killed. They created the impression that they were doing women a favor.
Not only did these abortionists [illegally] induce an abortion but they advised
a woman not to go to the hospital if she was bleeding or ill because prison
would then await her [and them]. And as a consequence, women would die
at home or come to the hospital already suffering badly from necrosis or septicemia. They would frequently arrive when there was nothing more that could
be done for them. Yet the state tried to make us doctors responsible for the
high number of maternal deaths due to botched abortions, to make doctors
the scapegoats. What could physicians do when women came after it was too
late? There were women who died in the emergency room as a result of septic
shock, septicemia, uterine necrosis, gangrene.

Of course, in some places, things were exaggerated. I learned from colleagues whose moral propriety cannot be doubted that, on many an occasion,
they were not only assisted by someone from the state police, but that this person took the liberty of offering his medical opinions. With respect to the prosecutor's office, we preferred to inform them from the very beginning if there
were any signs of violence having been done to a woman's body. If, for example, I found a perforated uterus or the woman arrived with peritonitis, then the
prosecutor was brought into the case.[29] I remember one evening when I called
to inform the prosecutor's office about the case of a young female doctor. They
told me to take care of the other cases first and to leave her until last because
they wanted to be present for her case.[30] I responded: "Very well, if you think
that female doctors cannot abort spontaneously." One half hour later, someone from the prosecutor's office called me back and told me to take care of
that case because they had no means of transport available and could not get
there. I then offered: "Sir [prosecutor], if you want me to send the hospital car
over . . . " He interrupted: "Never mind, Sir [doctor], I know it isn't a problem."
A tacit accord functioned as long as doctors were perceived to be credible.[31]

### Dr. G.T.

If a woman arrived bleeding in the middle of the night, and if the doctor considered the situation to be under control, then [the doctor] preferred to do
the abortion in the morning, in the light of day, because the hospital atmosphere was marked by suspicion. Every maternity hospital had its state or secret police representative whose role was to be an ever-present reminder [of
the decree's stipulations]. In Bucharest, they were more understanding, but
in the small provincial hospitals, some were pretentious enough to insist on
being present even during consultations, flagrantly violating the norms associated with medical examinations. A nonspecialist has no business in a gynecological examining room. The more zealous state police ignored this basic
principle.

### Dr. V.C.

I was a long-time party member—30-some years—the daughter of a communist. To me, being a communist meant to work hard, to set an example, to give

of yourself. . . . In general, I didn't accept anything [gifts] from my patients
until the last years. It was the going mentality: If you didn't accept anything,
it meant you didn't want to take care of the sick. That's how it was.[32]

By 1984 I seemed to have become a public danger for the party. I was the
chief of the gynecology unit, but Captain S. had the nerve to stand behind me
during a curettage. This was my specialty, not his. Moreover, women are not
cows, a statement I repeated to party higher-ups and for which I was regarded
poorly. . . . [33]

Once a doctor, a former student of mine, ended up on the operating table.
Other physicians, Drs. X.—a couple—had sent her to me; it wasn't my doing.
They set me up—and have since left the country. I was unaware that this fomer
student for whom I did an abortion was the wife of a secret policeman, that he
had the rank of a colonel. I didn't know until I was released from prison.

### Dr. M.

Can I, who had taken an oath, allow a woman to die? Can I say that it wasn't
genocide when the prosecutor, who had to authorize the interruption of a
pregnancy even in an emergency, came to the woman's bedside and while she
was in agony threatened her that if she didn't say who induced her abortion,
he would not permit surgical intervention?

What I'm telling you isn't something people talk about. I personally was
present during such scenes. Some prosecutors came to the hospital just to
amuse themselves; they'd put on a coat and enter unannounced into an examining room or operation to be present during a vaginal exam or gynecological
intervention. This defies any notion of medical ethics.[34]

Yet not all prosecutors were maniacs or inhuman. There were real people
among them, too. They knew full well that they also had wives, daughters, and
mothers.

### Dr. B.K.

In the obstetrics-gynecology clinics in the big cities, there was a small room reserved for the state policeman who was required to stay in the hospital at least
two hours a day. In the provinces, the prosecutors' and police offices had to
be informed about every curettage that was done. The policeman who had the
hospital as part of his beat ended up being integrated into the life of the hospital. Relations were established between him and the hospital staff, and in some
cases, even with patients. In this way, gradually, the formal and authoritarian
relationship took on the tone of a human one.

The chief of the medical department had a very important role. If he occupied this position because of his professional competence and prestige, then
the policeman respected the medical chief's authority. Under such circumstances, the official representative of the state repressive apparatus was clearly
dominated—so as not to say "controlled"—by the doctor. This deliberate subordination had certain advantages. Any person, no matter how high up in the
social or political hierarchy, sooner or later ended up in need of a doctor's
care. If not the person himself, then someone in his family, relatives, friends,
or someone to whom he was obligated in one way or another. . . .

If the chief of the department was in this position as the result of nonprofessional criteria (political interests or influence-peddling, for example), then he legitimated his presence through excessive conformity with police authority. That helps explain the fact that there were doctors who let women die because the policeman or the prosecutor had arrived too late or had not shown up at all.

The repressive political organs charged with "achieving the increased reproductive plan of the new socialist person" proceeded selectively in their surveillance of activities in the maternity wards. A system of informing was instituted whose utility was proved throughout the history of the regime. Denunciation and blackmail were hallmarks of this system. Even if all women and doctors were theoretically vulnerable to suspicion, not all were incriminated or interrogated. If a gynecologist was "clean"—that is, not in conflict with official institutions—then no one said anything; there was a tacit understanding that the woman had been admitted with a spontaneous abortion. It was not by accident that pressure was exerted only on some women who were hospitalized because of "spontaneous abortions." I'd say there was a quota of [those to be] sacrificed to make it appear that the system of sanctions was indeed functioning. Police collaborators within the hospital were drawn from among those whose punishment for transgressing the anti-abortion interdictions changed from the deprivation of liberty to the obligation to denounce. When you work in a maternity ward among so many women who recount their woes to each other, it is not difficult to find things to inform on. Hence, when a policeman or prosecutor interrogated a woman lying on an operation table to find out who had induced the abortion, in many cases their choice of which woman to interrogate had been made knowingly.

## Dr. M.

After I had served my prison term, I was deprived of my right to practice for one year. In order to live, I took a job as an ambulance medical assistant. But the deprivation of civil rights as spelled out in the civil code was not considered to be severe enough for the tastes of some of the higher-ups. Dr. Burghele, who at the time was minister of health, issued an order that all doctors who had been condemned for abortion activities were not to be permitted to practice in their area of specialization. I managed to escape this by the skin of my teeth. After I finished my year with the ambulance service, I worked at a different hospital from the one at which I had been working at the time of my arrest. Perhaps because of this or due to negligence, or human decency—because there were decent people—I was not denied the right to work in my specialty.

The most dangerous were those doctors who held important political positions or who were where they were in the professional hierarchy because of some compromise made with the regime. They were the most abusive and corrupt. Take Dr. S., who was notorious for being corrupt; he really screwed people. He decided on who was to be denied the right to practice in his or her specialty. However, everyone knew that he kept a kit with instruments for abortions at home. He was the husband of one of the capital's district vice-presidents.

## DOCTORS ON TRIAL

From time to time there were show trials of doctors, midwives, and backroom abortionists.[35] When medical personnel functioned as accomplices to an illegal abortion—having induced it, procured the necessary instruments, or acted as an intermediary—they could be, and often were, tried. Doctors were confronted by a fundamental contradiction: Although they had taken an oath to save lives, the state legislated the legal parameters of medical practice. By law, when a woman arrived at a hospital hemorrhaging from a self-induced abortion, the prosecutor's office required notification, meaning that this office was alerted to a case for which a doctor could be held liable. Yet humanitarian concern posed different sorts of problems for physicians who invoked various formal and informal rules and relations to justify their subsequent actions. For some physicians, the legal procedure became little more than convention. For others, the system of complicity, fear, and corruption functioned efficiently enough to keep them in check. Yet for a variety of reasons, others considered the risks worth taking.

On occasion, some doctors paid dearly for trying to work around the law. The following accounts represent two such cases. The first is a more typical account; the second relates the story of Dr. G., a gynecologist, whose experiences constitute one of the most notorious legal cases involving the ramifications of Decree 770. Dr. G.'s repeated encounters with the law stretched over more than a 25-year period. This history as read from the legal documentation would seem to be a straightforward story of breaking the law. But the formal rendering of events distorted the reality (and complexities) of daily life during the Ceausescu regime. Hence, Dr. G.'s battle with the system is reconstructed here through an analysis of legal documents and extensive interviews. As shall be seen, he is both innocent and culpable, humane and self-interested. Such are the dynamics of complicity and resistance. Before turning to this convoluted case history, let us examine that of Dr. M.

### Dr. M.
*(approximately 66 years of age, married, gynecologist)*

I had enough time to reflect [about all this] during my years in prison. Prudence and discretion had proven to be insufficient. I did my best to reduce the number of unknowns. But when you work with women, it's more difficult. Word traveled from one to the other that Dr. X. was obliging, understanding, humane; then, when a woman found herself in a situation that could have legal ramifications [needing an abortion], she sought this doctor out. How can you, as a doctor, explain to a woman that the professional assistance she is seeking is against the law? Especially when she presents arguments that, from a humane point of view, you cannot ignore: She has two or three children; salaries are inadequate; she doesn't have enough money to feed and clothe the children she already has; she has many debts; there is no one to take care of the children while she is at work; she is dead tired from overwork; and so on. What do you do?

Another unknown factor I tried to control to the best of my abilities was the issue of "institutional surveillance." We all knew that the Securitate had a person in each hospital, enterprise, school—in every institution, whether large or small. When you are constantly "hunted," you acquire a sixth sense about who is an informer, of whatever rank. But this knowledge did not mean you had escaped the varied forms of control omnipresent in the public sphere. One of the mechanisms used to foster a psychosis about taboos and intimidation was to create a "scapegoat." Those who were not politically inviolable were potential candidates for this role. I think I paid so high a price because of my own naiveté about my past, professional ethics, and the right to have my own opinions. In 1956, the year of the Hungarian revolution, I was in the sixth year of medical school. As you know, Romanian students were politically active, demonstrating our solidarity with the ideas and actions of the Hungarian people's revolt against Moscow's ideological and political hegemony. I was arrested with a group from my school and, after an infamous trial at the Ministry of the Interior, was sentenced to eighteen years' imprisonment. In 1964, when the last political prisoners were freed on grounds of the incompatibility between the victory of the proletarian dictatorship and the existence of political detainees, I was rehabilitated.[36] As the result of a decision by the minister of health, I and my colleagues were rematriculated. I finished medical school with a specialization in obstetrics-gynecology. But, for the regime, I nonetheless remained a "black sheep"; for the Securitate, a potential danger.[37] I believe that this played a role in my 1971 arrest. During this period, I was a doctor at a hospital in Bucharest. Every day I saw desperate women who had tried to get around the constraints posed by the banning of abortion. I also knew the reasons that motivated them to do so. I don't want to glorify myself by invoking the Hippocratic oath, but I cannot admit to having done illegal abortions only for the sake of material gain. What was the real motive behind the abortion law and who did it serve? How can a law be abided that ignores the dramatic conditions of women in a social [political] order whose consolidation presupposed the [paying of] permanent tribute on the part of women? We each had a wife, a mother, a sister, a daughter. How can you respect a law that condemns them?

So, in 1971, I was sentenced to one year and eight months' imprisonment for performing an illegal abortion. I curetted a woman who was the cousin of a long-time trusted patient of mine. When I saw this woman's cousin, she told me that she and her husband were workers; they had two children, one of whom was retarded. The operation went smoothly with no risk of secondary complications. When I was told to appear in court for a face-to-face meeting with the patient, I was not particularly alarmed. I knew that I had performed the abortion properly and that there had been no traces left to prove that an abortion had taken place. Not only had I never had a case in which subsequent complications had developed, but after four or five days even a medical biopsy would not have proven that I had interrupted the pregnancy. I didn't use cervical forceps precisely to avoid any trace. The meeting was short because of the psychological state of this poor woman, who was becoming acquainted for the first time with the style and means used by the police and prosecutors during an investigation. I took responsibility for everything. I confessed that I knew her because she had come for a gynecological exam. She had also declared this. I was certain that there were no signs on her cervix, and because a few days had passed, there were not even signs of my having dilated her. She was subjected to a biopsy at the Medical-Legal Institute. Both the woman and I maintained that she had not had an abortion but simply a gynecological examination. She was then subjected to another biopsy. The doctor from the maternity ward where this procedure was done claimed that there were traces of an abortion having been done. On the basis of this doctor's declaration, my guilt and the consequent verdict were established. I was guilty of interrupting a pregnancy and of retaining instruments illegally. These were found during a search of my household; they had been given to me by a widow after the death of her husband, who had been a doctor. My sentence was one year and eight months. I should add that what happened to the female doctor who had provided this "disinterested" denunciation confirmed for me that there probably is such a thing as divine justice.[38] Not long after this event, one of her patients died on her while she was performing an abortion. I don't mean to say that I was joyous about what happened, but I think there is retribution for everything that happens.

My appeal was denied, and so I did my time. By 1974, before the World Population Conference opened in Bucharest, I had been out for more than a year. The demographic statistics did not reflect what the state had intended. The conference would otherwise have provided Ceausescu with the opportunity to demonstrate the efficiency of "scientifically conceptualized" political demography to an international audience. However, the real situation . . . did not lend itself to utopian molding. In the interest of stimulating conformity to the strict application of the anti-abortion laws, the coercive-administrative mechanisms were revisited. At least for this occasion, it was thought necessary to tighten implementation of these laws as strictly as possible so that an increase in the birthrate would live up to the vainglorious conceits of the head of state under whose patronage the conference was to unfold. Among other measures taken was the review of the files of those who had violated Decree 770/1966. An extraordinary appeal tendered by the prosecutor general resulted in a number of cases being retried, among which was mine. I was again called before the court. Yet another time and as futilely as before, both I and the woman denied the accusation. The proof of the accusation, however, was the diagnosis presented by the doctor from the maternity ward where my patient had been reexamined after the fact. When it was over, my sentence of one year and eight months was considered to be too lenient in comparison with the gravity of the crime; an additional three years and four months were added to my punishment. The impartiality of justice? More like its subversion! The party wanted a high birthrate; the law hurried to carry out its orders. Thus, three years and four months more in prison! To serve the purpose of discouraging others, the punishments meted out were deliberately greater than warranted by the offenses committed. For a time, the news that Drs. X, Y, and Z had been sentenced to four, five, and six years of imprisonment had a numbing effect on other physicians. Such information spread rapidly throughout the medical establishment. We heard that a doctor's personal telephone notebook had been discovered and that, as a result of the investigation carried out by the state police, he was charged with performing 80 illegal abortions. He was given nine years.

But permit me to return to my case. I appealed. I knew from my own experience how roundabout the paths of justice were, so I decided to use whatever means necessary to be granted the right to offer counter-expertise. My case was being processed by a judge whom I had known fairly well because I had helped him resolve a personal "situation" that would otherwise have been a public scandal. I saved his professional career and his honor, even though this was for the sake of appearances regarding his family life. These two—career and honor—were linked, although the latter was believed to be one of the ethical precepts of the party that served as a condition for the former. I helped him save face and considered that he was indebted to me. Because I was jailed, I asked my brother and a lawyer friend to remind the judge of his unpaid debt and to grant me the opportunity to provide impartial expert opinion. Not only did he suffer amnesia with respect to my existence, but he also refused to admit the file containing counter-evidence.

I was incarcerated at the penitentiary in Slobozia. The prison doctor there was doing his required residency; because he commuted daily, he asked me to work as his assistant in the prison infirmary. Several months after my arrival in prison, an epidemic caused by food poisoning erupted. We were able to bring it under control quickly, a fact that contributed—as much as was possible for a prisoner—to the consolidation of my position. The director of the prison wrote a positive character report about me and requested that my sentence be reduced for good behavior. Thanks to him, I was released in November 1975, one year after my second sentencing.

The irony of fate and human meanness! These were the source of my deprivation of liberty for two years and seven months. Nothing would have happened, or at least not then, if the woman I promised to help had not told a neighbor in her apartment building that she was going to have an abortion on such and such a day for which she needed 800 lei, the cost of the abortion. Ironically, three or four days after the procedure, the apartment below my patient's was inundated with water; it happened to be that of the woman in whom she had confided. The neighbor asked her to take care of repainting the ruined apartment. The painting of an apartment was almost a luxury. The material circumstances of the persons responsible for the flooding did not permit them to cover the damages to their neighbor's apartment. Heated discussions ensued. In the end, the neighbor got her satisfaction through revenge; she denounced my patient to the police for having an illegal abortion. And that is how I became implicated in the tale I have just told you.

Dr. G.
*(born 1924, obstetrician-gynecologist)*

This case summary is drawn from an analysis of extensive legal documentation and from intensive interviews with Dr. G. and others.[39] A chronological summary of the legal investigations, trials, and sentences in which Dr. G. was involved offers a formal overview of the state's intrusion into and monitoring of his professional and personal life. However, a review of legal documents reduces the complexity and vicissitudes of lived experience to the wooden language of official discourse, homogenizing the ups and downs and ins and outs of this tangled history. Dr. G. was repeatedly accused of being more dedicated to breaking the law and pursuing a profit than to upholding professional standards. Yet his license to practice medicine was not definitively revoked, which would have been an appropriate measure if his professional competence had been at issue. Dr. G. consistently contested the accusations against him, maintaining that when he had done a curettage it was either to save a woman from the complications of an incomplete abortion or because another pathological condition required surgical intervention.

To be sure, "truth" was a matter of interpretation. Personal, political, and pecuniary interests played roles for almost everyone involved in each of the legal cases against Dr. G. Over the years, Dr. G. and the woman who was to become his second wife repeatedly experienced the depths of helplessness and despair; however, they also won small victories, which provided temporary respite from what otherwise seemed to be a relentless ordeal. Ultimately, Dr. G. was acquitted; both his and his wife's sentences were forgiven under the terms of an amnesty. The various actors implicated in these trials and investigations (including Dr. G.) engaged in both legal and illegal acts. Cynicism, blackmail, and denunciation were employed to varying effect. The nuances of interpretation were differentially dictated by self-interest. Neither the legal history alone nor Dr. G.'s personal reflections tell the entire story; however, combined they provide an ethnographic reconstruction of the politics of abortion as they affected one physician, Dr. G., in Ceausescu's Romania.[40]

At the age of 44, Dr. G. was a practicing gynecologist at the community hospital situated approximately ten kilometers from the city of Buzau. In June 1968, Dr. G. learned that he was under criminal investigation (Ministry of Health Order 524/1968). He became an object of press scrutiny; the case in which he was entangled was highlighted in several different publications. The story began late one evening when a pregnant 35-year-old mother of three children, accompanied by her own elderly mother, appeared at the maternity ward in the community in which they lived. The younger woman's labor pains had begun. However, the doctor, who resided in another community, was not there. The local midwife decided it was best to send the mother-to-be to the nearest hospital because the pregnant woman suffered from a deformed spine and respiratory problems, which could present difficulties. She was transported by ambulance to the hospital in community P, where she arrived before seven in the morning; upon arrival, she was taken to the emergency room for examination. Yet the doctor who was supposed to have been on emergency duty had signed off early in order to catch the train for Bucharest. Before leaving, she—Dr. R.—had written in her report that there were "no problems of special concern." The ambulance from the nearby community carrying the pregnant woman arrived after Dr. R. had departed. Dr. G. arrived at work at 7:30 that morning, though his shift did not officially begin until 8:00. He examined the woman in labor and decided to have her transported urgently to the regional hospital in Buzau. Dr. G. himself was unable to save the mother and child by surgical intervention because the operating room was locked, and the person who had the key, Dr. I., was away on vacation. (The relationship between Dr. G. and Dr. I. was tense; when the latter left on vacation, he irresponsibly failed to leave the key to the operating room for his colleague's use.) Dr. G. notified the hospital director of his decision, and, by 8:00 A.M., the woman was again in an ambulance. However, the driver refused to leave without proper authorization (despite the fact that earlier he had driven the doctor to the train station, seemingly without any orders). The director then told the driver to wait for him because he also had to go to Buzau. Although he had been told that this was an emergency case, the director kept the ambulance waiting for more than one hour; he wanted to meet the train from Bucharest on which Dr. I., who had been on vacation, and a staff nurse were arriving.[41] At long last, after a one-hour drive, the pregnant woman was taken into the operating room at the regional hospital. By then, it was too late; her uterus had ruptured. It was impossible to save either the mother or the child.

The dramatic events of this story reached the public in the wake of an investigative report by a journalist who attacked the Ministry of Health for the poor organization of health services and for the widespread lack of professional responsibility exercised by medical personnel.[42] Self-interest often seemed to outweigh sound medical practice, as the above case makes evident. The ministry came under moral fire for this tragedy. At the time that this report was published, the woman's husband (then the father of three motherless children) took legal action against the hospital. The notoriety of this case was such that the Ministry of Health was obliged to conduct its own investigation. The commission from Bucharest, assisted by the local medical bureaucracy from Buzau, determined that Dr. G. was the person most culpable—even though to others he seemed to be the least guilty. The hospital director, the doctor who was supposed to have been on emergency call, and the doctor who had left on vacation with the key to the operating room were reprimanded. Dr. G. had his right to practice suspended for one year.[43] Dr. G. contested this administrative sanction and brought charges against the ministry. In 1969 the case introduced by the victim's husband finally came to trial; the doctors implicated in his wife's death were accused of manslaughter. The single defendant found not guilty was Dr. G.; he was acquitted on January 3, 1970 (File 1089/1969). The others received punishments of varying severity; the director, for example, was given one year and six months' imprisonment. However, like his colleagues, he was excused from serving the sentence under the terms of a general amnesty (Decree 591/1969). Dr. G. did not find work until February 1971, more than one year after his acquittal in this sordid case.

During the period in which Dr. G. remained formally unemployed, he managed to support himself and his family with savings and alternative sources of employment. It was especially tempting for him to practice "informally"—or illegally—as a gynecologist because of the demand that had arisen after the issuance of Decree 770. The second economy in illegal abortions was a thriving market; although the risk was high, doctors were simultaneously able to satisfy humanitarian as well as monetary interests.

Dr. G. noted that he depended on his bank savings for survival. He pointed out that before 1966, when abortion was still legal, being a gynecologist was lucrative. In addition to a fixed monthly salary, a doctor was paid a 40 percent bonus from the money collected for abortions performed during a one-month period. During those years, a legal abortion cost 30 lei. If, for example, a doctor performed 400 abortions over the course of 30 days (perhaps doing 15 to 20 in a day's work), the hospital received 12,000 lei for these services. Of this total, 60 percent—or 7,200 lei—remained in the state budget, and the rest, 4,800 lei, was paid to the doctor (although it was taxable). This additional 4,800 lei per month was more than the equivalent of two months' salary. Dr. G. emphasized that he had deposited considerable sums into his account as a result of his earnings from legal abortions. Hence, his insistence that he had primarily lived off his savings can be viewed as credible.

In 1972 Dr. G. again became the subject of a criminal investigation (File 2174/1972). He was then employed as a senior staff physician in obstetrics-gynecology at the hospital in Giurgiu, in Ilfov county. The health department had alerted the prosecutor's office that Dr. G. had violated the provisions of Decree 770. In the official file of this case, Dr. G. was denounced for doing three illegal abortions. More egregiously, one of the women had died, allegedly because of his actions. The patient had been hospitalized in her second month of pregnancy. The illegally induced abortion had seemingly resulted in the perforation of her uterus and injury to the small intestine lining; this had developed into peritonitis, and in the end led to her death.

Dr. G.'s version of these episodes differs considerably from the official one (see, for example, File 934/1978). He insists that he did a curettage on the first woman for uterine bleeding caused by a benign uterine tumor, and not for purposes of interrupting a pregnancy. As to the second accusation, this patient had received official approval for an abortion from the special commission (which the prosecution contested, claiming the written authorization had been incomplete). The woman who later died—the third case—had been hospitalized for an incomplete abortion in her second month from which she had begun to bleed. She seems to have been curetted with legal permission.[44] Her condition remained stable during the first three days after the procedure; however, on the fourth day, she ran a high fever and an emergency operation was performed by the head of the obstetrics-gynecology section. By September 12, she had entered into a coma from which she did not recover. She died on September 17, 1968.

Dr. G. maintains that when he had first examined the patient, he had not found a perforated uterus, and that the perforation did not occur as a consequence of the curettage. He considers the criminal charges against him to be the result of a frame-up by the chief of the obstetrics-gynecology section, who wanted to get rid of him. According to Dr. G., he had established himself in a relatively short period of time as a significant presence in the hospital. Until he arrived at this hospital, the chief of obstetrics-gynecology—who owed his own position to political influence—had reigned over the ward's entire clientele. Dr. G.'s professional rank was higher than that of his superior, and as more and more patients began to seek him out, the chief of staff became increasingly irritated; his informal earnings (the "tokens of appreciation" from patients) had diminished noticeably. Resolved to do something about this situation, Dr. G.'s superior manipulated this financial vendetta into what became a judicial farce. In February 1973, Dr. G. was vindicated; the regional prosecutor's office ordered the criminal investigation closed for lack of evidence (Order 217/B/1973).

However, on December 12, 1974, the chief prosecutor of the same office ordered the case reopened (File 270/1974). He argued that the grounds previously presented to terminate the criminal investigation against Dr. G. had been unconvincing. In addition to the accusations already standing, two more cases were imputed to Dr. G., with yet another woman dying, allegedly as a result of his actions. He was arrested on December 23, 1974, and held under "preventive arrest" until January 7, 1976. On September 8, 1975, in the midst of the investigation, Dr. G. suffered a stroke and was taken to the hospital in a coma. When he had recovered sufficiently, he was returned to a prison cell. Because of the precarious state of his health, Dr. G. was conditionally released on January 7, 1976, in response to a plea from his family to the attorney general of the Socialist Republic of Romania. The family had asked that Dr. G. be granted a conditional release because of the poor medical treatment accorded him and the incompetence of the penitentiary's doctors. Together, these factors had contributed to the deterioration of Dr. G.'s health and might lead to his death. A panel of Supreme Court judges decided to grant the family's request. Between then and his final sentencing in 1979, Dr. G. was repeatedly hospitalized, often for lengthy stays.

The case reopened in 1974 focused primarily on the additional abortion accusations, although as before, no incontestable evidence was produced to prove his guilt. The legal files contain obvious inconsistencies. For example, accounts of state witnesses vary from one declaration to another. Contradictions exist with respect to details and critical elements. In one official statement it was claimed that one woman for whom Dr. G. had done an abortion had been in her fifth month of pregnancy (File 270/1974, p. 28; deposition of December 25, 1974). Yet in another it was noted that this same witness had been in her second month of pregnancy (File 270/1974, p. 29; deposition of April 2, 1975). Dr. G. formally requested that the medical records be verified, but to no avail. A partial review of this case suggests that under other political conditions, the evidence upon which his sentencing was based would have been considered insufficient. However, to Dr. G.'s misfortune, that was not the context in which he found himself.

According to the legal documents, shortly after midnight on August 9, 1974, a 36-year-old mother of three children, P.R., was hospitalized in the Giurgiu medical facility. Dr. G., the doctor then on emergency duty, diagnosed an incomplete abortion in the second month, accompanied by bleeding. He noted that there were no apparent signs of violence done to the uterus. She was admitted and medicated accordingly. The next day, Dr. G. left on vacation. The patient was examined by the chief of the gynecology section, Dr. F., who also diagnosed an abortion in the second month, but with peritonitis and perforations. The woman was operated on that afternoon; by whom remains unclear. Her condition worsened, and on August 14 she was transported to the Emergency Hospital in Bucharest: her blood would not coagulate; she suffered from renal-liver insufficiency and uremia. Despite emergency efforts, she fell into a coma and died on September 17, 1974, from acute post-abortive renal-liver failure. According to the medical-legal report, her condition resulted from the maneuvers used to induce the abortion. It was noted that the intestinal perforation had been caused by an instrument presumed to be cylindrical in shape and two centimeters in diameter.[45] In May 1977, following his trial, Dr. G. was declared guilty of manslaughter and was sentenced to eight years in prison and deprivation of the right to practice for five years (Penal Sentence 51, Ilfov county court; see art. 178, para. 2, of the Penal Code). He was also ordered to pay for the victim's funeral, and to pay child support for the victim's two children as long as they were minors.

As before, Dr. G.'s synopsis of the events leading up to his arrest and conviction challenges the above scenario (see, for example, File 934/1975), as do the accounts of witnesses cited in the case file. The criminal point on which Dr. G.'s culpability rested was the divergence between the diagnoses made by his section chief and himself. The section chief, in providing "expert testimony" against his colleague, Dr. G., asserted that Dr. G. had deliberately omitted evidence of the intestinal perforation in his write-up of the initial diagnosis. The chief claimed to have informed the police as well as the section personnel that Dr. G. had perforated the patient's intestine while performing an illegal abortive procedure. From the standpoint of the state's legal representatives, Dr. G. was a doctor with a criminal record; he was already considered a recidivist and a "social danger." The other physician, the chief of his medical unit, was a respected member of the community and an influential party member.

The prosecution argued that the patient had first arrived on August 8 around five in the afternoon—and not after midnight on August 9. Dr. G. had examined the woman and noted her pregnancy. He allegedly offered to do an abortion right then and there in his office. Although she had only 500 lei, he accepted this sum. He put her on the couch and locked the office door. While in the middle of this procedure, someone knocked at the door. Startled, the doctor had the woman get up so that he could answer the door. He then returned to finish the job. The woman—undoubtedly shaken by this unexpected interruption—felt him enter more deeply with the forceps than he otherwise would have done. It was this maneuver that was claimed to have produced the perforated uterus. Her cries were stifled by his warning to stay quiet; she endured the sharp pain in silence. After Dr. G. finished, he inserted a tampon to absorb her bleeding. He told her to go to the Polyclinic and ask for an admission slip that would enable her to be hospitalized if necessary. Contrary to his directives, she went home and told her husband what had happened. She felt increasingly ill and returned to the hospital that night, accompanied by her daughter, where she again met Dr. G., who was on duty.

However, the assistant who was on call that same night also challenged this official story, maintaining that it was a fabrication. She herself had been with the patient from the moment when the patient had been admitted until she was taken into the room where she had been medicated (Penal File 921/1979, municipal court). The assistant was perplexed by the fact that she had not been asked in detail about what had happened at the time of the initial investigation. She considered herself to be an important source of information because she had been on duty and had cared for the woman in question. She insisted that the abortion had occurred before the woman's hospitalization. According to this witness, the woman came to the hospital just after midnight on August 9; her daughter accompanied her. After Dr. G. did the examination, the assistant herself settled the patient "who entered on her own two feet" into a room with other women in it. While alone together, the patient had finally admitted that she had tried various methods to rid herself of the pregnancy. None had worked, so she went to a woman in the town who performed the necessary maneuver. The patient had gone to this same woman previously and refused to reveal this woman's identity.

According to the assistant's account, Dr. F., the section chief, ordered that the woman be taken that next day to a single room in a ward not reserved for gynecology.[46] Dr. F. also called his staff personnel to a meeting during the following days in which he told them that Dr. G. was on an excursion in Germany from which he was not going to return.[47] Moreover, he informed them that they would all be questioned by the authorities and should declare that Dr. G. had done the illegal abortion. This would have, by implication, simplified matters for everyone in view of Dr. G.'s departure from Romania. The assistant was incensed that her section chief had asked his staff to lie. It constituted an abuse of his authority. She also claims to have seen Dr. F. speaking subsequently with the victim's husband. He, as well as two women who shared a room with the unfortunate woman and the medical team who operated on her, had insisted that the victim had told them Dr. G. had done the abortion (in conformity with Dr. F.'s version). The hospital gatekeeper also declared that he had seen the woman enter the hospital on August 8 at the time when Dr. G. allegedly did the abortion.

Soon thereafter, the assistant left for her vacation at the seaside, where she ran into Dr. G., who was also vacationing there. She told him what had happened in his absence. She stated in her official declaration that she did not know what Dr. F.'s motives were; however, the tensions between the two doctors were hardly a secret. She had witnessed their arguments herself. Dr. F. had once said threateningly to Dr. G.: "I'll fix you!" The trial seemed to be a continuation—in a different milieu—of the conflicts between them. Dr. G. was convicted and sentenced in 1977. Like Dr. M., he believed in divine retribution: Dr. F., the section chief, died in the earthquake that hit Bucharest in 1977.

The other charges brought against Dr. G. in 1974 included the case of G.D.[48] Her role in the trial was a double one: she testified against Dr. G. as a witness for the prosecution at the same time that she herself was on trial for soliciting and having an abortion by him. Throughout the trial, the witness's statements proved inconsistent and contradictory. However, that did not affect their utility with respect to the indictment against Dr. G. A woman, G.D., claimed to have been on her way home in a trolley bus when she felt ill and fainted. Someone had kindly come to her rescue. It turned out that this person was a doctor, and—of critical importance to the prosecution—had offered to help her if she wanted to get rid of the cause of her physical condition. They exchanged phone numbers and addresses. Not long thereafter, the woman called on the doctor at the address he had given her. On the day of her medical visit, Dr. G. did a curettage for which G.D. paid him 1,500 lei. She was later escorted to the door by the same woman who had answered it when she arrived. That woman was Dr. G.'s "concubine" (as she had been characterized in the documents pertaining to her own case).

The "proof" of guilt was based on the discovery that Dr. G. had the address and telephone number of G.D., and that she, in turn, had his. Dr. G. and his partner were both found guilty: he for inducing an abortion illegally, and she for being his accomplice. Both were charged with illegally retaining instruments used for abortion in their possession. They were also charged with trafficking in narcotics. (During the search of their apartment, eleven vials of an analgesic drug were confiscated.) Dr. G. was sentenced to three years for the abortion. In addition, he received two years for drug trafficking and one for the illegal retention of instruments.

In this series of charges against him, Dr. G. was convicted of manslaughter for the death of another woman, C.A. This woman's pregnancy had not been registered in the health records of the community where she lived. She was examined by Dr. G. at the hospital in Giurgiu; he diagnosed an incomplete abortion with significant bleeding in the second month of her pregnancy. He intervened to stop the hemorrhaging. Later, Dr. F. accused Dr. G. of perforating her cervix while performing an abortion. Moreover, Dr. G. was charged with not treating C.A. for post-operative infection even though he was aware of what he had done. Yet again, Dr. F. contested that a botched abortion had been the reason for C.A.'s admittance to the hospital. He maintained that Dr. G. had performed an abortion for personal gain— and had done it carelessly. C.A. died of secondary complications, including septicemia. Dr. G. was sentenced to four years' imprisonment.

The final accusation contained in Dr. G.'s 1974 file was for an illegal abortion done for R.M.P. on July 18, 1974. R.M.P. was pregnant and unmarried. As noted in the indictment, R.M.P. had asked various friends if they could recommend someone who would help her out. A girlfriend told her about Dr. G. and gave her his address. When R.M.P. went to the address, she found an unfurnished apartment in which two other women were waiting for the same reason. After the curettage, she paid the doctor 1,500 lei. He also gave her a prescription to treat inflammation of the ovaries; the prescription was later allegedly "discovered" by the police in R.M.P.'s purse.

Among the witnesses for this case was a family who lived in the apartment next to that used by Dr. G., and the building administrator, who was a retired army officer (according to Dr. G.). In denouncing Dr. G., the building administrator noted that it seemed strange that so many women came to this apartment.[49] When the secret police entered the apartment to conduct a search, they discovered "some strong lights in the ceiling and others that indicated the illicit occupation of the accused" (File 921/1979). Even though Dr. G. did not admit to any of the above charges, he was sentenced to three years' imprisonment. R.M.P. received a one-year suspended sentence for arranging to have an abortion.

Final sentencing for the 1974 accusations against Dr. G. was not pronounced until June 2, 1979. Dr. G. appealed his initial sentencing in 1977, claiming judicial improprieties, among other grounds (see Supreme Court File 1400/1977; he had not been present at the original trial because of his health). Also in 1977, and as a result of the amnesty provisions of Decree 115 of that year, each of Dr. G.'s sentences was commuted, leaving him to serve a total of six years and eight months in prison instead of eight years (File 921/1979, Penal Sentence 65, June 2, 1979).[50] While the appeal was pending, Dr. G. did not continue to serve his remaining sentence, in part because of ongoing health problems.[51] On November 23, 1977, Dr. G. won the appeal; the Supreme Court granted a retrial to be held where the case had originally been tried, in the Ilfov county court (Penal Decision 2164/1977). However, the retrial was delayed by Dr. G.'s deteriorating health. He was scheduled to be reexamined on December 10, 1978, to determine whether he was fit to stand trial (Supreme Court File 1138/1978, Decision 1277). The result of these developments was that Dr. G.'s final sentence was not determined until June 1979.

Dr. G.'s next encounter with the state's repressive and legal apparatuses began in 1981.[52] On May 22, a representative from the police reported:

> Major S.M. of the Legal Division of the General Police Inspectorate, involved in the "general surveillance" of Dr. G., who has previously broken the abortion law and retained pertinent instruments [illegally], set out, accompanied by Lieutenant Major C.A., Sergeant Major O.T., and Lieutenant A.C., for street [X] and the entrance to building D.1 in order to identify women who were leaving apartment 26 . . . which belonged to M.T., Dr. G.'s concubine, following a telephone tip that he had performed an abortion for the caller; our scope was to detain and investigate the author of the crime committed.

Late that afternoon, Dr. G. left the building accompanied by a plump, blond-haired young woman "of about 26 to 28 years of age." As they neared the car in which the police were waiting, they were stopped. They resisted the attempts by these authorities to have them get into the police car to be taken to the station. The police decided to take them there by force. It was stated in the verbal report that Dr. G. fought with all his strength against being handcuffed. When they arrived at the station, Dr. G. "was faint, kept his eyes closed, and did not answer any of the questions put to him." The doctor called by the police determined that he had suffered a tachycardia [a racing heart beat] and recommended that he immediately be taken to the emergency room. Meanwhile, the woman who was with him was subjected to a medical-legal examination, the results of which incriminated Dr. G. Dr. G. nonetheless claimed that the young woman had come to the apartment to repair a camera, not to have an abortion. The denunciation against him had been made by a person "aware" of the activities that took place in apartment 26.[53] Dr. G. later learned that the building administrator as well as the occupants of the adjacent apartment had collaborated with the local police. He was arrested "preventively" in 1982; his pension payments were perfunctorily suspended. Dr. G. was condemned to three years' imprisonment, of which he served only thirteen months and three weeks, his sentence having again been reduced. He was released in 1984 because of his health and age.

Dr. G.'s final arrest occurred in 1988, when he was 64 years of age. The reason: performance of an illegal abortion and [illegal] possession of instruments (File 8068/1988). The official version alleges that he arranged to meet the husband of the woman who was to have an abortion. This man, L.M., escorted Dr. G., along with someone else, to an apartment where Dr. G. then did the abortion on L.M.'s wife. Dr. G. received 4,000 lei for his efforts. His hosts then called a taxi for him. However, as he left the apartment building, he was stopped by the police, who immediately confiscated his medical kit. Other police personnel took the woman who had just had the abortion to the Medical-Legal Institute for confirmation of her illegal abortion; she was then hospitalized. While Dr. G. was under arrest, the prosecutor's office searched his household and discovered a notebook containing names, addresses, and phone numbers. The investigation yielded "evidence" that Dr. G. had done seventeen illegal abortions during the year 1988, receiving 5,000 lei in exchange for each procedure. Based on these "findings," he was charged with having done 58 additional abortions before 1988 for which he was paid differing sums. In consequence of his actions, Dr. G. was accused of being a danger to society. The recidivist nature of his activities was emphasized and influenced his sentencing. He was given a sentence of seven years—five years for the first seventeen abortions, plus two years for the other charges.[54] Moreover, 305,364 lei were confiscated from his residence. Of this sum, the attorney general's office retained 251,000 lei. In the end, Dr. G. was required to pay only 3,636 lei and various legal costs. During the search of his residence, medical instruments which Dr. G. allegedly possessed and retained illegally were also confiscated.

Dr. G.'s version of these events again differs in detail from the official rendering. He maintains that an acquaintance—a woman who rented from family friends—had asked him to examine a friend of hers. The husband of the latter came to meet him and drive him to their residence. Dr. G. found that the woman was bleeding lightly after attempting to rid herself of her pregnancy. He counseled her to go to the hospital because it was possible that she would suffer from secondary infection. When Dr. G. left the residence, he was arrested. Not only did Dr. G. deny that he had induced an abortion, but he also denied possessing the appropriate surgical instruments, noting that these had been confiscated in 1974. The sums of money found in his household, as well as the address book, were related to the medical consultations he had done since 1981, when he became a pensioner. Dr. G. was acutely aware that these private consultations were not strictly legal, representing both fiscal and legal evasions managed through second-ary economic activities. Hence he conducted his business with the utmost discretion. He insisted that he had slipped up just this once out of a courtesy to a friend—and paid for it.

One evening at dinner with friends whose renter was the link to his fu-ture patient, Dr. G. had let his guard down. He had recounted to them how he had managed to buy an apartment in the center of Bucharest—a cov-eted address. Dr. G. believes that the renter lay in the shadow of the setup that then unfolded. As a divorced woman, it was unlikely that she would have been able to obtain her own apartment.[55] She presumably expected to be awarded Dr. G.'s desirable apartment as recompense for denouncing him to the police. To this end, she used both her friends and Dr. G. In view of the circumstances, Dr. G.'s suppositions do not seem far off the mark. The police conducted a search of his apartment, after which the keys were not re-turned to Dr. G.'s second wife, but rather to this divorcee, a police collabo-rator. For this criminal infraction of Decree 770, Dr. G. was sentenced to a total of seven years in prison. However, Dr. G. served only nineteen months and nine days of this last sentence.[56] On December 16, 1989, he was con-ditionally released. Ten days later, Dr. G.'s release became final. The Ceau-sescu regime fell on December 22, 1989. The Ceausescus were executed on Christmas day. On December 26, 1989, the provisional government of Romania made the abrogation of Decree 770/1966 one of its first decla-rations of liberation. Dr. G.—like so many others—was no longer subject to or victim of it. The Ceausescu regime had ended. Dr. G. was at last free to pursue restitution for the harm done him.

However, the majority of those harmed by this notorious decree and the policies accompanying it were the women of Romania who, over the long span of years, paid dearly with their health and their lives.

### WOMEN'S STORIES:
### PUBLIC HUMILIATION AND FEAR, PRIVATE PAIN AND RAGE

In the final section of this chapter, women express themselves. Theirs are not the most dramatic or unusual of tales, but rather represent the trials and tribulations typically endured by most women in Romania in direct conse-quence of the political demographic policies of the Ceausescu regime. The hardships of everyday life—physical, emotional, financial, and practical—color their recollections. These women describe the risks they felt forced to take. They speak about the thinking behind their decisions to abort or not to abort, which were often calculated in discussion with partners, par-ents, and in-laws. The lack of privacy in their daily lives is starkly evident. In its stead, the space of everyday life seems to have been permeated by fear, humiliation, pain, and despair. Especially for women, sexuality was fraught with tension and frequently led to the deterioration of relations between them and their partners. The threat of pregnancy alienated women from themselves. They too often viewed their own bodies—especially their reproductive organs—as the enemy within, capable of betraying their most personal interests and feelings. The tightening grip of the police state contributed forcefully to the internalization of rage and terror, and also to the complex dynamics of acquiescing to their own victimization. Indeed, the state's attempt to control women's fertility made many women experience their own bodies as the most intimate tool used by the regime to instill their lives with terror.[57]

Dr. L.I.
*(pediatrician)*

Many doctors, especially those who were waiting to be promoted in the professional or bureaucratic hierarchy, were guilty of being complicitous with the ruling power. Some were even more zealous than necessary. They hoped that their rewards would mirror the degree of their obedience and servility. What was unpleasantly surprising to us younger ones was the cynicism and careerism of those who occupied positions of authority in the medical system.[58] It was more than a simple inter-generational conflict. I will never forget the meeting to which the doctors from sector six were invited. It was in 1987, in the midst of the campaign to denigrate and blame doctors for the unfulfilled demographic indicators.[59] The director and chief of the obstetrics-gynecology unit of the Municipal Hospital presided over this working meeting. As on other occasions, we expected to be harshly reprimanded. But this isn't what stuck in my memory. What shocked me in particular was the hypocrisy and the disregard of basic deontological principles by certain doctors who had highly touted reputations. It was difficult for me to understand how it was possible to be a good doctor and, at the same time, lack backbone. One of the doctors who had taken it upon himself to accuse others claimed to have been outraged by the number of legal abortions which, inadmissibly, far exceeded the allotted number. One of the reasons frequently cited to obtain permission for a legal abortion was varicose veins. Even though this was on the list of ailments that qualified a woman for an abortion, the speaker implored doctors to be more devoted to the party's demographic politics than, by deduction, to medicine. The expression he used was astounding, if not outright inhumane, and disqualified him in my eyes. Making reference to women who suffered from varicose veins, the doctor's order was: "Determine who they are, operate on them, and get them back in circulation!" That is, get them back on the reproductive track, or as is said in zoo technology, breed them!

One of the recommendations by the organizers of this meeting about reducing the number of legal abortions . . . was to lower the number of cesareans.[60] A well-known gynecologist, a professor and chief of gynecology in a large hospital, asked if the legislation that granted women the right to abortion after two cesareans wasn't too lenient. The "scientific" argument he presented was that in some countries where abortion is forbidden on religious grounds, women with four and five cesareans do not renounce pregnancy and maternity. Why should Romanian women be different? Convinced that Romanian women were indeed as plucky as those to whom he had referred, he thought it was necessary to send a report "higher up" to the party and request that the legislation limiting cesareans to two be modified.

Then Dr. Milita, a highly respected colleague and competent doctor with a great deal of integrity, asked to speak. He cautioned that generalizations are sometimes dangerous. If, in the countries to which the distinguished professor had referred, the height of women was 1.70 meters, then transposing this solution [to our population] was not viable. In Romania, the average woman's height is 1.58 meters. Similarly, other anthropomorphic parameters such as bone structure and pelvic dimensions had to be taken into consideration. The response to his comment was as unprofessional as it was brutal: "You had best shut up because you are in last place in your district for fulfilling the gynecological exam plan!"

But there were doctors who helped patients as much as possible. It was known that during these years, 48 to 49 percent of the abortions that ended up in the hospital were "spontaneous." When they were on emergency duty and circumstances permitted, or when the doctor and assistant worked well together and trusted each other, then women hospitalized with hemorrhages were curetted and listed as having been treated for a spontaneous abortion.

The inverse was that some doctors, assistants, and women deferred to legal authority because of their sense of guilt about being involved in an illegal abortion. They became the subjects of blackmail by the prosecutor's office and the police: Collaborate or you will be condemned. Some chose the first option. I remember a patient who had a thyroid operation done by a renowned Romanian specialist; she left him an envelope containing 25 lei whose numbers were the first registered in the series. The police went into the doctor's office immediately after she left and took him to their office for accepting a bribe. He was released after a few days only because the hospital director had banged on all of the doors and invoked the dramatic situation of scores of sick persons scheduled for operations who risked irreversible aggravation of their conditions if the only specialist for this type of surgical intervention was detained because of a frame-up. There were doctors and doctors. Some were human, dignified, and moral. Others would let women who wouldn't reveal what they had done or who had induced the abortion die on the operating table; they didn't bother to look at them.

I was in my fifth month of pregnancy. I was commuting between a city in the north of the country where I was a pediatrician, and the other end of the country where I had my family and residence. It was in the second half of the 1980s. The provisioning of this city was so poor that we were starving, and I don't mean that metaphorically. I was tired, depressed, and suffering from various other symptoms caused by the lack of calcium. I couldn't go home weekly because my salary wasn't enough to enable me to pay for the train fare. My family, worried about the state I was in, insisted that I be hospitalized. The doctor who was following my pregnancy prescribed transfusions. After I finished this treatment and was released, he recommended two weeks of medical leave.

Moreover, he took me by the hand to the chief of the unit, who was a woman. He presented my case and explained the importance of a medical leave to help me recover. She said that five days' leave was sufficient. Regardless of his insistence, the decision was not changed. When we emerged from her office, an assistant who worked in this ward and who knew me offered an explanation for the chief's intransigence: "Lady, Doctor, you must offer her a little attention [a gift] and then it is virtually certain that she will give you two weeks."

How I came to practice in a Moldavian city is a long story. The year in which I finished medical school there were very few positions available. There were some in Bucharest and in the adjacent counties. My grades permitted me to choose the hospital in Giurgiu for the three years of required residency training. Not long after I began, I realized that many of my colleagues benefited from a six-month transfer assignment to Bucharest. To obtain such an assignment would have made it possible for me to avoid a daily commute [Bucharest–Giurgiu–Bucharest]. I inquired about the criteria for getting such a temporary transfer. And, as the saying goes, he who looks, finds. A transfer depended on how impressive the gift given to the director was—the director of the county health department. The ritual was as follows: You presented yourself to the director in his office with a package [or envelope]. After you made your case briefly, you were invited to leave your offering and to come back the next day. If the gift seemed to fit the request, then you would be assured that the response would most likely be positive. If it was deemed too little, he communicated his regret that nothing could be done. One colleague, in order to obtain this six-month transfer, gave him a gold ring as a gift.

When I finished my three years of required residency, there was an opening of jobs in the country. Most of the positions were in northern Romania. That's how I was named the pediatrician in a little town lost in the middle of nowhere, despite the fact that my grade-point average when I finished medical school was 9.58 out of 10. Even so, I was full of enthusiasm and ready to begin doing things. There were four of us, young, all pediatricians, and firm in our convictions. It didn't take us much time to ascertain that it was even worse than what we had imagined. The local medical system was dominated by a mafia whose principal interest was to earn ever more money and presents. Of all that was promised to us about our assignment, almost none of it was true. Several months after our arrival, all four of us still lived in a small room in the home for children. It was winter, very cold, and we didn't have anything on which to heat our food. As luck would have it, we didn't have much by way of food to heat either!

A temporary solution arose with my maternity leave. But I still had problems. They were caused by my direct experiences with demographic politics. I had a very difficult birth. The pregnancy had been relatively smooth. The infant was well developed, but also very large, weighing 4,200 grams [9 lbs., 4 oz.] at birth. I didn't want to give birth by a cesarean section, but in the last instance it seemed to be the solution most indicated for the child and myself. Before I entered the hospital, there had already been some fetal trauma. Two days before birth, the membranes had fissured and I began to lose liquid. My doctor told me to stay quietly in bed because he would be on duty in two days.[61] What could I do? When I entered the hospital, this liquid was already green in color and I was depressed, afraid that I would lose the child. I had no contractions. I was told to take some medications—I think nine of them. I began hyper-contracting. I felt that the fetus had turned into a ball and that the fetal cord could no longer be heard. I was in despair; I couldn't breathe and I was scream-ing that my child was dying. At that moment, they decided to use forceps be-cause I had not been approved for a cesarean by the professor who coordinated the maternity ward's activities. The refusal was due to the fact that if I had had a cesarean, it would have altered the number approved in the plan! So they used forceps. The child was large and the doctors fought hard to get him out. During these maneuvers, his clavicle was broken and when I saw his color, I be-lieved there was nothing more that could be done. He was put in intensive care. I was unaware of this until two days later when I regained consciousness. Be-cause of the emotional shock and my horror that something irreparable had happened to my child, I went into hemorrhagic shock. Neither my husband nor any one else from my family was allowed into the maternity ward; I survived because of the generosity of the women who were in the same room. When I was able to stand up, I went to see my child. He was bruised and very agitated. I told the doctor on call that I myself was a pediatrician and I wanted to know my child's condition. I learned he was spastic and agitated because he had a bit of encephalitis, and that he was being given Phenobarbital; they were trying to keep him alive. I wanted to throw myself out of the window. They restrained me. My husband was informed, and he began making phone calls and spurring relatives and friends into action. I had a breakdown. I couldn't control myself; I cried continuously. At last, a specialist was brought in to look at my child. That's how I learned that the spasmatic crying was due to the detachment of his clavicle, which produced a lot of pain every time he moved. I recovered from my psychological collapse with some difficulty. And for years I lived with the fear that my child might develop a physical or psychological infirmity.

S.M.

*(born 1951, researcher, married, one child)*

Even though it was many years ago, I still remember what I went through then, especially the emotional turmoil. . . . I married in the same year that I finished university; I was sent to work "in production." Before I knew what that really meant, I felt frustrated because I had wanted to conduct research or teach at a university. One year before the end of my university training, a law came into effect making employed service in a production unit mandatory (regardless of one's qualifications). This same law limited the possibilities for doing so in a large city. The idea that you were assigned to work in a production enterprise even if you had been trained in social sciences or education or culture was much less upsetting than realizing that you might be sent far away from your home and all that was familiar to you. . . . I had to consider myself lucky be-cause I was among the "exceptions" to the law; I was sent to a position in Bu-charest at a production enterprise that was, in fact, a department in a ministry. It didn't take me long to understand that my enthusiasm, my notions about

performance and creativity, were not in tune with the monotony of a bureaucracy. I realized I had to resist the temptation to succumb to bureaucratic routine and the danger of deprofessionalization. I had to be competitive at the
end of my three-year service if I was to have any chance at a university or research career.

One year after we married, with substantial help from our parents, we
bought an apartment. Also with their help, we managed to furnish it rather
spartanly. Our apartment looked more like a depot for family donations, all
of which contributed to some kind of aesthetic and degree of comfort. Our
debts exceeded our salaries. Six months after we had settled in, I gave birth.
Time passed. At the end of my first year working at this ministry, a rumor began to circulate about a competition for a research position. Assuming that
professional competence was to be the basis of the selection process—which
was not necessarily the case—the competition would be fierce because there
were few positions in the field in which I had prepared and, as a discipline, it
had just been abolished at the university. It would be tough, very tough, but
it was worth a shot. Meanwhile, our child was growing, but she wasn't yet old
enough for nursery school. Her grandparents were not retired, and we had
not found someone to take care of her when we were at work. We were young
and wanted to enjoy our youth.

It was spring when I realized I was pregnant again. Everything was in bloom.
I remember how much I enjoyed walking through the park on the way to the
continuing education course I was taking. Attendance was obligatory. I had
to miss two days; I wasn't feeling well. I couldn't miss any more days because
I knew I could not get a medical certificate justifying my absence. I couldn't
go to a doctor. And anyway, nothing happened. I had managed to overcome
my fear about what I was about to do. It was the first time for me, and I was
afraid of the darkness in the section of Bucharest where I was to go. I didn't
know the area well, and then I arrived at the home of a woman I didn't know
at all except for the phone call to establish a time. My husband wasn't able to
come with me because he was working second shift that week. I had promised
him I'd take a taxi home. We had decided not to tell our mothers because they
would not have agreed with our decision. They thought we had to have a second child, and even if the moment wasn't exactly the best, better early than not
at all. Moreover, they would have disagreed with my having an abortion because
of my blood type which was Rh-negative, although I understood that medical
problems did not typically accompany the first two births. We wanted a second
child, but not just then. First, I wanted to see what would happen with my job,
pay off some of our debts, and let our daughter grow up enough to be able to
go to nursery school.

I asked my friends and colleagues to recommend someone who could help
me out. A woman from work had a sister who was a medical assistant; she knew
a midwife who would do an abortion for 600 lei (one-third of my monthly salary). It was dark when I arrived at her house. When she opened the door, she
asked me if I had vials of saline solution. She took me into the kitchen and had
me get up on the table while she prepared her syringe and a transparent plastic tube, small in diameter, which was probably used for transfusions. While

she was doing that, I took in my surroundings. The room smelled of stew and of poverty. It is not by accident that kitchens are the chosen rooms for clandestine abortions. Water and fire for sterilizing are within reach, especially in the small kitchens that were the standard in socialist architecture. It was the one virtue of such kitchens. In this one, the table was in the middle; there was a sink next to it under which the garbage was kept. There was a stove. I watched her out of the corner of my eye. As soon as the syringe was sterilized over the stove's fire, she filled it with the saline solution and threw the vial in the garbage. She washed her hands and then took the syringe and introduced it into my uterus. She injected its contents into me. I stared with revulsion at a tapestry on the wall. A large flower, shocking blue in color, represented a futile attempt to brighten the color of poverty. I think that is why I consider such tapestries and the smell of onions frying to be signs of poverty and humility.

After she finished, she helped me get up and packed up the syringe. Quickly, all the other objects were removed from sight. I paid her and left. I went home and got into bed; I thought I'd read. After an hour or two, I began to feel cold and then colder. I covered myself with everything warm I could find in the apartment. Then I started to feel hot all over. I was burning and sweating. The only thing that didn't seem to have turned into liquid was a thought I had that I was melting; I would flow like incandescent lava. By the time my husband got home, just before midnight, I was again in a cold phase. I was shivering so strongly that I couldn't even manage to say that I thought I was going to freeze to death. Then I began to burn up again, then freeze, and back and forth. As morning neared, my husband said this couldn't go on and that we had to call the ambulance. The despair that this provoked was much worse than bearing the hot and cold! He didn't call the ambulance. By the next evening, I was much better. But nothing else happened, not what I was waiting for—not on the second day either. I had heard that for many women, a second intervention was necessary. I was horrified by the idea that I might have such a reaction again. But I couldn't turn back; I couldn't risk letting the pregnancy continue and bringing a malformed child into the world.

I had missed two days of classes. I couldn't miss a third. I had to go quite a distance to get there. As the bus neared the station where I got off, I felt that something was happening with me, in me. I took it as a sign that something no longer was a part of me; I sensed that I wouldn't need to go through this again. I was relieved—unaware of what was about to unfold. I entered the classroom and took my usual seat. I exchanged a few words with the person next to me, and then the lecturer, who wasn't much older than we were, began. We were a group of fifteen young men and women, all about the same age and with the same occupation. Not long before the end of the lecture, perhaps fifteen minutes before, I was suddenly overcome with the shock of what was happening to me. It had finally happened. I no longer heard anything. I saw my colleagues sitting near me and I panicked. What would I do at the break? How could I get up if any of the men stayed in the room during this pause? What will they think when they see the stained seat cushion? I would ask my neighbor to get them all out of the room. But then, how would I make it to the bathroom wearing this skirt when the hall would be filled with students enjoying the break between classes? I had no idea how I would manage, what to do. My horror at the humiliation of it all made it impossible for me to think straight. I was deeply ashamed; I couldn't think. I was only aware of this assault on my dignity. The chair—how would I clean it? As my colleagues began to get up and head toward the door, I, out of despair as much as humiliation, whispered to the women near me that I was hemorrhaging, that the chair was stained, and that I somehow had to get to the bathroom. I know that three of them surrounded me as we traversed the crowded hallway. Someone brought me cotton and I managed to wash out my skirt. Later, I left. Everyone knew by then but showed their solidarity by pretending not to. I took a few steps and felt that something was dragging me down, something much stronger than I. I remember thinking that somehow I had to hold my skirt so that it would not fly up indecently around me as I collapsed. I fainted. I don't know how long I was unconscious. When I revived, I felt a sharp pain in the area where the nose and forehead meet. When I opened my eyes, the person who was applying pressure to this point told me that he had heard this is what one should do when someone has fainted. I know that when I fell, my skirt was draped elegantly around my body. I have no idea whatever happened with the chair. But I think this is why I always associate humility with the form of a chair.

M.L.
*(born 1943, ballerina, married, two children)*

I had my first child soon after the decree, so my child was among the first generation of *ceausei*.[62] I wasn't even 23 years old then, nor had we even been married one year. I didn't want to keep the baby. I would have preferred to have had our own apartment first. My in-laws, with whom we lived, were very decent people, but they had two other children and space was tight. In the end, I gave in to my husband's wishes. My arguments were not convincing to him—that we had many hours of study, rehearsals, performances, tours. We were both in the theater. My in-laws agreed to take care of the child; it was their first grandchild. My pregnancy was very difficult. I could barely eat; I kept vomiting. Despite my condition, the child developed normally. However, the first few months following her birth were a nightmare.

Soon after my maternal leave ended, we moved into a studio we had gotten through the theater. I had to work hard to get myself back into shape to dance. Whenever there was a break between rehearsals and performances, we'd rush over to see our daughter at my in-laws. It was hard. You can't imagine my exasperation when I discovered that I was pregnant again! My daughter was not yet one. Luckily, if that's what you can call it, I had a cousin who was a medical assistant who induced an abortion for me. Unfortunately, nothing happened and she repeated the intervention. Then I bled, eliminating clots. I missed two days of work, but then I went back to the theater because I had no way to justify a longer absence. I had stopped bleeding. I had begun my warm-up exercises when a sharp pain took my breath away. My head hurt horribly. I felt as if an iron clasp had been clamped around my head and was being tightened. I was trembling. In between these fits of shaking, the pain in my head felt as if my brain would explode. My nails began to turn blue.

My colleagues were alarmed and went to get my husband. They took me to the theater's infirmary. The doctor took one look at me and moved into action. My temperature was over 41 degrees centigrade; my arterial blood pressure was five. I was taken to the emergency hospital. The pains continued and were intensified by my increasing fear. The hospital to which I belonged was that frequented by those "servants of the regime" who worked at the institutes of science, art, and culture. Many of the doctors there enjoyed high professional esteem, but it was also said that the selection criteria had been based on their "healthy origins"—that is, their good political backgrounds. I began to panic when I learned that the emergency doctor on duty was a woman who was known for her intransigence with respect to cases such as mine. I could tell from how she looked at me that she was certain of the cause of my condition; she didn't just suspect it. I was given three vials of calcium, and she told me not to be frightened, that she would deal with me gently. She sat beside me, and very calmly asked me, whispering, to tell her what I'd done so that she would know how to help me. She gave me her word of honor that she wouldn't tell anyone anything. She just wanted to determine what was the best treatment for me. I insisted that I hadn't done anything. I'd gone to work and all of a sudden, I was taken ill. Obviously, she knew I wasn't going to tell her the truth. She asked someone to bring me tea and to get me to a bed. The second day, they did various analyses and diagnosed that there had been an attempt to stop a pregnancy in the third month, and that I was hemorrhaging. I was put into intensive care to save the pregnancy. How could I take the prescribed medicines when I knew what I had done? How could I retain this pregnancy when I assumed that the chances were high that the fetus had been traumatized through my attempts to get rid of it? I couldn't take the medicines. I threw them into the drain in the shower room, which was close to my bed. I took steaming hot showers, as hot as I could stand. The person next to me in the room knew my story, and she allowed me to lift her and carry her around the room several times. I did this every day for the two weeks that I was hospitalized. Despite my efforts, nothing happened. I was released with the diagnosis of a pregnancy in the third month. Fatal! About a week later, I was on a bus on my way home. All of a sudden, I felt very ill. It was so bad, and I was so ashamed that I might do who knows what in the bus that I got off at the next stop. I leaned against one of the trees lining the sidewalk. I felt something warm in my abdominal zone. A good while later, I arrived home and went immediately to verify what had happened. There was something gelatinous, unformed. I wrapped it carefully in a lot of toilet paper with the idea that I would show it to the doctor who was required to track the development of my pregnancy. But by the next day, there was nothing in the packet; it had disappeared, so I didn't bother to go to the doctor's. Nothing happened for another ten days, and then, again, I felt sick. After a single tremor throughout my body, I felt the pleasant sensation of warmth. It had taken almost one month to eliminate the placenta. The next day I went to the hospital to recount what had happened. They were surprised by my story, and suspicious. I was examined. Since they did not find any signs of violence, the diagnosis was "spontaneous abortion." And that is how I escaped that time.

I think I had seven voluntary abortions. The first two were legal, having been before November 1966.[63] The fourth intervention is one I remember as clearly today as if it had been yesterday because it turned out I was pregnant with twins. It happened in 1973; I had been pregnant for seven or eight weeks. I had asked my cousin, the medical assistant, to talk with a gynecologist she knew. We agreed upon the conditions and the time. I was to pay 3,000 lei to the doctor and an assistant who would come to my house to do the curettage. At that time, 3,000 was quite a sum—my monthly salary. Despite the hardship this posed on our budget, it basically meant that the medical risk was minimal [because the procedure would be done by a gynecologist]. After all the fear and torment I'd been through the last time around, I wasn't about to try that again. The morning of the day when the doctor was supposed to come, I was chatting with my coworkers about having found a doctor to do a curettage. One of them commented that it seemed terribly expensive and that she knew someone who would do it for half the price. It was true that I would have to go to the residence of this person, but my colleague said that she was very competent. She said she had arranged such meetings for many of our colleagues, and she could do so for me also, even for that very evening. The cost was the decisive factor for me, but I had no idea how to cancel the arrangement I already had. A savings of 1,500 lei meant being 1,500 lei less in debt. I was very aware of this fact. I told my colleague I had decided to opt for her solution, but that we had to invent an excuse to give to the doctor. All of my colleagues came with suggestions, and eventually a workable scenario emerged. When I arrived home, I told all of this to my husband and about his role in the small theatrical piece that would be enacted when the doctor arrived. I must say that he played his part extremely well. When the bell rang, I hid in the bedroom with my ear glued to the door so that I could listen to how my husband explained to the doctor that there was a small problem:

"Sir, doctor, I think it my duty to inform you of my own uneasiness. My wife, like most women, talks more than she should on occasion. And it turns out that she told our neighbor that she was going to have a curettage done. Our neighbor seems to be okay, but do I know for sure? Perhaps it might be better to put this off a bit." To which the doctor responded: "Sir, if your wife's dumb, that's her problem." And he left rapidly.

I called a taxi and went to the address my colleague had given me. When I entered into the apartment, I had second thoughts about the person in whose hands I had been placed. A woman, rather young, welcomed me. She was small and very thin. She looked like she didn't have an easy time of it. But it was too late to change my mind. She gave me an anesthetic and had me climb up on the kitchen table. She said she wanted to finish before her husband returned. When she began, I calmed down because it was clear to me that she knew what she was doing. I thought she had finished and was about to get up when she told me to stay put. She wanted to make sure. Immediately, she commented: "Stay still, don't move because you've got another." That's how I learned I had twins. After I got off the table, I felt very dizzy from the anesthetic. It wasn't obvious how I'd get myself to a taxi. Just then, her husband came in. He looked at both of us, and then said he'd escort me home. When I got out of the car, I saw my worried husband gazing out of our apartment window that opened onto the street. It was already midnight.

### G.D.
*(born 1949, divorced, telephone operator)*

G.D. was a key witness in one of the cases against Dr. G.; she also served as a principal informant against his wife, who was charged with being an accomplice to his crime. More than 20 years later, in 1994, she related her side of the story.[64]

In 1973, when I was 23 years old, I lost my virginity to a classmate and friend of mine whom I had known for six years. Not long thereafter, I discovered that I was pregnant. I confided in him; after all, I considered him to be my fiancé. What a shock! My father had died the previous year; next, I learned that my "friend" felt no responsibility with regard to my predicament because he claimed that he was sterile. He told me to do whatever I thought I had to, but that I could expect no support of any kind from him. Time passed, and I felt the symptoms of my pregnancy more frequently. Taking a bus or trolley had become quite an ordeal. I had to get off at each stop to vomit. Finally, I told my mother who, under the circumstances, really acted admirably. I decided I had to get rid of the pregnancy. My mother offered to give me the money for a clandestine abortion. I had to find someone to do it. My best friend learned about Dr. G. from someone else and contacted him. She then took me to the designated place as pre-arranged with him. I didn't pay much attention to my surroundings. I knew that we had gone to an apartment in the Taberei area. When we arrived, we rang the bell and someone answered. I don't recall who it was. After all these years, I can't remember the password I used to be let in. I was six weeks pregnant. Dr. G. gave me a local anesthetic and then a general. It went very well. When he finished, I got off the table and stayed a half-hour more to recover a bit. I gave him 1,500 lei and walked home with my girlfriend. Dr. G. had asked me to call him if there were any problems. I recovered quickly and without any difficulties, so I didn't speak with him again. I consider him to be a very competent specialist. After all that happened, I know how much I owe him for what he did for me at that time. Through all these years, I've lived with my guilt about him. But what was I to have done? I was so young; I had personal and family problems, and my fear of the police and prosecutor was greater than my gratitude. In the trial against him, I identified him as the person who had done my abortion.

In April 1974, when I came home from work, I found a summons from the Ilfov prosecutor's office in my mailbox. I was invited to appear at their Rahova office. On the day and at the time noted in the "invitation," I was met by a policeman who told me that Dr. G. had been arrested for doing illegal abortions and that my name and number were found during the search of his apartment. I tried to deny that I knew the accused, but my interrogator was much stronger than I. Even now, after all these years, when I think about what happened, I feel afraid again. I was paralyzed by fear, and especially then. I really didn't have much choice: I could either be accused or accuse. I didn't have the strength of character to opt for the former. After I signed a statement saying that Dr. G. had interrupted my pregnancy in his own apartment—a pregnancy of six weeks and for which he had received 1,500 lei—I was taken in a police van, along with other women, to a hospital for a gynecological exam. They found that I was not then pregnant.

Soon thereafter, I was called again to appear at the station. That time, I was expected to recognize from among a line-up of women the one who had opened the apartment door for me. I was so frightened that I don't know whom I recognized. I don't know if they suggested to me or not whom I was to pick. All I know is that I stated that I recognized one of the women in the line-up as the one who had opened the door, even though that wasn't quite true because I didn't remember who had received us.

The worst was during the trial. Before I entered the room, I swallowed half a box of mild sedatives. I didn't know how to get a grip on my fear. I was really out of it. I know that when asked whether my statements had been true, I maintained that they had been. They asked me to recount how I came upon Dr. G. I couldn't bring myself to implicate my friend in this mess, so I invented the story about the trolley bus. I claimed that I had met Dr. G. on my way home. I was pregnant, and particularly when I rode in such vehicles, I became ill. And that is how I met Dr. G. I became ill and he came to my assistance. We got off the bus together and he told me he was a doctor and that he could help me out. That's also how I explained why I had his phone number and he mine. With this tale, I saved my girlfriend. After the trial ended, I came home and slept a day and a half. The pills had taken effect.

I was left alone after that and didn't hear any more about this whole story. But one night, several years later, I had the sense that someone was following me. (I worked the night shift at a hotel near my apartment.) I walked faster; just before I entered the hotel, I realized that the person following me was Dr. G. I can't tell you how frightened I was. I assumed he was looking for me to pay me back for what I did during the trial. He seemed like a crazed man to me. I called two close friends of mine from high school who knew the whole saga and asked them to come quickly, telling them that Dr. G. had followed me and I didn't know what he was likely to do with me. These two friends, two bruisers, came and threatened Dr. G. that if he didn't leave me alone he'd have to deal with them. Knowing that I was "covered," I asked Dr. G. what he expected from me and how he had learned where I lived. He told me that he was appealing his sentence and he had come to convince me to change my deposition. To get my address, he had used a ruse. He had called my house, and when my mother answered, he said he was an operator for the telephone company and that they needed my address. I refused to help him and begged him to leave me alone. For many years, my life was a nightmare. In every shadow, I saw Dr. G.! Really, he is an extraordinary doctor. And despite it all, I knew how much I owed him!

Anonymous

My abortion experiences in Rumania are not totally normal, but they are typical of the experiences every woman in my country goes through.[65] My difficulty in finding a doctor, getting together enough money, overcoming fear, and having five abortions between the ages of 18 and 23—all that is normal for Rumanian women. Although my experiences are typical, I must add that if I remain healthy and alive after all my experimental abortions, it is because I have a somewhat privileged position.

My parents were Communist Party members before 1939 and fought with the Underground during World War II. After 1945 they were rewarded with good jobs which gave them privileges, such as special health care. These privileges extended to their children even after my parents lost their high posts in the "housecleaning" of 1952. . . .

### My First Abortion

My first abortion took place in the period before it became illegal. All I had to do was to go to the hospital—my mother had spoken earlier with the doctor— and pay 30 lei; at the time, the average monthly income was 1,500 lei. I was put to sleep, and when I awoke the world was again in order. That same year, in the fall of 1966, the right to abortion was repealed. . . .

### My Second Abortion

I got pregnant again in the spring of 1969. I began to discover the different ways one could get rid of this "thing" without having an abortion. I learned about lifting heavy objects and taking hot baths, in fact, so hot that one must get drunk beforehand . . .

The hot baths, the large quantities of vodka, the heavy lifting and the overdose of quinine did not help. Since neither my friend nor I had the money to pay for an expensive illegal abortion (between 3,000 and 5,000 lei), I was forced to tell my parents. Fortunately, my mother was friends with a gynecologist who performed the abortion for free after hours in his office. The fear that I was going to be caught was felt by everyone involved. In case something unforeseen might happen, I only received a local anesthetic. The operation hurt a lot but only lasted five minutes and went well. After it was over, I promised myself, and my mother, that the next time I would really be careful, since I now knew how bad it could be. . . .

### My Fifth Abortion

Four years had passed since the anti-abortion law was put into effect. Doctors and patients had adjusted to the new situation. It was now easier to get an illegal abortion. Everyone knew "somebody"—a doctor, a midwife, a medical student—for a price. I knew of a doctor whom some of my friends had gone to. I told my aunt I needed 4,000 lei. She immediately gave me the money. Twice the doctor postponed the operation. Finally, the day came and I learned what had become "usual" in the last four years for so many women in Rumania. I had to go alone; I was not allowed to know the doctor's name and the abortion was to be performed in someone's apartment. And at the door I had to use a special signal.

Upon arrival I received a sedative and a local anesthetic. A long, low coffee table, with books placed under two of its legs to create a tilt, served as an operating table. Two stools held my legs. A bucket was at the lower end of the table. A tape recorder was turned up loud. Two unknown men, only one of whom was a doctor, performed the operation. From the previous abortions I had learned how much it could hurt and that it would all be over in five or ten minutes. This time it hurt more and seemed like it would never end. The doctor was swearing, the assistant held my hand attempting to calm me, but the tape recorder could not drown my moans. After a half hour, which seemed like eternity, it was over. . . . I had a fever the next morning. When my temperature did not go down the next day, I became concerned and went to my doctor at the clinic. He examined me and found that half the fetus was still in me. He immediately sent me to the hospital and I was lucky to get Dr. X. again.

After I told him the story, he said to me: "Hopefully, your uterus is not punctured. From the color of your face I'm afraid it might be."

On the next day I received my second curettage during which the doctor discovered that my uterus had been punctured and I was bleeding internally. I was operated on within a half hour.

Everything went so quickly that there was no time to conceal the matter. The doctor was forced to inform the police of the operation. An official representative of the police was present during the operation, and when I woke up he was at my bedside. The first interrogation began. I told him I did not know what had happened. He said that the "case" was so clear that there was no need for an interrogation or confession. I only needed to say who had performed the abortion.

After ten days I was released from the hospital. At home I found a summons. I went to the police and maintained my story that I had not done anything and did not know how the puncture had occurred. About every three days I had to report to the police always with the same tiresome questions. . . .

In the meantime, my whole family and all my friends had been informed about the incident. I was threatened with a three-year prison sentence. With the help of Dr. X., I tried to find a solution. Finally help came from my parents' friends who were friends with one of the highest judges in the country. They called him and explained the situation: The daughter of R., you remember him. We fought together in the Underground, etc., etc. Well, anyway, the daughter is in trouble. . . . He promised to take care of everything.

At the next interrogation, there was a new official. He said that he had the task of resolving the case fairly. . . . I went with him again to the Institute for Legal Medicine and to Dr. X. A medical explanation of the perforation was patched together. On December 12, eighteen days before the 23rd anniversary of the founding of the Republic, the case was dropped because of insufficient evidence. My new investigator whispered to me that I would not have gone to jail anyway, since there was an amnesty in honor of the 23rd anniversary. He still wanted to know whether I was really innocent. I reassured him that I was.

E.M.

*(born 1957, worker, married, three children)*

I married in 1980, and in that same year I became a mother. I became pregnant again the following year. My first child was still very little and I, very young.

A colleague of mine recommended a woman who was not medically trained but who had a "clean" method to interrupt a pregnancy. She came to my apartment and, using an improvised instrument, introduced a solution of water and vinegar into my uterus. I paid her 1,500 lei which, at the time, was about twice my monthly salary. A few hours later, I began to have abdominal pains. They felt like cramps. The next day, I began to bleed. The bleeding continued, and became heavier. However, by the end of the day, I eliminated a gelatinous mass. The hemorrhaging continued throughout the night. My husband became very frightened and called my mother. She is a courageous woman and knows how to get things done. She decided I needed to be taken to the hospital. She took care of everything. She prepared some "small attentions," that is, gifts for the nurses and assistants, and I was hospitalized for a spontaneous abortion. I had a curettage through which I learned that I would have had twins.

From then on until 1987, I had abortions approximately twice per year, with the exception of the year in which I gave birth to my second child. I became pregnant easily. On the one hand, I loved my husband and didn't want to deprive him of the right to a normal intimate life. At the same time, the only method we used to avoid my getting pregnant was the calendar, and we didn't manage that with much rigor. We had tried to obtain birth control pills. This was difficult in and of itself, and then there were the secondary problems associated with them. I only used them for a short time. A colleague of mine told me that some women introduced one or two tablets of vitamin C into their vaginas before having sex. I tried that only once; my husband found out that the citric acid in vitamin C might lead to vaginal ulcerations. That was the end of that.

In the spring of 1984 I found that I was again pregnant. I already had two children. I suffered from psoriasis, so I went to get an approval for a therapeutic abortion. Unfortunately, I learned that this ailment was no longer on the list of medical grounds for a legal abortion. Then I taught myself to inject water and vinegar [into myself]. I'd fill a yogurt jar three-quarters full with boiling water to which I'd add vinegar up to the neck of the bottle. When the temperature of this solution was tolerable, I'd introduce it into myself. (I checked the temperature just as I did for my children's baths—with my elbow.) I struggled with this in the beginning until I learned to introduce the solution correctly, but I never made a mistake. Cramps and hemorrhaging followed. Then the problems began. Even though I'd bleed heavily, I had a hard time eliminating the fetus. On one occasion, I found myself lying in a bath tub of bloody water while my husband massaged my abdomen—to no avail. I was losing a lot of blood and became very pale; my husband called an ambulance. I arrived at the Municipal Hospital in a coma; my pulse was four. That was the second time I was hospitalized for a spontaneous abortion.

In 1987 I was hospitalized a third time. I went during the day in order to reduce the suspicions of the hospital personnel. I was bleeding. A resident did the curettage. I note this because he was very young and a person of color. The release papers for a spontaneous abortion in the second month of pregnancy were signed by the head of the section. Three months later, I found a summons from the local police station in my mail box. I was "invited" to pay them a visit.

You can't imagine how frightened we were, both my husband and myself. The interrogation lasted for three hours. My husband was not allowed to be present with me; he remained in the courtyard of the station. The officer who interrogated me was very young and very aggressive. I wasn't beaten, but I was threatened with physical violence. The manner in which the interrogation was conducted had the desired effect. I admitted that I had induced the abortion myself. They threatened to search my apartment to find the instruments I used. I said I didn't use any because my method didn't require any. I explained that I drank boiled red wine and then climbed into a very hot tub and began massaging my abdomen. When I began to bleed, I went to the hospital. I was interrogated twice more after which my file was sent to court. One of the interrogations was after a gynecological exam; I knew I was pregnant but I was too afraid to do anything. That is why I gave birth seven months later. Before the trial, I was called to the court by the prosecutor who was to deal with my case. He asked me to provide witnesses. I said I couldn't because there weren't any. I then learned that without a witness the case cannot be brought to trial. Because of that, I was introduced to an officially provided witness. It was a man that I saw for the first and last time during the trial! Needless to say, this did not present legal difficulties.

I was given six months of imprisonment, with the sentence to be carried out at the place where I worked. Luck was on my side; the official formalities associated with applying my sentence took so long to complete that by December 1989, I had still not begun to serve it, meaning that I still received my full salary. (The state retained 80 percent of your pay while you carried out a sentence at the place of your employment.) Even today, I don't really know what happened to cause the delay from which I benefited. I know that I had been presumed guilty from the very start, a recidivist. For the police, the fact that I had been hospitalized three times for spontaneous abortions was all the evidence they needed. Moreover, it was demonstrated that the institutions designed to maintain public order had done their jobs efficiently—I, of my own free will, had recognized that I had broken the law.[66] On the day of my trial, there were quite a few others taking place. One woman was accused of inducing an abortion by introducing the neck of a beer bottle into her vagina in order to tear the membranes. And that was nothing in comparison with another case that had happened while I had been hospitalized. A woman had introduced a battery-operated light into her vagina, hoping that the dilation produced by the energy source would cause the egg to separate. Instead, she was rushed to the emergency hospital because the light had exploded in her vagina.[67]

R.T.

*(born 1951, worker, married, one child)*

I wasn't able to keep a pregnancy, not even the first, without injections. As soon as my period was late, I started to have strong abdominal pains. I gave birth in 1980. In February or March 1980, instead of my period, I had very strong pains down below, and I didn't know what was happening. On the third day, I went to the doctor. He said, "I'll treat you . . . so your period will come."[68]

My husband told me, "Go back and tell him you're married. So what if you're pregnant? [Her husband misunderstood the doctor's intentions.] I want us to have a child." So I went back. The doctor commented: "What on earth—if your period comes, it means that you aren't pregnant. Otherwise, the treatment will stabilize your pregnancy. You aren't going to be able to keep a pregnancy without being treated. You can have as many children as you want, but only under medical supervision."

I wanted to have a child so I had to begin treatment; I don't remember what he did. Nonetheless, I still had terrible pains. The doctor told me I had to decide either to continue on with the pains or to give up the pregnancy. And this during Ceausescu's time! The doctor said, decidedly: "If you want, we'll get rid of it." There were medical grounds in my case. He also told me that if I was determined to have the child, I would have to risk continuing with the treatment. I was examined every month, for nine months; it was awful. I was nauseous, in pain. But the birth was fine: three and a half kilograms, and half a meter long. And four months later I was pregnant again! I don't know how it happened. Needless to say, I was beside myself. I hadn't yet forgotten the nine months of trauma, the treatment and exams, what the doctor had said. This was all that went through my mind, incessantly, like a bell ringing. I knew I couldn't have any children without medical treatment. Naturally, I was frightened.

I would have liked to have had many children because I really love children. I had told my mother that if I didn't marry I would adopt a child—that's how much I wanted to have children. But when I learned about the necessity of medical treatment I didn't want more. In fact, I had all three of mine this way. I didn't think of myself as sicker than others, but I didn't want this treatment. Then I found out that I had spasmatic crises, lack of calcium, etc. I was afraid to have another child. So the second time I became pregnant, a doctor took care of it. He did abortions for others, and, despite the secrecy, I heard about him. When I made up my mind that I couldn't go ahead with a second pregnancy, I went directly to him. I knew him and after this we became good friends. He told me not to be afraid and whenever something happened, to come to him. He did the abortion at home. The proper instruments had to be registered and were kept under lock and key, so he couldn't get them. Even though he was a doctor, what he did was primitive. I ended up having to go to the hospital.

But, naturally, because things didn't work out well the first time and I had to be curetted at the hospital anyway, I wasn't about to go to him again. I would pay anything to have it done in the hospital, properly. By my third pregnancy, my husband saw how badly off I was. He said no matter what it cost, we would go to a doctor. That was in December. You can imagine—we still owed 100,000 lei on our house, which was quite a sum, and with Christmas coming up. . . . On December 6, I was hospitalized. That was in 1984. My husband went to all of our acquaintances to arrange for us to go to a doctor in X who did abortions. He was known to many, including a more distant family relation of my husband's. When you are desperate, you find out what you must. I was desperate and afraid. My husband's cousin, several times removed, didn't want to tell us to whom to go. She told us to manage on our own.

Both my husband and I began to cry because we didn't know what to do. He said, "Don't worry. Even if we have to go straight to Ceausescu, we will. We have proof that you can't have more children; it's not that you simply refuse to go through another treatment." He reassured me that I'd get rid of the pregnancy, no matter what. Finally, someone else who had been to the doctor in this city agreed to show us where he lived. I was parked on another street in the event that someone called the police. . . . Later, as I had been instructed, I waited for him at the hospital. He came to examine me. By that time, I had already been very ill and had had to stay in bed a week. I couldn't get out of bed, and it was obvious I had to have medical treatment or get rid of the pregnancy. If I hadn't been so sick, I could have waited another month to see and finish paying for the house, but for me, it was urgent to resolve this one way or another. So when I met him at the hospital, I told him that no matter what, he had to do something for me. He asked if I knew how costly it was, to which I responded that I didn't care. You can't imagine what that meant—that we had 100,000 to pay on our house and yet I didn't want to discuss the price with the doctor. His assistance mattered more than anything to us.

He suggested that it could cost up to 10,000 lei, of which 5,000 had to be given to the doctor who actually did the procedure. He himself was the head of the section and had an entire group of doctors under his supervision.[69] A young woman was going to do it. To express my gratitude, I gave him a service of knives and had his suit dyed at a factory. I'd do anything for him! He didn't ask us for anything, except, well, for the dyeing of his suit. My husband had that done immediately and then went to pay the other doctor 5,000 lei. In fact, we gave 6,000 lei to her and 4,000 to him. He didn't ask us for anything. He said he didn't need anything, but, as you probably understand, we virtually forced him to take the money we offered. We were afraid of what might happen in the future; maybe we'd need him again. But he insisted that we only had to pay the doctor who had done the procedure, and what we thought was appropriate. Of course, he told us what others had given and, naturally, we added a bit to that so that if I had problems, I could go back to her. And once I did. My stomach hurt. I went to her and she took me immediately and treated me. I gave her a bottle of wine.

When she had done the curettage, someone from the prosecutor's office was present. Always, when a medical kit for a curettage was opened, the prosecutor appeared. I was already on the operating table when I was asked what had happened to me. The policeman was dressed in civilian clothes. The doctor intervened immediately, but he kept on: "What is your name? Let me see your identity card." The doctor's assistant also tried to save the situation: "Oh, we've got a problem because she left it in her father-in-law's car." The policeman was reading from my medical file—a false name. "You've had a curettage done before. Legal motive." (Those who had four or six children—I don't even remember anymore—had the right to a legal abortion.)

The problem was that the head of the section who had arranged for my legal abortion had written a false name on my medical record so it would all seem legal, and this policeman wanted to see my identity card. When I heard that, I fainted from fear. I don't recall when I came to. There were girls in the hospital who were waiting for someone from the prosecutor's office to come and get them. These girls had induced abortions themselves, and after the doctor had saved them, they were turned over to the prosecutor's office so the doctors would come out smelling clean. These women were hoping to get better; they needed blood, everything. It was . . . I can't even express it. It was like a war; only a war could create more fear. While you were waiting your turn, you'd see the prosecutor and police arrive to take someone away, handcuffed. She'd be arrested and locked up. These were the conditions in which we lived then.

My doctor repeatedly told me not to worry, that absolutely nothing would happen to me. But this had little effect; I was a prisoner of terror. . . . I had an acquaintance in Alba who did curettages for others and she was arrested. Two years . . . I didn't know anyone else. In the hospital, I heard about people. I saw how girls were arrested. The ward in which I stayed was full of women who had aborted, but whenever anyone met in the hospital corridors, of course, no one had had an abortion. Everyone was there for all sorts of feminine ailments, but not for having a curettage. . . .

We women talked amongst ourselves. For example, when I was still unmarried, I heard about a funeral for a 20-year-old girl. She had been pregnant and had stuck some sort of plant root into her vagina and poisoned everything. We talked about such things. Abortion was legal until the 1960s. It was easier for our parents. Times were still good enough during our childhoods, but the rest went from bad to worse. We grew up with problems. By the 1980s, we knew that doctors would be held accountable for the death of a child.[70] The Securitate were really active then . . . doctors were really under the gun.

Those were tough times; it pains me to think that it even happened. It was torture for women.[71]

## A.T.
*(born 1946, peasant, one child)*

I kept wondering, what to do not to have this child? I found a root, wormwood. It's a root from a kind of long grass. I managed by myself. I had heard about this weed from a midwife, may she rest in peace. She told me her story once: "My, what happened to me! I was young and there was no way I could have this child because I'd made him with another man, not my husband. I simply had no choice; I had to do this, and manage it as well as I knew how." She explained it to me, so I decided I'd try the same. I went and found a hoe—we used to hoe corn—and a shovel, and I got some of this root from along the margins of the field. I took a good one—long, thick as a finger. I washed it carefully, and cut a slit in it. Then I tied some thread to it—a long piece so I could tie that around my thigh. I introduced it into my uterus and kept it there some twelve hours.[72] Later, a bit of my period began; the pains started. My stomach hurt, and things like that. But by the end of the week, the child was gone.

I never went to the hospital; nothing I did ever resulted in my having to go to the dispensary. No one ever heard that I had gone there for so much as a pill. I managed to resolve my own troubles. Sometimes I improvised, using a very thin tube. No matter how many problems, I dealt with them. God forgive me, but I was even arrested because of an abortion. The first time I aborted myself, I used the root. I did it to myself five times; I never went to anyone else. But, you know, in those moments, well, when you're most down on your luck, you need someone to bring you a brandy, a tea. . . . I even managed at six months [in the sixth month of pregnancy]! I wasn't able to get rid of it in the first or second months; I couldn't. I tried to induce an abortion, but to no end. . . . What to say, I had a strong uterus. So it happened at six months. Heaven forbid, but when you looked at it! Like this, with a finger resting against its little head, like that. . . . That's how it died, with its fingers like that. . . . I buried it outside. No one saw me. I hadn't said a word to anyone. I never had any trouble, not even at six months. Ask the village midwife; I never ended up needing her. I knew how to take care of myself. I worked with wormwood, or an irrigator, a douche with chamomile tea. I worked well; I never had to be cleaned out afterward by the midwife.

I also did abortions for others. My arrest was accidental; I helped another woman. She had come to me crying that she had three children; her husband was away in the countryside trying to earn money, and it was very hard for her. "Oh my, oh my. I am going to kill myself. I will not have more children!"[73] I told her she couldn't do such a thing, to go and kill herself. So she went and got some saline solution from the pharmacy and then I introduced it. I did this at her house, in the kitchen where it was warm. She didn't have problems because of what I did, but she ended up with a partial paralysis. Here's what she did: After I finished, she then went to a neighbor's, who took her to work in the fields. She also gave her plum brandy, which she drank, and a sparkling wine. And then she got sick. She kept crying, "I am dying! I am dying!" and so they called the doctor. The doctor, a woman, was not from our community. She came and gave the woman an intravenous injection. All of a sudden, her face was contorted. But this wasn't because of what I'd done, but because she'd drunk plum brandy and wine. May the devil take her, why she did that!

Oh, she'd had plenty of abortions done by others, but those who had helped her before had gone to find work elsewhere in the country, so she came to me. And me, fool, jackass that I am, I hooked up with another fool! I mean, I decided to help her because maybe her husband was a drunk or had cheated on her. Ha! And later on, they claimed that I had received stuffed pillows, a thick woolen blanket . . . if I saw any of these, then strike me blind. I never received anything from them.[74] They didn't pay me anything, not even as much as the dirt under my nails! They said they'd given me rugs! And for that, her mother and her whole family accused me. After the doctor had given her the intravenous, she had been taken to the hospital in Baia Mare. The doctor never returned to our community again after that.

That night, I was at my mother's when I heard what had happened. I was afraid. I knew they'd all say, "You, you killed her!" I was so afraid; I was shaking so much that I was good for nothing. I knew that everyone was cursing me. I couldn't sleep or eat. I was a wreck. I don't wish anyone to be in the situation in which I was.

They took her to the hospital, and then they interrogated her and then me. They arrested me. They took me to B, and then V [small towns], and they kept me under arrest for a week. I was threatened—that I would have to pay for her hospitalization; I wouldn't be able to, no matter how much I worked. It was her family that accused me, no one else. During the interrogation, I said it wasn't because of me. I didn't deny that I'd done the abortion. I told Mr. H., our policeman, that I wasn't guilty at any price; she went off drinking. They came with a commission and searched my house. No one said anything about my having broken that law about doing abortions. They only asked what she ate, what she'd had to drink. Her blood was poisoned. If it had been because of me, there would have been something with her uterus; they would have had to take it out, or do who knows what. It wasn't my fault.

After they took me there, she acted like a spoiled child. God only knows; she acted like she didn't know me at first. Then they put her in front of a large mirror and asked her if she knew that woman, who she was. "My neighbor," she said. "She's the one who did the abortion?" "Yes." "And what did she give you to drink?" "She didn't give me anything." "What did she give you to eat?" "Nothing. I drank some brandy and wine, and I went to the fields, and when I came back, I got really sick. The doctor came and gave me an injection, and I don't remember anything else about what happened to me." She did abort, and there were no traces that someone had done anything to her down there. The doctors were surprised that I'd been arrested when she hadn't hemorrhaged or anything; there was not one sign of anything having gone wrong. But if it was to be prison, there was no way out.

Before the trial, I was kept in the penitentiary in Baia Mare, and from there I was taken to the trial dressed in prison clothes. They couldn't get me to name anyone else [who did abortions]—there were six or seven—although she did. But God gets to everyone in good time. Her children are all pretty cursed. They also tried to get me to name the others for whom I had done abortions, but I didn't want to say and do harm to someone else so she'd end up in prison. It was enough that I was there! The witnesses were the woman's husband, mother, and family. There were no strangers there. No one else from the village was there. My case was publicized in the local newspaper. I was sentenced to three years, and did one year and ten months. I wasn't a party member. In prison there were doctors, engineers, priests, midwives—all sorts were there. And those who were there weren't idiots, only smart people were there in prison, from all over our country.

I got along with all the guards. I didn't make trouble. I didn't like to stay put, so I asked to work. I worked in the fields—that's how my sentence was reduced from three years to one year and ten months, through work. When I'd come back to my prison cell, I'd bring whatever I could from what we'd worked that day—tomatoes, onions. I'd walk as close to the cells as possible to give to the others what I knew they missed so much. From prison, you missed basic things a lot—fresh air, liberty, everything.

There were all kinds in prison. Many were there for embezzlement. I was in Jilava for a while. There was a midwife who'd been arrested for doing an abortion using parsley. I don't know what she did exactly, but the stem broke off and entered into the woman's uterus. It rotted in there and she got an infection from it. The child was lost because of the complications. Both the midwife and the woman were interrogated. The midwife was old and all that she wanted was to get out of prison before she died, not to die there. She said the prosecutor had asked why she'd done the abortion. She had responded that the woman was suffering; she felt sorry for her. But the woman died a few months later and the midwife ended up in prison for life. How she cried! She wasn't even allowed to get the monthly package and postcard that we got.

Then there was a doctor—handsome, tall. He was a gynecologist. He had done a curettage on someone who had an infection; in the process, he perforated something and she died on the spot. He was sentenced to ten years and one day. That [additional one] day meant life—beyond ten years, it was forever. Ceausescu was having a canal built. Prisoners were taken to the White Gate to work.[75] We weren't permitted anywhere near the place. I don't know what went on there, but many got sick there. It was obligatory labor. You had no choice. If an order was given to shovel a trainload of dirt in one day, it had to be done. If not, you were beaten to death. That meant a good journey to the other world. It was a very strict prison there. I don't know who intervened for the doctor, but whoever it was was very important and highly regarded. He was taken back to Jilava. There were other doctors like him. They didn't risk their lives for some small sum, but rather for a serious amount. They didn't give away their daily bread for just anything. But such is the risk. Sometimes it doesn't work out.

I got out in November 1981, I think. When I came home from the Rahova women's colony, barefoot, I didn't find anyone at home. They were all out working. They didn't know what to do when they saw me—my mother, child. They had heard I had escaped, that I had died. They couldn't believe their eyes.

Oh, from time to time, I'd done abortions for others when they were really down and out. I helped people in trouble. I didn't receive money. The women usually didn't have any, and I really did feel pity for them. That's how I am. Once, there was a doctor who had a niece. He was a dentist. He came to me and told me he had this niece, and, well, he fixed my teeth and I fixed the girl. She was three months pregnant. I used a thin tube and solution with her. He took me to B, where she stayed with her sister. I didn't take a root to do it that way because it was winter and you can't dig then; you can't even find it then. In the winter, you have to manage other ways. Anyway, there was no problem. I did an abortion now and then, but I was really afraid. And especially after I got out of prison; I wasn't going to end up there again. I said to myself, "They can harness oxen and horses for me, give me Ceausescu's villa, but never again." Once bitten, twice shy, as they say! After I got out, one came to me. H. [the village policeman] had warned me to be careful, that someone might come to me to have me do an abortion for her. If so, I was to let him know who it was. And one did come and said she was pregnant. Three months. I asked her if she wanted me to do something, and she said she wanted my help, if only with a word. I interrupted her, saying that she wanted to do me harm, which she denied. She only wanted to see herself free. I was afraid. It was nighttime when she came;

in the morning, I went to H. and told him: "Look, Mrs. C. came, and asked me to help her . . . " And so he made sure that her pregnancy was recorded at the dispensary, and she had the child.[76] And I was off the hook. H. was no longer afraid that I'd do any more abortions. And I didn't, except for myself. But for others, I didn't do that again.

Many women died. Most were married. There was a bad case once. A woman drank from the root *spins*. It's a yellow-colored poison. They found the root in a pot. She was poisoned by it. She left behind a little girl. A commission came to do a report. And then there were the village gynecological controls. They checked all of us. There was a girl, or so they think, who had a child whom she abandoned. The child was found thrown into the water. It [the child] was normal. Then they came to check everyone who was able to have a child. Only the old escaped. The midwife can confirm this; they checked all of us. They wanted to find out who the child's mother was, but they never found out. For all they knew, she was from another village. Whoever did what she did didn't hang around here. She took off.

Times were hard. They are now. I wouldn't do an abortion for anyone. I have sinned enough. It is a sin to do such a thing. It is an unforgivable sin perhaps; God knows, because he passes judgment on us all. I'm Orthodox. Around here, at Easter and Pentecost when everyone goes to confession, you have to come clean with what you've done in your life. I did. Oh, if I were to get pregnant again, I'd take care of myself because I can deal with my own sin, but not someone else's, only mine.

N.G.
*(born 1943, unmarried, medical assistant)*

The following story was related by N.G. about another woman.

In the more than 25 years that I have been an anesthetist, I've seen a lot of suffering and many cases of desperation. Needless to say, in the operating room or the recovery room, we need to concentrate on the patient's medical rather than emotional condition. That's not because our occupation makes us insensitive, as some would have it, but because, when intervening medically, nothing should interfere with the speed and certainty of a decision or gesture. It is a rule that we impose on ourselves and try to respect; it's generally in the patient's best interest. Of course, it is sometimes difficult to do. I'll tell you about one such case because the emotions and compassion I felt then, I feel as strongly today. It happened in 1982. I was on call. All of a sudden, the surgeon entered into our assistants' room and asked if there was an operation scheduled. I told him there wasn't. Without giving me any details, he asked me to go to the anesthesia room where there was a student who was in very serious condition. When I saw her, I was sickened. Her face had turned purple-black and she looked as if she had been tattooed. Her complexion was the color of indigo and covered with tiny dots the color of an eggplant. Only the two of us were in the room. I went up to her and, whispering, asked her to tell me what she had done. I assured her that whatever she said would remain confidential between us; I also told her that her condition was serious and I needed her help to know how to prepare for the operation. I reminded her that I too was a woman, that I was not that much older than she, that the doctor who was going to operate on her was a good person, and that we both wanted to help her and she could trust us. I kept on—that I could be her sister and that she should tell me what happened just as she'd tell her. I believed what I was saying, and I think she knew that; she also sensed that her condition might be grave. She told me she was a second-year philology student, and that her fiancé was a student in military medicine. Three weeks before, he, assisted by his mother, had injected saline solution into her uterus. She was in the third month of pregnancy. She had tried other methods, but nothing worked. Her student friends advised her to go to the cleaning woman for the German language department who would resolve her situation for 300 lei. Having heard that quite a few of her colleagues had suffered complications after seeing this woman, she had been frightened off. Her fiancé was also against this option, so they decided he should introduce a solution into her. After this, she took antibiotics. Everything was fine until that very morning. When she awakened, she looked just as she did then. I got her ready and took her into the operating room. When the surgeon opened her up, I saw that her uterus was in an advanced stage of putrefaction. We took her immediately to the emergency hospital to have her put on dialysis. It was too late. Her family retrieved her body from the emergency hospital's morgue. Later, I learned that she had been the daughter of the head of the secret police from a region in the east of the country.

M.P.

*(born 1951, engineer, married, two children)*

I married in 1977. I had finished university two years before and commuted about one hundred kilometers between Bucharest and the locale where the combine enterprise to which I had been sent was located. After we got married, we lived with my in-laws in a two-room apartment in a standard [socialist] building. My in-laws gave us their bedroom and moved into the living room. To get to the bathroom, you had to go through the living room. When my husband and I stayed out late in the city, we preferred to stay over at friends' rather than wake up my in-laws. On workday mornings when I got up early so I wouldn't miss my train, I felt guilty with respect to my in-laws because they, too, had to get ready for work. In addition to my exhaustion from commuting, each of us lived with the irritations of daily life in these cramped circumstances, which we each felt but which none of us would admit to the others. Fortunately, our relationship was warm and filled with mutual respect, each of us making an effort so that our communal life would be tolerable.

Not long after we married, I became pregnant. The decision that emerged from a family discussion was that I would keep the baby, despite the sacrifices this would mean for all of us. Actually, the fact that we wanted to have children and my in-laws wanted grandchildren from their only child was not a strong factor in our decision. We could have waited, resolved our housing problem, even if all that meant was that I found a job close to home so that I wouldn't have to commute every day. We were very young; we had time to have as many children as we wanted. After much reflection, what really influenced our decision were pragmatic matters. A pregnant woman could obtain a medical leave more easily if commuting became too overwhelming. And in general, people are more tolerant of a pregnant woman. In this condition, a woman benefited from a reduced work load, and from pre- and postnatal leaves. During this period, family, friends, acquaintances, and connections could all be mobilized to concentrate their efforts on helping me arrange a job in Bucharest. The facts that my husband had a position here and that I was pregnant were not in and of themselves sufficient reasons to get me off the hook from commuting. But during this time—almost a year, if we figured in additional sick days that I could use while pregnant—it would be possible to work on the mechanisms by which I could get a new job or promote myself professionally. That required my cultivating influential relations and informal arrangements, all of which involved financial expenditures, but ones that had to be made. The aim was for me to find a job closer to home. That's how we all thought about the situation; we were all in agreement. And, my husband and I wanted a child anyway—in fact, two. My husband had been an only child and he especially wanted us to have two. Our first came sooner than I would have liked, given the circumstances, but so it was. I became a mother.

My in-laws' optimism about our being able to kill two birds with one stone with this decision was rewarded by the end of my maternity leave; I found a job as an engineer at an enterprise in Bucharest. But by then our housing problem had become acute. It was very difficult for four adults and one child to live in two rooms. Hence, the savings that my in-laws had built over a lifetime of work was transformed into an advance toward an apartment for us. In those years, the state gave loans to those who were building or acquiring their own residences. We contracted for an apartment into which we hoped to be able to move within the year; meanwhile, our child was growing fast.

Not long after I stopped nursing I again became pregnant. Since we had gone that far, then why not all the way! So I had our second child. And then our problems really began because we were firmly decided against having more than two children. In the aftermath of a mass media campaign at the end of the 1970s about those who broke the anti-abortion law, doctors and other medical personnel were so frightened that it became terribly difficult to find someone who was willing to risk his or her liberty and career for the sake of doing an illegal abortion. Indeed, the doctor who had done a curettage for me before I was married had been arrested.

After I had given birth to my second child and until the middle of the 1980s, I became pregnant five more times. Four times I rid myself of the pregnancy by introducing something inside; once I had another curettage. In 1985 I finally succeeded in getting an IUD put in. I had acquired the IUD in 1981 but had been unable to get it fitted because I had not been able to do what was necessary to have someone do it. Just when I thought I had at last managed to arrange everything, I found myself with child again! And so I had to start all over: time and money to find someone to help me out, fear of the procedure itself and of the potential medical and civil consequences, recuperation, and so on. I believed each time would be the last because I was going to get the

IUD inserted, and, then, bam! I'd find myself impregnated again. After each of these traumas, a simple gesture of tenderness from my husband caused me to recoil. It was only with great effort that I managed not to dissolve into a hysterical crisis. I didn't know what other excuses I could invent to put off his advances. My obsessive fear about what might happen to me again was much greater than my need for affection. I began to hate the approach of nighttime. I began to feel guilty about what I was forcing my husband to live with. I rebelled against him, against myself, against everyone. I cried all the time. My nerves gave way, which broke the smoldering tension that so often filled entire days. Frustration, humiliation, and despair pitted us against each other. Tormented by this much turmoil between us, we'd try to remember that we were but two miserable passengers on the topsy-turvy vessel of life; our compassion would turn into lovemaking. And it would begin all over again! To prevent the deterioration of our relationship, my husband did all that he could to acquire that IUD. Eventually, he bought it for 1,500 lei from someone who had returned from Switzerland. Getting it fitted cost us 2,000 lei more plus several packs of cigarettes and coffee.[77]

It took me a while to get used to being free of this ever-present worry. The fear of becoming pregnant had become a part of my daily existence. The fear, the sense of humiliation, and memories of pain and hardship only slowly lightened their grip on me. Surgical interventions were done without anesthesia because it was increasingly difficult to obtain anesthetics; these had also fallen victim to the "rational use" of medicines that the regime had imposed. My fear of the excruciating pain and hemorrhaging that too often followed the sound method was exacerbated by a nagging feeling that perhaps something had remained inside;[78] that if I later arrived at the hospital and declared that I had had a spontaneous abortion I would be betrayed by my own body. It was humiliating to feel always like a hunted beast, or to wait endlessly in the desolate, dirty halls of a hospital permeated by an atmosphere of suffering and poverty, which somehow made just breathing all the more difficult. I was hospitalized four times for hemorrhaging and diagnosed for incomplete abortions. Fortunately, there were no visible signs of cuts, punctures, or lacerations on my cervix. I then had legal abortions done at the hospital. In fact, the last two times, the doctors didn't bother to ask questions. They obviously knew the real story.[79] And my official medical history already contained two or three spontaneous abortions; if there was ever to be an investigation, the doctors were covered. They could invoke a particular pathology—viral infections, fever, whatever— which had left my body vulnerable and weakened.

I already said that during these years I had had one curettage and four interruptions of a pregnancy using a sound. I made contact with the gynecologist who had done the curettage through a family friend who was a doctor, although with a different specialty. This procedure cost us 5,000 lei. I actually considered myself lucky because, by then, a curettage usually cost 7,000. The "discount" resulted from my having been one of two patients who was scheduled in such a way that the doctor only had to "lift" the necessary instruments once.[80] These procedures were done in the home of a close friend of the gynecologist; that the doctor only had to carry the instruments one time from his residence to his friend's enabled the other woman and myself to benefit from a preferential price.

To arrange for the abortion with a sound, I called upon a friend whose cousin was an assistant herself. It's true that she was not a specialist in gynecology, but she worked "cleanly."[81] She was experienced, and it only cost me 800 lei—because I was the friend of her cousin; otherwise, it would have cost me 1,000 lei. Moreover, since she worked in a hospital, if complications did arise, she could be very useful. This method did not work on the first try. It was only a few days after the second attempt that the elimination occurred. It seems simple, but it wasn't—at all. I hemorrhaged on the third day after this double-sound treatment, and with this, the fetus was finally eliminated. It already was ten or twelve weeks old. Things had begun to worsen on the second day of this episode; I began to bleed heavily and it wouldn't stop. I called the person who had induced the abortion, but to no avail. I couldn't imagine that I had so much blood and that I was losing it with such intensity. After several hours of waiting, during which time I tried to remain as immobile as possible, my husband decided to go find the person who had induced the abortion for me. He eventually found her and brought her home to see if she could stop the bleeding. We asked ourselves if something hadn't happened that would betray us. She told us I had to go to the hospital; there was nothing else to do in this situation. She reassured us that there were no visible signs of an intervention and that we had nothing to fear. My husband called the ambulance. The ambulance physician took my blood pressure. It was seven. He gave me vitamin K and something to stabilize my condition. When we got to the hospital, to my surprise and shame, I recognized the doctor on call. We had gone to high school together. He looked over my chart, examined me, and did not pose any questions. Of course he knew what I'd done. He asked how my children were, how we were getting along financially, and he told my husband to take care of me because I was very weakened from the loss of blood. I hadn't been too strong to begin with. He verified that nothing was left in my vagina, but had me remain in the hospital for three days so that my body could regain its stability.[82]

My husband and I were horribly traumatized, especially psychologically, by the reality of yet another abortion. It affected both of us profoundly, and for a long time we were afraid of another such situation. My pregnancy was quite advanced—more than twelve weeks. I had tried all kinds of methods. I even tried a concentrated infusion made from the flower of a plant that decorates the green spaces of the city and people's courtyards. A colleague at work told me it was effective. I knew it was quite toxic, but I didn't hesitate to try it. However, it didn't produce the desired effect, so I again resorted to an induced abortion. I was at home, several days after the procedure by injection. I felt that all of my blood had collected in one point and that it was going to be eliminated; there was no barrier within me strong enough to hold it back. I ran to the bathroom in a panic. I just made it to the tub and it gushed out of me. When I finally had the courage to look, I saw a small mass of blood that was moving in the stream of blood which oozed toward the drain. My scream escaped involuntarily from deep within me. It was no longer fear, nor humiliation, pain, guilt, nor despair. It wasn't even pity. It came from the emptiness inside of me out of which the quiet of death had been squeezed. Its life had been along the path of my scream. My husband wrapped the inert morsel in newspaper. But what to do with this little package? Where could we dispose of it? If we threw it in the garbage and someone found it? The simultaneous shock and fear made us paranoid; we began to imagine all manner of horror tales. Later on, when it was dark outside, my husband threw the little packet into a garbage can far from our house. We were unable to sleep that night; nighttime was a time for the innocent as well as for sinners. We sat facing each other. There was nothing to say. What could we have said? We smoked; we cried. We kept on crying.

Decree 770 was the underlying cause of the physical and emotional anguish suffered by so many women with regard to their reproductive lives. Their partners and families also felt the effects of the criminalization of abortion. For all practical purposes, modern contraceptives were unavailable. As a result, sexual intimacy was fraught with fear and anxiety lest another encounter result in a pregnancy. Despite the propagandized representations of a paternalist state that saw to the welfare of its citizens, these much-heralded "optimal conditions for the raising of large and healthy families" eluded most Romanians. Especially during the 1980s, Ceausescu's population shivered in dimly lit homes or stood endlessly in lines in the hope of minimally providing for themselves and their families. Shortly after the Ceausescu regime fell in 1989, its dark legacy began to come to light both in Romania and within the international arena. The tragic consequences of this epoch in Romanian history are the subject of the next chapter.

## CHAPTER 7

# Legacies of Political Demography

*"There are three kinds of lies: lies, damned lies, and statistics."*
MARK TWAIN, *Autobiography*, ATTRIBUTED TO DISRAELI[1]

*And when they believed in him, he devoured his children.*
VLADIMIR LEVCHEV, "STALIN (SATURN-SATAN)"

"Planned motherhood" as dictated by the Ceausescu regime affected the physical and emotional well-being not only of individual women, men, children, and families, but also of society as a whole. The consequences of the political demographic policies cast a dark shadow over the radiant past of the Socialist Republic of Romania's "golden era." Social and biological reproduction had become daily dramas, increasingly in conflict with each other. Sexuality and intimacy were fraught with fear—of an unwanted pregnancy, of having a confidence revealed to the secret police. This often intangible fear reverberated throughout the body politic that constituted Ceausescu's Romania, making citizens simultaneously complicitous with and resistant to the will of the Party/State.

With respect to pronatalist politics, among the tangible effects associated with resistance or complicity were an increase in the number of illegal abortions—and relatedly, maternal and infant mortality—and an increase in the number of unwanted children, many of whom were abandoned to the streets or to state institutions. An infant AIDS epidemic spread, especially among the children in institutions, although this fact was deliberately hushed up lest the image of Ceausescu's golden era be tarnished. Husbands and children too often found themselves widowers and orphans because a wife and mother had died in a desperate attempt to avoid bringing yet another innocent being into the harsh conditions of everyday life. A regime that celebrated women's contributions to the building of socialism, and that demanded the birth of children to that end, became the source of the deaths of too many women and children. In spite of the glittering rays of ideological propaganda, the multilateral deterioration of the physical, social, material, and spiritual conditions of life in Romania continued, officially unseen.[2]

Because the basic aims of research were politically manipulated, it became virtually impossible for specialists to evaluate the effects of the pronatalist policies. Empirical studies and reports ordered by the party hierarchy remained unavailable to the general scientific community, let alone the general public. Marked "for internal use" or "professional secret," their circulation was strictly regulated. However, since the fall of the Ceausescu regime, its dark legacies—particularly regarding political demography—have been revealed and are the subject matter of this chapter. Abandoned children, an infant AIDS epidemic, and international trafficking in children through private adoptions are but the most internationally publicized consequences of state-orchestrated childbearing. Other medical and social problems, such as high maternal and infant mortality rates and the emergence of street children as an urban phenomenon, also resulted, at least in part, from the pronatalist policies.[3]

## MEDICAL CONSEQUENCES

News of an infant AIDS epidemic, whose existence had been publicly suppressed during the final years of the Ceausescu regime, filled the world's media shortly after the regime's demise in 1989. But infant AIDS was not the only dramatic physical consequence that afflicted the politicized bodies of Romanian citizens. Maternal and infant mortality rates soared; the population's health in general was affected. Few epidemiological studies exist, however, and the data available are incomplete and unreliable.[4] Ultimately, politics dictated the parameters of medical research as well as of medical practices and determined the limits of social and scientific knowledge. Therefore, in attempting to make sense of the medical consequences of the pronatalist policies, existing data can only be interpreted in the context in which they were produced and used.

A cautionary word is appropriate about attributing too much power to demographic policies alone in determining what are complex social outcomes. On the one hand, age-specific male mortality has been consistently rising in Romania, as it has been elsewhere in the region, marking a demographic change. It is, however, clearly not a direct consequence of the pronatalist policies.[5] On the other hand, changes in the shape of the population's age distribution were indeed significantly affected by pronatalist policies; however, other factors such as urbanization, mass education, and widespread health care contributed to this process as well. Whereas the baby boom attributable to the 1966 law looks dramatic in sheer numerical terms, this cohort's incorporation into the educational and employment systems, as well as the marriage market, was mitigated by complex sociopolitical and institutional responses. The sociological significance of demographic trends differs markedly from their demographic characterization.

## Induced Abortions and Maternal Mortality

As elsewhere in the Soviet bloc, abortion was the primary method of fertility control in Romania, which was the extreme case among these countries (table 7.1).[6] It is generally assumed that Romanian women had, on average, between five and seven abortions during their reproductive lives. In Romania, the restricting of legal abortion combined with the lack of modern contraceptive options led to a dramatic increase in the practice of illegal abortion, in consequence of which many mothers ended up on death's doorstep. The relation between restricted access to legal abortion and modern contraception and increasing maternal mortality rates is a historical and comparative constant that varies little across cultures.[7] Indeed, Romania's maternal mortality rate skyrocketed over time. By 1989 it was the highest in Europe.[8]

It must nonetheless be emphasized that abortion-related statistics are highly variable and notoriously inaccurate.[9] The classification of an abortion as legal or illegal depended on a variety of factors. The official category of registered abortions included abortions that were legal according to the dictates of the law and legal according to the license taken by physicians who interpreted certain non–legally induced abortions as legal. As discussed in the preceding chapters, it was in the interest of individuals and institutions who provided abortion statistics to "round them down"—that is, to lower their numbers. This practice was applied to many other domains of statistical production, with statistics being manipulated according to the needs of the "plan." For example, in reporting agricultural and industrial production figures and natality figures, statistics tended to be inflated. Collusion was systemwide.

The purpose of numerical manipulation was to avoid sanctions, especially pecuniary ones. Again, the personnel at any hospital—from administrators to the medical cadre—knew that it was in their best interests to declare the smallest number of abortions possible. The number of legal abortions for which certificates were based on legitimate therapeutic grounds was relatively low, and varied little from year to year (see table 7.2). Recall that until 1985, women who were 40 years old or who had four or more children in their care were eligible for legal abortions. In 1985 the age limit and number of children were increased, the effects of which are seen in the table: in 1986 the number of incomplete abortions rose, meaning that more women had ended up in the hospital as a result of illegal abortions; fewer women were able to seek legal abortions on the grounds of age or number of children, and more abortions were attributed to medical causes. Regardless of the legal changes, the number of abortions continued to rise, and many of them were illegal, at least when initially performed (figure 7.1). Whenever political measures were reinforced throughout the hospital system, a temporary suspension of or adjustment to abortion-related prac-

TABLE 7.1   Abortion in Selected Countries, 1987

| Country | Abortions per 100 Live Births |
|---|---|
| Bulgaria | 102.8 |
| Czechoslovakia | 72.5 |
| Finland | 21.9 |
| France | 21.0 |
| GDR | 42.2 |
| FRG | 13.5 |
| Hungary | 67.3 |
| Italy | 33.9 |
| Romania | 131.1* |
| Sweden | 32.0 |
| England and Wales | 22.5 |
| Scotland | 14.1 |
| Yugoslavia | 102.2* |

SOURCE: Patterns of Fertility in Low-Fertility Settings, 1992, table 29, p. 70.
*Data for Romania are for 1985; for Yugoslavia, for 1984.

TABLE 7.2   Classification of Abortions by Reason, 1979–1988

| Year | Incomplete | Five Children* | Age of 45 Years** | Medical Cause |
|---|---|---|---|---|
| 1979 | 47.5 | 35.9 | 9.1 | 7.5 |
| 1980 | 47.5 | 36.1 | 8.6 | 7.8 |
| 1981 | 48.5 | 35.5 | 7.9 | 8.1 |
| 1982 | 49.9 | 34.8 | 7.2 | 8.2 |
| 1983 | 47.9 | 36.1 | 7.1 | 8.9 |
| 1984 | 41.3 | 41.4 | 7.7 | 9.6 |
| 1985 | 41.0 | 42.4 | 7.2 | 9.4 |
| 1986 | 68.6 | 14.1 | 0.9 | 16.4 |
| 1987 | 66.1 | 16.9 | 0.6 | 16.4 |
| 1988 | 60.1 | 22.8 | 0.5 | 16.6 |

SOURCE: Roznatovschi 1989.
   *Between 1979 and 1985, the woman could have been over 40 years of age.
   **Between 1979 and 1985, the woman had to have given birth to and have in her care four children.

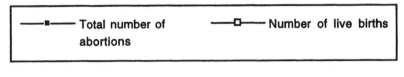

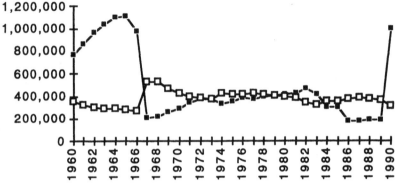

Figure 7.1: Number of Abortions and Live Births, 1960–1990.
*Sources:* Data courtesy of the Ministry of Health, Bucharest;
*Anuarul statistic al Romaniei, 1990.*

tices occurred. However, the heightened surveillance that was applied when the repressive screws were tightened did not endure indefinitely, and abortions resumed.[10]

Abortion statistics were falsified in various ways. For example, medical and statistics personnel devised broad statistical categories that allowed the facts to be obscured and facilitated shifting cases between legal and illegal categories. In this way, the medical profession managed to circumvent the political controls of the state to a certain degree. To illustrate, a report following up on a U.S. Agency for International Development (USAID) site visit to Romania provided interesting statistics on legally sanctioned abortion for the years 1983–1987, from which politically motivated statistical adjustments may be inferred (see table 7.3):[11] In 1985, for example, rape was cited as the underlying cause of 127,601 legal abortions. But in 1984, rape had officially accounted for only 32 abortions. The 1985 figure shows clearly how statistics became constructs of political necessity: despite further broadening of the anti-abortion law, rape still constituted a legal basis for abortion. Furthermore, because 1985 happened to be the last year in which already having four children remained a legitimate reason for a legal abortion, the number of abortions in this category was high.[12] This table also indicates consensus among physicians in their responses to political constraints on medical practice.

TABLE 7.3     Legally Sanctioned Interruptions of Pregnancy, 1983–1987

| Year | Spontaneous Abortions | More Than Four Children | Rape |
|------|----------------------|------------------------|------|
| 1983 | 199,867 | 151,846 | 54 |
| 1984 | 121,045 | 120,782 | 32 |
| 1985 | 20 | 128,372 | 127,601 |
| 1986 | 1 | 59 | 4,516 |
| 1987 | 118,390 | 30,388 | 29 |
| *Five-year total* | 499,323 | 431,447 | 132,232 |
| *Percent* | 30 | 29.4 | 9 |

SOURCE: *Women's Health, Family Planning, and Institutionalized Children in Romania,* 1991, p. 32.

Spontaneous abortions or miscarriages also offered physicians a great deal of classificatory latitude. In 1983, the year in which the natality figures reached their lowest level since 1966, there were 199,867 spontaneous abortions recorded. In 1985, after political-disciplinary measures had been reestablished throughout the hospital system, only 20 such abortions were recorded. Because of the political climate, physicians were reluctant even to report miscarriages. In 1986, but a single spontaneous abortion was noted. As surveillance lessened and everyone adjusted to the newer version of Decree 770, the reporting of spontaneous abortions resumed. By 1987, 118,390 miscarriages were on record.

According to an age-specific analysis of induced abortions (see figure 7.2), the greatest number of abortions occurred among women between the ages of 25 and 34, as did, coincidentally, the highest number of abortion-related deaths.

Following the issuance of Decree 770, the number of recorded abortions dropped sharply, from 973,447 to 205,783. Noticeable declines also occurred after the tightening of abortion measures in 1973, and again between 1983 and 1985. However, as already discussed, these subsequent declines were not nearly as dramatic, suggesting that by then the population had learned how to adapt more quickly to the imposition of additional restrictions. The number of abortions again crept up while the number of births slid back down.

Abortion data for the period 1979–1988 reveal other trends associated with the banning of abortion and lack of modern contraceptive alternatives.[13] Of the total number of registered abortions, approximately 60.1 percent were due to incomplete abortions. These women arrived at the hospital in need of emergency treatment for post-abortion complications. Note this estimate does not include women who died before reaching a hospital.[14] Medical doctors and clients alike attest to the fact that women ended up in the hospital out of dire necessity, already in the throes of

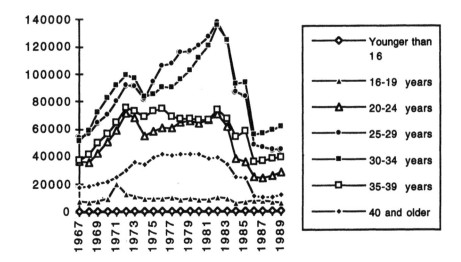

Figure 7.2: Number of Abortions by Age Group, 1967–1989.
*Source:* Data courtesy of the Ministry of Health, Bucharest.

secondary complications.[15] In 1989, for example, at one of Bucharest's largest maternity clinics, 3,129 women were hospitalized for complications associated with illegally performed abortions.[16]

As noted above, self-induced abortions often meant that many mothers died, leaving the children they already had motherless. From a reading of a selection of files at the Ministry of Health, it was painfully evident that many of the women who died as a result of illegal abortions left three or four children behind. Some of these women had had as many as ten abortions before this final tragedy. According to Mezei, 1,193 children were left motherless in 1989 from the consequences of illegal abortions.[17] It is generally accepted that women who already had one or two children were more likely to try to abort another pregnancy than a woman who had not yet given birth to a first or second child. In a recent study jointly conducted by several institutions, it was determined that the number of maternal deaths due to abortion generally increased in direct relation to the number of children to whom a woman had given birth. Among women who had previously given birth to one or two children, there were 18 abortion-related deaths per 100,000 live births; for women with three or four children, the number of deaths jumped to 48 per 100,000 live births. The death rate for women with more than four children was higher still, 67 per 100,000 live births.[18]

A word of caution in interpreting the category of maternal mortality is appropriate. In most of the available data, maternal mortality is specified and refers to the deaths of women who are already mothers. Hence, maternal mortality statistics do not typically include deaths of women who have not already borne children (who are not yet mothering). Young women who had become pregnant out of wedlock and married women who were not yet ready to have a first child are not usually included among these statistics.[19] Nonetheless, it seems that such data exist, although they are not readily accessible. Age-specific Ministry of Health data for 1984 concerning a sample of 449 women indicated that abortion-related female mortality was highest (174 deaths) among women who had two children (excepting those aged 40 and older). However, the next highest number of deaths (92) occurred among women who had no children, most of whom were between the ages of 15 and 24. The figures then return to the general pattern: there were 78 and 75 deaths recorded for mothers who already had one or three children, respectively.[20]

As discussed in chapter 5, to combat the rising incidence of illegal abortion and its link to maternal mortality, the all-too-familiar formulaic "intensification and diversification of health education for women" was recommended. Propaganda and instructional activities (e.g., conferences, slide shows, and films) illustrating the "evil consequences of abortion, the danger to the health and life of the woman, to [her] family, and society" were to be held throughout the country in enterprises with high numbers of female employees, in youth groups, and in villages. Films were to be shown in theaters around the country and in Bucharest.[21]

Throughout the years in which the pronatalist measures were in force, illegal abortions and their consequences contributed significantly to the disturbing increase in maternal deaths that earned Romania the highest maternal mortality rate in Europe. The French demographer Blayo estimated that in 1988 there were 204 deaths per 100,000 declared abortions in Romania; in the same year in the Soviet Union there were only 10 per 100,000. In France the data showed a variation between 0.5 and 1 death per 100,000 declared abortions over the years.[22] As may be seen in figure 7.3 (and table 7.3), abortion was the primary cause of maternal death.[23] Maternal deaths due to causes other than abortion-related practices generally decreased. However, there was a relatively consistent relationship between the number of maternal deaths due to obstetrical risk and restrictive legislative activity: the number of maternal deaths due to causes other than abortion rose each time the abortion-related legislation was tightened—for example, in 1968, and again in 1973 and 1986 (after which obstetrical risk again declined). Although such increases may be attributed in part to "politically correct" statistical manipulation, these temporary shifts better reflect the increase in the number of births and decrease in the number of illegal abortions immediately following abortion-related proscriptions. With the benefit of experience, social adaptation (including partial accommodation by the health system) to legal constraints occurred with greater rapidity.

The effects of the political demographic policies may be seen in the

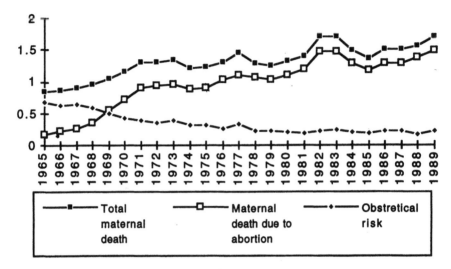

Figure 7.3: Indicators of Maternal Mortality per 100 Live Births, 1965–1989.
*Source:* Data courtesy of the Ministry of Health, Bucharest.

abortion-related maternal mortality figures given in table 7.4 (and figure 7.3). In 1965, the last year when abortion was legal, of a total of 237 maternal deaths, 47 were due to complications stemming from abortion. In 1967, after Decree 770 had been in effect for one year, the number of maternal deaths had tripled, to 143 abortion-related deaths (of a total of 481 deaths). By 1989, 545 out of 627 deaths were due to post-abortion complications. As can be seen, the obstetrical risk for abortions initiated in hospitals was low. Over the years, the maternal mortality rate rose from 86 deaths per 100,000 live births in 1965 to 169 per 100,000 live births in 1989; of those, 87 percent were related to abortion.[24] It has been estimated that during the 1980s, "every year approximately 500 otherwise healthy women of childbearing age died from postabortion hemorrhage, sepsis, abdominal trauma, and poisoning."[25]

Despite the state's glorification of motherhood, between 1965 and 1989 approximately 9,452 women were said to have died from abortion-related complications.[26] The heartbreaking and chilling irony of Ceausescu's pronatalist policies was that illegal abortion was the predominant method of fertility control as well as the predominant cause of mortality among women of childbearing age. If the state punishes physicians who, for humanistic or financial reasons, perform illegal abortions where legal abortion is severely restricted and modern contraceptive options are unavailable, an increase in maternal deaths due to unsafe abortions is inevitable.

Upon the fall of the Ceausescu regime in December 1989, most women's

TABLE 7.4    Maternal Mortality, 1965–1991

| | Deaths from Post-Abortion Complications | | Deaths Attributable to Other Obstetrical Causes | | Total Maternal Deaths | |
|---|---|---|---|---|---|---|
| Year | Number | Per 1,000 live births | Number | Per 1,000 live births | Number | Per 1,000 live births |
| 1965 | 47 | 0.17 | 190 | 0.68 | 237 | 0.85 |
| 1966 | 64 | 0.23 | 171 | 0.63 | 235 | 0.86 |
| 1967 | 143 | 0.27 | 338 | 0.64 | 481 | 0.91 |
| 1968 | 192 | 0.36 | 314 | 0.60 | 506 | 0.96 |
| 1969 | 258 | 0.55 | 233 | 0.50 | 491 | 1.05 |
| 1970 | 314 | 0.73 | 183 | 0.43 | 497 | 1.16 |
| 1971 | 363 | 0.91 | 159 | 0.40 | 522 | 1.31 |
| 1972 | 370 | 0.95 | 136 | 0.35 | 506 | 1.30 |
| 1973 | 364 | 0.96 | 148 | 0.39 | 512 | 1.35 |
| 1974 | 381 | 0.89 | 136 | 0.32 | 517 | 1.21 |
| 1975 | 385 | 0.91 | 131 | 0.32 | 516 | 1.23 |
| 1976 | 432 | 1.04 | 110 | 0.26 | 542 | 1.30 |
| 1977 | 469 | 1.11 | 145 | 0.34 | 614 | 1.45 |
| 1978 | 447 | 1.07 | 89 | 0.22 | 536 | 1.29 |
| 1979 | 422 | 1.03 | 92 | 0.22 | 514 | 1.25 |
| 1980 | 441 | 1.11 | 86 | 0.21 | 527 | 1.32 |
| 1981 | 456 | 1.20 | 77 | 0.20 | 533 | 1.40 |
| 1982 | 511 | 1.48 | 78 | 0.23 | 589 | 1.71 |
| 1983 | 471 | 1.47 | 76 | 0.24 | 547 | 1.71 |
| 1984 | 449 | 1.28 | 73 | 0.21 | 522 | 1.49 |
| 1985 | 425 | 1.18 | 68 | 0.19 | 493 | 1.37 |
| 1986 | 488 | 1.29 | 83 | 0.22 | 571 | 1.51 |
| 1987 | 491 | 1.28 | 84 | 0.22 | 575 | 1.50 |
| 1988 | 524 | 1.38 | 67 | 0.18 | 591 | 1.56 |
| 1989 | 545 | 1.49 | 82 | 0.22 | 627 | 1.71 |
| 1990 | 181 | n/a | 82 | n/a | 263 | n/a |
| 1991 | 114 | n/a | 69 | n/a | 183 | n/a |

SOURCE:  Data courtesy of the Ministry of Health, Bucharest.

bodies were liberated from the grip of the centralized state. The day after the execution of the Ceausescus, abortion was fully legalized in Romania.[27] Urban and rural women alike expressed gratitude for the legalization of abortion. The fear of unsafe abortion had colored sexuality in Romania, especially the sexual lives of women, married or not. The decriminalization of abortion had an immediate effect on the number of legal abortions recorded, as well as on the number of abortion-related maternal deaths. In 1990 abortions outnumbered live births by a ratio of three to one. The total fertility rate quickly fell below replacement level, although a clear distinction between urban and rural rates was evidenced: city women had "almost one child fewer" than rural women.[28] By the summer of 1990, the principal hospitals in Bucharest alone were each reporting 70 to 100 abortions performed daily.

Within one year, a dramatic drop in abortion-related maternal deaths was also recorded: from 545 to 181. Although the maternal mortality rate declined to 83 per 100,000 inhabitants, abortion-related deaths still accounted for 66 percent of the 1990 total.[29] So great were the traumas associated with the pronatalist policies that, months after the legalization of abortion, the Ministry of Health still received files of mothers who had died as a result of illegal abortions, unaware of the momentous changes. Moreover, according to Serbanescu et al., because nonmedical abortionists may be "more accessible, more affordable, or more familiar, the practice of illegal abortion is likely to continue, especially among women who seek abortion beyond the legal gestational limit of 12 weeks."[30]

Here it is important to mention that abortion remains the predominant method of fertility control. Modern contraceptive knowledge and use in Romania were limited before 1989, a consequence of the political demographic policies as well as traditional beliefs and practices. Because contraceptive use is generally related to educational level, without a concerted campaign to educate the population, including men and medical practitioners, abortion will continue to be the method of choice for women to resolve fertility issues. Contraceptives are increasingly available; however, their cost in the current period of economic inflation is often prohibitive. Early on, doctors voiced their concerns that raising the price of legal abortions would tempt poor women in particular to seek cheaper abortions performed by unqualified persons, thereby reproducing the unsafe conditions of the recent past. Wealthier women escape these problems by paying for private services, which provide personal attention, privacy, and more sterile conditions. Unfortunately, adjusting prices upward is easier than introducing family planning and sex education on a widespread scale, or ensuring the production and distribution of contraceptives. This has meant that women's health, especially among the poor and less educated, remains hostage to other interests that are considered to be of greater priority.

These same physicians stressed that women must be dissuaded from using abortion as the primary method of fertility control. However, men and women are reluctant to use contraceptives for a variety of reasons, among which are fear of side effects (which, as useful disinformation, were highly publicized under the regime), partner resistance (particularly by men), price, and difficulty of obtaining contraceptives and contraceptive knowledge.[31] It has been widely recognized that a multifaceted educational campaign about sexuality and contraception is critical to changing sexual and reproductive habits in Romania. This situation is aggravated by the lack of behavior modification among those who are knowledgeable about modern contraceptive use.[32]

A host of other problems affected women throughout the period of pronatalist policies. Doctors noted that women complained regularly about depression, nervous disorders, sexual problems, and social isolation.[33] Although post-abortion morbidity data are virtually nonexistent, health officials readily refer to problems that frequently resulted from illegal abortions: "damage to the uterine cervix, chronic infection, and severe anemia that, in turn, increase the risk of postpartum hemorrhage and infection, infertility, preterm birth, and low birthweight."[34] Serbanescu et al. have estimated that "nearly 20 percent of the 4.9 million women of reproductive age are thought to have suffered impaired fertility."[35] Despite an assumed relationship between political demography and morbidity, there is little evidence to substantiate anything other than probable influences. It is extremely difficult to disaggregate factors that emerged from the consequences (intended or otherwise) of centralized planning and increasing neo-Stalinist state control, which, in turn, gave rise to diverse socio-psychological and physical ailments. It is the totalizing context of the Ceausescu regime itself that must ultimately be analyzed.[36] For women, the state's "multilaterally developed" attempts to control their fertility were a source of tension throughout the childbearing years. To this were added everyday stresses—social, economic, medical, sexual—caused by the precariousness of existence in Ceausescu's Romania.

## Infant and Child Mortality

Ceausescu's pronatalist policies did contribute to an increase in the birthrate. Ironically, however, these policies also contributed to an increase in infant and maternal deaths (see table 7.5). Over the years of communist rule in Romania, infant mortality declined markedly: for example, in 1948 there were 142.7 infant deaths for every 1,000 live births; by 1989 that number had dropped to 26.9 infant deaths for every 1,000 live births.[37] Nonetheless, relative to infant mortality rates in other industrialized countries, the Romanian rate remained high. Moreover, the figures are unreliable. Infant mortality rates in the former communist countries were generally underreported; in Romania, statistical distortion was politically motivated. Although the number of infant deaths dropped more or less continuously after the interwar years, the infant mortality rate varied in accordance with a number of factors, not the least of which was the number of births. As has already been discussed, the birthrate also tended toward decline—in spite of the political demographic legislation, but in keeping with modern trends in industrialized countries. Like the birthrate, infant mortality rates

TABLE 7.5    Infant Morality and Maternal Death
from Abortion, 1965–1991

| Year | Number of Abortions | Number of Maternal Deaths from Abortion | Infant Mortality Rate per 1,000 Births |
|------|---------------------|------------------------------------------|-----------------------------------------|
| 1965 | 1,112,704 | 47 | 44.1 |
| 1966 | 973,447 | 64 | 46.6 |
| 1967 | 205,783 | 143 | 46.6 |
| 1968 | 220,193 | 192 | 59.5 |
| 1969 | 257,496 | 258 | 54.9 |
| 1970 | 292,410 | 314 | 49.4 |
| 1971 | 341,740 | 363 | 42.4 |
| 1972 | 380,625 | 370 | 40.0 |
| 1973 | 375,752 | 364 | 38.1 |
| 1974 | 334,621 | 381 | 35.0 |
| 1975 | 359,417 | 385 | 34.7 |
| 1976 | 383,220 | 432 | 31:4 |
| 1977 | 378,990 | 469 | 31.2 |
| 1978 | 394,636 | 447 | 30.3 |
| 1979 | 403,776 | 422 | 31.6 |
| 1980 | 413,093 | 441 | 29.3 |
| 1981 | 427,081 | 456 | 28.6 |
| 1982 | 468,041 | 511 | 28.0 |
| 1983 | 421,386 | 471 | 23.9 |
| 1984 | 303,123 | 449 | 23.4 |
| 1985 | 302,838 | 425 | 25.6 |
| 1986 | 183,959 | 488 | 23.2 |
| 1987 | 182,442 | 491 | 28.9 |
| 1988 | 185,416 | 524 | 25.3 |
| 1989 | 193,084 | 545 | 26.9 |
| 1990 | 992,265 | 181 | n/a |
| 1991 | 866,834 | 114 | n/a |

SOURCE: Data courtesy of the Ministry of Health, Bucharest.

were affected by the abortion legislation. As Baban and David point out, the infant mortality rate had been at 46.6 in 1966 when Decree 770 went into effect; by 1968 it had climbed up to 59.9, giving Romania one of the highest rates in Europe—a distinction that would be maintained until the demise of the regime.[38] Nonetheless, infant mortality did decline after 1968, until the next legislative decision, after which another slight increase occurred in 1974. An almost continuous decline followed, lasting until the next round of abortion-related legislation. Not surprisingly, infant mortality increased in 1984 and 1985, and hit a high in 1987. Although by 1989 the infant mortality rate had dropped to 26.9 (see table 7.5 and figure

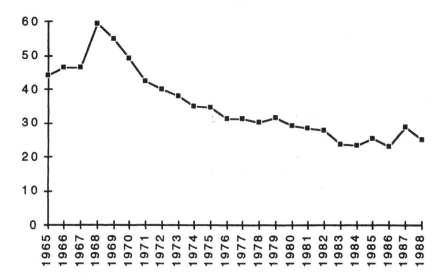

Figure 7.4: Infant Mortality Rate per 1,000 Live Births, 1965–1988. *Source: Anuarul statistic al Romaniei, 1990*: 67.

7.4), it was still among the highest in Europe.[39] In comparison with most other countries, Romania fared poorly. In Hungary, the infant mortality rate was 15.7 deaths per 1,000 live births; in Bulgaria, 13.6 deaths per 1,000 live births.[40] In 1990 Romania's infant mortality rate remained high, with 25.3 deaths per 1,000 live births recorded in the first six months.[41]

The positive relation between the criminalization of abortion and an increasing maternal mortality rate is stronger than that between criminalization and an increasing infant mortality rate. Again, it is difficult to attribute direct causality, particularly in a context of worsening socioeconomic conditions. During the winter months, the lack of heating itself constituted a threat to infant survival. Pediatricians often mentioned this, also noting that hospitals in Bucharest were better off than most others in terms of infrastructural resources. One physician whispered that the infant wards were the only ones heated regularly in Bucharest, an arrangement secretly agreed upon among medical personnel; this was an attempt to reduce the number of infant deaths. This same doctor doubted that hospitals outside of the capital possessed the necessary backup energy sources.

Among the principal causes of infant death in Romania were malnutrition, respiratory ailments, and congenital anomalies.[42] Infants especially at risk were those whose mothers were 40 years of age and older (49.2 percent had mothers in this age group), infants who weighed less than 5.47 pounds at birth, and those who were born in rural areas. (In 1988 infant mortality in rural areas was 27.8; in urban areas it was 23.)[43]

Just as physicians were politically responsible for promoting the birthrate plan, so too were they responsible for reducing the high infant mortality rates. Doctors were called to task for "[not] respecting the obligatory program of home visits to evaluate a child's development and to detect the first signs of illness."[44] By 1988 the registration of live births was delayed, often up to 15 days. The official rationale for this delay was that those in rural areas where communication networks and transportation were more problematic would then have adequate time to report live births, deaths, and so on. But as many commented, this two-week period allowed time to determine whether an infant was likely to survive the first difficult phase of life, and to adjust infant mortality figures accordingly.[45] If an infant died during this grace period, a doctor might attempt to convince the mother to agree to list the child as a stillbirth. A physician explained: "If you are not registered alive, then you are not registered dead either [i.e., as an infant mortality statistic]."

However, not all mothers were prepared to cooperate with this strategy. Some were intent on receiving the minuscule financial compensation to which they thought they were entitled for bearing children, but in order to do so the infant had to be in the mother's care. A mother had to be convinced that declaring a child a stillbirth was a humanitarian gesture. Otherwise, the physician was potentially vulnerable to accusations and political trials. If the mother did not agree to reclassify her child's birth status, then the physician was subject to the fines related to not fulfilling the infant mortality plan.

Children between the ages of one and four were also vulnerable to premature death. In 1988, Romania had the highest European mortality rate for children in this age group (2.2 percent); respiratory ailments, accidents, and congenital anomalies ranked as principal causes.[46] Children living in rural areas, as well as adult males, were at higher risk than those in urban areas or adult females. Yet again, it is difficult to posit a direct causal relationship between child mortality and political demographic policies. For example, a party activist, reporting in 1977 on the demographic situation in the Constanta region, summarized the diverse potential factors contributing to deaths among young children. Among these factors were the prevalence of infectious diseases, especially for children attending nursery school, where contagion was more likely. In this same discussion, attention was drawn to the problem of nutrition and its role in promoting good health. The quantitative measure of caloric intake suggested that the daily intake of children at nursery schools or kindergartens was actually somewhat higher than the "necessary 1,300 calories per day." However, this caloric "excess" was qualitatively problematic, most of these calories having come from processed carbohydrates such as flour and sugar products. The caloric intake from proteins, fruits, vegetables, and fats was insufficient.[47]

The divide between quantity and quality widened steadily in the 1980s. Quantitative measures became the literal representations of the "new socialist person." Scientific or rational nutrition provided this newly constituted being with correlated height, weight, and caloric intake prescriptions. Pregnant women were instructed about proper diets so that the future labor force would consist of healthy, fit bodies. Quantitative data were modified as necessary. However, such sleights of hand could not be applied to everyday experience. Infants, children, and women—the objects of intense scrutiny—continued to die, despite the "ideal conditions" accorded their care by the paternalist state, which discursively championed their significance in the development of socialism.

## AIDS in Romania

Political demography, combined in diabolical fashion with the willful neglect of the general population's living conditions, contributed to the horror that became one of the most highly publicized legacies of the former regime: an infant AIDS epidemic. Infants abandoned to hospitals, orphanages, and the streets ended up in state institutions. The first case of AIDS was reported in 1985; however, knowledge about it was firmly and deliberately repressed by the regime. Despite this censorship, in 1988 a lengthy paper on the pathogenesis and diagnosis of AIDS was published by the Ministry of Health. It concluded "with the instruction that it was forbidden to enter a diagnosis of AIDS or HIV infection on medical certificates; one was only permitted to refer to an opportunistic infection or pneumonia."[48] Statistical evidence was again consciously distorted; medical practice was again subjugated to political interest.

One result was that blood was not screened, which, in turn, served as a source of a quietly burgeoning infant AIDS epidemic. In one of the more cynical examples of a disinformation campaign, the dangers of AIDS transmission were minimized in a brochure issued by the Institute for Hygiene and Public Health:

> Persons at high risk for infection must be conscious that they can transmit this illness to others, and consequently they must be excluded from donating blood, plasma, organs, etc. *Furthermore, the danger of transmitting AIDS through blood transfusion or the administration of blood-based preparations is practically eliminated through measures taken with respect to the selection of blood donors and exclusion of those contaminated with the HIV virus, laboratory screening of blood to identify and exclude contaminated blood.*[49]

As the Rothmans discussed in their Helsinki Watch report, Romania was not an obvious high-risk country for an AIDS epidemic. Drug trafficking through Eastern Europe was extremely limited during the socialist era (although Eastern Europe became an East-West corridor after 1989); moreover, most Romanians were too poor to support drug habits. Homosexuality was culturally and politically condemned, and punishable by law. Travel to and especially from Romania was insignificant, hence "the handful of cases that appeared in the mid-1980s might still be a handful—if not for the additional fact that some one or another of them donated blood."[50]

The insidious role of the political demographic policies in contributing to a tragedy in the making was woven into the webs of institutional complicity and negligence. To combat high infant mortality, doctors attempted to control the afflictions to which infants succumbed and for which they themselves could be held accountable. To this end, injections of antibiotics were routinely given. However, these injections were given with unsterilized syringes that were used repeatedly. Disposable needles did not exist, and those administering injections rarely took the time to sterilize a syringe after it had been used.[51] Curiously, microtransfusions of blood were also given to failing infants. Microtransfusions were thought by some to endow these children with "proteins, hemoglobin and antibodies, and . . . boost the infant's immunological system and nutritional system."[52] Instead, they challenged the fledgling immunological systems of their recipients. Recent data indicate that by the end of 1990 there were 1,094 registered cases of infant/child AIDS (zero months–twelve years of age) although the mode of transmission varied (see table 7.6).[53] It must be noted that because the available data do not distinguish between persons who are HIV-positive and those who have AIDS, it is difficult to make firm claims about the prevalence of AIDS in Romania.

After the execution of the Ceausescus, the world learned of the institutionalized hell to which abandoned and orphaned children had been consigned. Medical personnel, human rights workers, and international organizations offered compassionate assistance to the Romanians. Western media were filled with heart-wrenching stories: "Romania's AIDS Babies: A Legacy of Neglect"; "Fight against AIDS Lags in Romania"; "W.H.O. Emergency Team Is Sent to Romania to Assess AIDS Cases."[54] Foreign aid donations supplied disposable syringes. Romanian medicine became the focus of international attention, but the multiple problems confronting the medical profession and medical practice were (and remain) daunting. As one Romanian physician concerned about the poor state of public health in his country commented: "Here, people do not have respect for their own bodies." He attributed much of this to the destructive effects, understood in their totality, of the former regime. Some physicians still insisted in 1990 that AIDS was not a real problem in their country, claiming that the epidemic among children was confined to that population. Such attitudes do not disappear overnight.

TABLE 7.6    AIDS Cases by Age Group, 1990–1993

| Age Group | 1990 | 1991 | 1992 | 1993 |
|---|---|---|---|---|
| 0–11 months | 392 | 461 | 469 | 475 |
| 1–4 years | 700 | 1,124 | 1,588 | 1,860 |
| 5–9 years | 0 | 9 | 39 | 121 |
| 10–12 years | 2 | 5 | 5 | 5 |

SOURCE:    Data courtesy of the Ministry of Health, Bucharest.

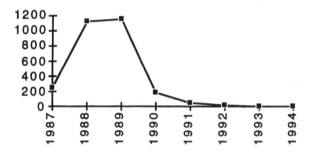

Figure 7.5: New AIDS Cases among Children,
1987–1994. *Source: Situation de l'infection HIV-SIDA
dans le monde et en Roumanie*, 1995.

Combined Romanian and international efforts may have stemmed the
tide of the infant AIDS epidemic, as suggested by figure 7.5.[55] However, the
figures presented in figure 7.5 and table 7.6 (both from Ministry of Health
data) do not readily correspond, unless the definition of "children" differs.
According to the table, in 1993 there were 475 cases of AIDS diagnosed
among infants zero to eleven months of age (up from the number of cases
registered between 1990 and 1993). The reliability of these data has been
questioned by some foreign specialists, who are concerned that the dramatic drop indicated in figure 7.5 may reflect distortion of the actual situation in the interest of convincing Western institutions that substantive
progress has been made.[56]

Although the infant/child AIDS epidemic may have been attributed
largely to the consequences of the pronatalist policies (i.e., increased institutionalization of unwanted children) combined with the administration
of microtransfusions of tainted blood and the use of unsterilized syringes,
the rise in the number of adult cases cannot be attributed to these same
causes. Nonetheless, it is worth noting that adult AIDS has increased steadily since 1990. The deliberate suppression of HIV and AIDS data in the

TABLE 7.7    AIDS Cases by Age and Gender, 1990–1993

| | 1990 | | 1991 | | 1992 | | 1993 | |
|---|---|---|---|---|---|---|---|---|
| Age Group | Male | Female | Male | Female | Male | Female | Male | Female |
| 13–14 | 0 | 2 | 1 | 2 | 2 | 3 | 3 | 4 |
| 15–19 | 3 | 2 | 3 | 2 | 3 | 2 | 3 | 2 |
| 20–24 | 7 | 6 | 9 | 7 | 10 | 12 | 10 | 17 |
| 25–29 | 6 | 7 | 8 | 7 | 10 | 8 | 11 | 15 |
| 30–34 | 10 | 5 | 13 | 9 | 13 | 12 | 17 | 17 |
| 35–39 | 4 | 4 | 7 | 8 | 10 | 11 | 14 | 15 |
| 40–49 | 7 | 3 | 12 | 4 | 14 | 7 | 16 | 12 |
| 50–59 | 7 | 2 | 8 | 5 | 8 | 6 | 10 | 6 |
| over 60 | 0 | 0 | 1 | 0 | 3 | 0 | 3 | 0 |
| Total | 44 | 31 | 62 | 44 | 73 | 61 | 87 | 88 |

SOURCE: *Anuarul statistic 1994*, 258–59.

mid-1980s transformed the spread of adult AIDS into an unintended consequence of the demographic policies and raises familiar questions about the reliability of the number of cases reported, and about the incidence of maternal transmission of HIV/AIDS to infants. There was an official total of 75 adult AIDS cases reported in 1990; in 1991 the total rose to 106; by 1992 it had increased to 134; and by 1994 to 175 (see table 7.7).

The total number of infant/child and adult cases reported between 1985 and 1994 was 3,119. Of these, 92 percent, or 2,885, were among infants or children. The young also accounted for 92 percent of the total AIDS deaths during this period: 1,067 children died out of a total of 1,157; among known adult cases, 87 died.[57] The highest incidence among adults has been among heterosexual men and women, and among people living in Bucharest (52 percent) and the port city of Constanta (24 percent).[58] The rise in female AIDS cases is most likely a result of increased prostitution, unsafe sex practices, and drug use.[59] Radio Free Europe/Radio Liberty reported in one of its final editions (no. 240) that the Romanian minister of health, Iulian Mincu, had proposed that brothels be legalized as a means of combatting the growing incidence of adult AIDS. The minister of health would be well advised to also implement nationwide sexual and contraceptive education. As discussed above, numerous studies on contraceptive knowledge and use conducted since 1989 have made it clear that, despite improvement, both knowledge and practice remain inadequate. Otherwise, cases of adult AIDS and sexually transmitted diseases will undoubtedly continue to grow in number.

SOCIO-INSTITUTIONAL LEGACIES:
ABANDONMENT, INSTITUTIONALIZATION, AND ADOPTION

*You read this, reread it, and it's not possible to believe what's going on. . . . At this*
*children's home, all manner of things . . . in flagrant contradiction of educational*
*norms, of human decency ultimately, with the particular care accorded children by*
*our country, especially children without parents.*

Scinteia, DECEMBER 11, 1988

Soon after the Ceausescu regime fell, the plight of Romania's abandoned children surfaced. The political demographic policies bore directly on the institutionalization of children, many of whom—unwanted by their families—were abandoned to the "family" of the state that had demanded them. International humanitarian efforts mobilized quickly to help the Romanians deal with the macabre institutionalized "care," which, like AIDS, had been kept hidden from public view. Organizations and individuals of all ages from the world over joined the Romanians in alleviating the immediate pain of these hapless *ceausei*—the children so named after Ceausescu's pronatalist policies.

Abandonment and institutionalization are not recent phenomena in Romania or elsewhere; however, the conditions surrounding both are unique in Romanian history. The institutionalization of abandonment as social practice forms part of the broader history of policing reproduction. Kertzer has detailed the development of infant abandonment in Italy. The institutional system that evolved there spread "throughout much of southern Europe, and later into Russia." He has raised paradoxical issues that are relevant to, although radically different in context from, the Romanian situation: "How, in this most family-centered of Western societies, could so many babies be cast out from their families? How, in a population so famous for its distrust of and aversion to government, could people so regularly give up their babies to civil authorities?"[60]

Romanians are family-centered, and, especially during the 1980s, feared their government. Yet, during the later years of the Ceausescu regime, there were more children than beds in the state institutions designated to care for them. A confluence of factors led to the overcrowding, among which were poverty, exhaustion, and perverse disinformation about the generosity of the state to its citizens, especially to those in need.

The establishment of surrogate "care" and "educational" institutions was consistent with the state's exercise of its paternalist obligations. If and when families did not fulfill their parental roles, then the state took on the "fostering" of these children. In the 1980s abandoning a child was often the consequence of despair combined with an internalized dependence on the state for the basics of life: the state generally controlled when and how much heat, water, and light households and state institutions had. Centralized production and distribution affected what families had to eat. (In this respect, the rise of the second economy paralleled that of illegal abortions; these were the means through which people managed their daily lives.)

Some mothers left their infants in the hospital; others abandoned them to state institutions on a temporary or long-term basis; still others left them to the streets.[61] Infanticide is not common, although punitive statutes exist(ed) in the legal code, as in article 177. The care of children by people other than their biological parents is culturally embedded.[62] However, during the Ceausescu years, increasing numbers of parents were unable either to call upon such networks or to support another mouth to feed.[63] They frequently left their children at state institutions with the intent of bringing them home at a later date. Those who failed to find the children they had entrusted to the care of the paternalist state learned why—as did the rest of the world—when the regime collapsed.[64] The squalor of human existence that lay hidden from sight did not figure in the rhetorical representations of the socialist public sphere and the role of the ideal socialist family within it. Tragically, that role was simultaneously exalted verbally and abused materially, to the detriment of generations to come.


## The Institutionalization of Children

The institutions in which the fates of too many children had been sealed were not all orphanages. Some provided long-term residential care for diverse categories of children, among whom were orphans whose parents were dead or unknown to them. Many others were (and are) "social orphans," children who have been abandoned or voluntarily given over to state institutions by living parents. Parents may jointly institutionalize a child; in many instances, however, it is mothers—single or divorced—who did (and do) so. These women also tend to have limited financial, educational, and emotional resources to offer their children, the majority of whom are "legitimate." (In Romania, legitimacy is based on the father's formal recognition of his child, regardless of the parents' marital status.)

The Romanian institutional system was byzantine in organization, with the care of minors divided among the Ministries of Health, Education, and Labor depending on the child's age and physical and mental condition.[65] The Ministry of Health was responsible for children age one to three. A majority of these children had been abandoned at birth or as infants for socioeconomic reasons; over time and as a result of the medicalization of their care, what had been attributed to the social origins of many of their problems instead became "medical cases."[66] After the age of three (and until the age of eighteen), "normal" children were transferred to children's homes overseen by the Ministry of Education or Labor, which was responsible for turning them into productive citizens (through knowledge and work). Yet again, each ministry focused on its specialty—education or work—as the primary means of satisfying the needs of their wards.[67]

Some of these institutions housed children who had been diagnosed as "unrecoverable." These children from whom God seemingly had looked away (to borrow from the Romanian surrealist poet Mircea Dinescu) were disabled in various ways. Some were blind, others were mentally deficient, yet others had physical handicaps. Thought to be incapacitated by such ailments, these children were condemned by Darwinian notions separating the fit from the unfit. Labeled "nonproductive" in a society ideologically dependent on production, the handicapped were effectively sentenced to death. "It is a place they go to die," said one medical director of a facility from which the productive and nonproductive were selected to be sent to other institutions, where they awaited their fate.[68] Consigned to oblivion, the handicapped became the victims of systematic, institutional neglect. Many of the physically and mentally handicapped were assigned to the Ministry of Labor (rather than, for example, the Ministry of Health).[69] The logic behind this bureaucratic allocation was linked to the formation of productive new socialist citizens. However, as unproductive members of society, these children were virtually ignored. The Ministry of Labor was neither interested in nor professionally prepared to deal with their special needs. Conditions in these institutions exaggerated those on the outside. Heat, hot water, adequate clothing and food were even scarcer.

The human needs of these youngsters had been officially obliterated by the designation of a label: "unrecoverable."[70] Their vacant stares and traumatized small bodies provided international photo opportunities, the results of which captured the hearts of the world and brought international assistance to post-Ceausescu Romania. Journalists provided stomach-turning and poignant tales about the dire plight of the "handicapped." It was clear to specialists that many of these children could have been productive members of society had they been offered therapeutic or rehabilitation programs and basic human warmth. Newspaper articles were filled with stories such as the following:

> Down the hall, other cribs hold smaller children, pale skeletons suffering from malnutrition and disease. Despite the heat of the day, several of the children are wrapped in dirty blankets. From one still bundle, only a bluish patch of scalp is visible. Asked if the child inside is alive, an orderly says, "Of course," and pulls back the covers. The tiny skeleton stirs. . . .

> Approximately 100,000 children and adolescents up to 18 years of age remain in the care of the state, many confined to institutions indescribable in their filth, degradation and misery—understaffed and ill-equipped nurseries, preschool orphanages and homes for the handicapped and "unrecoverables."[71]

Aid of all kinds poured in. Foreign and Romanian humanitarian organizations filled the reopened spaces of civil society. Some orphanages became home to groups from several different countries attempting to address the diverse needs of the orphanages: infrastructural rehabilitation (ranging from the painting and sanitizing of buildings to the installation of electrical and water systems and the acquisition of educational resources), care training, care giving, and the like. A multilanguage monthly newsletter underwritten by the UN Children's Fund (UNICEF) and the European Community in conjunction with the Ministry of Health was inaugurated, aimed at circulating information to governmental and nongovernmental organizations assisting children.[72] In 1992 legislative measures were passed regarding the handicapped (Laws 53/1991 and 57/1992). After its establishment in March 1993 by governmental decision (Decision 103), the National Committee for Child Protection opened an office to help coordinate the activities of these organizations so that their efforts might be more efficient as well as beneficial to those most in need. By the end of 1994, more than 300 aid organizations were operating in Romania. Some deal specifically with orphans, some with foster care, others with street children or the handicapped; still others perform multiple humanitarian tasks.

In a study done in 1991 on the causes of institutionalization of children between the ages of one and three (and later, up to the age of six), and of those suffering from malnutrition and other physical problems, it was determined that most of them were "medically fragile." They came from socioeconomically vulnerable groups: Roma (Gypsies),[73] single women, families with more than two children, as well as families with low levels of education. "Developmentally delayed" children, stigmatized in society at large, were frequently institutionalized. According to one official source, as of April 1993, there were approximately 158,078 institutionalized children.[74] Here, it is important to point out that the number of institutionalized children initially decreased after the fall of the regime (as a result of more adoptions and the legalization of abortion) and then began to increase again as a consequence of postsocialist economic instability.[75] Although political demography is no longer a primary factor leading to institutionalization, the hardships of daily life have continued. With growing marketization, class differentiation has become visible. Poverty compels many parents to institutionalize their children. The material conditions of these institutions have been enhanced since Ceausescu's execution, although the prospects for long-term infrastructural improvement warrant concern. In June 1995 the international relief organization Doctors without Borders announced that it would terminate activities in Romania, asserting that too little had been achieved on behalf of the institutionalized children. The number of children committed to institutions has continued to grow, yet the approach to their care remains too medicalized.[76] Furthermore, resource constraints (of all kinds) relative to the number of children institutionalized keep the related issues surrounding adoption ever present. It is to these that I now turn.

## Children for Adoption, Children for Sale

Caught up in the postrevolutionary fervor of 1989, foreigners began traveling to Romania with hopes of adopting the children whose images had inspired international humanitarian compassion.[77] The French and Belgians had previously reacted with outrage to media reports about Ceausescu's village systematization plans by creating goodwill ties with villages in Romania; after 1989 they were among those who went to salvage the children incarcerated in institutions. In this small way, they joyously participated in the "return to Europe" that was the promise of the day. Other prospective parents came from as far away as New Zealand.

As the word spread among the international community of individuals and couples wanting to adopt, Romania became an adoption hot spot. It was projected that at least one-third of all international adoptions in one year's time would be from Romania.[78] Law 11 of 1990 granted foreigners the right to adopt Romanian children. Yet for reasons elaborated below, provisions of this law proved inadequate to handle problems arising from the influx of adoptive parents.[79] According to a report issued in 1991, foreigners had adopted 1,457 Romanian children during only the three-month period between August 1 and October 31, 1990.[80] By the end of that year they had adopted 2,951 Romanian children; another 1,741 children had been welcomed into Romanian families (a development underplayed by the foreign media). The U.S. Embassy reported that by June 11, 1991, American citizens had adopted 1,451 children, up from a total of 480 for all of 1990. (The Immigration and Naturalization Service claimed there had been 2,287 adoptions by Americans as of early September 1991.) The 1991 figures also reflect what had become a lucrative business in privately arranged adoptions.[81]

Foreign adoption of Romanian children had been permitted in very limited numbers during the latter years of the Ceausescu regime. This little-publicized practice was another facet of the "commerce in human flesh" that had enabled Jews and Germans to be bought from Romania. (Hungarians wanting to emigrate to Hungary were not so fortunate, the Hungarian currency not having been convertible.) Children also had hard-currency price tags attached to them and were among Romania's exportable goods, in direct contradiction to the stated ideological goals of the pro-natalist policies.[82] G. Dupoy's article "Romania: Ceausescu even sells abandoned children," which appeared in *Le Quotidien de Paris*, took issue with Ceausescu's cynical machinations: "With his great clairvoyance, he realized that many families in the West wanted to adopt children, and that the market was tight. But, in Romania . . . there were beautiful blond babies with blue eyes. They would command a hefty price."[83] In 1981, French couples adopted 145 Romanian children; by 1983 the number had fallen to 92. Thereafter, foreign adoptions became ever rarer, or simply better hidden.

This changed dramatically in 1990, when foreigners flocked to Bucharest, as well as to other Romanian towns from which they might "save" a child. Many whose journeys had been prompted by a humanitarian response to the media images projected around the world were nonetheless overwhelmed by the conditions they confronted face-to-face upon arrival at the state-run institutions. A British woman expressed her deep revulsion: "I have never believed in abortion . . . but I did think that for many of them death would have been preferable to the way they were living. And this is Europe, not Ethiopia."[84] Foreigners scoured the orphanages, looking for the child that would inspire an affective bond. Prospective adoptive parents often arrived in groups, each waiting to be shown available children. These were confusing, traumatic times, especially for Romanians. To cope with the increasing number of adoption requests, the Romanian government formed the National Adoption Committee in early 1990. Among its tasks was the coordination of data on institutionalized children eligible for adoption. However, lack of adequate staff and a computerized information system led to bureaucratic inefficiency and may well have encouraged institutional corruption.

Gradually, as the channels through which children were obtained changed, the emotional rhetoric about the humanitarian rescue of children from the abysmal conditions in the orphanages lost its force. In its stead, a more generalized rhetoric emerged about saving children from the difficult living conditions in Romania and giving them the opportunity for a better life in the West. Before the July 1991 modification of the adoption law, which was designed to stop private adoptions and abuse, many if not most children were acquired via private connections, a fact usually overlooked in the media accounts of the baby trade in Romania. According to U.S. consular representatives, a majority of these children were of Roma origin. Though they are notably darker-skinned to the Romanian eye, Westerners do not generally consider them to be markedly different in appearance. Indeed, it is believed that Romanian children, including Roma, are popular in Western adoption circles because they are Caucasian. In view of the widespread prejudice against the Roma (throughout the region and not only in Romania), it was argued that adoption offered a humane road out for some of these children, whose chances at productive lives were otherwise slim. Many Romanians considered the adoption of Roma children a legitimate means of ridding Romania of them at the expense of foreigners. Others resented the squandering of Western altruism and resources on "tigani" (Gypsies).[85]

The creation of the National Adoption Committee inadvertently encouraged expansion of the private market, or what became known as trafficking in babies, rather than facilitating the adoption process. Hence, many foreigners eager to adopt a Romanian child opted for private networks. This route was faster than the official bureaucratic procedures; it was also more expensive, very arbitrary, and subject to coercion, corruption, and foreign complicity with these acts (conscious or not).[86] As one Romanian official put it: "The child is the object of a traffic in money and goods . . . in which Romanian citizens as well as foreigners participate, whether we are talking about the natal or adoptive families, or intermediaries. . . . It's as though potatoes are being sold at the market!"

Contrary to Western media coverage, the victims of this process were not only foreign adoptive parents, but also poor and single Romanian mothers, many of whom were Roma. Poor women are especially vulnerable to the demands of others, some of whom consider their bearing of children to be little more than the means of production that yields a valuable commodity; others assume that rescuing a child from poverty is a justifiable end, regardless of the means.[87] In this respect, international adoptions—especially private ones—have too often been used as vehicles for legitimating what has amounted to a self-serving, class-differentiated notion of whose family values are better. What is posited as in the child's best interests frequently sacrifices the otherwise revered mother-child relationship in favor of a materially based, affect-laden argument about the child's future. Hypocritical rhetorical flourish similarly serves to mask scrutiny of what has become a form of surrogacy transaction using Third World women who may ultimately have little say in the matter.[88] This is not to say that international adoption is intrinsically exploitative. However, lack of regulation opens the paths to exploitation.[89]

Private adoptions did contribute to the exploitation of some women's reproductive labor, to which I now turn. For example, responses to a U.S. Embassy questionnaire for the month of June 1991 indicated that at the time 39 of the children waiting to be adopted were living in private homes, 15 were in a hospital, and 13 in an orphanage.[90] Here, the ambiguity surrounding the definition of a child eligible for adoption came into play. If both parents were alive and the child was in their care, it had to be determined that they were unable or categorically unwilling to care for the child.

Not surprisingly, before the change in the adoption law in July 1991, visa problems arose more frequently when a child's status was questionable. In such circumstances, the U.S. Immigration and Naturalization Service (INS) investigated, but even if the INS ruled against the granting of a visa because the child was not deemed legally adoptable, the consulate had the authority to grant one by invoking a special clause for "humanitarian parole."[91] This option, although not specific to adoption, was widely used in these situations, enabling would-be parents to circumvent INS decisions and take their adopted children home. Irate adoptive parents called upon their congressional representatives to pressure the embassy and were as much to blame as anyone else for the ethical compromises, cast in terms of humanitarian interests, that such decisions often required. As one representative of a U.S. agency working on such problems commented to me: "In a sense, we exploit the horror of the [recent] past; no one can play God—but we do!"[92]

For all of the legitimate adoptions, there were those that simply were not. Coercion of Romanian mothers happened in various ways. Many adoptive parents considered themselves at the mercy of "adoption entrepreneurs"; and indeed they often were. The author of one of the many articles written by Westerners about their experiences in adopting Romanian children quoted another adoptive parent: "What can we do? said one Irishman out of earshot of the rest. They know their way about, they have the contacts, they get the job done. They're not buying children or coercing anyone; none of us would care for that at all."[93]

By law, a mother had fifteen days to change her mind about consenting to the adoption of her child. However, when a mother did have a change of heart, her decision was not necessarily accepted graciously by the foreigners or their negotiators. In one instance, a Romanian mother was threatened by the translator for the would-be U.S. adoptive parents. She was told that she would be responsible for the costs—emotional and financial—accrued during the stay of the American adoptive parents. No Romanian could conceivably cover such expenses. Whether the Americans knew of the translator's methods is not known. That the translator had much to lose if the adoption fell through, however, is obvious, as is the fact that the American woman intended to appeal to her congressional representative. Most adoptive parents in privately arranged situations turned a blind eye to possible coercion, and in view of the language barrier, this was easy to rationalize.[94] If they had allowed themselves to know, they would have had to succumb to their own pain over the loss of a child with whom they might already have bonded. It was easier to believe that adoption was simply in the best interest of the child.

U.S. consular officials, representatives of the INS, and professionals working with orphanages and with the National Adoption Committee had all heard stories involving varying forms and degrees of coercion. Few doubted their veracity. Some had their own variants to tell: Doctors reported about the adoption rings operating in the hospitals at which they worked; an INS investigator told of being offered a child for adoption by an "enterprising" father. The father felt he had the patriarchal right to impregnate his wife in order to have babies for sale. In the course of my limited fieldwork on private adoptions, I had similar experiences in a village from which there had been a number of privately arranged adoptions:[95] A local entrepreneur who had staked out his territorial claims offered to search the area for a child fitting my preferences and then bring the child to Bucharest for my approval. A Roma woman later introduced me to her pregnant daughter who lived in a small hut on the outskirts of the village. Two of her children had already been sold to foreigners through private adoption arrangements.[96] With the money from the children's sale this family had bought clothing and a conspicuous radio-cassette player and had plastered and painted one of their two rooms. The mother-to-be was traumatized by the thought that my presence meant her husband had already contracted the child she was carrying to another foreigner. Her own mother wailed in fear that the purpose of this supposed contract was to obtain baby parts, a rumor that circulates widely among the poor whose children—often against the will of their mothers—end up in the homes of wealthier others.[97] Amidst the sobs of these two women, it was gradually revealed that the young woman's husband had obtained her "agreement" to give up her children by beating her. She dreaded the childbearing years that loomed ahead and would be the source of ongoing emotional and physical pain for her. She recognized that bearing babies had become a lucrative endeavor for some in this time of economic instability. Indeed, a nineteen-year-old Roma father waited for me outside this woman's hut. He wanted to sell his four-day-old boy in exchange for a radio-cassette player and $1,200. The infant's father insisted unconvincingly that his wife would agree to this arrangement. I was relieved to learn that the young mother and child were still in the hospital.

To counteract the abuses that had surfaced as a result of the trafficking in children, President Ion Iliescu signed Law 48/1991 on July 16, 1991.[98] This law modified the terms of Law 11/1990 granting foreigners the right to adopt Romanian children. Henceforth, foreigners would be able to adopt only children registered with the National Adoption Committee (meaning that the children were officially eligible for adoption).[99] The intent of governmental regulation was to eliminate the profit motive, which had given rein to exploitation and corruption, as well as to slow the exodus of Romanian youngsters. Among the law's provisions is the necessary institutionalization of orphaned children as a means of preventing their sale and determining the legality of their legal adoption status. Children had to reside in an institution for a minimum of six months. This "trial" period gave the parents time—if the child was a social orphan—to change their minds or for adoptive families in Romania to be found. The preferential treatment accorded Romanian citizens in adopting Romanian children is meant to address the demographic problems posed by a declining birthrate and increased infertility, as well as to avoid the problems that may accompany intercultural adoptions experienced by children as they grow older.[100]

The law provoked public outcry both in Romania and abroad. Private adoptions had become lucrative for many in Romania: local "dealers," mothers and/or their families, translators, lawyers, and judges, as well as orphanage and hospital personnel;[101] allegedly, consular employees were also involved. Abroad, the law subjected foreigners to the frustrations that adoption procedures entailed elsewhere, especially in the United States. However, this law marked an important step toward the recognition and protection of citizens' rights, especially those of women and children, and should be applauded for its attempt to apply the "rule of law" embraced in the West.

The effects of Law 48/1991 may be seen by looking at the annual adoption figures presented in table 7.8. The number of adoptions in Romania has increased steadily since 1990, whereas the number of foreign adoptions has declined noticeably. However, a rise in the latter since 1994 may reflect the consequences of both increased bureaucratic efficiency and international diplomatic pressure.[102]

In part as a concession to continuing international insistence, a critical legislative decision defining legal abandonment, Law 47/1993, was finally issued. The ambiguity about the legality of a child's adoption status had contributed importantly to bureaucratic procrastination on the part of the Romanians and frustration for foreigners.[103] Caught in the midst of a legal limbo, children remained institutionalized; they were neither claimed by their parents, some of whom had not made any effort to see them, nor eligible for adoption because their parents had not relinquished their rights. The new law specified that a court had the authority to annul parental rights after six months of "evident lack of interest in the child."

As mentioned, diplomatic pressure has had a positive influence on the formulation of certain legislative decisions. While all of the above laws have been necessary, the controversies surrounding the adoption of Romanian children have also brought to the fore the complexities of, and international engagement in, the global politics of reproduction. Despite the tremendous benefits that international involvement has brought, not all of these efforts have been laudable. These latter raise questions about whose interests are at stake. With respect to Romanian-American relations, the granting of most-favored-nation trade status was delayed partially in the name of altruism for the sake of the children, particularly those who are handicapped. The distinction between medical assistance and adoption processes has often been deliberately blurred to skirt legal constraints. I do not mean to suggest that the desire to help vulnerable children is misplaced. Global humanitarian intervention has been crucial to bettering the treatment of institutionalized children, whether handicapped or abandoned.

I do, however, mean to shift attention to the use of the emotion-laden rhetoric that has served as an effective lobbying weapon for groups hoping to influence the adoption process in accordance with their own goals. Ma-

TABLE 7.8    Number of Adoptions, 1990–1994

| Year | Adoptions in Romania | International Adoptions | Total |
|------|---------------------|------------------------|-------|
| 1990 | 1,741 | 2,951 | 4,692 |
| 1991 | 2,343 | 7,159 | 9,502 |
| 1992 | 2,647 | 157 | 2,804 |
| 1993 | 3,208 | 891 | 4,099 |
| 1994 | 4,830 | 2,038 | 6,868 |
| Total | 14,769 | 13,196 | 27,965 |

SOURCE:  Data courtesy of the Ministry of Justice, Bucharest.

nipulation of the dire situation of handicapped and institutionalized children has not been confined to profit-seeking Romanians, and they are not the only ones who have tampered with legal parameters. American interest groups have used the media to help win support for their causes, occasionally relying on inaccurate representation in order to play upon sentiment.

Indeed, the legacies of the pronatalist policies discussed thus far readily lend themselves to humanitarian and media attention, including sensationalism. In some instances, the violation of international laws under the guise of humanitarian assistance has been quietly tolerated by Western governments. For example, in the fall of 1994 a British couple was sentenced in Romania for violating the adoption laws by resorting to the illegal private market. Diplomatic intervention eventually enabled the couple to leave Romania. The diverse crises associated with the institutionalized children have caused the Romanians much embarrassment and soul-searching.[104] Yet it would seem that some foreigners might also benefit from self-examination. Prospective adoptive parents do not have the right, regardless of their good intentions, to disregard laws in order to satisfy their emotional needs or humanitarian convictions. While the rationales are many, the ends do not justify the means. The hypocrisy entailed in practices such as breaking the law is especially problematic in a period in which the institutionalizing of democratic practices is so fragile.

But as has been demonstrated throughout this book, rhetoric and practice rarely mirror each other. Here I briefly explore how discursive distortion predicated on presumptions of moral legitimacy has contributed to the manipulation of adoption-related issues. On March 19, 1993, the television program "20/20" aired a segment about a home for the severely handicapped in Sighetu Marmatiei and the "courageous, caring" efforts of an American citizen to rescue these "unsalvageable" children from this locale. Congressional lobbying efforts included testimony by well-meaning actresses and the presentation of heartbreaking, but highly selective, reporting. The interweaving of misinformation contributed to the emotional force of the program. Dated footage and inaccurate statistics were utilized to heighten the dramatic effect of the rescue mission. This television program failed to reveal that Dutch nurses had been placed at this particular institution and had witnessed slow but steady improvements. The intimation that little had changed for Romania's forgotten children discounted the progress that Romanians had made in this domain since 1990, as well as the effective contributions of international organizations established in the homes or orphanages since then.[105]

While the cause of helping handicapped children is noble, capitalizing on sentiment to excuse the disregard of international laws is unacceptable. The "freedom-bound" mission described in the television program involved the spiriting away of nine children, without institutional authorization, across international borders and has raised questions about the legality of parental or legal guardian approvals for a foreign citizen to take Romanian children to the United States. Clearly, the "escape" from the orphanage in Sighetu Marmatiei necessitated the active complicity of intermediaries, including personnel able to issue visas. These children were ostensibly taken to the United States to receive medical treatment; however, it remains unclear whether they will be returned to Romania following treatment, or instead become available for adoption in the United States.[106] As troubling as the circumstances confronting these children are, this television program has raised disturbing questions about the lengths to which individuals, foundations, and government representatives will go to achieve their ends—in violation of existing laws.

The problems associated with adoption are only partly a result of pronatalist policies. Profiteering emerged within and across Romanian borders in the context of institutionalizing market practices. The politics of reproduction in Romania today are different than they were during the Ceausescu period. Under Ceausescu's rule, the masses were forced to reproduce in the service of the state. Presently, as Romania struggles with socioeconomic and political transformation, and as Romanian society becomes more visibly class-differentiated, those persons who are most vulnerable, such as poor and single women, have often been forced to reproduce in the service of market demands. Adoption laws help to diminish one source of abuse suffered by women coerced into giving up their children. To reiterate, the measures approved by the Romanians are in compliance with international practices and should be respected on their merits. Moreover, Romanians and foreigners alike should uniformly heed international laws.

## Street Children

Not all abandoned children have been institutionalized, adopted, or reintegrated with their families. Others have joined the ranks of the world's urban street urchins, a phenomenon unknown in communist Romania. Today, they hover around the streets, markets, and train stations of the capital city, which is said to host the greatest number of them (an estimated 1,500 children in Bucharest out of a national total of 5,000).[107] Street children are a consequence of both the pronatalist policies that contributed to the birth of unwanted children and the economic turmoil that has affected so many families in the immediate post-Ceausescu period of change. Among these children are the homeless who have lived on the streets for several years, "circumstantial vagabonds" (that is, children who have recently fled their homes or institutions to live on the streets), and those who "work" on the streets to contribute to their families' incomes. These latter beg, "wash car windows, transport packages, distribute handbills, etc."[108] Roma children, who allegedly make up the majority of street children, are frequently associated with such activities, as well as with the rise in urban juvenile delinquency attributed to them and to street children.[109] Although drug abuse is not readily recognized as a problem in Romania, Romanian authorities have noted that the inhalation of volatile substances has become popular, especially among street children: "In 1993, 223 persons (42 under the age of fourteen, 170 between the ages of fourteen and eighteen, and 11 over eighteen years) were identified who had consumed these kinds of substances. . . . It must be noted that the majority of users come from the category of 'street children.' "[110]

The growing number of street children in urban areas suggests that this phenomenon warrants attention. To date, media, government, and socioethnographic interest has been limited. Yet the infrastructural problems that have contributed to the emergence of this urban phenomenon continue to exist. Children born to parents whose economic conditions have worsened may well find themselves living in the streets.

Society's reactions to the political-economic constraints detailed in the preceding chapter have contributed to the complexity of the demographic outcomes described in this one. As is evident from a general summary of the legacies of Ceausescu's political demographic policies, the artificial and short-term increase in the birthrate resulting from the issuance of Decree 770 occurred at the expense of the overall well-being of the Romanian population. The virtual banning of abortion gave rise to alarmingly high infant and maternal mortality rates and compounded the problems associated with the basic material and "spiritual" impoverishment of society. Unwanted children inadvertently became a burden to the very regime that had dictated their births.

When the immediate post-Ceausescu legalization of abortion made legal abortion the primary means of fertility control,[111] fewer unwanted children were born, and fewer children were institutionalized (at least initially).

Nonetheless, the fear that had pervaded reproductive practices for so many years contributed to the deaths of women who, unaware or uncomprehending of the liberalization of abortion, still resorted to illegal abortions. Years of anti-contraceptive propaganda conjoined with the expense and difficulty of obtaining contraceptives prompted an apprehensive and uninformed populace to avoid using them. "Liberty" and economic interests influenced the flourishing of prostitution and the marketing of sex and sexuality. However, "safe sex" was not included in the commodification or liberalization of sexual habits, reflecting a combination of ingrained cultural notions (particularly about the use of condoms), a lack of knowledge concerning AIDS and other sexually transmitted diseases, and an embodied sense of national immunity (e.g., "AIDS and STDs afflict foreigners").[112]

The bearing of children remains problematic, especially for poor women. Poverty differentially affects the global politics of reproduction. It is poor women who primarily experience the brunt of restricted access to legal abortions when and where modern contraceptive options are unavailable to them. During the Ceausescu regime, most women struggled to control their fertility. Those privileged with economic or other resources arranged for "safe" illegal abortions.[113] Too many others ended up as maternal mortality statistics. Women who gave birth to unwanted children often abandoned them to the institutions run by the paternalist state. Many of those children have also ended up in the statistical roster of Ceausescu-era legacies. Since 1989, women have also given up or sold their own children to foreigners through adoption arrangements. Some women have done so willingly; others have been coerced.

The medical, social, and psychological effects of Ceausescu's political demographic policies became a focus of international engagement shortly after the fall of his regime. Numerous studies on their consequences have been done since 1989, often with international collaboration. It has become axiomatic that data collected before 1989 were consistently distorted. To meet the political goals of centralized planning, statistics were over- or under-represented, frequently by medical personnel who colluded in the "doctoring" of abortion-related and infant mortality figures. Although recent studies contain the requisite disclaimers concerning reliability, the data are nevertheless generally treated as if they are representative of the circumscribed empirical phenomena under examination. Yet the data on which analyses of the same problems have been based—even though obtained from the same institutional source—vary from study to study. For example, as observed throughout this chapter's notes, mortality figures differ. The recorded discrepancies suggest that some people are unaccounted for. Despite their absence, death-related statistics seem to have acquired the force of objectivity.[114] While the numbers themselves are revealing, they do not facilitate a nuanced analysis of the dimensions of human experience they are purported to represent.

In view of the context in which such statistics have been produced (or not produced, as the case may be), caution is warranted with respect to their interpretation. Formal fulfillment of "international standards" may gloss over the particularities of research practices and policy formulation in post-Ceausescu Romania (irrespective of whose interests are served). The institutionalization of democratic procedures cannot be uncritically predicated on idealized discourses about democracy and the objectivity of science. The relationship between what is said and what is done bears careful scrutiny.

Taken in this light, the 1995 announcement by Doctors without Borders concerning their withdrawal from Romania after five years is deeply disturbing and underscores the significance of cultural factors in any understanding of the process of transformation under way there (and throughout the former Soviet sphere). The deterioration of everyday life that took place especially during the last decade of Ceausescu's rule makes health, education, and the environment critical sites for societal change. Pollution of the physical body, the mind, and the environment was pervasive at all levels of Romanian society and impedes the transition from the past to something different, let alone something better. The state's intrusion into and systematic violence upon the bodies and souls of its citizens have scarred the body politic itself. The legacies of the political demographic policies must be treated effectively if the public and private selves of the populace are to be reconciled.

## CHAPTER 8

# Coercion and Reproductive Politics
## *Lessons from Romania*

*Romania's experience in the realm of reproductive health can guide policy makers, health system administrators, and reproductive health professionals throughout the world. The high number of maternal deaths during the past 25 years vividly illustrates the consequences of restrictive reproductive health policies: In their determination to control their fertility, Romanian women risked their health and lives; as a result, vast numbers of women died or were permanently injured. Romania's experience also clearly demonstrates the difficulty of reversing the effects of misinformation or lack of information.*

C. HORD, H. DAVID, F. DONNAY, AND M. WOLF,
*Reproductive Health in Romania: Reversing the Ceausescu Legacy*[1]

*Everyone who has had a happy sexual life or children they love should try and understand the world of Norma McCorvey and Ceausescu's Romania. Maybe then they will comprehend what happens when safe abortion is not available.*

EDITORIAL, *The Lancet*[2]

The Ceausescu regime endured 24 years, during which the inhabitants of Romania became increasingly alienated from their country's leadership as well as from each other. The legacies of this period discussed in the preceding chapter primarily highlight the negative consequences of the paternalist state's demographic policies. An ethnography of Ceausescu's rule as gleaned through an analysis of these policies has shed light on the problematic and paradoxical aspects of the relationship between regime politics, social relations, and reproductive practices, and between the body and the body politic. This concluding chapter discusses in more general terms the lessons that may be drawn from experience with coercive reproductive policies, of which banned abortion was the legislative centerpiece. First, however, a summation of the politics of duplicity, which at once both fed the Ceausescu regime and depleted it of basic human resources, is in order.

## A MOVEMENT OF RAGE: AGAINST THE REGIME

The institutionalization of political will designed to engineer the construction of socialism shaped and was shaped by everyday social experience.

In practice, the rhetorically antagonistic us-versus-them dichotomy noted throughout this analysis was not as sharply defined in daily life as this heuristic classificatory device suggests, either in Romania or elsewhere.[3] But unlike other countries in the region, Ceausescu's regime steered the Socialist Republic of Romania on a course of ever-increasing hard-line politics and daily hardship. Duplicity as communicative style and complicity as communicative act marked the public servitude of "the population" and the disintegration of any notion of civil society as well as of the self. As one person reflected, "If I had to define my life before 1989 with one word, it would be "duplicity."[4] In Romania, the "spoiler state" was particularly adept at fulfilling its mission of "spoiling individuals."[5] Dissimulation and lying served as important regulatory mechanisms for a system whose legitimacy had long since not rested on revolutionary zeal.[6] On the one hand, lying protected the official version of socialist reality; on the other, it also protected the actual reality that people lived. Persons attempted to adjust their behavior according to their interests and those of the system. They lied to retain their positions.[7] They spent large sums greasing the goodwill of persons with redistributive power in the attempt to care for their extended families or to arrange an illegal abortion. Yet the unflinching rhetorical dedication of the regime to the needs of its children rang hollow, particularly by the 1980s.

People knew that the official discourse consisted of lies and that they themselves lied; the communicative system was transparent to all. And, as Kundera has written: "Ah, the beauty of transparency! The only successful realization of this dream: a society totally monitored by the police."[8] Whether society was totally monitored by the police is open to debate; but it is widely assumed to have been. Therein emerges the regulatory function of lying: it increased everyone's vulnerability to the arbitrariness with which power was wielded.[9] This arbitrariness was also diffused at all levels of society. The much-dreaded Securitate was organized hierarchically, its ranks swelled by low-level informers. The everyday fear among the populace was tied to the gnawing uncertainty that anyone—a friend, colleague, or family member—could be an informer who sold the lives of others to fortify his or her own interests. To quote again from Kundera, "When it becomes the custom and the rule to divulge another person's private life, we are entering a time when the highest stake is the survival or the disappearance of the individual."[10]

Not everyone participated in all lies all of the time. Some issues remained abstractions until they affected one's personal life directly. The banning of abortion, for example, was not especially noteworthy until a mother, sister, wife, or lover needed one. Then, people often became willfully entangled in a web of lies and deception. Although virtually everyone lied, no one knew when or to whom they might be held accountable for doing so. Lying transformed individuals into the pawns of power; heightened vulnerability made people susceptible to manipulation, particularly if the well-being of their families was at stake. Again, it was made clear that failure to cooperate could be translated into reprisals against family members: A child would be denied entrance into school, a spouse could lose his or her job.[11] To jeopardize the security of another for what was represented as one's selfishness was a responsibility most ordinary persons were reluctant to take. Uncertainty often mocked self-dignity. Fear and distrust of *puterea* (roughly, the power elite) and of each other were the constants of social relations as well as the end products of compromised, vulnerable selves.

In keeping with the reciprocal dependency between the regime and its citizens, it must also be recognized that the vulnerability felt by the population was mirrored in the growing vulnerability of the state. As so nicely characterized by Jan Gross: "Superiors and subordinates alike contributed to perpetuating the regime. . . . This novel society required both the participation and the vulnerability of all . . . all were custodians and wards simultaneously."[12] Distrust of the publicly loyal masses found expression in repressive and coercive measures. Those at the top were themselves increasingly at risk for greedily embracing Mephistopheles in exchange for privileged lifestyles that could be ruined without notice. Most notorious among the Faustian troops were the secret police, themselves instruments of the very power they manipulated in their own self-serving "ideological" defense. The Securitate supplied muscle to what had become, for all practical purposes, an illegitimate system heavily dependent on administrative repression for survival.[13] Moreover, mass participation in the falsification of empirical realities made it more difficult for people to trust in common sense, let alone that which was officially claimed as "truth." Rumors, phantoms, and conspiracies acquired credibility in an environment in which plausibility had lost critical meaning.[14] Everyone participated in their creation.

Public posturing by and for everyone became both modus vivendi and modus operandi. The beneficial achievements of Ceausescu's socialism were celebrated by the propaganda apparatus. Bounty was rhetorically weighed in inverse proportion to the actual material conditions of daily existence. As the latter steadily deteriorated, the former flourished. Building socialism, creating new socialist persons and families with many happy and healthy children were speech acts performed to the script of Ceausescu's "golden era."

However, the intentional power of words does not automatically transform them into tangible realities. By the mid-1980s, the gap between what was said and what was experienced had become irreconcilable. Romania's inhabitants could not live adequately on the fantasized stage set that the Socialist Republic of Romania had become. Alienation from the regime became widespread across all spectrums of society, including the privileged. Almost everyone felt the tightening squeeze in which they were clasped. They felt themselves repeatedly betrayed by the paternalist regime—Romanian at that—which had vowed the satisfaction of their needs in exchange for filial loyalty. Although the public performance of socialist (sur)realism continued unabated, people's dependence on informal networks and secondary economic activities increased.[15] The public and private were interpenetrated from below as well, with the public sphere being pillaged by those who nonetheless ritually recognized the power in it.

If seeing is believing, then the Ceausescus were blinded by the luster of the radiant future that their golden era allegedly presaged. While communism in the rest of Eastern Europe was collapsing peacefully, appearance suggested the inviolability of Romania's insulation from outside "forces of destruction." Fatally seduced by the very power they coveted, complacent in their fully distorted selves, the Ceausescus did not recognize the fragility of the false world constructed in their images.[16] Ultimately, they became victims of the political economy of duplicity and dissimulation they themselves had commanded. First in Timisoara, then in Bucharest, inhabitants of Romania did the unspeakable: They spoke their hearts and minds. *Jos Ceausescu!* Down with Ceausescu! *Timisoara!*

"In the beginning was the Word . . . " and so the beginning of the end finally erupted in the belly of the beast, in Bucharest. What had endured 24 years publicly crumbled in 24 hours.[17]

> Maybe something will happen by itself? It will never happen as long as we daily acknowledge, extol, and strengthen—and do not sever ourselves from—the most perceptible of its aspects: Lies. . . . And the simplest and most accessible key to our self-neglected liberation lies right here: Personal non-participation in lies. Though lies conceal everything, though lies embrace everything . . . let them embrace everything, but not with any help from me. This opens a breach in the imaginary encirclement caused by our inaction. It is the easiest thing to do for us, but it is the most devastating for the lies. Because when people renounce lies it simply cuts short their existence. Like an infection, they can exist only in a living organism.[18]

A ritualized performance of public support for "Ceausescu-Romania" turned into a "movement of rage" against the paternalist regime of socialism in one family.[19] In a dramatic variation on a classic theme, the nation's children murdered their parents.[20] Paradoxically, in liberating themselves from Ceausescu's dictatorship, the atomized and alienated citizens of Romania momentarily realized the power of the population.

With the abrogation of Decree 770 by the provisional post-Ceausescu government, abortion became and remains legal in Romania. Without question, the heartbreaking and chilling irony of Ceausescu's pronatalist policies was that illegal abortion became the predominant method of fertility regulation among a beleaguered population. In view of the real conditions—and limitations—of daily life in Ceausescu's Romania, a woman's decision to seek an illegal abortion was a rational one. Insensitive to the lived experiences of most Romanian citizens, the regime focused on formalist interpretations in all domains of everyday productive and reproductive life. The consequences of banning abortion without regard for the actually existing circumstances of daily life contributed to Romania's tragic achievement of having the highest maternal mortality rates in late twentieth-century Europe, a Europe not then embroiled in war.

The politics of reproduction in Romania are now different than during the Ceausescu period. Under Ceausescu's rule, the masses were forced to reproduce in the service of the state. Women's reproductive lives were blatantly exploited. Today, as Romania struggles through the rigors of economic and political transformation and as Romanian society becomes more explicitly class-differentiated, those women who are most vulnerable—poor and single women—have often been compelled to reproduce in the service of market demands. Poverty in particular constrains women's reproductive options in ways strikingly different from those of women with access to diverse resources, especially financial ones. Under Ceausescu, poverty became the generalized socioeconomic condition of Romania's population. In postcommunist Romania, as elsewhere in the region, poverty has become the mark of an increasingly class-differentiated society. Not surprisingly, poverty has also become increasingly feminized, as it is in the West.[21]

## BANNED ABORTION: LESSONS FROM ROMANIA

What may be learned from Romania's stringent reproductive policies? Why do health professionals from democratic countries insist on the importance of understanding the ramifications of Ceausescu's banning of abortion? To be sure, the personal dramas confronted by average Romanian citizens coping with Ceausescu's dictatorship are of a different order of magnitude than those familiar to most middle-class citizens living in Western democracies. Yet the personal despair experienced by Romania's impoverished population may be more readily likened to that faced daily by the poor in the West. In these final pages, I suggest various links among reproductive politics, poverty, and the feminization of poverty. The connections between them must be acknowledged publicly rather than consigned to the abstraction of morally charged rhetoric about an idealized world in which few people have the privilege to live.[22]

The political control of human reproduction—whether promoted in terms of the regulation of population growth, sexual practices, abortion, or adoption—is now a universal policy concern. Government efforts to influence fertility behavior call attention to an important prerogative of the modern state: political intervention in private life, intimacy, and sexuality.

Technological developments have facilitated the bureaucratic regulation of the body as well as of medical practice, to positive and negative effects. Moreover, the enormous expansion of the state into the bodies and lives of citizens has radically blurred cultural boundaries between public and private interests. Until the twentieth century, fertility regulation was typically managed by and in the context of families, which were patriarchal in their social-sexual organization.[23]

The twentieth century has witnessed extreme manifestations heretofore unfathomed of the political control of fertility behavior. Analyses of such extreme case examples, of which Ceausescu's Romania is certainly one, make explicit their relations and mechanisms of domination. Analyses also shed light on processes related to fertility regulation in general that otherwise tend to remain hidden. Hitler's antinatalist policies were directed against those "unfit" to reproduce the Aryan essence; compulsory sterilization was used as a technique of biological genocide. The Communist Parties of China and Romania have subjected their populations to widely publicized and broadly penetrating anti- and pronatalist policies. Under totalizing or authoritarian regimes such as these, the reach of the state is maximal, and the rights of persons as individuals are broadly denied. Instead, persons as members of the social body (the "people-as-one") are considered properties of the nation-state to which they belong. Such regimes readily embrace coercion as a means of accomplishing designated goals.

However, coercive policies only "succeed" at great cost to human life. In Romania, the intent of the political demographic policies was to increase fertility and give birth to new socialist persons. But in the end, "Romania represents the most striking failure of a coercive public policy designed to influence reproductive behavior."[24] The construction of socialism and nationalism is among the rhetorical devices used to link fertility behavior to the state and thereby legitimate the state's control over human reproduction.[25] The paternalist state usurped the patriarchal and patrilineal "right" of men to "protect" women's sexuality and wombs, granting neither men nor women legal control over female fertility. However, the state's intrusion into its citizens' intimate lives inadvertently fostered male/female solidarity against the state and institutionalized illegal abortion. Elsewhere, and not only in communist countries, coercive policies designed to decrease fertility have also involved "terrible social sacrifices" for which "there is little evidence that they are more effective in reducing birth rates than serious programs of collaborative action."[26] Whether pro- or antinatalist, coercive policies have always been resisted and always at significant human risk.

The fundamental lesson of Romania's political demographic policies, the centerpiece of which was the re-criminalization of abortion, is that legal and safe abortions must be protected by law. The comparative, historical records of maternal mortality in countries where abortion is banned make clear that women will seek illegal abortions when effective options to prevent and terminate unwanted pregnancies are not available to them. In short, women risk their lives in order to gain control over their fertility. Clearly, access to contraceptive knowledge and methods by women *and* men is a critical aspect of responsible sexual and reproductive practices, and, of course fertility regulation.

The criminalization of abortion speaks loudly to the politics of duplicity across the globe. Criminalization has never eradicated abortion and invariably pushes abortion underground, making it invisible in the public sphere. Women the world over, as well as their families, partners, and friends, have responded creatively as well as despairingly to the criminalization of abortion. They have organized feminist abortion collectives, traveled as "abortion tourists" to countries where legal abortions are obtainable, and sought doctors or midwives working in the illegal, underground economy of abortion provision or back-alley abortionists.[27] Others have experimented with traditional and contemporary methods to self-induce an abortion. Again, whatever the means, women without recourse to legal and safe alternatives will pursue the termination of unwanted pregnancies illegally.

It is important to underscore that protecting abortion as a legal right (in all countries) is *not* synonymous with advocating abortion as a method of fertility regulation. In general, abortions involve surgical intervention, and all surgical interventions open the body to the possibility of secondary complications. Although the development of RU486, the so-called abortion pill, may dramatically alter abortion techniques, it is unlikely to be accessible to all or even most women. This raises a critical issue regarding abortion rights. Abortion must be legally protected as a last resource. Yet, just as the legal protection of abortion does not mean that abortion should be promoted as a method of fertility regulation, so the existence of legal abortion does not enable all women to have access to safe abortions performed by qualified medical or nonmedical personnel. The right to abortion constitutes rhetorical equality for women; however, the availability of and access to legal abortion in actuality remain stratified. Poor women are generally disadvantaged on both counts.

In this respect, the Romanian case is instructive. During Ceausescu's rule, only a privileged minority of women had relatively easy access to the staples, let alone luxuries, of everyday living; these same women were better positioned to acquire modern contraceptives or clandestine abortions by trained providers. By contrast, the majority of Romania's women of childbearing age struggled along with their families to furnish the basic necessities of daily life. Many of these same women struggled through the ordeals of unsafe, illegal abortion, becoming the victims of such practices. Here, in the United States, the lives of poor women are similarly stressed in an everyday sense, and it is they who will be most egregiously affected by any recriminalization of abortion.

For those who would revisit *Roe v. Wade*, Romania's recent history stands as a tragic and poignant lesson. Those who uphold absolute "moral" or political values (as was the case in Romania) over the all too real exigencies of daily life privilege ideology over lived experience. The fervent rhetorical defense of the sanctity of life denigrates the sanctity of the embodied self while eschewing any consideration of the empirical factors that constrain women's and families' childbearing *and* child-rearing possibilities. Recriminalizing abortion would further alter an already transformed war against the poor into a war against poor women in particular.[28] Despite claims made by anti-abortion advocates, there is no empirical evidence suggesting that women seek abortions for frivolous or primarily selfish reasons.[29] However, incontestable historical and comparative evidence repeatedly demonstrates that criminalizing abortion reconstitutes illegal abortion as an unsafe method of fertility regulation.

The social inequalities that limit the reproductive or contraceptive options of poor women cannot be reduced to class-biased notions of the sexual irresponsibility of poor women—often women of color. Because poor women often lack access to reliable means of contraceptive knowledge and practice, the consequences of their sexuality and fertility behavior are less shielded from bourgeois public scrutiny than those of women with more resources. Poverty stigmatizes women's sexuality, childbearing and child-rearing, just as it also contributes to the stratification of those aspects of women's lives.

Poverty calls attention to women's reproductive capacities in complex, paradoxical ways. For example, it is poor women, often of color, who are typically entrusted with the care of children other than their own; these women are customarily valued for their presumed "natural" mothering skills. Yet these same women are denigrated for their purported lack of sexual control and mothering skills when it comes to their own offspring. It is also poor women who rent their bodies more frequently for the pleasure of men, or to bear children for those unable to do so. And poor women are often expected to give up their babies for international adoption under the guise of humanitarianism. The politics of reproduction and of duplicity are yet again coupled in relations that mask the unequal gender hierarchies—male and female—which lend shape to the stratification of reproduction across the globe. Class and race intermingle to disproportionally disadvantage certain women.[30] Regarding abortion and the politics of reproduction in general, poor women are decidedly more vulnerable to circumstances beyond their control.

As the Romanian case demonstrates, ignoring the social conditions of re-production—the actually existing constraints or opportunities of everyday life—has profound social consequences. Unwanted pregnancies too often result in neglected children deeply scarred by the lack of love and support as well as by the harshness of their young lives.[31] And while the banning of abortion is especially problematic for poor women, it is no longer clear—should abortion again be criminalized in the United States—that women with the resources to afford illegal abortion services would be readily able to do so. The changing practice of medicine in the United States will nec-essarily and adversely affect the provision of illegal abortion: For example, the increasing centralization of care-delivery systems facilitates their surveil-lance, thus reducing the possibility of furtive and illegal work in hospitals.[32] Malpractice insurance combined with limited training of abortion tech-niques in medical schools and extremist violence against abortion providers reconfigure in unprecedented ways the context in which illegal abortions may be obtained, compromising the safety of the procedure. Furthermore, it can only be assumed that legal action against nonmedical abortion provid-ers such as midwives and feminist collectives will be instituted to discipline their activities. Hence, if abortion is re-criminalized in the United States, travel abroad would become a preferred option for women with the means to do so. The hypocrisy of abortion tourism warrants no additional comment than that noted in the introduction.

Herein lies another grim lesson from Romania's experience. All of the techniques of the modern state were brought to bear on the systemwide in-stitutionalization of repressive reproductive politics, for which the banning of abortion served as legislative catalyst. Law became the instrument of and for oppression. The modern state depends on legal rationality to legitimate and extend its control throughout society. The rule of law run amok, as was the case in Ceausescu's Romania, offers an important cautionary tale about the power of law to subvert, and pervert, its own objectives. History has al-ready demonstrated that democracies are not immune to tyranny by law.

In this respect, the criminalization of abortion poses persistent and vex-ing problems: Law by and for whom? Democracy by and for whom? The criminalization of abortion defines women's legal rights as citizens as es-sentially circumscribed by biology. All women, unless infertile, can poten-tially become pregnant. Hence, because of their fertility, women are created unequal before the law. In sharp distinction, men's legal rights as citizens and their participation are not fundamentally constrained by their sex.[33] The criminalization of abortion is a critical means by which the patriarchal control of women is formalized and legitimated by law, whether in the pa-ternalist states of the former Soviet sphere or the patriarchal ones of the West.[34]

For example, a "moderate" ideological position on the re-criminalization of abortion in the United States proposes certain exceptions under which an abortion might be performed. Two of these exceptions, rape and incest, are especially revealing of male presumption and reflect the duplicity of anti-abortion rhetoric. These exceptions in particular unmask the reality that they represent: women's bodies are not considered to be their own property, even when they are adults. Rape and incest, the latter of which is assumed to be more prevalent in father-daughter relations, breach basic taboos associated with the ideal-typical bourgeois family. Only when women are demonstrably victimized by male sexual violence that violates the norms of patriarchal propriety (that is, when the limits of male self-control are breached) may women be exonerated from bearing a resulting pregnancy.[35] The circumstantial exception to a law that otherwise denies women control over their reproductive lives serves to remove the evidence against the perpetrator and what would amount to the enduring shame of being viewed as a criminal.[36] The exception proves the rule, so to speak: the criminalization of abortion legally protects male domination of female sexuality and fertility and deprives men and women of accountability and responsibility for their actions.

Indeed, rape and incest, when proven, highlight a truism of human reproductive and sexual history: men are rarely held accountable for their uncontrolled sexual behaviors.[37] Historically, virility has been projected as a powerful representation of maleness. Yet, it is not virility and male sexual irresponsibility that have been targeted for taming, but rather women's allegedly inherent libidinous desires that have required male control and "protection."[38] Women—not men—customarily must answer for their sexual conduct. The misplaced sexual urges and excesses of men, from rape to the refusal to use condoms as a routine matter of safe sexual practice, are generally tolerated and excused. Self-indulgent rationalizations suffice to account for a man's "right" to endanger the well-being of a partner in pursuit of his own immediate pleasure.[39]

Unwanted pregnancies are not the mysterious products of divine conception. Indeed, conception without sex obviates the issue of unwanted pregnancy. This method of conception has been made possible by the new reproductive technologies that have emerged from scientific intervention. The factors that contribute to unwanted pregnancies are many and complexly related. However, to date, women bear the primary burden of such pregnancies. Men must take responsibility for their sexual interests and activities.[40] Social change rather than reinvigorated social control is necessary. Just as democratization of household labor is a necessary condition of women's equality, so too is the democratization of sexual and reproductive responsibility. Until responsibility for sexual and contraceptive behavior becomes gender-neutral, women will remain unequal in the public and private spheres of everyday life.

However, the slow change in the division of household labor suggests that optimism about the democratization of sexual and contraceptive knowledge and practices is idealistic. This makes the necessity of legal abortion ever more urgent. But keeping abortion legal has attendant responsibilities. For example, physicians must have the right of conscientious objection with respect to performing abortions, just as women must have the right of full information and access to safe abortions.[41] There must be forthright efforts to educate all citizens regardless of their gender, race, class, and ethnicity about contraceptive options, and to create the foundations of a political and cultural environment that encourages citizens to take responsibility for their lives, as well as for their fertility choices.[42]

Again, re-criminalizing abortion will not stop abortion, just as prohibiting liquor and drugs has not stopped their manufacture, distribution, and consumption.[43] Nor would banning abortion strengthen "the family"; banning abortion would, however, create an unenforceable policy, the consequences of which would differentially hurt poor women and give rise to a culture of hidden pain and overt hypocrisy. Madison understood that the test of democracy lies in its treatment of its minorities, society's most vulnerable members, among whom are women and children.[44] As long as women lack the freedom to control their reproductive lives fully, they will be unable to participate in the public sphere as full and equal citizens, and in their private lives as full and equal partners.

Demanding that women bear children, as was the case in Romania, and legislating that they do so, as some hope will again be the case in the United States, are facile and misguided approaches to social and human reproduction. Pronatalist or, for that matter, antinatalist cultures need not be coercive or restrict other social arrangements. The criminalization of abortion reduces the experienced realities of everyday life to abstractions, the results of which are detrimental to health, liberty, and the quality of life. The value of life-as-lived is thereby transformed into life as a material to be maximized, for example, for reproduction of the labor force or for the will of God. From such an ideological or theological perspective, there is ultimately nothing sacred about life other than its being. "Meaningful lives" become meaningless in these terms, the prerogatives of the privileged.

Detailed analysis of the political demographic policies of the Ceausescu regime, of which the criminalization of abortion was the central legislative act, has made it possible to focus on the social implications and human costs of restrictive reproductive legislation and policies, especially as they affect the lives of women and children. When reproductive legislation and policies are formulated according to abstract principles rather than in consideration of actual socioeconomic factors that influence the quality of human life, then the lived consequences are too often tragic, particularly for women and children. Ceausescu's Romania offers a glaring case study of the consequences of banning abortion and limiting the availability of and access to the resources that make everyday life livable. The Romanian case must be borne in mind by those who would ban abortion in the United States (or elsewhere). Otherwise, for those of us in the United States, the American dream will become an American nightmare to which we will all bear witness, and for which we will all share responsibility.

# APPENDIX: COURT CASES

The following are summaries of typical abortion-related court cases. They represent a diversity of circumstances as well as sentences. Copies of court files were obtained in 1990; their selection was arbitrary and in response to my request to the Ministry of Justice. (The one case specifically requested was not provided; the archives were in disarray, mirroring the turmoil of the immediate post-Ceausescu months, and it was said to be impossible to locate. While there is undoubtedly more than a kernel of truth to this claim, it should be noted that the case was a politically sensitive one involving a party activist, a gynecologist, who had been arrested in the 1980s.) File numbers for each case are given.

## CASE 1: FILE 10273/1987

The accused, E.M., was a 30-year-old married worker and mother of two children at the time of her trial in 1987. She had been indicted for a self-induced abortion through abdominal massage. She had been in the second month of pregnancy and was hospitalized for severe hemorrhaging. A uterine curettage was done, and it was determined that she suffered the consequences of a self-provoked incomplete abortion in the second month of pregnancy. Her case was presented to the prosecutor, who gave the reason for her indictment as the social danger of her action. She was sentenced to six months' imprisonment, which was commuted to correctional labor at her place of work. (She had no previous blemishes on her record and was judged to be otherwise well-behaved in her family, society, and place of work.) She was fined 350 lei to cover court costs.

## CASE 2: FILE 8094/1987

The accused was a 37-year-old married worker, the mother of two children (minors) at the time of her trial. She had been arrested for her activities in conjunction with arranging for the illegal interruption of her fourteen-year-old daughter's pregnancy.

Two other women were also implicated in this case. When, in December 1986, the accused learned of her daughter's pregnancy, she had called upon one of the co-defendants, a 60-year-old retired medical assistant. The accused had asked her to recommend someone who could examine her daughter. These three then visited the principal defendant, a retired 78-year-old doctor, to confirm the pregnancy of this minor. At that time, they also agreed on a date for the termination of the girl's pregnancy to be done at her home. The retired physician received 5,000 lei for her troubles; the other, who assisted her, received 2,000 lei. At the end of December the girl had a uterine curettage done. In January 1987, she was hospitalized with a diagnosis of post-abortive pelvic congestion. A medical exam revealed that her uterus had been enlarged. An immunologic test for pregnancy came back positive. The reasons for the indictments involved in this case included an induced abortion, illegal termination of a pregnancy, and illegal retention of instruments. The mother was sentenced to six months in prison, to be served through correctional labor at a socialist enterprise; the retired physician received a sentence of two years' imprisonment, confiscation of gynecological equipment, and a fine of 5,000 lei; the third adult was sentenced to a one-year prison term and a fine of 2,000 lei for assisting in an abortion and acting as an intermediary. Each of the accused was required to pay the state 1,200 lei to cover court costs. (The minor was not sentenced.)

### CASE 3: FILE 12379/1986

The accused, C.C., was a 28-year-old married office worker at the time of her trial. She was charged with consenting to terminate her normal pregnancy by means of the services of another person. Having learned that she was pregnant, and not wanting to keep the child, she had called a friend who put her in touch with an acquaintance. This latter was a 29-year-old hairdresser, D.C., who had no previous criminal offenses. The accused and her friend went to the house of the hairdresser, where they encountered Dr. G., a 78-year-old retired physician with previous criminal charges. He examined the accused and established that she was in her second month of pregnancy. Assisted by the hairdresser, he performed a curettage in exchange for 5,000 lei. Because of subsequent medical complications, she was hospitalized. It was determined upon examination that she had had an illegal abortion. A search at the residence of the doctor yielded surgical instruments forbidden by law to be in a doctor's personal possession. Moreover, vials of the narcotic hydromorphine-hydrochlorine were also found, for which he did not have authorization. The accused was sentenced to one year in prison with forced correctional labor at a socialist enterprise for the duration of her sentence. Dr. G., charged with doing an illegal abortion and with possession of illegally retained instruments and narcotic substances, was sentenced to two years and six months in prison and stripped of his civil rights for one year after his release; the 5,000 lei were confiscated from him, as were the surgical instruments and medications. He also had to pay hospital costs of 2,538 lei. The hairdresser, D.C., was sentenced to one year in prison because of the social danger her behavior represented and for assisting in an illegal abortion. The friend, whose participation in this criminal act was minimal, was fined 3,000 lei for her complicity. To cover court costs, Dr. G. was fined 1,600 lei; each of the others was fined 300 lei.

## CASE 4: FILE 10388/1986

The accused, C., was a 25-year-old married worker at the time of her trial. She was charged with consenting to an illegal abortion. In May 1986, in her third month of pregnancy, she had asked an acquaintance to recommend someone to whom she could go for an illegal abortion. The acquaintance gave her a sound and put her in touch with G.E., a 43-year-old married worker who was the mother of two children (both minors). The accused went to the residence of G.E. who introduced the sound into her uterus in order to induce an abortion; she received 500 lei in exchange. G.E. twice induced an abortion. Following these attempts, C. was hospitalized for an incomplete abortion during the third month of pregnancy, which resulted in infection, according to the medical-legal report. Because of the "social danger her actions represented," and for seeking an illegal abortion as well as carrying illegal abortive instruments, C. was sentenced to one year's imprisonment, to be served through correctional labor at a socialist enterprise. G.E. was condemned to two years and six months' imprisonment, fined 2,150 lei for doing five illegal abortions for sums of 300 to 500 lei each; in addition she was forced to surrender a one-half kilogram packet of "Vegeta," and to pay 3,234 lei to cover the hospital's costs and 406 lei for the clinic's. She was fined 2,150 lei to cover state costs, and 150 for court costs. The acquaintance was sentenced to one year and six months' imprisonment for twice assisting in abortions and for retaining and trafficking in abortion-related materials, as well as for serving as an intermediary between the other two guilty parties. Both C. and the acquaintance were fined 150 lei to cover court costs.

## CASE 5: FILE 457542/1987

The accused, C.A., was a nineteen-year-old unmarried worker at the time of her trial for an illegal abortion. At her residence, she had tried to induce an abortion during her third month of pregnancy by introducing her finger into her vagina while simultaneously rubbing her abdomen. As a result of her actions, she hemorrhaged. She was hospitalized with the diagnosis of an incomplete abortion in the third month of pregnancy. A curettage was done, and fetid, infected fragments were removed, along with pus. C.A. was sentenced to one year of imprisonment, to be served through correctional labor at the enterprise where she worked. The leniency of her sentence was due to her sincerity throughout the investigation, the positive reviews about her received from her place of work, and to her being unmarried. She was also fined 250 lei to cover court costs.

## CASE 6: FILE 4105/1987

The accused, M.L., was a 26-year-old unmarried worker who was tried for having induced an abortion. In her second month of pregnancy, M.L. had sought the assistance of C.V., a 36-year-old married nurse who was the mother of four children (all minors). C.V. introduced a rubber sound into M.L.'s uterus; she then injected a mixture of water and penicillin through the rubber sound. Four days later, M.L. was hospitalized and had a curettage done; the remainder of a previous ovulation was extracted. The medical-legal examination confirmed an abortion attempt in the second month of pregnancy. The rubber sound was found during a search of the residence of C.V. For having had an illegal abortion, M.L. was sentenced to eight months' imprisonment, to be served through correctional labor at her place of work. For doing an illegal abortion and for retaining abortion-related instruments, C.V. was sentenced to one year and four months' imprisonment, confiscation of the sound and of 1,000 lei received, and payment of 717 lei to cover the hospital's costs. Each was also required to pay 500 lei to cover court expenses.

### CASE 7: FILE 8196/1986

The accused, F.C., was a 57-year-old married women who worked at an agricultural cooperative; she was also a recidivist. She was charged with participating in the abortion of C.E. and with obtaining abortion-related materials that led to the permanent physical infirmity of C.E., who suffered a critical wound. C.E. had found herself pregnant from an extramarital affair with N.E., a 32-year-old clerk who was married and the father of one child. In June 1985 she had sought her lover's assistance in arranging for an abortion. N.E. begged G.G., a 43-year-old worker, married with two children (minors), to help him resolve this problem. G.G. asked his aunt, who lived in a community near Bucharest. She knew F.C., in her community, who did abortions. In July 1985 the two men escorted the pregnant woman to G.G.'s aunt's house. There, F.C. tried to induce an abortion. She told her client that if nothing happened in the next three days to return to try again. F.C. received 1,000 lei for her services. After three days, F.C. went to Bucharest and in the home of N.E. repeated the abortive method until she induced hemorrhaging. After a period of time, C.E.'s health deteriorated and she was hospitalized with a diagnosis of an incomplete septic abortion in the third month. Because of her toxic-septic state of shock and gangrene, a full hysterectomy was done, which resulted in a permanent physical infirmity. A medical-legal report confirmed that mechanical abortive maneuvers can interrupt a pregnancy and induce the eventual expulsion of the fetal matter. In this case, F.C. was sentenced to three years' imprisonment, to which were added the remaining 619 days from a previous sentence. A part of her punishment for performing an illegal abortion had been pardoned in 1984. However, because she had consciously committed another infraction of the law within three years of being pardoned, the benefits of that pardon were revoked; she was required to fulfill the remainder of her former sentence, which had not been executed. In 1986 she was charged with doing an illegal abortion, being a particularly serious social danger and a recidivist, and having illicitly increased her earnings. One thousand lei were confiscated from her to be paid to the state. N.E. was sentenced to two years and four months in prison for his complicity in inducing an illegal abortion. G.G. was sentenced to two years' imprisonment for complicity. The accused were required to pay the obstetrics-gynecology hospital a total of 6650 lei compensation, with a legal interest rate of 6 percent. Furthermore, each of the accused had to pay a 500 lei fine to cover court costs.

## CASE 8: FILE 5884/1987

F.F.P. was a retired physician who was charged with doing an illegal abortion and with the illegal possession of gynecological instruments found at his residence during a search. It was determined that in 1986, I.E., in her second month of pregnancy, had asked her mother to intervene to get the retired gynecologist to induce an abortion. F.F.P. had agreed to help her and went to the pregnant woman's residence to do so. He did not expect or receive any material gain (financial or otherwise) for his efforts because of their friendly relations. After this abortion maneuver, I.E. was hospitalized and treated; a uterine curettage was done. [The file was incomplete; no sentence was noted.]

# NOTES

## ACKNOWLEDGMENTS

1. It was there that I wrote the report *The Handmaids' Tale: Policy, Gender Ideology and the Body Politic in the Socialist Republic of Romania* for the National Council for Soviet and East European Research. This report was transformed into my articles "The Politics of Reproduction in Ceausescu's Romania: A Case Study in Political Culture" (1992a), "Abortion and International Adoption in Post-Ceausescu Romania" (1992b), and "Political Demography: The Banning of Abortion in Ceausescu's Romania" (1994), which are variously incorporated into this volume.

2. The circumstances of the unexpected rupture in our collaboration are described in Notes and Comments, "International Cooperation and Intellectual Property Rights: A Romanian Case," *East European Politics and Societies* 19(2) (1996): 328–32.

3. Some of the ideas and data contained especially in chapters 2 and 3 were independently published by Mezei during the period of our collaboration, without her informing me. I am now aware of the following such publications; there may be others. See, for example, Mezei, "Régulation politique et comportement démographiques en Roumanie" (1994); and "A Demographic and Sociological Review of the Romanian Demographic Policy and Its Consequences" (1993); "Famille roumaine et transition vers un autre système social" (1993). Also see Mezei, "L'Odysée de la famille roumaine" (1991), which I read in draft when we agreed to collaborate.

## INTRODUCTION

1. In a culture that favors sons, limiting the number of children to one per family means that female babies are at risk. Presumably, abortions are among the means used by women to rid themselves of unwanted female babies, with ultrasound assisting in the detection of the sex of the fetus. Female infanticide, child abandonment,

and maternal suicide are also practiced (see, for example, Greenhalgh and Li 1995). Girls constitute the majority of Chinese children eligible for adoption. (In Romania their corollary was Gypsy or Roma children.) Abortion in China is legal. It is difficult to determine whether the neglect of Chinese orphans is the result of state policy. However, the eugenics legislation is decidedly state-ordered, yet has received little mass-media attention in the West (see Dikotter 1996: 4–5).

2. Abortion became a feature of a woman's reproductive life usually after she had given birth to her first or second child. In response to the anti-abortion policies, Romanian women tended to marry at a younger age and finish childbearing at a younger age; illegal abortion was a primary method employed to limit fertility.

3. Abortion, although hotly contested in Ireland, remains illegal. This rough estimate of abortions performed in England and Wales is based on the number of women who provided their home addresses in Ireland for hospital records. See *World Abortion Policies*, May 24, 1994, published by the UN Department of Economic and Social Information and Policy Analysis. Hoff cites a figure of 5,000 abortions performed abroad annually (see Hoff 1994: 627).

4. The post-1989 intrusion of the Catholic Church into the intimate lives of Polish citizens was tempered by the liberalizing of abortion in Poland in fall 1996. A papal visit in spring 1997 prompted reconsideration of the legality of abortion, which remains a contested issue.

5. On the number of abortions in Brazil, see Barbosa and Arilha 1993: 408–17.

6. Bohlen 1995.

7. I invoke "the state" in its fully objectified form. Throughout this book, I follow popular Romanian usage and interchangeably refer to "the state," "the party," "the Party/State," or "the secret police." Although ethnographically "correct," these terms conceal or misrepresent the complexity of the institutionalized personal relations they are meant to represent.

In a totalizing state, individual interests and rights are subordinated to those of the state. The state controls freedoms of, for example, movement, speech, and reproduction. In effect, individuals are both members and properties of the nation-state.

8. These are but a few of the concerns that fall under the rubric of reproduction. Sexual practices (e.g., homosexuality) and the thorny issues associated with new reproductive technologies (e.g., surrogacy, fetal tissue and property rights) also form part of the spectrum of reproductive politics. The literature on any one aspect is broad, and its review is beyond the scope of this introduction.

9. Other policies in different state formations may be more revealing of the relationship between a state and its citizens. For example, in the United States, an ethnography of the tax system would provide an illuminating lens through which to study state-society relations: all citizens are subject to taxation, and many express their individuality through various forms of resistance and evasion. (I am indebted to Jack Katz for a useful discussion on the ethnography of the state.)

10. Among a vast literature ranging from rites of rebellion in peasant and industrial settings to the impact of second economies, I mention two standard works, both of which are by James Scott (1985, 1990).

11. I wish to thank Jack Katz for this insight about self-enrichment, which nicely captures the notion of social agency. Also, note that democratic systems present

more possibilities for engaging in acts of defiance than do totalitarian or totalizing states, a point to which I will return.

12. See Sayer 1994: 367–77. I thank Katherine Verdery for bringing this illuminating piece to my attention. Later in this introduction, I modify Sayer's insight somewhat: complicity is accompanied by related forms of duplicity.

It is beyond the scope of this book to take up classic issues of state legitimacy, consensus and coercion, and revolutionary social transformation.

13. Here I quote Ginsburg and Rapp (1995: 1), because they have already stated what I would otherwise have to rewrite. They point out, in relation to reproductive policies, what the critique of totalitarianism also emphasized: that "the power to define is not unidirectional." Top-down orders are rarely implemented fully as intended.

14. Sayer 1994: 369.

15. Bureaucratization has similarly routinized and formalized social exchange; the "faceless bureaucrat," like the "faceless masses," is an image that captures this distinction between individual subjectivities and objectified "bureaucrats."

16. See Lefort 1986, especially "The Image of the Body and Totalitarianism," pp. 292–307.

17. Again, it is beyond the scope of this introduction to discuss the critique of the state at length. In addition to the above references, see the useful article by Abrams (1988). Sayer reminds us that "even if the state . . . never stops talking, we cannot be sure that anybody is listening" (p. 370). Perhaps it is useful to qualify this statement further, pointing to the selectivity with which persons "listen." To what instrumental ends may also be queried.

18. The arbitrariness with which "could" was interpreted functioned as an important mechanism of control.

19. See Ginsburg and Rapp 1991: 311. I acknowledge my debt to these authors; their focus on the politics of reproduction provided a conceptual framework through which to pursue my research in Romania.

20. This characterization, which I have reproduced from Kligman 1992, was influenced by Ginsburg and Rapp 1991. See also Ginsburg and Rapp 1995 for analysis of diverse but related aspects of the politics of reproduction.

21. See Anderson 1991.

22. The banning of abortion is often heralded in the name of preventing the death of the nation. See, for example, Gal 1994. The ethnic cleansing campaigns in the dissolution of the former Yugoslavia employed this same logic.

23. The literature on fertility regulation is extensive. Hartmann 1995 offers a controversial overview of key issues and struggles around them.

24. Ginsburg and Rapp (1995) present richly illustrative materials.

25. This is not to suggest that women are solely responsible for their reproductive lives. For example, young women are often forced into sexual relations by older, stronger men. The Personal Responsibility Act contained in the Republican Congress members' "Contract with America" cynically specifies that mothers must identify fathers "as a condition for receiving AFDC [Aid to Families with Dependent Children]" but does not specify comparable "disciplinary" measures aimed at men who are unwilling to take responsibility for their sexual acts. Although efforts to compel men to pay child support are becoming more prevalent, the pro-male bias of this

document is hypocritical and, sadly, predictable. See Gillespie and Schellhas 1994: 65–77. For a more equitable application of the Personal Responsibility Act, see Pollitt 1995: 120.

26. Costello 1995. She wrote in defense of the need to protect late-term abortion techniques. Approximately the same proportion of Catholic women have abortions as do other women, a point for which I thank Henry David.

27. Debates about individual rights offer a venue through which to pursue an ethnography of the politics of reproduction. In the United States, the exercise and protection of one's rights are fundamental to the effective operation of democracy. Not surprisingly, "rights" are hotly contested by those whose differing interests make claim to them. See, for example, Petchesky 1990; Luker 1984; Ginsburg 1989.

28. See David 1994: 346.

29. This point is also made in Petchesky 1990: 156. On the risks associated with illegal abortion, see Miller 1993.

30. Katherine Verdery observed in a discussion that the Catholic Church was interested in the production process, whereas Ceausescu's regime was interested in the products themselves. For each, bodies served instrumental purposes.

31. The collusion between the Vatican and the Soviet Union at the World Population Conference in Bucharest in 1974 speaks to certain shared interests (Jean-Claude Chesnais, personal communication).

32. I wish to acknowledge Carolyn King for noting this point in a paper for my seminar on women, gender, and democracy offered at Georgetown University.

33. Although women are able to travel abroad to have abortions, this tells us little about the conditions in which abortions are performed.

34. Pronatalist policies are meant to alter behavior to promote higher fertility rates; they vary considerably in content and implementation. Romania's pronatalism was coercive.

35. Some who came to abhor these policies had failed to heed earlier warnings. For example, prominent international human rights organizations eschewed involvement before 1989 on the grounds that raising the complex issue of banned abortion might jeopardize funding in other important domains of their critical work.

36. Quoted in Zlatescu and Copil 1984: 14, and translated from the French.

37. Quoted in Serban 1988: 1. It is important for the reader to understand that 1988 was a year of extreme hardship for the majority of Romanians. The cynicism of such glorified pronouncements is total.

38. See Zlatescu and Copil 1984: 6. As chapter 4 discusses, the Second World, or Soviet-bloc countries, occupied an ambiguous position in the struggle between approaches to population policies and population regulation. Ceausescu adroitly manipulated this ambiguity to his advantage.

39. According to Pietila and Vickers (1994: 77), "hard though it is to believe" the preparations for the Population Conference in Romania initially did not include any recognition of "women's role in population questions."

40. Parvu 1988: 22.

41. Zlatescu and Copil 1984: 20.

42. Trebici 1975: 45.

43. Quoted from the Program of the Romanian Communist Party in Parvu 1988.

44. Ibid.

45. Zlatescu and Copil (1984: 31) provide a useful diagram of the interrelated economic and social policies. The section "L'utilisation rationnelle du fonds biologique, de réproduction (femmes de 15 à 49 ans)" succinctly lays out the "scientific" rationale behind the organization of political demography. Other diagrams such as "Le potentiel de la réproduction humaine" and "Le système des sciences" merit perusal. See pp. 26–37.

46. The literature is extensive; I cite but two works pertinent to this discussion because of the explicit link between population and governance. See, for example, Donzelot 1979 and Foucault 1991: 87–104.

47. Trebici 1979: 174.

48. Zlatescu and Copil 1984: 7. See also Ceausescu 1979. Ceausescu underscores that the socialist conception of democracy, and also of human rights, is based on the "necessity to ensure full equality between persons, to achieve equitable economic and social relations, which enable each citizen to lead a dignified life, with free access to schooling, culture, science, with the possibility of participating directly . . . in the governing of the entire society" (p. 109).

49. See Parvu 1988: 22; Trebici 1975: 48.

50. The objectification of such terms has been critically discussed with respect to the implications for academic writing. I use these terms intentionally throughout this book, with the understanding that the usage is problematic.

51. Foucault 1991: 100. I wish to thank Katherine Verdery for bringing this article of Foucault's to my attention. It helped to focus my ethnography of the Romanian state.

52. See Donzelot 1979: 48. This work has been influential to my approach.

53. Serban 1988: 1.

54. Ibid.

55. This study, in part, offers a case study of Foucault's trenchant contributions to our understanding of power, sexuality, discourse, and institutions. A readily accessible discussion of key Foucauldian concepts and methods of power as they apply to the analysis of the former communist states is presented by Horvath and Szakolczai (1992). They characterize a technique as a "procedure . . . close to the common meaning of things" (p. 27); techniques of power are directed at individuals. See also Gordon 1980, especially Lecture Two, pp. 92–108.

56. As Foucault noted, statistics reveal that "population has its own regularities, its own rate of deaths and diseases . . . ; statistics show also that the domain of population involves a range of intrinsic, aggregate effects, phenomena that are irreducible to those of the family, such as epidemics, endemic levels of mortality, ascending spirals of labour and wealth" (1991: 99).

57. Parvu 1988: 22.

58. On the use of statistics for disinformation, see Todd 1990: 17–21 in particular. Also see Alonso and Starr 1987.

59. See Asad 1994: 78, 79.

60. On the role of the intellectuals during Ceausescu's rule, see Verdery 1991a.

Regarding the social sciences, the absence of political science and psychology from the list is intentional. Political science as it is known to most readers was not taught; instead, Marxism-Leninism was the basis for instruction in political thought. Psychology had existed in Romania; however, in the 1970s a scandal emerged, provoked by the fascination of certain psychologists with transcendental meditation. Because meditation in any form provided individuals with a mode of escape from mind control and from an environment saturated by Communist Party symbols and practices, it was considered dangerous and was abolished as an academic discipline and research focus. Sociology was also considered to be a "dangerous" discipline that offered too much room for idiosyncratic interpretation. It too was abolished as an academic discipline in the 1970s, although sociological research was allowed to continue. The consequences of the decimation of the social sciences are now coming to the fore.

61. Just as doctors attended to the physical body, so priests ministered to the soul. Romania was not quite a godless state. The Orthodox Church officially represented the spiritual life of the Romanian nation. On the roles of priests and doctors in the management of sexuality and reproduction from the late eighteenth century on, see especially Donzelot 1979: 171–88.

62. Quoted in Zagorin 1990: 24.

63. Bourdieu attributes this reflexive process to the "ways of seeing and being" in which the acceptance of the world "as is" results because "their mind is constructed according to cognitive structures that are issued out of the very structures of the world." See Bourdieu and Wacquant 1992: 168.

64. Ibid.: 167. Others have written about this type of violence in related terms. For example, M. Simecka wrote of "civilized violence" and M. Marody of "covert repression" (Simecka 1982, Marody 1988: 113–32, both as cited in Sampson 1990). Some may argue that the distinction between cultures of fear and terror is academic; however, physical force wielded arbitrarily yet systematically in the public sphere is nonetheless different from physical force used under specific circumstances or from administrative repression as an effective control strategy. Ceausescu, for example, used physical force in a more circumscribed fashion than his predecessor, Gheorghiu-Dej. Under Ceausescu, terror became embodied in the sexual lives of women.

65. See Kornai 1992. The literature on the socialist system, command economies, and the like, is broad. For the purposes of this discussion, I also recommend Verdery 1991b and Campeanu 1988.

66. The quoted definitions are taken from the *Random House Dictionary of the English Language,* 1967: 443 (duplicity), and *The Oxford English Dictionary,* vol. 4, 1989: 616 (complicity).

67. Bourdieu aptly noted: "Any symbolic domination presupposes on the part of those who are subjected to it a form of complicity which is neither a passive submission to an external constraint nor a free adherence to values." In Bourdieu and Wacquant 1992: 168.

68. This is generally applicable to all authoritarian regimes of this sort, whether fascist or communist. Recall that in Romania, communication via mail and phone was subject to surveillance.

69. Sayer 1994: 374. The Havel essay, "The Power of the Powerless," is reprinted

in Havel 1990. The literature on power, hegemony, and resistance is extensive and cannot be treated here.

70. *Ketman* was introduced by Czeslaw Milosz in *The Captive Mind* (1990: 54–81). See also Sampson 1994: 12. Some may ask what distinguishes *dedublare* from *smecherie*, the art of cunning (typical of swindles, for example), which has enjoyed a long cultural history in Romania. *Smecherie* is more akin to a talent that some cultivate; *dedublare* became a virtual communicative mode as well as survival mechanism during communism. *Smecherie* as a cultural practice was individually realized. *Dedublarea* was a cultural practice present in all strata of society to greater or lesser degrees.On dissimulation as "refuge" from repressive structures, see Zagorin 1990.

71. I am aware of the reified quality of my intentional use of the self in terms of distinctive entities. Totalizing regimes recognize the danger of individual thought and attempt to control it through brainwashing, a powerful propaganda apparatus, and other means. The popular literature on this subject (e.g., George Orwell's *1984*) is extensive.

Scott's emphasis on the performative aspect of compliance is relevant to this discussion. See Scott 1990, especially on public and hidden transcripts.

72. The split self brings to mind problems of split consciousness. The split between official and private lives was recognized by East European authors. See, for example, Hankiss 1990: 97, 121. Gabor elaborated on the "schizophrenic duality" of socialist economies in "Second Economy and Socialism: The Hungarian Experience," in Feige 1989: 339–60.

D. Winnicott discusses the concept of the false self in psychoanalysis, which is suggestive with respect to understanding *dedublare*. The false self as I understand it corresponds readily with performative dimensions of getting needs met and with the infantilizing practices of the regime (to which Romanians themselves refer). (I thank Jeff Prager for the reference to Winnicott's chapter, "Ego Distortion in Terms of True and False Self," in Winnicott 1965: 140–52.)

In Romania, there are ritualized expressions (in word and deed) that offer respect through the kissing of the hand. A more problematic usage invoked by Behr in his book entitled *Kiss the Hand You Cannot Bite: The Rise and Fall of the Ceausescus* (1991), speaks to the power relations engaged in certain exchanges: anger is displaced by a kiss. It is a profoundly humbling gesture.

73. On the one hand, *dedublare* was internalized, becoming "second nature." This suggests that such behavior was not deliberate. On the other, *dedublare* has been labeled by Romanians themselves as a recognized behavioral mechanism. Having it both ways serves varied purposes.

74. It is important to recall that in totalizing regimes, individual options for participation or nonparticipation are quite limited. Hence, assessing degrees of complicity is both necessary and complicated.

75. Ginsburg and Rapp have used the term (1995: 3), defined by Shellee Colen to mean that "physical and social reproductive tasks are accomplished differentially according to inequalities that are based on hierarchies of class, race, ethnicity, gender, place in a global economy, and migration status and . . . are structured by social, economic, and political forces" ("'Like a Mother to Them': Stratified Reproduction and West Indian Childcare Workers and Employers in New York," in Ginsburg and Rapp 1995: 78). Stratified reproduction also pertains to concerns about surrogacy

and the effects of illegal abortion. It powerfully captures the essence of Nazi reproductive policies. See especially Bock 1991: 233–55.

CHAPTER 1.
BUILDING SOCIALISM IN CEAUSESCU'S ROMANIA

1. The quotation is from p. 297; see also pp. 292–306. John Thompson summarizes Lefort's characterization as: "The People-as-One forms a social body which is held together and sustained by a Power-as-One, a power which simultaneously embraces and stands for the whole." Quoted in the editor's introduction to Lefort ·1986: 24.

2. On nation-building strategies, see Jowitt 1971.

3. The "nationalization" of industry on June 11, 1948, represented the "real dialectical moment, the 'threshold' at which the backbone of the old society was broken" (Ionescu 1964: 163). This act was followed by a series of decisions of equal import. Collectivization, another "threshold" strategy, was unveiled in March 1949. See Jowitt 1978 and Kideckel 1993.

4. Ideological goals were to be achieved through the implementation of five-year plans, themselves devised through "rational planning." Indeed, the "plan" was the quintessential representation of rational control. See, for example, Verdery 1991b: 419–39; Lampland 1995, chapter 5.

5. Teitelbaum and Winter 1985: 100.

6. See, for example, Berelson 1979: 209–22; David and Wright 1971: 205–10; Moskoff 1980: 597–614; Pressat 1967: 1116–18 and 1979: 533–48; Teitelbaum 1972: 404–17. Note that modern contraceptives were unavailable.

7. The quotation is from Verdery 1991a.

8. In the 1980s Ceausescu declared that Romania would achieve economic independence through repayment of its international debt obligations. This was done at enormous cost to the population.

9. Balcony speech by Ceausescu, August 21, 1968, on Czechoslovakia; printed in full in *Scinteia*, August 22, 1968.

10. Ceausescu's emphasis on self-determination was inspired by Tito's insistence on self-independence; Ceausescu's ideological conviction was further cemented by his introduction to Kim Il-Sung's ideology of self-reliance. In the 1970s Ceausescu was also prominent in the Non-Aligned [Nations'] Movement, and, in addition, made overtures to the West, the Middle East, and the Far East.

11. Ceausescu's rehabilitation of Patrascanu served as a vehicle through which he isolated rivals within the party and discredited his predecessor, Gheorghiu-Dej. This political "rehabilitation" increased consensus about Ceausescu's rule. See "Hotarirea C.C. al P.C.R. cu privire la reabilitarea unor activisti de partid," 1968: 63–73; Ceausescu 1969: 67. See also Hodos 1987; Tismaneanu, forthcoming.

12. Ceausescu's power was not yet secure, hence his resistance to these trends was conveniently hidden.

13. See Fischer 1989; Durandin 1990.

14. Ceausescu, as translated by Verdery 1991a: 117.

15. For example, J. D. Rockefeller, a member of the American delegation, praised Ceausescu for his concerns about the role of governments in ensuring their

population's well-being: "It is gratifying and encouraging that you say this because I do not believe there are many heads of state who cast the problem of population in this perspective." Quote from the stenogram of a meeting between Ceausescu and Rockefeller during the 1974 World Population Conference. (Courtesy of Romania's Department of Defense and the archives under the authority of the army, 1994.)

16. See, for example, Sampson 1984c. The systematization plans were made public in stages, even though they had been discussed in the Executive Committee of the R.C.P. as early as 1967. (I was able to read the transcript of this meeting in June 1994, courtesy of the Ministry of Defense, which had authority over these archival materials.) By the mid-1980s, the more fully elaborated "systematization" plans were condemned throughout the West, as were the political demographic ones cited above.

17. For example, in regard to the U.S. opening to China, see Isaacson 1992: 243, 338. Ceausescu's visits to China and North Korea during this period planted the seeds for his own "cultural revolution" and personality cult. Ion Iliescu, the first post-Ceausescu president of Romania, referred to this in his memoir, *Revolutie si reforma* (Iliescu 1993: 22).

18. The formal political valorization of the family and of motherhood has been typical of totalizing regimes. See, among many others: Koonz 1987; de Grazia 1992; Moeller 1993; Lapidus 1978; Jancar 1978; Stacey 1983.

19. In relative terms, international in-migration of labor was minimal. In the former Eastern bloc, the GDR and Czechoslovakia were exceptions, importing labor from other "fraternally" related, less-developed countries such as North Vietnam, Cuba, and Angola. The Soviet Union regularly imported "fraternal" workers (from North Korea, Romania, Bulgaria, North Vietnam, and other communist countries) on temporary contracts. The conditions under which these guest workers labored were usually slave-like. In Czechoslovakia, for example, Vietnamese workers rioted to protest the conditions in which they were forced to live. (I thank Jean-Claude Chesnais for information on "fraternal" labor in these countries.)

20. At the Tenth Party Congress in 1969, Ceausescu introduced the concept of the "multilaterally developed socialist society" in which the material and spiritual realms of society would be created according to socialist principles. (I thank Vladimir Tismaneanu for pointing out that Ceausescu did not invoke this phrase until the Tenth Congress.) At the Ninth Congress, he referred to the "improvement in the building and final victory of communism in our country." See also Shafir 1985, part 1.

21. See Trebici 1981. Also see David and McIntyre 1981.

22. At the beginning of the twentieth century, the average number of children per woman was five; before World War II, it had dropped to four (see Trebici 1991: 42; I acknowledge Smaranda Mezei's initial input into this discussion). Four and five children per woman were the figures dictated in the abortion laws as modified during the Ceausescu reign.

23. Especially during this initial period when communist rule was imposed, the Romanian Communist Party (like the others in the Soviet sphere of influence) mimicked the policies of Big Brother. At the time, the Romanian leadership was generally Soviet trained and controlled. This set the stage for intense internal struggle within the party over foreign or domestic determination of policies.

24. It may be argued that collectivization and the heavy industrialization drives were enforced during their "second wave" implementation phases, from 1958 to 1962 for collectivization, and continuously for industrialization. The use of violence in the early phase had a different function than later on; in the initial years, violence pertained more to the radical destruction of the "past;" in later years, to disciplining the population. See Jowitt 1971: 92–173.

25. Jowitt discusses the nation-building strategies of Leninist states in particular. He defines "breaking through" as the "*decisive alteration or destruction of values, structures, and behaviors which are perceived by a revolutionary elite as comprising or contributing to the actual or potential existence of alternative centers of political power*" (1971: 1; original italics). It is noteworthy that Jowitt, in this seminal work, does not mention the abortion law, itself central to demographic control and transformation.

26. The state's liberalization of abortion publicly formalized a popular practice of last resort. In this manner, the state transformed peasant norms. On the traditional peasant family, see Kligman 1988. Shortly after the end of World War II, 76.6 percent of the population lived in rural areas; approximately three-quarters of the active "work force" was engaged in agricultural work. By 1977, 56.4 percent of the population continued to live in rural locales. Although many rural inhabitants were no longer agricultural workers, they nonetheless lived primarily according to the norms of their communities. It is beyond the scope of this work to discuss the ambivalent role of the peasantry for the Romanian Communist Party.

27. See, for example, Verdery 1983; Kligman 1988; Kideckel 1993.

28. Commuting was instituted by the regime and fit well with the systematization plans. Although commuting resolved a host of infrastructural problems, it contributed to local atomization. While extended family relations could be maintained, they were transformed. Some male heads of household, for example, returned to their villages only on weekends. Although they remained members of their families and communities, they lost touch with the rhythms of daily life.

29. See *Anuarul statistic al Romaniei, 1990*: 51. For more differentiated data on social structural changes in Romania, see, for example, Cazacu 1988. Also, see Muresan 1996. According to her data, the urban population increased by 4.9 percent between 1948 and 1956. This rapid growth gradually slowed; between 1956 and 1966, the urban population increased by 2.3 percent; between 1977 and 1992, by 1.86 percent.

30. From 1956 to 1965, the birthrate declined to 14.6 per 1,000. See *Anuarul statistic al Romaniei, 1990*: 66–67.

31. For specific trends, see Trebici and Ghinoiu 1986: 48.

32. See Chesnais 1992, appendix A2.4, pp. 547–48. The Hungarians did not adopt the policies instituted in Romania. Instead, they turned to maternity incentives.

33. The issuance of this decree coincided with Ceausescu's insistence at the Ninth Party Congress on collective leadership. Chivu Stoica, who signed the decree, was later removed from his leadership position, and collective leadership as a style of governance was also abandoned.

34. On the use of terror as a political instrument during the Dej period, by and large modeled after Stalin, see Jowitt 1971, especially chapter 6.

35. A joke captures the nature of reciprocal complicity, which served as a form of social contract: The five paradoxes of the Romanian Socialist Republic are:

—Even though no one works, the plan is fulfilled beyond expectation.
—Even though the plan is fulfilled beyond expectation, nothing is available.
—Even though nothing is available, everyone eats.
—Even though everyone eats, they are not satisfied (thankful).
—Even though they are not grateful, everyone claps their hands.

(The last refers to people showing their adoration for Ceausescu by clapping on command even though they despised him.) See Itu 1992: 11.

For ethnographically informed studies of workers, see Haraszti 1978; Burawoy and Lukacs 1992.

36. The drama of Romania's abandoned children became public upon the fall of the Ceausescu regime, after which the orphanages became the focus of intense international assistance. This background describes the context in which they were created. In Ceausescu's Romania, adults were frequently "abandoned" to prisons or psychiatric institutions.

37. From 1948 to 1989, there was little variance, with men constituting approximately 49.3 percent of the population; women, 50.7 percent. See *Anuarul statistic al Romaniei, 1990*: 50. In general, women constitute the majority of the population because male mortality is higher than women's.

38. See Lapidus 1977: 136.

39. It is worth noting the distinction between "presence" and "representation." Jan Gross makes a similar distinction between embodiment and representation (J. Gross 1992: 56–71).

Also, certain women wielded enormous power. Most notable among them were Ana Pauker, minister and Central Committee secretary between 1947 and 1952, and Elena Ceausescu. Both of these women were reviled and feared.

40. According to Ceausescu, in his address to the 1985 National Conference on Women, 126 of the 446 members and adjunct members of the Central Committee were women. In the regional committee bureaus of the party, women constituted approximately 40 percent of the active members (Ceausescu 1985). That women participated in the public sphere in this manner bears directly on the backlash against them in the postcommunist transition. This is a general phenomenon in the region, and it must be analyzed in terms of the accession of men to their "traditional" roles as the holders of power in patriarchal orders.

Note that Gheorghiu-Dej's politburo was all male after Ana Pauker's ouster. There were no women among the alternate members. (I thank Vladimir Tismaneanu for calling my attention to this.)

On class fractions and relations of domination, see, in particular, Bourdieu 1984.

41. It is important to point out that men were also, if differently, subject to the double burden under socialism through their labor in the second economy. See, for example, Kligman 1992: 364–418; Goven 1993: 224–40.

The problematic relationship between women's roles in the family and in the broader society was recognized early on by sociologists and demographers, who noted a "negative correlation . . . between fertility and the affirmation of women's status in society" (see Trebici 1974, 565).

42. For brief, summary data, see the National Report prepared for the World Conference on Women, Beijing, 1995: *The Condition of Women in Romania (1980–1994)*. This figure is cited on p. 40.

43. While maximization was stated as a goal, contradictory policies addressed different ideological concerns. For example, when women were brought into the labor force, retirement occurred at a relatively young age: normally 57 for women, 62 for men. Retirees frequently became unpaid laborers as childcare providers in the private sphere.

44. Regrettably, there are no statistics to demonstrate macro trends, much less differentiated statistics at the micro level. The "feminization" of certain occupations was characteristic throughout the region. Wage differentials between men and women working in similar positions were customary throughout most of Eastern Europe, with women's salaries being significantly lower. On gender inequality, see, for example, Molyneux 1982; Rueschemeyer and Szelenyi 1989: 81–109.

45. For example, in 1989 women constituted 53.4 percent of those involved in telecommunications; 62.5 percent in services; 58.6 percent in the arts, culture, and education (*Anuarul statistic al Romaniei, 1990*: 116).

46. The contradictions between women's socially productive and reproductive labor highlight the evident slippage in a set of murky categorical distinctions that have long plagued the relationship between Marxism and feminism.

47. The legislation of pro- or antinatalist reproductive rights necessarily engages states in the private lives of their citizens. Protection of rights differs fundamentally from state legislation of reproductive behavior. The latter usurps citizens' rights to privacy and intimacy.

48. Classic writings on this point by Marx, Engels, Lenin, and Stalin are found in *Women and Communism* 1950. Among the extensive literature on the topic, see also Mill and Taylor 1870; Levi-Strauss 1969; Barrett 1988.

49. The conflation of "bourgeois" family relations with peasant family organization contributes to the "disappearance" or "silencing" of women (or backlash against them) in the current transition. The relationship between paternalism and patriarchy is seminal. See, for example, Pateman 1988.

50. I thank Pat Merloe for this comment about socialist language characterizing the relations between the state and its citizens: the language itself creates duties or obligations for citizens; the only rights protected are those of the state over its citizens.

51. This point is consequential in that men lost their "right" to women as private property.

52. This 1973 statement on gender homogenization concludes with his noting: "Nonetheless I believe that women must work more intensely toward the liquidation of the negative attitudes that still dominate in these domains." In effect, it was the responsibility of women to combat sexism (see Ceausescu 1973a: 9).

53. Pateman 1989: 185.

54. On socialist paternalism, see also Bruszt 1988: 43–76; Goven 1992; Verdery 1994: 225–55. The relationship to the family differed importantly in the "bourgeois" state. There, the state historically depended on patriarchal authority to maintain order; the "head of family was *accountable* for its members. In exchange for the

protection and recognition of the state, he had to guarantee the faithfulness to public order of those who were part of that order" (Donzelot 1979: 49). Donzelot 1979 is useful historical-comparative reading on the relationship between the state and families.

55. This quotation from Ceausescu's opening address to the National Conference for Women in 1966 signaled the regime's "right" to supervise the family in the interest of socialist well-being. Quoted in *Femeia* 10 (1966): 2.

56. Such tactics were employed shamelessly during the Gheorghiu-Dej era. During collectivization, villagers were traumatized with threats that if they did not join the collective, a child would be denied entrance into school or a relative would be denied a job. The role of the family—official and unofficial—merits serious treatment. I regret that Smaranda Mezei did not write the study on that topic that she claimed to be writing for a doctoral thesis; it is of profound importance for a nuanced understanding of complicity and resistance.

57. Here, regime mobilization techniques were often called upon to heighten people's sense of insecurity in other domains. For example, dependence on the paternalist state was strengthened by Ceausescu's manipulation of national independence. Ultimately, Ceausescu's brand of nationalism turned against the Romanian people themselves.

58. Consistent with such multilaterally developed microcosms whose internal organizations conflated the boundaries between public and private, gynecological exams to determine the health of women of childbearing age were carried out at state-enterprise medical facilities whenever possible. The building of agro-industrial complexes as dictated by the systematization plans followed a similar logic, which emerged from the central projects of creating "the new socialist person" and building socialism (discussed below).

59. One viable option was to drop out of the official sphere and work as a seasonal migrant laborer in construction, agriculture, or the like. In many cases, such labor was lucrative. At the same time, it led to social dislocation. An attempt to manipulate the issue of residence permits is presented in the case of Dr. I.G. discussed in chapter 6.

60. In 1974 state Decree 225 was issued prohibiting the residence, however temporary, of almost all foreigners in the homes of Romanians. This had particular consequences for researchers and tourists as well as relatives other than close ones. In the 1970s, legal foreign guests could be accommodated in private homes provided they were registered with the local district militia. Any person who did not register a guest risked being heavily fined and put on the "watch" list. The ever-present building "super" gave the state's eyes perfect vision, unless something blocked the view—such as a bribe. My first field research in Romania began in 1975. Many of the foreign researchers were housed in the same building, making surveillance easier. With the exception of the building administrator, the Romanian residents avoided the foreigners.

61. I am grateful to Nick Andrews for calling attention to this point. Ceausescu's father, however, was said to have been a drinker and irresponsible. Popescu notes that Ceausescu was like a harsh father whose love was expressed through severity (see Popescu 1993: 237).

62. See Jowitt 1978; Tismaneanu 1992: 287; Georgescu 1985. This was not the only regime in which "socialism in one family" was characteristic; the same was true in North Korea, for example.

63. Another popular meaning was associated with the interpretation of PCR: *pile, cunostinte si relatii* (pull, connections, and relations)—which again characterized the way things were accomplished. With respect to political positions held by extended family members, see de Flers 1984: 165–73; and Brucan's octopus diagram in Brucan 1992: 273. On traditional family organization, see Kligman 1988.

64. See Kligman 1988.

65. Elena Ceausescu's nefarious influence on the formulation of legislation and policy is asserted by most Romanians. She was universally perceived as a dragon lady. Even Nicolae Ceausescu is often said to have been victim to her cunning. Assumption weighs more heavily than empirical evidence in accounts about this much-hated couple.

66. I wish to thank Jean-Claude Chesnais for these figures. By 1965 the infant mortality rate had fallen to 44 per 1,000.

67. Jokes provided a venue for the popular expression of opinion. In one, Ceausescu visits a collective farm in the southwest of the country. In his speech to the workers amassed to hear him, he proclaims: "I need many children!" and exhorts women to bear them. When he finished his speech, one of the organizers of this gathering asked if anyone had any questions. No one did. He asked again, and again. Finally, one of the Gypsy women present raised her hand to inquire: "Comrade Ceausescu, to make this happen, do we come to you, or will you come here to us?"

68. As times became harder, it was more difficult for families to manage. In urban areas in particular, grandparents (often pensioners) took on more unpaid household responsibilities such as childcare, cooking, and shopping. In the 1980s, the latter was more akin to hunting and gathering. In this regard, social reproduction had become the responsibility of women and the elderly. It was often the elderly who were left to spend endless hours standing in line to obtain scarce necessities for daily needs. They were jokingly referred to as *soimii pietei*, falcons of the markets (in contrast to the *soimii patriei*, falcons of the nation, mentioned below).

69. Although heredity is a primary factor in the label *neam bun*, other factors came into play as well: honor, moral fortitude, hard work, wisdom, prudence, and decency (see Kligman 1988: 31–35).

70. The Uniate, or Greek-Catholic, church was introduced into Transylvania in the 1700s during the Austro-Hungarian empire. Some argue that this was deliberate on the part of Hungarians to destabilize Transylvania. The Uniate church was outlawed during the communist period. It was the confessional church of a large segment of the population, especially in Transylvania. It was also the church to which National Peasant Party leaders such as Iuliu Maniu belonged.

71. Proper sexual behavior was propagandized by exalting the virtues of marriage and families with many children. Homosexuality, deviant because it was said to defy the natural laws of reproduction, was punished by law under article 200 of the Penal Code.

72. See Toranska 1987. Elsewhere in Central Europe, the private sphere became

the locus for the reemergence of civil society, although not for the transformation of gender relations within this sphere. See, for example, Einhorn 1993: 58–68.

73. I have translated *om* (customarily connoting the encompassing category, "man") as "person" in keeping with the ideological intentions of homogenization.

74. Ceausescu 1972a: 74–75.

75. "Fraternal" relations always had a double connotation. In addition to the ritualized political reference, there was also the traditional one: "You choose your friends; siblings are God-given." For example, Romania had fraternal relations with the Soviet Union and "friendly relations" with France.

76. Council of State Decree 153 of March 24, 1970, published in *Buletinul oficial,* no. 33, April 13, 1970. See also the "Ethical Code of the Communist Party." For a discussion of parasitism under National Socialism, particularly with regard to Nazi body politics, see Bock 1989: 271–96.

77. To illustrate, when someone applied to emigrate, his or her employment was usually terminated. A subsequent visit by a member of the security apparatus to ascertain what this individual did with his or her time would reveal that said person was unemployed. After such an interview, the person could be imprisoned from one to six months on the grounds of parasitism in accordance with article 1 of Decree 153/1970.

Decree 153/1970 was invoked in the trial that followed the interethnic violence of March 1990 in Tirgu Mures and was used discriminatorily against Roma in particular (see Helsinki Watch 1991: 15–24).

78. The collapse of communist regimes throughout the Soviet sphere was dramatically marked by "the people" reclaiming public spaces. The world was treated to repeated images of the weighty monuments of communism being brought down—often with difficulty. See, for example, Kligman 1990: 393–438.

79. J. Thompson, in his explication of Claude Lefort's work (1986: 24) notes that the state (as the "people-as-one") "forms a social body which is held together and sustained by a Power-as-One, a power which simultaneously embraces and stands for the whole." In Ceausescu's Romania, homogenization was the fulfillment of "wholeness."

The armed forces served as an important milieu for disciplining young men into new socialist persons. The socially productive role of these forces grew as production in certain domains became more dependent on militarization: the military was expected to harvest crops as well as to construct the House of the People and the Boulevard of Socialist Victory.

80. By the late 1980s the overall plan became known outside of Romania as the village destruction plan, although the most significant actual destruction was to the capital city itself. See, for example, Giurescu 1989.

81. Scientific nourishment is discussed in chapter 5.

82. I highly recommend J. Gross's succinct discussion on the "totalitarian style of language" as a technique of social control. Referring to one of Stalin's phrases "utterly divorced from the evidence of the surrounding reality," Gross notes that "under the rules of totalitarian language usage, Stalin had the copyright on defining reality" (see J. Gross 1988: 236–39).

83. See Lefort 1986: 299.

84. Ceausescu's defense of the nation was a source of pride in the late 1960s and the 1970s. By declaring the rights of nations to self-determination, he took a stance against the Soviets, although he did not waver in his commitment to communism. His brand of communism was Stalinist; however, his nationalism (also Stalinist) was intended to castigate the non-Romanian implementation of communism in Romania. The reference is to the large number of Jews and Hungarians in leadership positions in the late 1940s and 1950s. It is not surprising that Ceausescu's "Romanian" origins were called into question immediately after his execution; to accept his indigenous roots, so to speak, is to accept recognition of complicity with his rule.

85. See Sampson 1987. By the 1980s, living in a village proved easier in many respects than in "modern" urban areas. Villagers usually had access to forests. Despite the nationalization of forests, poaching of wood was widespread. Rural dwellers were able to be warm and to heat water on their wood-burning stoves. In response to similar government edicts during the following winters, urban dwellers improvised alternative heat sources, such as installing tiled wood-burning stoves, often vented through windows. But alternative heating was filled with risks: some using gas stoves to warm themselves forgot to close the gas valve when that source of centrally controlled energy was shut off. The remaining gas pressure was too little to maintain heat, but sufficient to result in death by asphyxiation.

86. The literature on the state and civil society and the relationship to a public sphere is the topic of intense debate. It is beyond the scope of this chapter to review it.

87. See Lefort 1986: 285–86.

88. To what degree this contributed to the lack of samizdat literature in Romania is unclear. However, registering typescripts did not facilitate circulation.

89. By the mid-1980s, people were supposed to acquire approval to meet with a foreigner before the encounter, in contrast to the practices of the 1970s, when written reports were expected to be submitted after a meeting had taken place by plan or chance.

90. There were odd twists to these reshaped relations. In the village where I lived, family members who lived in the nearby city often sent tomatoes procured in their local market to their families in the village because weather conditions had damaged the expected vegetable yield in the family private plot. For related analyses, see Kideckel 1993; Kligman 1988; Verdery 1983.

91. As has been seen with respect to the abortion legislation, repression and concession frequently went hand-in-hand. Ceausescu attempted to use the tactic of offering concessions to his disgruntled population during his final balcony speech on December 21, 1989; however, by then symbolic gestures had lost their efficacy. Promises of pension and family-allowance increases were perceived as what they were: too little, too late.

92. These privileges ranged from access to special stores, hotels, and hospitals to high salaries. The Orthodox Church was considered by many to be married to the Communist Party. The chief rabbi also represented the party line in exchange for certain privileges for the small Jewish population.

93. This applied to almost all domains of acquisition. For example, it was typical to enter a restaurant with unoccupied tables and be told that none were free—

until money or cigarettes magically made them so. Again, the literature on the second economy is too extensive for citation. See also Feher et al. 1983.

94. See Sampson 1984a.

95. Self-financing and global accord were economic strategies by which workers were designated as responsible for their own successes. These strategies constituted other distorted forms of individual social action promoted by the regime.

96. On the sociology of standing in lines, see Campeanu 1994. Campeanu also notes that the competition inherent in this activity contributes to the destruction of social solidarity, as mentioned above.

97. The state attempted to determine what its citizens had the right to ingest, although the rationing system did not guarantee that all items were adequately supplied. Individuals could go to acquire the allotted quantities at their convenience rather than wasting hours in lines. Whether a particular item was available is a different matter. When I returned to the village where I did extensive field research, I arranged with local officials for my own ration "rights."

Rationing varied across the country, the capital being least affected. But, according to one informant, allotments per person per month in Cluj were: 1 kg. of sugar, 1 kg. of flour, 1 kg. of cornmeal, approximately 6 oz. of butter, ten eggs, 750 ml. of cooking oil, ten to twenty liters of gasoline. By contrast, in Bucharest each person had the "right" to 1.5 kgs. of sugar, 1 liter of cooking oil, and 40 liters of gasoline. The rest were not rationed per se. Again, availability was another matter. Distribution was at best arbitrary. Like their village counterparts, Bucharest residents learned about deliveries and lines worth standing in by word of mouth. Although rationing was limited to oil and sugar, a person could buy only limited quantities of other items at one time. Hence, one person waiting in line might be allowed to purchase only one packet of butter, one kg. of meat, etc. Children became important pawns in the art of standing in lines. "Families with many children and little money lent their children to those who had money but few children," a friend explained to me. (See Wedel 1986 for a description of the underground professional organization of lines that developed in Poland.)

Endless jokes about lines circulated. Their blackness varied; here is one: "At a long line for meat, one citizen nervously said to the person next to him: 'Please keep my place. I'm going to murder Ceausescu!' After a while, he returned. When the person who was keeping his place saw him, he asked: 'Well, how did it go? Did you murder him?' 'Not yet—but I left someone holding my place in that line too'" (Itu 1992: 20). The situation in rural areas was much more severe: receipt of one's rations depended on meeting one's production quotas.

98. It is an intriguing coincidence that the word for seller, *vinzator*, also means "traitor." Ironically, *vinzatori* were key people whose activities kept the system going yet contributed importantly to its demise. In effect, they "sold out" their country.

99. The case of dissident writer Paul Goma, who was forced into exile in 1977, perhaps chastened other intellectuals with similar aspirations. In comparison with other East European intellectuals, the Romanians generally remained, at their best, passive. See Verdery 1991a; Tismaneanu 1992.

100. This point seems pertinent to understanding Mikhail Gorbachev's misunderstanding of the social dynamic unleashed by *glasnost* and *perestroika* in the Soviet

Union. Gorbachev, the benevolent paternalist leader, seemed baffled by the "in-gratitude" shown him for liberalizing the state's treatment of its citizens, as manifest most immediately in the emergence of interethnic strife.

## CHAPTER 2.
## LEGISLATING REPRODUCTION UNDER SOCIALISM

1. Translated from the republication of the Romanian original in Zlatescu and Copil 1984: 10: "Décision du comité politique executif du comité central du P.C.R. concernant l'accroissement de la responsabilité des organes et des organisations du parti, des organes d'État et du personnel médico-sanitaire dans l'accomplisse-ment de la politique démographique et pour assurer une croissance adéquate de la population."

2. The quoted expression is taken originally from Mitchell 1974: 231. Moeller quoted it in 1993: 2.

3. Laws were issued both by the Council of State and the Grand National As-sembly, the legislative bodies of the Socialist Republic of Romania. Laws were signed by the president of the assembly, and usually the president of the country. Decrees were issued by the executive branch of the government and were signed by the prime minister. The former had to move through a lengthier process. The instru-mentality of decrees lay in part in their immediate efficacy. Instructions to laws and decrees were then elaborated by the ministries charged with supervising their im-plementation. Throughout this study, laws and decrees are treated interchangeably inasmuch as their societal effect was interchangeable. Also, the reader will note that the date of a law's signing did not always correspond with the date of its public un-veiling through publication in the official bulletin. The date of official publication is the one that legally affected the population.

The Council of State was a legislative body that issued laws and decrees; it was also responsible for the scheduling and organization of the Grand National Assembly. The Council of Ministries was an executive body that issued decisions and was largely responsible for the formulation and implementation of policy. See Fischer 1989; Shafir 1985: 94–104; Graham 1982: 65–67.

4. The founding principles are contained in the Constitution of the Popular Re-public of Romania, written and approved in 1948 and further elaborated in 1952.

5. The Family Code was adopted under Law 4, 1953, and published in the *Bule-tinul oficial*, no. 1, January 4, 1954.

6. Decree 456/1955 (published in *Buletinul oficial al Marii Adunari Nationale a R.P.R.*, no. 30 [November 1,1955]) modified the 1948 text (of art. 456 of the Penal Code), noting that a medical abortion is legal if the pregnancy represents a danger to the woman's life or if one of the parents suffers from a grave hereditary illness.

7. See Decree 571, published November 5, 1956.

8. See especially Trebici 1974: 564–73; quotation, 565.

9. I thank Katherine Verdery for this insight. Contraception provided indepen-dent options for managing one's relationship to the Party/State. Also see Zielinska 1993: 55–56.

10. See Zlatescu and Copil 1984 for an overview of this relationship. Also see Nydon 1984.

11. See Trebici and Ghinoiu 1986: 43. The classic demographic transition theory has been the focus of substantive critique. The assumed three stages of transition have been questioned on the grounds of over-generalization. Some critics have pursued analyses more sensitive to socioeconomic levels, noting differentiation of transition processes based on class, for example. See, for example, Greenhalgh 1990; Kertzer and Hogan 1989; Schneider and Schneider 1996; Watkins 1986.

12. Trebici and Ghinoiu 1990: 78.

13. I thank Jean-Claude Chesnais for the TFRs from 1946 to 1989.

14. Jerzy Berent noted that the number of births recorded in 1966 was only 60 percent of that in 1955. See Berent 1970: 35.

15. Chesnais 1992: 584. The unreliability of historical data must be considered, although we can reasonably assume that mortality was still higher in earlier periods.

16. Infant mortality rates are not as directly linked to urbanization and formal educational levels as fertility rates. The former may be affected by educational and public health initiatives, such as those undertaken, for example, by UNICEF, the United Nations, and other international organizations.

17. See Kligman 1988: 65–66. The socialist state, wanting to medicalize gynecological practices according to scientific standards, forbade the continued activities of unlicensed midwives. This was another attack on customary village life.

18. New immigrants to town were generally employed in jobs for unskilled workers (e.g., construction, heavy labor).

19. Oral histories and literary works are good sources from which to gain information about these methods; reliable statistical data or systematic studies are unavailable.

20. See Istrati 1969: 85. These observations are about events in a provincial Romanian town in the 1930s.

21. See *Anuarul statistic al Romaniei, 1990*: 210; Zlatescu 1984: 41. The prosperity of the late 1930s was sometimes referred to as a small Romanian economic "miracle." See *Enciclopedia Romaniei*, vol. 4, 1943: 941–72.

22. The relationship between class and access to abortion is comparatively and historically consistent, except when abortion is liberalized and made available at low cost to all.

23. The liberalization and criminalization of abortion in Romania (as well as in other Soviet bloc countries) followed patterns similar to those in the USSR. In the USSR abortion had been liberalized in the 1920s; in Romania it was liberalized in 1957. In the USSR, abortion was banned in 1936; in Romania it was banned in 1948 and 1966. Over time, ideological positions were changed to meet political-economic needs.

On the comparative enactment of similar Moscow-inspired laws, see Zielinska 1993: 52, note 14.

24. Between 1949 and 1957, the birthrate decline represented about five in 1,000 women, dropping from 27.6 percent to 22.9 percent. The decline in fertility was more impressive: from 3.34 children per woman in 1949 to 2.73 per woman in 1957. (I thank Jean-Claude Chesnais for these figures.)

25. In the 1950s, the Palatul Justitiei (Palace of Justice) was renamed the Tribunalul Mare, or High Court. "Palat" (palace) was an inappropriate label for an institution in a state predicated on the dictatorship of the proletariat.

26. The name "Avortorium" was imported from the USSR for this particular gynecological section of the hospital. In 1955 abortion was again liberalized in the Soviet Union. The places where abortions where done were called "Abortariums," nicknamed "meat grinding machines." As many as 300 women per day had abortions, with anywhere from two to six being done simultaneously. See Heinen and Matuchniak-Krasuska 1992: 71. The jurist's recollection was provided by Smaranda Mezei.

27. See Decree 463 published in the *Buletinul oficial*, September 26/30, 1957.

28. See Teitelbaum and Winter 1985: 101.

29. The lack of commentary about this revision is noted in Zlatescu 1982: 238.

30. See Zielinska 1993: 50, 53; Berelson 1979. Regarding previous anti-abortion laws in the Soviet Union, see, for example, Goldman 1993.

31. Jean-Claude Chesnais suggests that the decriminalization of abortion in the USSR may have been a strategy meant to affect what had become a demographic imbalance. The years 1933–1945 were characterized by de-kulakization, purges, famine, and deportation; after the war and a return to peace, there was a significant baby boom, which created problems for the Soviets with respect to childcare facilities, housing, education, and budgetary allocations. Liberalization of abortion in 1955 may have served internal political demographic "corrective" interests. (Personal communication.)

32. The general repression of the late 1940s was redirected in the late 1950s, notably against intellectuals and peasants. (The final phase of forced collectivization was ordered in 1958.) Propaganda was heightened, and marked by public scapegoatings of persons alleged to be guilty of not fulfilling quotas and other transgressions. Deportations to the Baragan area followed. See *Cartea alba a Securitatii* 1996, vol. 2: 21; vol. 3: 12, 38, 587.

33. The decrease in the number of offspring did not affect the popularity of marriage. In general, couples married at a young age.

34. These phases are approximate. For example, the abortion law was revised in 1985, although related policies began to change in 1984.

35. Divorce also aggravated infrastructural problems, such as that generated by the housing shortage. Cases of divorced persons having to continue living together because of the lack of alternatives were common.

36. See Decree 680 published in the *Buletinul oficial*, no. 106, October 7, 1969; Decree 312, in *Buletinul oficial*, no. 96, August 31, 1977. Refer to Zlatescu 1982: 245–48.

37. See Ioan 1988: 251. Divorce is the subject of pp. 244–314.

38. See art. 37, para. 2 of the Family Code, and Decree 779 of October 8, 1966.

39. Ceausescu 1972b. This was Ceausescu's welcoming speech to university students, who would be among those soon forming families.

40. See Ioan 1988: 259–60 for a more complete listing. That battery has only recently figured among human rights concerns may be better understood in view of these practices. That reconciliation after attempted murder was thought worthy of consideration speaks volumes about the state's attitude toward violence in everyday relations. On domestic violence, see, for example, the report "Lifting the Last Curtain: A Report on Domestic Violence in Romania," prepared by the Minnesota Advocates for Human Rights, February 1995.

41. These sums varied over time, as did salaries. Nonetheless, in 1979, an average salary was 1,289 lei per month, with which the cost of initiating divorce proceedings may be compared.

42. It would be interesting to know who those 48 were. As one colleague queried, somewhat cynically: "Members of the nomenklatura, perchance?"

43. See Zlatescu 1982: 248.

44. See, for example, Mihailescu 1987: 520–28.

45. See *Anuarul statistic al Romaniei, 1990:* 67.

46. Petchesky has also made this point with respect to legalizing abortion in the United States: "Shifts in state policies regarding abortion or fertility have usually been responses to, rather than determinants of, changes in the economic and social conditions that structure women's work and marital patterns and birth control practices. . . . The Supreme Court decision in 1973 was not the 'cause' of rising abortion rates but an accommodation to social changes that began long before *Roe v. Wade* was decided" (Petchesky 1990:102, 103).

47. Ghetau 1991.

48. Replacement thresholds are calculated with respect to female reproduction and mortality before the age of childbearing; in any age cohort, each woman theoretically replaces herself with another who lives through childbearing years. Jean-Claude Chesnais provided these figures.

49. Berelson 1979: 212. Berelson also notes the impact of Decree 770, which contributed to an estimated 39 percent more births than would have otherwise occurred if "the birthrate had been equal to the East European average." In this regard, the policy was effective (see pp. 214, 217).

50. Again, the opportunity for Ceausescu to affirm publicly the relationship between the population and the nation was poignantly provided by the Warsaw Pact invasion of Czechoslovakia in 1968, which Ceausescu denounced. In other words, his nationalist project, however embryonic, was already conceived. Dej himself had moved hesitantly in this direction. (Katherine Verdery observed that Dej nationalized the means of production; Ceausescu, the means of reproduction.) The invasion offered a convenient stage for its unveiling. Silviu Brucan summarizes the numerous reasons that prompted the Romanian leadership as early as 1956 to find ways to articulate "gradually a more independent Romanian position in the international arena, which will show, especially to the Romanian people, that we accord priority to our own national interests, and not as has been the case until now, those of the Soviets." Ceausescu was then a member of the Political Bureau of the Romanian Workers' Party, and was involved in the strategy for "de-satellization" (see Brucan 1992: 73).

51. Quoted in Wright 1975: 254. I have been unable to verify the original source cited by Wright, who attributes this quote to *Pravda.* The Romanian banning of abortion in 1966 was reported in *Pravda* without comment (no. 282, October 9, 1966, p. 5).

52. See *Ministerul Sanatatii si Prevederilor Sociale, Instructiuni No. 819,* October 19, 1966, to Decree 770/1966 for the control of a pregnancy's development.

53. The instructions lend a more elegant twist to this form of control. They stated that the file would be returned to the woman's doctor so that her pregnancy could be institutionalized; tracking the smooth development of her pregnancy became the

institutional responsibility of the medical unit to which she was assigned. The appropriate medical personnel would be held to account for any "mishaps."

54. A sound is a medical instrument introduced into the uterus to cause it to dilate. Medical instruments are used by physicians, but a catheter-like tube may also be improvised for nonprofessional use. See chapter 6 for greater detail on the kinds of implements used by women to induce an abortion.

55. See Dorobantu 1985: 8–9. It must be noted that, in most cases, the sources from which statistical "evidence" was drawn are not presented because these sources were not available for public consultation, but rather circulated "for internal use" only. It may often be assumed that statistics were based on data obtained from the Center for the Calculation of Health Statistics, although it would be virtually impossible to obtain the exact sources. Abortion-related complications are discussed in chapter 7.

56. See, for example, article 186, para. 1; article 188; and article 483.

57. Punishments were further specified in related decrees. See, for example, Council of State Decree 218, "Anumite masuri tranzitorii privind sanctionarea si reeducarea prin munca a persoanelor care au comis acte prevazute de Codul Penal, July 12, 1977" published in the *Buletinul oficial*, no. 71, July 17, 1977.

58. Ceausescu 1973a: 12–13.

59. Ibid.: 9.

60. See "Decisions of the Plenary session of the Central Committee of the Romanian Communist Party, June 18–19, 1973, with Attention to the Growth of the Role of Women," 1973, p. 27 (italics added). The relationship between a public address and a party decision was sacrosanct. What was proclaimed, was.

61. The UN Decade of Women was 1976–1985; International Women's Year was 1975. See Pietila and Vickers 1994: 74–83.

62. See Instructions, no. 27, January 17, 1974, published in the Bulletin of the Ministry of Health, Supplement 2.

63. See Section IV, art. 2.

64. This generalization does not hold in Muslim populations, however. (I thank Murray Feshbach for his close reading of this chapter and for this observation.)

65. The incidence of Down's syndrome was noticeably higher among children whose mothers were older than 38 when they gave birth. Dr. Teodoru George from the Polizu Hospital provided this information to Smaranda Mezei, citing U.S. literature. Prenatal diagnosis is not generally available in Romania.

66. See Instructions, 1974, Section V, art. 29.

67. Ibid.: art. 24, para. 2.

68. Ibid.: art. 25, para. 3.

69. See Law 18/1968, art. 35, authorizing the state to verify the source of an individual's or family's property. The publication of this law implicitly acknowledged the functioning of a second economy and was an attempt to limit the scope of such activities.

70. On July 1, 1974, the population of Romania was 21,028,841, according to the *Anuarul statistic al Republicii Socialiste Romania, 1975*. The planned figures projected that the population should reach 25 million by 1990. (The population in 1990 was 23,206,720.) This was noted at the Party Congress held in November. See "Directivele Congresului al XI-lea al Partidului Comunist Roman cu privire la planul cin-

cinal 1976–1980 si liniile directoare ale dezvoltarii economico-sociale a Romaniei pentru perioada 1981–1990," 1975.

71. The full equality of individuals before the law as postulated in the constitution and invoked repeatedly in official discourse was adjusted to the realities of everyday life. The following joke, which circulated in the 1970s, illustrates that Romanians considered these laws to be instruments of domination: "The law is a barrier over which lions jump, under which cats crawl, and in front of which oxen come to a standstill." In other words, the law was regarded as a hurdle over which those in power jumped and those with ability got around; the inept were simply blocked.

72. An ordinance issued by the Ministry of Health, no. 473/1983, stated that histo-pathological analyses were required to establish diagnoses of incomplete abortions. In this way, one group of medical specialists controlled the diagnoses offered by other specialists.

73. See Zlatescu 1982: 241. In 1986 an ordinance from the Ministry of Health forbade the use of intra-uterine devices (IUDs) and surgical sterilization of women. See Ordinul 300/18 published in the *Buletinul Ministerului Sanatatii* (for internal use), 1987, p. 61.

74. A joke about the reasons for the unavailability of condoms captured the perversity of political demography à la Ceausescu: What does he do in his free time? [The following were high-ranking Communist Party officials]: Maurer? He hunts; Chivu Stoica? He drinks; Ceausescu? With a shoemaker's awl, he punches holes in condoms! (I wish to thank Mihai Nicolae for this as well as other jokes; See Nicolae 1992: 52.)

75. All of these were part of the popular repertoire of "old wives' cures." Among the panoply of practices that were revived or modified, substances such as iodine combined with soap and others containing estrogen hormones were also injected directly into the uterus. For a more detailed list of drinks, injections, and physical methods, see, for example, Ciortoloman 1966: 1.

76. Here it suffices to illustrate the general tendencies in demographic behavior. However, data differentiated in terms of social categories or residence patterns (urban, rural) would provide a more nuanced picture. Early marriage remained relatively constant throughout the Ceausescu period, the median age of marriage for men being approximately 25; for women, 22. See, for example, Muresan 1996: 823, table 7, constructed with data from INED, Paris; the National Commission for Statistics, Bucharest; and the Council of Europe. Also see Trebici and Ghinoiu 1986: 110–11. They calculated that a second child was usually born by the time a woman was 25.5 years old (p. 111). In the United States, 44 is the maximum age considered for age-specific groups.

77. The crude birthrate was 14.3 per 1,000 inhabitants in 1966 and in 1983. The total fertility rate was 1.9 children per female in 1966; 2.06 in 1983.

78. Resistance of this kind came at great cost to women in particular, and to family life in general. Sexuality had become embedded in fear, anxiety, and despair. In the summer of 1981 a hard-working couple living in the far north of the country requested a confidential chat with me. They were at their wits' end. They were already financially strapped. They had two children, a small apartment. The wife was desperate: "If I sexually reject my husband because we can't afford another child, then he will go to someone else, which I can't endure. And, it is not right to deny him

sexual access. Can you help us [acquire contraceptives]?" Sadly, this was not an isolated case.

79. See Stefanescu 1991: 85.

80. See, for example, the internal report "Studiul asupra cauzelor care influenteaza fertilitatea populatiei feminine" prepared by the Ministry of Health, Bucharest, 1986. The number of live births was correlated with such factors as years of marriage, income, and occupational and educational levels. Predictably, regular studies showed that the relationship between years of education and number of children was an inverse one. See also Muresan et al. 1977. Data collected in 1974–75 were compared against those for 1967–68 for women age 15 to 49, in their first marriages. Among the questions analyzed were those pertaining to a woman's reasons for not wanting children, or more of them. The most frequent concerns expressed were lack of childcare possibilities or financial resources, inadequate housing facilities, female sterility, and poor health.

81. This reasoning should be juxtaposed against that which had motivated the drop in the age limit to 40 back in 1972 as discussed above, as well as against biological process: female fecundity decreases after age 40.

82. Extramarital relations were common. When discreet behavior gave way to public expression, society's hypocritical scorn emerged.

83. In Stefanescu 1991: 85.

84. This may be seen by comparing the crude birthrate, the total fertility rate, and the number of abortions per 100 live births during the period 1983–1989. In 1983 the birthrate was 14.3 per 1,000 inhabitants; by 1986 it had risen to 16.5 per 1,000; 1987, 16.7 per 1,000; 1988, 16.5 per 1,000; 1989, 16 per 1,000. In 1983 the figure for the total fertility rate (number of children per 1,000 women between the ages of 15 and 49) was 2.0; 1986, 2.4; 1987, 2.4; 1988, 2.3; 1989, 2.2. Regarding abortions: in 1983 there were 131 abortions per 100 live births; by 1986, 49 abortions per 100 live births; 1987, 48 per 100; 1988, 49 per 100; 1989, 52 per 100. These figures were drawn from the Comisia Nationala pentru Statistica and the Ministerul Sanatatii, Centrul de Calcul si Statistica Sanitara. See also Ghetau 1991: footnote 35.

85. Published in *Buletinul oficial*, no. 69, September 13, 1983.

86. Smaranda Mezei reported the dentist's tale.

## CHAPTER 3.
## "PROTECTING" WOMEN, CHILDREN, AND THE FAMILY

1. Ceausescu 1988: 19.

2. In 1989 the contributions from the state budget to a household's resources were approximately 12 percent. The money generally went toward covering health care, maternity care, pensions, assistance to invalids and widowed persons, and family allocations. See *World Bank Country Study* 1992: 41.

3. See Decree 410 of the Council of State regarding state allocations and benefits for children, mothers with many children, and military wives, as well as indemnities for birth. *Buletinul oficial*, no. 76, December 26, 1985. (The 1956 law about allocations for children was modified by Decree 197/1977.); see also Law 10 of November 23, 1972, *Codul muncii din Republica Socialista Romania*, published in *Buletinul*

*oficial,* no. 140, December 1, 1972; Law 3 of July 6, 1978, *Asigurarea sanatatii popu-latiei,* published in *Buletinul oficial,* no. 54, July 10, 1978; Law 1 of July 8, 1977, *Contributia persoanelor angajate in unitatile de stat si care nu au copii,* published in *Buletinul oficial,* no. 60, July 8, 1977 (modified by Decree 409 published in *Buletinul oficial,* no. 76, December 26, 1985, to increase the amounts); Law 3 of March 26, 1979, *Regimul protectiei anumitor categorii de minori,* published in *Buletinul oficial,* no. 28, March 28, 1970; Decree 65 of February 17, 1982, *Organizarea activitatii creselor si gradinitelor si stabilirea contributiei parintilor care au copii in aceste unitati,* published in *Buletinul oficial,* no. 20, February 17, 1982; Decree 190 of June 27, 1977, *Decoratiile de Stat in Republica Socialista Romania,* published in *Buletinul oficial,* no. 65, July 9, 1977 (representing the amended Decree 195 of November 8, 1951, published in *Buletinul oficial,* no. 109, November 8, 1951). See also Zlatescu and Copil 1984: 205-13; Ceterchi, Zlatescu, and Copil, 1974.

4. Law 1/1977 was published in *Buletinul oficial,* no. 60, July 8, 1977, but was modified in State Council Decree 409 of December 26, 1985, published in *Buletinul oficial,* no. 76, December 26, 1985. This decree increased the monthly contributions of childless persons. Although various circumstances exempted certain persons from this tax (such as children acquired through marriage who were then under the couple's care), the law penalized people unable to bear children because of sterility or for other reasons. The functional gender bias of pronatalism is evidence of the instrumentalization of the female body.

5. Family allocations existed throughout Eastern Europe, although the amounts varied, as did their intent. Some countries encouraged second or third births, for example, while discouraging larger families because of the strains on housing and other infrastructural resources. A comparative table is presented in Klinger 1991: 520. The reliability of the information is questionable; nonetheless, the general trends are suggestive. For Romania, the positive incentives associated with pronatalism were limited, especially in light of the repressive measures that had been instituted. See Zlatescu and Copil 1984; Ceterchi et al. 1975: 65-95; Moskoff 1980: 605-8; and *Throughout the World—1989* 1990. Country summaries include basic laws and types of programs; see "Family Allowances" (coverage, source of funds, qualifying conditions).

6. The limits of maximum and minimum salaries in socialist economies were scaled and fixed. The ratio of the smallest and largest salaries could not be greater than 1:5. For average monthly wages, see *Anuarul statistic al Romaniei, 1990,* p. 123.

7. The allocation for children appeared as a lump sum added to one's monthly salary, from which various taxes had already been deducted. The total allocation was calculated as a cumulative sum: for a family with three eligible children and a salary of less than 2,500 lei, the allocation per month would have been 1,080 lei. It has been extremely difficult, however, to ascertain how the sums were actually calculated, and the decrees do not specify this. Various specialists have repeatedly assured me that the monthly payments were not figured cumulatively. Yet numerous women (with three children) emphatically insist that they were. The interpretive difference is not insignificant. If the sum were not cumulative, the monthly allocation for a family with three children and a minimum salary would have been 430 lei; calculated cumulatively, the sum would have been 1,080 lei for all three children. Moreover, if calculated cumulatively, the pro-family incentives actually favored only the first child.

8. For example, in Hungary, Bulgaria, and Czechoslovakia the main goal of pro-natalist measures was to encourage second or third children.

9. I wish to thank both Jean-Claude Chesnais and Eva Fodor for their assistance in revising this section.

10. The longitudinal study of family budgets done by the Central Bureau for Statistics was not accessible to the public, having been considered a "state secret" until the fall of the regime. It contains useful, if minimal, data for analyzing the family costs of raising and educating children. Individual expenditures represent the average for a family according to the number of family members, regardless of their age and age-specific expenses; see appendix 2.5.

11. Family allowances in table 3.1 were calculated according to the 1985 levels as above (which had not been adjusted). Table 3.2 describes the costs of living; it is unclear how this table was constructed.

12. Comparison of various quality-of-life measures illustrates the absence of the "luxuries" of everyday life in Romania. For example, in 1988 there were 279 televisions per 1,000 population in Hungary, 191 in Romania, 379 in West Germany, and 812 in the United States. In the same year, there were 164 automobiles per 1,000 population in Hungary, 50 in Romania, 472 in West Germany, and 631 in the United States. There were 3.5 doctors per 1,000 population in Hungary, 2.1 in Romania, 3.5 in West Germany, and 2.7 in the United States. Data are from the *Hungarian Statistical Yearbook* 1990: 350–51.

13. For example, even though a wage earner with four children and a monthly salary of 2,827 lei received an additional 1,250 lei per month, or 44 percent of the state salary, this did not amount to much in the harsh conditions of scarcity characteristic of the 1980s. This calculation does not include other supplements to wages, such as an additional sum allocated monthly to women with many children. The point nonetheless pertains.

14. Another problem that stems from working with these data is that the aggregate expenses per person as stated were not differentiated by generation. Expenses for children and adults are not identical.

15. According to Smaranda Mezei, a study on unequal access to Romanian education revealed that 93 percent of students and 97 percent of their parents considered university education to be most important for personal success. See Cazacu 1991: 215. An analysis of who actually achieved their higher educational goals would be necessary to evaluate the mechanisms that regulated unequal access.

16. Data that would make it possible to evaluate the quality of education are unavailable. Moreover, data regarding average enrollments per school mask the differences between urban and rural milieus. In general, Romania's urban population rapidly increased as a consequence of migration, resulting in many overpopulated schools. By contrast, in rural areas, depopulation and aging of the population led to under-enrollment in certain grades and schools. The same kinds of variations occurred in regions where birthrates remained high.

The ratios of students per teacher remained roughly constant following the "boom" years. The demographic effects of the pronatalist policies were felt most dramatically after the 1966 banning of abortion. Again, they varied by region.

In response to budgetary constraints (not directly correlated with political demographic policies), the number of students per teacher in primary and secondary classes was increased. Often, there were 30 to 40 students per teacher in secondary-level classrooms (see, for example, table 4.17 "Romania—Student per Teacher Ratios by Level," *World Bank Country Study: Romania.* 1992: 199).

17. Smaranda Mezei provided this information without documentation; it is, nonetheless, plausible.

18. Ibid. This figure was 63 percent among children whose parents themselves had higher degrees.

19. This interview, conducted by Smaranda Mezei, is revealing with regard to the value of money, especially when considered in terms of post-1989 inflation.

20. It is worth noting the logistical arrangements. The children slept in the bedroom, and the parents slept on a pull-out couch in the living room. One child studied in the bedroom, the other in the living room. A. recalled many a time that she and her husband sat quietly in the kitchen so as not to disturb the children. Only members of the nomenklatura enjoyed the type of living space to which middle-class families in other countries are accustomed.

21. See Decree 410/1985, sec. 3, art. 6, para. 2. Decree 410 covers many categories, not all of which are mentioned here. For this and other decrees cited below, see also *Digest of General Laws of Romania* 1987: 43–56 (hereafter *Digest*).

22. The monthly sums for children whose parents were cooperative members were: 100 lei per month for the first and second children; 200 lei per month for the third and fourth children; 300 lei for the fifth and any additional children (see Decree 410/1985, sec. 2, art. 16, para. 1, in *Digest*, p. 49). The amount allocated for a first child was one-third of that designated for an urban family's first child.

23. For examples of the functioning of this quota system, see Kideckel 1993.

24. See Decree 410, arts. 18, 19, 20, in *Digest*, p. 50.

25. Decree 410, sec. 3, art. 25, increased the sum granted as a kind of maternity bonus in Decree 197/1977, sec. 3, art. 25, from 1,000 to 1,500 lei (see *Digest*, p. 52). These bonuses were one-time payments, again primarily symbolic in their effect. They did not have any influence on demographic trends. Calculated in terms of monthly median salary, Romanian women received smaller bonuses than women in other Eastern bloc countries. This is noteworthy in view of the obsessiveness of the pronatalist ideology in Romania. In the German Democratic Republic, Czechoslovakia, and Hungary, birth bonuses were not linked to number of births. See Klinger 1991: 516.

26. Published in the *Buletinul oficial*, no. 36, April 27, 1977. Women were paid by the liter; it did not matter whether they donated milk on a daily, weekly, or other basis. See *Digest*, p. 152.

27. When in Romania during the 1980s, I acquired Chinese-produced powdered milk from the diplomatic shop (paid in lei) for many desperate and exhausted Romanian friends.

28. See Decree 10/1972, arts. 152–58, in *Digest*, pp. 38–39.

29. If a woman had been employed without interruption for at least twelve months, she received 85 percent of her salary; 65 percent if she had worked less than one year but more than six months; 50 percent for less than six months of labor. Women who had given birth to at least three children received 94 percent of their salary for maternity leave, regardless of the length of employment. See Decision 880 of August 21, 1965, in the *Colectia de decizii a Consiliului de Ministri*, no. 33, August 21,

1965, art. 15, further amended in the Council of Ministers Decision 1356 of June 26, 1968. Reproduced in *Digest*, pp. 74–76.

30. See Decision of the Council of Ministers 1356 of June 22, 1968. Note the gender bias in this maternal "right": fathers did not have the same right to take leave for childcare.

31. Art. 158/1972 of the Labor Code.

32. Needless to say, such prescriptions came with a price tag. Here, it is also important to note the impossibility of generalizing about the uniformity of receipt of bonuses.

33. Law 3/1978, art. 94, paras. e–g, in *Digest*, p. 85.

34. Retirement ages in Romania were quite low for men and women. In view of the insistence on an active labor force, it is paradoxical that the regime did not raise the retirement age. Instead, it demanded more children. The system was production-oriented in theory and inefficient in practice. The retirement age may have represented a nod toward the reality of surplus labor and hidden unemployment. Pensions were also tied to retirement age, which has had particular consequences for women in the immediate postsocialist period.

35. See Law 3, "Asigurarea pensiilor de stat si a asistentei sociale," of June 30, 1977, and published in *Buletinul oficial*, no. 82 of August 6, 1977, art. 18, paras. 1–2.

36. See Council of State Decree 190, "Decoratiile de Stat in Republica Socialista Romania," of June 27, 1977, published in *Buletinul oficial*, no. 65, July 9, 1977. Note that the articles of this decree elaborate on those in Council of State Decree 195 of November 8, 1951, which was Stalinist in origin. In 1944, Stalin introduced a series of measures regarding "protection of the family," among which was the valorizing of mothers with many children, who were honored as "heroine mothers."

37. The organizers of this event were party activists in the health field. The invitation to participate in the festivities was not one that could be declined; acceptance of the invitation was mandatory. Smaranda Mezei provided this anecdote.

38. The most detailed version is found in Council of State Decree 65 of February 17, 1982, published in *Buletinul oficial*, no. 20, February 17, 1982, about the organization of nurseries and kindergartens, and parental fees.

39. Monthly parental fees for daily nursery school attendance: 270 lei for income up to 5,000 lei; 295 for income between 5,000 and 6,000 lei; 320 for income between 6,001 and 7,000 lei; 340 for income over 7,000 lei. Monthly parental fees for weekly daycare services for the same accumulated earning levels were, respectively, 320, 385, 445, 500. For daily kindergarten (until 5 P.M.), the amounts varied between 256 and 320 lei; for weekly periods, between 270 and 340. See Council of State Decree 65/1982, art. 6 (in *Digest*, p. 102).

The 1982 decree regulated parental fees even after 1985, but the fees were calculated according to mechanisms other than legislative ones. State enterprises determined these for the childcare centers associated with them by the authority vested in them under "self-management." The fees did not include money the parents spent on gifts and "small attentions" for staff members with which they tried to ingratiate themselves on behalf of their children. Similarly, the cost of medicines was not included. Although medicine was free, its scarcity meant that procuring it was quite costly. On self-financing and self-management, see, for example, Fischer 1989.

40. The way in which aggregate figures were constructed must be qualified. In

the published statistical data about the age structure of the population, age variables were determined by calendar-year intervals rather than by months. The potential childcare population was not calculated for children between the real ages of one and three and three and six, as is the case in the annual statistical review. Consequently, the population for whom the number of places available in childcare institutions was reported differed from the actual population requesting them. The school year encompasses two calendar years; for an accurate representation of the school population, age should be detailed by months, not calendar years. For example, on July 1, 1985, a child who was five years and eleven months old figured in the cohort of five-year-olds in the age structure of the population. However, in the school statistics for 1985–86, this same child was considered among the six-year-olds (see table 3.4).

41. Such an assessment requires, for example, evaluation of the supply and demand relationship between the population of childcare-age children, infrastructural availability (number and capacity of childcare centers), and the number of persons staffing those institutions, correlated with information on female employment and the existence and extent of alternative childcare arrangements for preschoolers.

42. The actual number of kindergartens decreased slightly, meaning that there were more children enrolled in each institution. See, for example, *World Bank Country Study: Romania*, 1992: 182, table 4.1. The decrease in the number of kindergartens reflected changing financial allocations. In 1990–91, the first year labeled "postcommunist," the decreased proportion of children enrolled may have been due to a variety of factors, important among which were increased financial costs in a time of economic uncertainty and emigration.

43. The conditions under which these institutions functioned in Romania merit note. Teachers had to contend with inadequate supplies of all materials, ranging from those used for instructional purposes to food and basic emergency medical supplies—not to mention the frequent lack of water, heat, and electricity.

44. See, for example, Law 3, March 26, 1970, published in *Buletinul oficial*, no. 28, March 28, 1970; Council of State Decree 545, December 30, 1972, published in *Buletinul oficial*, no. 162, December 30, 1972, in *Digest*, pp. 123–45.

45. See Law 3, 1970, art. 1, in *Digest*, p. 123.

46. In 1989 there were 89 hospitals and homes with 15,926 slots (children lived and received treatment in these institutions); 3 vocational boarding schools with 1,090 slots; and 14 boarding schools with 4,465 slots. There were also 36 special state instructional institutions with 16,627 pupils (deaf-mute, blind, retarded, handicapped, and delinquent). As Romanians and the world came to know, the number of institutions noted on paper fulfilled propaganda purposes rather than the needs of the children. The number of institutions in existence to care for these children revealed nothing about the quality of care offered. The plight of Romania's orphaned and abandoned children is discussed in chapter 7.

In 1990 there were 60 nurseries at state enterprises with 8,535 children; 22 special kindergartens with 2,101 children; 155 children's homes with 23,701 children; 121 special general schools with 25,686 children; 27 special professional training schools with 11,434 children; 7 special high schools with 1,398 children; 148 state boarding schools with 2,588 children; 2 vocational boarding schools with 577 children; 25 special homes for abandoned children, vagabonds, and otherwise homeless youth with 3,196 children; and 2 rehabilitation centers with 1,010 children. It is disturbing to note that abandoned children, many of whom were the products of forced pregnancies, were indiscriminately institutionalized with delinquents. The implications of the classification of these children are sobering. (I thank Jean-Claude Chesnais for this observation.)

CHAPTER 4.
INSTITUTIONALIZING POLITICAL DEMOGRAPHY

1. In *Aspects Sociopolitiques et Démographiques de la Planification Familiale en France, en Hongrie et en Roumanie*, 1977.

2. Jan Gross's distinction between "embodiment" and "representation" is useful; the Grand National Assembly did not comprise representatives of society (see J. Gross 1992: 59).

3. See *Decisions of the Commission for Health, Labor, Social Security, and Environmental Protection of the Grand National Assembly*, 1987.

4. On semantic manipulation, see, for example, Voicu 1993: 22–23. A classic work is that by Thom (1987).

5. The Ministry of Tourism's role in fulfilling reproductive norms was to encourage the "use of natural cures offered at [mineral] spas for the treatment of and recuperation from gynecological ailments." Together with the Ministries of Health and Labor, the Institute for Spa Therapy and Medical Recuperation, and others, the Ministry of Tourism was charged especially with combating sterility and infertility. The institutional division of labor and responsibility with respect to these policies was outlined in the "Program pentru aducerea la indeplinire a sarcinilor si masurilor stabilite de Comisia pentru sanatate, munca, asigurari sociale si protectia mediului a Marii Adunari Nationale asupra indeplinirii cu mai multa fermitate si raspundere a directivelor de partid si a reglementarilor referitoare la cresterea demografica a populatiei" issued by the Ministry of Health in 1987. (I am grateful to the physician who provided me with this set of directives.)

6. See Decree 541 of July 29, 1969, published in *Buletinul oficial*, Part 1, no. 81, July 29, 1969.

7. The constitution of the National Demographic Commission was formalized in Law 3, March 18, 1971, and published in *Buletinul oficial*, no. 35, on that day; it was modified by Decree 58 of the Council of State on February 27, 1974, and Decision 27 of the Council of State, March 5, 1974. Modifications spelled out the creation of county and municipal demographic commissions subordinated to the National Demographic Commission. On the NDC, see Zlatescu and Copil 1984, esp. pp. 17–22.

8. "World Population Plan of Action," The Population Debate: Dimensions and Perspectives. Papers of the World Population Conference, Bucharest, 1974, vol. 1 (New York: United Nations), p. 166.

9. Paul Demeny, "Population on the World Agenda—1974," as quoted in Berelson 1979: 218. This lengthy quotation reflects the serious consideration accorded Romania's population policy in the 1970s. Readers should note that China's demographic policies aimed at controlling overpopulation were not greeted in the West

with similar detachment. China endorsed abortion as a means to enforce an anti-natalist policy in "the public interest," which conflicted with Western "moral" discourse.

10. Ethical concerns were taken up later. See, for example, Berelson and Lieberson 1979.

11. As already discussed, after Romania announced its anti-abortion legislation in 1966, the USSR responded negatively. The silence of the West in part reflected abortion politics there: France and the United States also had restrictive abortion laws. (These were liberalized in 1975 and 1973, respectively.) It was only after the World Population Conference that criticisms about the Romanian population legislation began to circulate publicly. In 1974, while the liberalization of abortion was being debated in France, an article in *Le Monde*, "Romania: Severity Reinforced," reported: "One year ago, the Ministry of Health issued a series of measures meant to stimulate natality. These reinforced the severity with which those who transgressed the 1966 law were treated. In effect, privileged women resorted to the services of doctors while the others have been forced to seek clandestine practices. . . . Conversely, the severity accompanying the application of this law, as has been seen in Romania after 1966 or in Bulgaria after the restrictive decision of 1968, translated into rapid increases in the birthrates. . . . In Bulgaria and Romania, the registered improvement [in the birthrate] was of short duration" (November 27, 1974). France is pronatalist, although its population policies are encouraged through positive incentives rather than the draconian, coercive measures employed by the Ceausescu regime. On abortion rights in France, see Allison 1994. The ideologically grounded Reagan-Bush anti-abortion approach blinded the United States to the horrors provoked by the regime's banning of abortion.

12. Ceausescu 1974: 494. I thank Stelian Tanase for a copy of this speech.

13. The creation of CEDOR in Romania was approved in 1973. See Comunicarea Cancelariei C.C. al P.C.R. no. 1635/1603, April 9, 1973, and no. 2810/2762, June 6, 1973. Elena Ceausescu expressed her skepticism about the relevance of this center at a meeting of the Executive Committee of the Central Committee of the PCR on July 3, 1974: "We don't have computers for industry but we're supposed to provide them for demographers!" (see stenogram of the sedinta Comitetului Executiv, Arhiva MAN, vol. 1, no. 930). CEDOR was closed in 1984 after allegations of espionage activities (personal communication, Jean-Claude Chesnais).

14. On December 11, 1970, at its plenary session, the UN General Assembly: "1) proclaimed 1974 as the Year of World Population, 2) recognized that the elaboration and application of demographic policies were internal to each state and, therefore, international actions in the realm of population had to adapt to the different needs and requests of member states, 3) asked the secretary general to establish, in consultation with interested member states, a detailed program of activities and measures to be taken in 1974 . . . , 4) invited interested UN organizations to assist the secretary general in elaborating this program for the Year of World Population, 5) invited members states to participate in full in the Year of World Population according to their possibilities and political inclinations, 6) underscored that UN organs and interested member states should continue to offer their assistance upon request in the elaboration and application of dynamic political demographic programs" (reproduced in Trebici 1975: 378).

15. See ibid.: 379.

16. For a more complete description, see Zlatescu and Copil 1984: 18, from which this partial list has been drawn. As close reading of the laws clarifies, people in commissions and other institutions were designated to formulate and apply policies. The power of the state was constituted by the actions of individuals.

17. Zlatescu and Copil 1984: 19.

18. I wish to thank Vladimir Trebici and Vasile Ghetau for their contributions to this chapter. Also, it should be noted that after the World Population Conference in 1974 funds were no longer allocated to support the effective functioning of the NDC. See, for example, *Comunicarea Cancelariei C.C. al P.C.R.*, 1973. Between 1974 and 1976, the budget for "population" decreased from 7.5 million to 5.3 million lei, a decline that continued. Instead, the budget underwrote the salary of the secretary general, the political intention of which was clear.

19. This was customary practice. Assigning nonspecialist activists in positions of institutional authority was a means of maintaining control and surveillance. Ritualized presentations of scientific arguments were well developed by the 1980s. Trebici recollected that on March 7, 1984, he and other specialists were invited to a meeting of the Central Committee. Lina Ciobanu (member of the Political Executive Committee and vice–prime minister of the government, charged with overseeing the Higher Council on Health) instructed them ahead of time on official protocol pertaining to the Ceausescus' entrance into the room. Contrary to expectations that the discussion would focus on Romania's demographic situation, the participants were informed about the number of doctors arrested for performing clandestine abortions. Hours were spent discussing abortion and concerns related to it. At one point, Lina Ciobanu took the floor and, on behalf of her gender, proclaimed women's support for the party's programs. The meeting was as much about discipline and punishment as it was about conformity.

20. Much has been written about this dynamic in such economies. See, for example, Kornai 1986; Rev 1987: 335–50; Verdery 1991b: 419–39.

21. Trebici recalled a chat with Emil Bodnaras who, in his role as mediator between Ceausescu and the NDC, claimed that the NDC's demographic studies were stopped somewhere in the hierarchy before reaching Ceausescu. Bodnaras, a vice-president of the Council of State, had been charged with coordinating the NDC's activities. Manea Manescu, also a vice-president of the Council of State, seems to have supplied the leader with demographic information. At the time, Manescu was politically responsible for the "productivity" of the Central Bureau of Statistics. (He later became prime minister of Romania.) Trebici attributes the political demographic measures to both Ceausescu's peasant cultural mentality and the interested interventions of various counselors and ministers of health.

22. For example, Ceterchi, Zlatescu, and Copil 1974 and 1981; Zlatescu and Copil 1984; the NDC together with the Ministry of Health also carried out three national fertility surveys as part of a UN longitudinal project on world fertility patterns. See Muresan et al. 1977.

23. The NDC was not disbanded; it simply ceased to function meaningfully. Just as a person who was removed from office was often placed in some lesser position or relocated, in this instance, it was an institutional structure that was silenced.

24. See Council of State Decree 116, published in *Buletinul oficial*, no. 109, October 28, 1975.

25. Ceausescu 1984b: 1–3. The previous chapter discussed the fetishism of laws. Statistics were similarly fetishized.

26. See Presidential Decree no. 210, published in *Buletinul oficial*, no. 62, of August 13, 1983.

27. On the relationship between political demography and demography as politics in this context, see Trebici 1988: 69–78. In an interview with Smaranda Mezei, Professor Trebici underscored that, over time, demographic study in Romania had been reduced to the analysis of abortion data.

28. Huff 1954, *How to Lie with Statistics*, is a classic work. Also see Alonso and Starr 1987.

29. This assertion is plausible. It was in the interest of all institutional representatives to confirm a decline in the number of abortions. Since everyone had mothers, sisters, wives, and daughters, most persons were complicitous in statistical distortions. This same specialist argued that it was more difficult to distort mortality and birth figures. He contends that it is less likely that the infant mortality rates were "reworked." If fewer cases had been declared for 1989, then it would be expected that the "real" figures would be high for 1990, which was not the case. While this may be statistically true, it is sociologically questionable. By the 1980s, infants were often not recorded as having been born until two weeks after birth, during which time their official status could be negotiated. In some cases, an infant who died in the first week of life was officially registered as having been born dead. This type of statistical manipulation was not systematic, giving rise to sociological dilemmas if not statistical ones. See chapter 7 for additional discussion.

30. In the yearbook for 1986, the section "Population and the Labor Force" consisted of four pages of data (pp. 16–20); by comparison, the data presented in *Anuarul statistic, 1978*, was quantitatively different. Statistics on population and the labor force were not combined, but rather were reported in separate sections (see pp. 47–82 on population; pp. 105–18 on the labor force).

31. The first president of the Higher Council of Health after 1983 was Alexandrina Gainuse. She embodied all of the qualifications appropriate to this function: she was a woman with a high governmental profile and a member of the Political Executive Committee. Rubenesque in shape, she symbolized the "ideal type" of woman in communist iconography. Devoted to the cause of the party and to the *Conducator*, Ceausescu, she embodied the image of a "goddess of maternity." This embodiment of the female communist ideal was reproduced in Elena Ceausescu's choice of her successors: Lina Ciobanu and Aneta Spornic were considered "reliable" and had similar merits. *Conducator* is *Führer* in Romanian. This title was first used by General Ion Antonescu, Romania's military dictator between 1940 and 1944.

32. The following persons in the Council were not from the public health system: state secretary of the Ministry of Agricultural and Industrial Production; state secretary of the Ministry of Electrotechnical and Electronic Industry; the adjunct minister of the Chemical Ministry; Central Committee secretary of the Front for Democratic and Socialist Unity; the vice-president of the National Council of Women; the party secretary of Timis; the secretary of the Central Council of the General

Confederation of Romanian Trade Unions; the president of the National Council for the Youth Organization, who was simultaneously the secretary of the Central Committee of the Union of Communist Youth; the adjunct director general of Romanian Radio-Television; the minister and state secretary of the National Council for Science and Technology; the vice-president of the Council for Problems pertaining to the Local Councils; the vice-president of the National Council for Physical Education and Sport; the adjunct ministers of the Ministries of Labor and of Education and Instruction; the secretary of the Council of State for Environmental Protection; the secretary of the party committee from Prahova; the minister and secretary of state of the State Planning Committee; the adjunct minister of the Minister of Tourism. Note the overlap with members of the NDC. (This list was provided by Smaranda Mezei.) Moreover, the breadth of institutions represented suggests the encompassing character of the endeavor. This is a good example of what is referred to as a totalizing state. All domains were drawn into taking responsibility for abortion.

33. See Rochat 1991: 32.

34. At one of the innumerable meetings in the early 1980s at the Ministry of Health on this subject, to which all the directors of large hospitals had been "invited," the ministry's party activists placed all of the blame for the spread of infection and the manner in which hospitals were managed on the shoulders of physicians. At that time, intra-hospital infection critically affected most newborns and infants. Rumors of this notorious meeting circulated throughout the country because a member of the audience, Dr. Alessandrescu (the director of the maternity section at the hospital Polizu), had the courage to speak the truth. He demonstrated in detail that the major causes for the alarming spread of infection through the hospitals were: the lack of electric current, which affected the ability to sterilize medical equipment; the lack of heat; the poor quality of hospital food; and acute lack of detergents and disinfectants, which affected the hygiene of all hospitals. Smaranda Mezei provided this macabre anecdote.

35. This was proposed and finalized at the meetings of the Political Executive Committee on August 3, 1987, and the Plenary Session of the Central Committee on October 5, 1987.

36. Jean-Claude Chesnais noted that in the People's Republic of China political and medical surveillance were also coordinated to maximize control over individual women's reproductive lives. On China, see, for example, Croll, Davin, and Kane 1985; Tien 1991; and Greenhalgh and Li 1995.

37. It would be interesting to ascertain the number of penal proceedings begun during the mid-1980s against infractors of the abortion laws as a means to highlight the "success" of this aggressive ideological campaign. All of my efforts to do so have failed.

38. Ceausescu 1984a: 14.

39. See *Principalele obiective si masuri tehnico-organizatorice de ocrotire a sanatatii in anul 1988*, which contained a series of measures prepared by the Ministry of Health for distribution to all medical units. This information was accessible to a very limited "public." Such publications were stamped "for internal use." By the mid-1980s, "for internal use" generally was equated with "state secret." Those who received such publications were at risk if they disobeyed this convention. (I thank the physician who provided this document.)

40. Report Regarding the Causes of the Birthrate Decline and the Measures to be Imposed by the Higher Council on Health, the Ministry of Health, and the National Demographic Commission to Better the Demographic Indicators, 1984: 7.

41. Ibid.: 11.

42. See Foucault 1979: 184–85, on the exam, "which combines the techniques of an observing hierarchy and those of a normalizing judgment."

43. Gadea 1966: 10. The social significance of reproduction was a leitmotif of demographic policy from its inception in 1966 to its demise in 1989.

44. After the fall of the regime, the Western press exaggerated the extent and frequency of these exams. In interviews conducted with factory workers, peasants, intellectuals, and medical practitioners in the capital and in the countryside, I was unable to verify from women that they had been subjected to the much-heralded monthly checks. Indeed, the organization that would have been needed to manage such an undertaking on a national scale precluded such a possibility, especially in Romania. Doctors admit to having checked for pregnancies without informing their patients. The farther from Bucharest, the less rigid the system. The exams were indeed ordered; how they were carried out is quite another matter. The Western press has little justification for sensationalizing an already horrendous situation.

45. "Metodologia luarii precoce in evidenta a gravidelor si supravegherea medicala a sarcinii in primul trimestru," *Muncitorul sanitar* 17, April 4, 1987, 6. I am grateful to the doctor who gave me first-hand information regarding the enterprise's report on these matters.

46. Note that the reliability of the finding that all were virgins is questionable; what is more important, however, is that this finding is culturally believable for those who need to believe it.

47. V. Petrescu, "Sanatatea unui oras-uzina," *Munca*, February 4, 1988.

48. I. Coman, "Preocupari sustinute pentru imbunatatirea indicatorilor de sanatate a populatiei," *Informatia Bucurestiului*, April 18, 1987, 2.

49. I thank Dr. Bogdan Marinescu for his helpful insights.

50. Lazarescu 1988: 6.

51. Ibid.

52. Lazarescu 1987: 6.

53. The activities of the secret police in the policing of the body are central to a full accounting of how the system functioned; however, such privileged information is not available to researchers, especially foreigners.

54. The following is a truncated version of an ongoing saga, the intricacy of which exceeds the space available. A summary based on recorded interviews and review of official documents is provided. I, as well as Smaranda Mezei, thank those interviewed and the Ministry of Justice, which perhaps inadvertently provided the "key" to them.

55. Conditions in Romanian detention institutions were sorely inadequate. Families could be granted the opportunity to bring detainees food and clothing.

56. Under the Romanian communist legal system, the accused was assumed guilty until proven otherwise. In this case, M.T.'s guilt was by association, aggravated by the fact that she did not live according to the more puritanical social norms of socialist society, which were invoked when convenient. (By the 1980s, the hypocrisy of these norms was exposed by the regime itself when it suggested that unmarried

pregnant girls should be socially tolerated. It seems that in the 1970s it was enough to be consenting adults to provide a pretext for imprisonment.)

57. She offered this observation in the lengthy interview done by Smaranda Mezei. I interviewed her husband, Dr. G., the principal accused in this case, who is discussed in detail in chapter 6. The issue of legal residence and its dubious conflation with "concubinage" and associated illicit activities should be clarified. Labeling M.T. a "concubine" was meant to degrade her. Humiliation and degradation were standard tools of the state repressive apparatus. In regard to Dr. G.'s residence status, to be a legal resident in a larger city, one had to possess a permanent resident card, which was officially recorded at the district militia's local population bureau. A person had the right to live at another address if a commuter visa had been issued. Although Dr. G. was a legal resident in the city where his wife lived, he also had a commuter visa for Bucharest. Hence, his cohabitation with M.T. was proper from a legal residence standpoint.

58. This false promise of imminent release was a ruse to get her to forgo her hunger strike. Dr. G. had gone on a full hunger strike twice during his incarceration: once for 28 days; the second time for eighteen. Ultimately, he was released for "reasons of health." (Health reasons have been repeatedly applied since the fall of the regime to excuse those few nomenklatura members sentenced for their participation in the regime.)

59. Tampons and sanitary napkins were unavailable in Romania. In urban areas, women resorted to cotton, which in the 1970s was more readily obtainable than in the 1980s. M.T.'s son was not permitted to bring any other items for his mother.

60. Dr. G. later demonstrated the false credibility of this particular witness upon whom M.T.'s case as an accomplice was built. In her official declaration given in December 1974, G.D. claimed the abortion had taken place in her fifth month of pregnancy (see file 28). In another declaration, taken in May 1976, she stated that she had been two months pregnant at the time of the abortion. The official documents are filled with contradictions and evasions. In a declaration given in April 1975, the same witness described M.T.'s apartment in detail, which she "could not remember" by the time of her May 1976 statement. Two witnesses gave the identical phone number as that which they had dialed to contact Dr. G. at M.T.'s apartment. The authorities failed to verify the number, which in fact belonged to a Bucharest resident but to neither of those accused. More evidence of investigative and rhetorical laxness emerged via Dr. G.'s formal written account describing the deliberate set-up of M.T. With regard to the charge that instruments used for abortions had been found in the apartment, he noted that the instruments found were not those prohibited by the Ministry of Health's Ordinance 886/1966. Dr. G. also questioned why no one verified whether the witness's pregnancy had indeed been officially registered at the Polyclinic to which she was assigned. The reason for not checking this detail is self-evident.

61. Whether these items were found in the apartment because Dr. G. had them or because they were planted there is ultimately immaterial. See, for example, a recounting of similar evidence in Verdery and Kligman 1992: 134, footnote 29.

62. For example, Dr. G. proved that the eleven vials considered to be narcotics had been prescribed for his brother, a cancer patient. Because his brother had

been under Dr. G. and M.T.'s care at the time of his death, the vials remained in the apartment.

63. Being labeled a social danger was tantamount to public or official death. No institution would assume the responsibility for engaging such a person.

64. It was assumed that she had acquired these items illegally—from the profits of the abortions to which she had been an accomplice. Law 18 authorized state authorities to confiscate goods illicitly obtained.

65. There is nonetheless at least a kernel of veracity to his remarks. While detained at the Directorate, M.T.'s cell mate informed her that she had heard that the prosecutor of M.T.'s case had received expensive gifts from Dr. G.'s legal wife, G.G. The cell mate, who most likely was an informer herself, claims to have overheard this while cleaning the building offices. Such information could only increase M.T.'s anxiety, even though it was meant to show solidarity among prisoners. M.T. had already been accused of being a concubine; next, she learned that Dr. G.'s wife, who lived in another city, was lavishing attention on the Bucharest district prosecutor handling her case.

66. Her sentence had been suspended. Both she and Dr. G. appealed to the Supreme Court to have their records corrected. The charges against trafficking in narcotics and keeping instruments for abortion at home were annulled.

67. This is taken from the record of the Executive Committee meeting of the National Women's Council, April 26, 1974, 10.

68. See Cancea 1976: 155. According to Suzana Gadea, the National Council for Women became active in 1958; it had been officially created in 1957. Party membership in these early years was not mandatory; many years later, it became an issue. See note 74 below.

69. Official rhetoric about the relationship between the female political body and the "beloved leader" relied heavily on metaphorical constructions drawn from the symbolic and emotional repertoire on paternalist family relations. For example, formulations such as "we women, we are engaged under the leadership of our beloved party," suggest that the inauguration into communist activities was more akin to their "harem-ization" (Smaranda Mezei's apt characterization), noting that in the socialist context, these institutionalized practices gave birth to the "unique people" and the "socialist nation." See *Normele de organizare si functionare a Consiliului National, a comitetelor si comisiilor femeilor,* 1979, p. 11. Similar relations between women and the party were construed in the official pronouncements of other East European Communist Parties; the national element was more highly developed in Romania. (Nazi Germany is another well-known case in point.) Personality cults lend themselves readily to a discursive personalization of the relationship. Also note the parallel between the relationship of the Communist Party to "the people" and of Jesus as bridegroom to the soul and to the Church. See Kligman 1988: 219–20.

70. See *Normele de organizare si functionare a Consiliului National, a comitetelor si comisiilor femeilor,* 1979, p. 5.

71. It is impossible to decipher how the women's organization was supposed to lessen women's household burdens when the organization's financing was extremely modest. As specified in the Code of Organizational and Functional Norms, p. 27, disposable funds derived from the organization's publications: *Femeia, Sateanca, Dolgozó*

*Nő*, and the annual, *Almanahul Femeii;* and from their cultural and public activities, donations, and subventions.

72. Code of Organizational and Functional Norms, p. 8–9.

73. During these years, women who held high office in the council fought for the emancipation of women out of their own conviction, which fortuitously coincided with the needs of the party. Suzana Gadea did not become a member of the party until 1975. I acknowledge her for the interviews granted in the summer of 1993.

74. I wish to remark upon the fervor with which Gadea recounted her experiences in those "formative" years of work in the National Council for Women. She herself became involved after the war, when there were many hardships to endure; her activity in this organization stopped when she became Minister of Education. However, her commentary on that period was marked by what might be labeled revolutionary zeal. During her active years in the women's movement, Gadea spoke of holding seminars from six to eight P.M. almost daily—after she completed a full day of teaching duties at the Polytechnic Institute where she was a professor. She noted that in the beginning women did not understand the value of education. But gradually, as they witnessed others being promoted and getting ahead, they joined in. She spoke of how movement activists adapted their methods to draw in peasant women; their proselytizing was planned for Sundays after church services.

75. See *Organigrama miscarii de femei*, 1975: 147. This "women's movement" was organized from above and bears no resemblance to a grassroots social movement; this was a social movement in ideological terms only.

76. Women's roles are discussed more fully in chapter 5.

77. Ciobanu 1974b: 6. Note that the magazine *Sateanca* (*Village Woman*) was produced for rural women.

78. See Rodica Geta Constantinescu, "Infractiunea de avort," *Femeia* 1, 1974, 35. In 1974 an order was given that more articles with themes based on "atheist-scientific education" appear in the magazine. See the Plenary Session of the National Women's Council, April 26–27, 1974.

79. *Femeia* 8, 1966, 25.

80. Ceausescu 1986: 1.

81. The increasing disjunction between what was said and what was done was repeated throughout the system. While the president of the Women's Council may have thought women to be tireless, the women themselves seem to have thought otherwise. They were exhausted. In 1983 all workers were expected to produce more for less.

82. See *Regulament-cadru privind organizarea, functionarea si continutul activitatii cluburilor 'Femina,'* 1984, 4.

## CHAPTER 5. SPREADING THE WORD—PROPAGANDA

1. See Ceausescu 1971: 65.

2. A useful discussion of propaganda as mass mobilization in a Leninist regime is found in Kenez 1985. It is regrettably beyond the scope of this chapter to treat the style and function of propaganda in any detail. It is important to note that propaganda campaigns varied in form and content over time. Regarding Romania, see, for example, Magureanu 1979. On disinformation activities, see Turcu 1991: 113–34.

3. In this respect, the mission of such political formations resembles both that of the Catholic Church and fundamentalist movements (see, for example, Lane 1981). Some compare the methods of ideologues and "theologues" as well: unquestioning devotion, confession (à la self-criticism), ritualization, and so on.

4. In the initial period at least, there is reason to believe that Communist Party members believed in what they were doing and approached their work with fervor. Over the years, enthusiasm and fervor seem to have been tainted by opportunism and cynicism—or sheer exhaustion.

5. The Stalinist character of propaganda was maintained throughout the communist era; however, its functioning within the broader party system varied. In the 1940s and 1950s, and again from the mid-1970s, propaganda, ideology, the police, and the administration were tightly coordinated. In the 1960s and early 1970s, as a result of power struggles at the top of the party hierarchy, these units experienced a period of relative relaxation and autonomy with respect to their operation. (I thank Stelian Tanase for this note.)

6. Leonte Rautu's "longevity" in terms of political influence is incontestable. After serving as head of Radio Moscow's Romania service during World War II, he returned to Romania, where he was the driving force behind the propaganda apparatus between 1945 and 1965. (He was succeeded by Dumitru Popescu in 1971.) Under Ceausescu, he continued to serve as a Central Committee secretary and as deputy prime minister in charge of education until 1981. In that year, his resignations from the Political Executive Committee and from the rectorship of the Stefan Gheorghiu Party Academy were accepted. Ironically, this consummate communist ideologue lost his position because of his daughter's application to emigrate. Rautu died in 1993 at the age of 83. (I thank Vladimir Tismaneanu for the content of this note.)

7. Again, *compliance* should be underscored and distinguished from belief. This distinction contributes to an understanding of the structural dynamics of dissimulation.

8. See Bourdieu 1977: 237, note 47. The author's definition of symbolic violence is: "that form of domination which, transcending the opposition usually drawn between sense relations and power relations, communication and domination, is only exerted *through* the communication in which it is disguised."

9. The perception of resources as being finite among peasant societies was categorized as the "image of limited good." See Foster 1965: 293–315. The striking parallel to socialist organization was noted by Jowitt 1978.

10. In P. Gross 1990: 98.

11. See Ioan Moraru, "Inalta grija si raspundere pentru fondul uman al tarii," *Scinteia*, October 4, 1966: 1.

12. Stefan Milcu, "Medicul si responsabilitatea lui fata de generatiile viitoare," *Scinteia*, October 22, 1966: 1.

13. See Bulgaru, "Expresia inaltei responsabilitati a generatiilor de azi pentru viitorul poporului roman," *Scinteia*, November 26, 1966: 1–2.

14. According to D. Popescu, Ceausescu was disturbed by the fact that he was the leader of a small country, rather than of a superpower. Political demography was in part a way for him to compensate for this situation. See Popescu 1993: 307, note 5. (I thank Stelian Tanase for bringing this to my attention.)

15. On the manufacturing of consent as a propaganda role of the media, see, for example, Lippmann 1932; and Herman and Chomsky 1988. The relationship between propaganda functions (in totalizing and democratic contexts) and conspiracy theories is apparent in these texts.

16. See Moraru, "Inalta grija si raspundere pentru fondul uman al tarii," p. 1.

17. One of the functions of propaganda was to sensitize the population to political developments and create consensus. Normally, the press "prepared" the population for policy changes by publishing the "debates" held among party functionaries on a particular issue. This form of offering opinions gave the appearance of democratic politics.

18. Suzana Gadea, "Raportul consiliului national al femeilor din Republica Socialista Romania," *Femeia*, no. 7, 1967: 11; emphasis added. *Femeia* published a supplement reproducing the entire report, the full title of which is: "Report of the National Council of Women of the Socialist Republic of Romania, with attention to the activities that have unfolded since the last national conference and to the responsibilities of the women's movement in light of the decisions taken at the Ninth Congress of the RCP."

19. Suzana Gadea, who served at different times as minister of culture and minister of education, paid for her obedience to the party. Had she devoted herself only to her professorship at the Polytechnic University, she would probably have been much happier, if less comfortable materially. She was not a leading party ideologue; she was a good example of a loyal, high-ranking party hack. Incarcerated after the fall of the regime, she was released from prison on medical grounds. She died in 1996.

20. This speech served as an important indicator of what was to come. See Ceausescu 1966: 1–2.

21. See C. Roman, "Miini harnice," *Femeia*, no. 6, 1966: 7.

22. See Luiza Vladescu and Gheorghe Vlad, "Familia si educatia patriotica a copilului," *Femeia*, no. 8, 1966: 25–27. It should also be noted that no one in the 1960s imagined that Romania would become a neo-Stalinist state by the 1980s.

23. During this period, Zaharia Stancu was president of the writers' union which, like any other professional association, was subordinated to the party. Furthermore, the party used all of its powers of seduction to court the union's members into doing their bidding. Many literary and art figures gave in to this political pressure. For example, the president of the writers' union could only be a writer invested with political authority (meaning he or she had the stamp of party approval). This also obliged him or her to serve as a leading figure in the unceasing quest to legitimate the regime.

24. Academician Zaharia Stancu, "Traditia caselor pline de copii," *Scinteia*, September 24, 1966: 1. What is not necessarily obvious in such responses is that seven, nine, or eleven refers to those children who survived infancy.

25. Dialectical reasoning was valorized because of its semiotic power. Every contradiction could be resolved through its antinomy. For example, the contradictory demands associated simultaneously with being mother, wife, wage laborer, and political or social activist were transformed into harmonious being under the encompassing rubric of the "dialectics of the feminine ideal." See Geta Dan Spinoiu, "Dialectica idealului feminin," *Femeia*, no. 3, 1967: 3–4, 36–37.

26. See Natalia Stancu, "Maternitate," *Scinteia*, September 25, 1966; "Maternitatea," *Femeia*, no. 9, 1966: 5–6; "Tot respectul femeii-mame," *Femeia*, no. 10, 1966: 2; Lucia Demetrius, "Rasplata anilor lungi," *Femeia*, no. 11, 1966: 5; Dr. C. Stanca, "Elogiul mamei," *Sanatatea*, no. 11, 1966: 4; Maria Serban, "Copilul meu, cel mai frumos din lume," *Femeia*, no. 11, 1966: 2–3.

27. See Ursula Schiopu, "Puterea miraculoasa a copilului," *Scinteia*, August 27, 1966.

28. "Atmosfera de familie," *Scinteia*, October 5, 1966.

29. See "Tot respectul femeii-mame," *Femeia*, no. 10, 1966.

30. See *Dictionarul explicativ al limbii romane*, 1975: 229.

31. The power relations inherent in different welfare state arrangements create relatedly different dependency relations. This type of subordinate relation between state and citizen is hardly unique to socialist states; however, it is a structural and generalizable feature of them.

32. "Society, it is I." See Trotsky 1947: 421. Also see Clark 1981, chap. 5, for a discussion of the father-family state relation during Stalin's reign. (I thank Richard Stites, in particular, for this reminder.)

33. By the 1980s, Ceausescu was not only the embodiment of the Communist Party but of the nation as a whole. Lest anyone be unaware of his omnipresence in Romanian history, a song filled the airwaves daily to remind them about the secular but nonetheless holy trinity: "the party, Ceausescu, Romania." See also Verdery 1994: 225–56. According to D. Popescu, Ceausescu "didn't consider himself to be the spokesman of the people, but, more to the point, a parent of them." See Popescu 1993: 237.

34. "Santierul poate deveni o familie?" *Scinteia*, August 27, 1966; "Sarbatoarea fertilitatii pamintului romanesc," *Scinteia*, October 3, 1966. Refer to the discussion in chapter 1 on dynastic socialism in Romania.

35. See the following articles on diverse but related themes, some of which were more "scientifically" than sociologically slanted: "Pastrarea sarcinii-cerinta fiziologica a organismului sanatos," *Scinteia*, September 29, 1966; "Multa grija si afectiune noilor generatii," *Sanatatea*, no. 10, 1966: 2; Dr. Ion Georgescu, "Evolutia si controlul sarcinii," *Sanatatea*, no. 12, 1966: 14–15; Dr. Cornelia Gabreanu, "Cum folositi concediul pre si post natal?" idem; George Popovici, "Procreatia," *Sanatatea*, no. 1, 1967: 10–11; Dr. Al. Manole, "In asteptare," idem; Aneta Danila-Muster, "Avortul si echilibrul endocrin," *Femeia*, no. 1, 1967: 22; Dr. Ion Mates, "Avortul empiric," *Femeia*, no. 2, 1967: 23; "Retrospectiva asupra asistentei sanitare a mamei si copilului," *Sanatatea*, no. 6, 1969: 4–5.

36. In the 1980s, a campaign began in earnest in support of "rational alimentation." The intent of this healthful eating plan was to regulate caloric consumption and nutritional benefit. Unfortunately, by the time the plan was publicly introduced, Romanians had to forage for food on a daily basis. It was impossible to take the plan seriously, and most held it in utter contempt. Rational alimentation was the butt of many a joke, none of which satisfied hunger pangs. For example: What is the best political joke? To wish someone "good appetite" at the beginning of a meal!

37. See "Masuri pentru reglementarea intreruperii cursului sarcinii," *Scinteia*, October 2, 1966: 1.

38. Ibid.: note 30.

39. Health and productivity were ideologically linked. The definition of a sick person as a potentially nonproductive citizen had dire consequences for handicapped children, for example. Although many would have become reasonably healthy and productive individuals elsewhere, in Ceausescu's Romania their differences consigned them to institutional hells, circumstances that later tugged at the hearts of most of the world.

40. *Femeia,* no. 10, 1966. Medical specialists presented their opinions about birth, abortion, and women's health. One of the section headings was titled: "Medicii au cuvintul" ("Doctors Have Their Say"), p. 7.

41. Dr. Theodoru granted an interview to Smaranda Mezei in the summer of 1992. By then, his opinion about abortions was much more nuanced. He stated that abortions done by doctors were safe, regardless of the traumatic nature of the operation. But, because of the surgical intervention, minor post-abortive problems might emerge. Given the potential pathologies associated with abortion, he considered other methods of fertility control to be preferable.

Another specialist from the Titan hospital offered his opinion on the subject: "If an abortion is done under good conditions, there is no risk to the woman's health given that the mucous lining regenerates monthly. But it is obligatory that this be done by a specialist in the best hygienic environment." In view of the fact that abortion was the principal method of fertility regulation in Romania before and after 1966 (and today), Romanian gynecologists are quite skilled. He also maintained that if Romanian hospitals were equipped with aspirators, then these tools for intervention would present fewer complications than other modern contraceptives.

42. The relationship between national identity and population practices is invoked by almost all nationally inclined political figures in eastern Europe. The crucial cultural fears in Romania pertain to the Gypsy birth rate; the Hungarian "threat" was (and is) not significant in this regard because the Hungarians' natality rate is lower than that of the Romanians. According to the population and residence census from 1992, the average number of children per woman was: for Romanians, 1.8; Hungarians, 1.7; Germans, 1.5, and Roma (Gypsies), 2.7 (see *Recensamantul populatiei si locuintelor din 7 anuarie 1992,* 1994: xxxi). More recently, the number of children per woman among the Roma was estimated at 4.35 (see Muresan 1996).

43. *Femeia,* March 1967, p. 4. This socio-psychological study was done at a factory in Bucharest at which some 18,000 women worked. It is not possible to identify the author of the research, or for whom it was done. This was a deliberate tactic of manipulation; in part, it made it impossible to verify the results.

44. See, for example, "Femeia in viata sociala, un important factor de progres," *Femeia,* no. 10, 1967, p. 8; "Prezente active in viata sociala," *Femeia,* no. 8, 1968: 7; "Directoarea," *Femeia,* no. 6, 1968: 3–4.

45. For example, in *Femeia,* no. 11, 1968, the importance of motherhood as an occupation was underscored in this way: "A millennial 'occupation' that will continue into the future as long as human life exists, and that must be recognized as the most noble: the 'profession' of being a mother! At 46 years of age, M.B. from Reghin has achieved a human record of having sixteen children."

46. *Femeia,* no. 19, 1966: 2. On divorce as a socio-political problem, see Ciurea Codreanu 1968.

47. Corneliu Vadim Tudor, "Femeie creatoare, slava tie!" *Almanahul Femeia,* 1984: 24. This fragment is part of the prolific "literary" production of the 1970s and 1980s. Literary production of this type was among the very few industries that exceeded plan targets; it constituted a productive processing industry of pulp literature, so to speak, through which the "court poets" were able to create and sustain the illusion of Ceausescu's personality cult. One of the greatest apologists for Nicolae and Elena Ceausescu was the author of this ode dedicated to Ceausescu's wife, Elena. The viciousness of Vadim Tudor's attacks on others was rivaled only by the degree to which he used words to prostitute himself to his masters. Vadim Tudor, at the time of this writing, is a member of the Romanian senate; director of the newspaper *Romania Mare* (*Greater Romania*), which is dedicated to chauvinist, xenophobic interests; and president of the Romania Mare Party. Vadim Tudor carries on the Ceausescus' legacy through his political and journalistic activities and is one of the most fervent advocates of nationalism in post-Ceausescu Romania.

48. See Ceausescu 1973a: 9. (See also my earlier comments on this quotation, on page 27.)

49. *Hotarirea plenarei C.C. al P.C.R. din 18–19 iunie 1973 cu privire la cresterea rolului femeii in viata economica, politica si sociala a tarii,* p. 27.

50. See Ceausescu 1978. Again, the need to change the household division of labor between men and women was not mentioned.

51. Fischer 1989: 174.

52. Ibid.: 175. Fischer quoted a fragment from the volume, *Omagiu,* that was dedicated to Ceausescu on his 55th birthday. UCY is the Union of Communist Youth.

53. See Greenwald 1986: 33.

54. "Prezente feminine prestigioase in cel mai inalt for stiintific al tarii," *Femeia,* no. 3, 1974: 3–5; Aneta Dumitriu, "Traditia de a fi fruntasi se pastreaza zi de zi, ceas de ceas (un episod din cronica feminina a intrecerii socialiste)," *Femeia,* no. 10, 1974.

55. Ciobanu 1974: 5. The complicity of Western states in bolstering the fictional achievements of Elena Ceausescu is now an embarrassing chapter in international relations of that era. In the United States, for example, she received an honorary degree in chemistry, though not from a top university. Richard Stites reminded me about the Soviets who lit the way for their East European comrades. For example, Nadezhda Krupskaia (Lenin's wife) served a similar purpose in the 1920s, as did Valentina Tereshkova, the cosmonaut, in the 1960s.

56. Elena Ceausescu did not, however, qualify for a "heroine mother" medal. Motherhood was not her strongest representational quality. But this detail did not detract from the accolades: "Inalt omagiu stiintei romanesti," *Femeia,* no. 1, 1974; "Stralucit mesager al stiintei romanesti," *Femeia,* no. 3, 1974 (in which there was a section devoted to the prestigious presence of women in the highest scientific forum of the country; the photographs of four other female academicians surround the principal portrait); Ciobanu 1977.

57. See *Rolul femeii in viata economica, politica si sociala a Romaniei socialiste,* 1973: 158.

58. Activist women publicized new job possibilities for women. See, for example, "Meserii feminine, meserii masculine?" *Femeia,* no. 2, 1974; Spornic 1975.

59. *Rolul femeii in viata economica, politica si sociala a Romaniei socialiste,* 1973: 162.

60. "The publications of the National Women's Council will make their central preoccupation the increase in women's (city and village) contributions to the

realization of the party's policies, and the popularization of female workers, cooperative peasants, intellectuals as sources of material and spiritual goods, of women—mothers, educators of the young generation." Ibid.: 164. The women's club, Femina, was created in part to help fulfill this task (see Gabriela Ionescu and Zenia Grigore, "Clubul 'Femina'—o tribuna de educatie," *Femeia*, no. 1, 1974: 16). For the period, see also Deliman 1977. The author offers a compilation of party directives on the subject and gives them a "socialist"-feminist interpretation.

61. Measures also targeted increased participation of women in diverse institutions and enterprises. See *Femeia*, no. 1, 1974: 8.

62. Deliman 1977: 96.

63. For details about these provisions see ibid.: 160. They were reiterated by Ceausescu in various venues throughout the 1970s. See, for example, Ceausescu 1978.

64. As discussed in chapter 2, contraceptives were *not* forbidden by law; however, they were unavailable. This meant they could only be obtained through illegal, black-market connections. Abortion, on the other hand, was illegal. Western reporting on this matter has been consistently inaccurate. Illegality and unavailability are not necessarily synonymous. Births were avoided through illegal abortions, abstinence, coitus interruptus, and various other traditional methods. Women workers whom I interviewed frequently explained that they did not want children because they did not have apartments or they commuted long distances to work. They were traumatized by childcare problems.

65. See Teitelbaum and Winter 1985: 102.

66. Babies were also included on the list of exportable goods when hard currency was the price. This is discussed in chapter 7.

67. See "Hotarirea Comitetului Politic Executiv al C.C. al P.C.R.," 1984. A joke that circulated shortly thereafter noted: By presidential decree, the genital organs have been nationalized! The play on the word "organs" (state organs/genital organs) is pointed.

68. Cited in "Hotarirea," 1984. On March 6 an editorial appeared in *Scinteia* titled "The firm, steadfast application of the demographic policies for the nation's vitality, youth, and vigor." It reiterated and further elaborated the major points of the decision, marking the debut of an aggressive indoctrination campaign that became characteristic of the style of propaganda until the brutal end.

69. Ceausescu 1984b.

70. See *Regulament-cadru privind organizarea, functionarea si continutul activitatii cluburilor 'Femina,'* 1984: 13–14.

71. See Constantinescu, Negritoiu, and Stativa 1987: 4–5.

72. *Femeia*, no. 3, 1967: 4.

73. The formulaic nature of propaganda content made the shift from four to five children easy to manage. See chapter 2 regarding the legal policy change.

74. See M. Mincu 1988: 16.

75. See Dr. Dragos Serafim, in *Flacara*, no. 7, February 14, 1986: 12. The reference to a depraved society is to Romania in 1934.

76. Madeleine Maicanescu-Georgescu, "A avea sau a nu avea copii," *Sanatatea*, no. 1, 1984.

77. This phrase comes from the title "Handsome and Healthy Children for the

Vigor and Youth of the Fatherland" (*Scinteia tineretului*, January 28, 1986). This title, which appeared twice in March in the Communist Youth League paper, was among those used for pronatalist propaganda. It reproduced one of the arguments frequently invoked by Ceausescu to spark (or discipline) the population into fulfilling the population plan.

78. Throughout the 1980s, the headlines were filled with political demographic propaganda. Additional titles included the following which are meant to be representative, not exhaustive: Lucian Huiban, "Copiii-bucuriile familiei Trifa," *Sanatatea*, no. 3, 1984: 7; Dr. Lidia Oradean, "Sanatatea copiilor—bogatia viitorului," and Dr. Sebastian Nicolau, "Bucuria vietii," both in *Sanatatea*, no. 4, 1984: 3–4; Sanda Faur, "Imensa grija cu care tara isi vegheaza copiii," *Femeia*, no. 3, 1985: 9; Silvia Netcu, "Copiilor tarii—dragostea si grija intregii tari," *Femeia*, no. 6, 1985: 3; Valeria Chilau, "Copiii-viitorul tarii," *Sanatatea*, no. 6, 1987: 3; George Radu Chirovici and Sava Bejinaru, "Copiii sint soarele omului: reportaj dintr-o comuna suceveana, unde a avea multi urmasi constituie o lege traditionala a colectivitatii," *Scinteia*, February 23, 1986: 2; George-Radu Chirovici, "Casa cu multi copii, semnul raspunderii de bun cetatean pentru viitorul natiunii: venirea pe lume a unui copil este un miracol ce concentreaza in el intregul univers," *Scinteia*, March 2, 1986: 1–2; Silviu Achim, "Familia numeroasa—temeiul dainuirii si statorniciei prin vremi: perene invataminte ale istoriei romanesti," *Scinteia*, September 18, 1986: 4; M. Stefan, "O bogatie mai presus de orice," *Scinteia tineretului*, March 5, 1986: 1, 5; Maria Predosanu, "A darui viata—o optiune ce sta in puterea femeii," *Sanatatea*, no. 12, 1987: 8; etc.

79. A very black joke of the times posed the following paradox: What is even colder than cold water? Hot water. See Stefanescu 1991: 91. Hot water in each city was controlled from a centralized source. In the 1980s the provision of water was severely limited. Hence the black humor: when the hot water knob was turned on, the water was ice cold (if it emerged at all).

80. Parvu 1988: 21. The link between demographic and economic factors was meant to legitimate the pronatalist policies of the regime. Needless to say, this legitimating argument was first invoked in the 1960s; it did not change substantively over time.

81. "Noi, botosanenii, iubim familiile trainice, cu copii multi si sanatosi," *Femeia*, no. 6, 1984: 14. Botosanenii are the people from Botosani.

82. Ibid.

83. This pertains to the period before the banning of abortion in 1966.

84. Trebici and Hristache 1986. The authors reproduce a regional typology whose classification system is based on the level of socioeconomic development attained according to synthetic indicators. Botosani is placed in category VI, regions characterized by limited development. The same results applied to this region's industrialization. See also Sandu 1987.

The region in which I did the most extensive fieldwork also had one of the highest natality rates in the country and was similarly celebrated in the state media for its contributions to the population plan. (See, under the formulaic title, "O indatorire de inalta raspundere fata de societate, fata de viitorul natiunii noastre socialiste" [A duty of the highest responsibility for society, for the future of our socialist nation], *Scinteia tineretului*, March 8, 1986.) However, village residents quickly pointed out, despite public profession of Eastern Orthodoxy, they remained Greek Catholics, which is why their natality rate was generally so high. The state's pronatalist policies themselves were considered irrational.

85. This region was located along the Soviet border in the northeastern corner of Romania; the political leadership deliberately avoided developing important industrial interests in such areas.

86. Educational levels are frequently associated with changing fertility patterns; increased education is positively correlated with decreased family size. The "enlightening" role of political-educational activities remained limited in Romania.

87. See "Familia cu multi copii—o lege a vietii si implinirii umane, o nobila indatorire patriotica," *Scinteia*, March 9, 1984: 1–2.

88. As reiterated by Dobbs 1990c: 1, 8A.

89. I. Mincu 1982: 75. This very same Mincu became minister of health, serving throughout much of the Vacaroiu government during Iliescu's second term (1992–1996). On scientific alimentation, also see I. Mincu 1978; Mincu and Boboia 1975; and I. Mincu, Mihalache, and Cheta 1985.

90. Ibid.: 104.

91. See Rosca and Popescu 1989: 19. This is discussed further in chapter 7. Also see the *Romanian National Nutrition Survey*, 1991, prepared for the Ministry of Health and UNICEF, Romania.

92. See, for example, Doina Mosoiu ("Femeii-mama—sprijinul material si pretuirea intregii societati," *Scinteia*, March 5, 1986), who presented the adjusted monthly allocations for children then in effect. Until December 31, 1985, mothers with five or more children received 200 lei per month; thereafter, they received 500.

93. See "Cresterea si educarea noilor generatii," 42.

94. The first title, "Fratii despartiti: divortul este intr-adevar un dezastru familial," appeared in *Femeia*, no. 12, 1988: 13; the second, Areta Sandru, "Gaseste-mi un loc linga inima ta," in *Scinteia tineretului*, May 20, 1987: 2.

95. See "Raspuns catre o mama," *Femeia*, no. 12, 1988: 13.

96. The world witnessed ex post facto and with horror the "good care" provided for orphaned children in Ceausescu's Romania. It is even more tragic that most Romanian parents had little way of knowing the truth.

97. See Teodoru 1985; M. Mincu 1988; Badea 1987.

98. On educating the public on health, see especially Dorobantu 1985: 26–67, from which this is summarized.

99. Ibid.: 94.

100. Madeleine Maicanescu-Georgescu, "A avea sau a nu avea copii," *Sanatatea*, no. 1, 1984: 12; note that coitus interruptus was one of the few "natural" methods available to the masses.

101. See *Muncitorul sanitar*, January 28, 1986. Only the first of the five objectives of this competition issued by the committees representing the party, the trade union, the workers' council, and the communist youth union of Suceava's Health Directorate have been reproduced herein.

102. Dr. Valeria Bobocea, "Angajati in realizarile epocii marilor infaptuiri socialiste," *Muncitorul sanitar*, January 28, 1986.

103. See *Sanatatea*, no. 3, 1984: 2. Both of these winners' statements must be taken with more than a grain of salt.

104. M. Mincu 1988: 30.

105. Stefanescu 1991: 43.

106. To have yelled "demonstration" in public would have resulted in arrest. The means (menstruation) led to the desired end: the flowing of blood, specifically that of the Ceausescus. Political jokes were the nemesis of propaganda. They were told among a private public—that is, among trusted kin and friends.

107. Ana Blandiana, *Amfiteatru* 1984. This, as well as several other poems, appeared. Blandiana was not punished in any significant manner, resuming publication elsewhere after a short while. The editor of the paper was demoted. These poems were allegedly photocopied and distributed by Roma in Bucharest. It was implied that Blandiana's past and her personal relations protected her from enduring ostracism. See, for example, M. Nitescu, *Sub zodia proletcultismului: dialectica puterii* (Bucharest: Editura Humanitas, 1995), p. 299.

## CHAPTER 6. BITTER MEMORIES

Smaranda Mezei conducted the interviews in this chapter with D.N., N.G., G.T., V.P., B.K., M., M.L., G.D., E.M., and M.P.; Katherine Verdery conducted the interview with I.D., and I conducted those with V.C., Dr. G., L.I., S.M., and A.T., or as otherwise cited. Both Mezei and I interviewed B.M. at various times between 1990 and 1994.

1. Recall that from an ideological standpoint, the socialist state planned the eradication of differences, including gendered identities.

2. Recall that article 200 of the Penal Code criminalized homosexuality.

3. There has been a tendency to romanticize the role of the family under communism as a site of refuge from the state. While a semblance of privacy and freedom was maintained in family life, the agents of state repression also successfully and insidiously manipulated interpersonal, intimate relations (see note 4). Moreover, gender relations within the family were not critically reformulated.

4. The manipulation of private relations was a common technique in the former socialist states. In addition to partners informing on each other, in the German Democratic Republic women linked to the Stasi infiltrated women's groups and informed on them. See, for example, Kukutz and Havemann 1990.

5. Ceausescu's Romania offers yet another example of physicians' participation in politically motivated medical practices. The Nazis were among those who used their professional skills to the most nefarious of ends. See, for example, Mitscherlich 1949 and Lifton 1986.

6. See Sawicki 1991: 81. I draw upon Sawicki's outline of a Foucauldian feminist analysis, which "would focus not only on the dominant discourses and practices . . . but also on the moments of resistance that have resulted in transforming these practices over the years."

7. Quoted from Rita Bashaw, "Examining the Invisible: Gendered Identities in GDR Protokolleliteratur," seminar paper, Georgetown University, 1994.

8. Year of birth, gender, and profession are given in parentheses when possible. It is also difficult to posit that most obstetrician-gynecologists in Romania were male, as many Westerners assume.

9. The consequence referred to was pregnancy. Such advice did not include information about "safe sex" practices to avoid sexually transmitted diseases. In interviews conducted with prominent doctors in 1990, several of them claimed that AIDS was not a problem that affected adults in their country.

10. Recall that citizens of socialist states were adept at reading between the lines, which was, said differently, a form of subtle or implicit communication. What could not be stated verbally or in writing was nonetheless communicated.

11. Recall that by 1980 contraceptive devices were obtainable only on the black market.

12. This account distinguishes between doctors taking risks in hospital or clinic settings and those who did abortions on their own. There is no hard evidence available to support the claim regarding the class difference in maternal mortality statistics.

13. It is important to note that women did not generally mention the gynecological exams when talking about their lives during the regime unless prompted to do so because many were unaware of the political pronatalist aspect of these seemingly routine medical exams. Most women recounted the daily ordeals associated with becoming or not becoming pregnant and terminating an unwanted pregnancy. The gynecological exams were considered to be relatively minor inconveniences in comparison with the ever-present problems of dealing with their sex lives. Women opposed to these exams (for a host of reasons, including political ones) managed not to show up on the appointed day. Others were rudely made aware of the politics of reproduction if they had the misfortune of being examined by a zealous party activist. One way or another, the ubiquitous gynecological exams, however draconian, were not nearly as straightforward as they were made out to be by the Western media.

14. It was not possible to confirm this assertion; however, the number of kits produced and sold annually between 1983 and 1989 suggests that there was a relationship between political interests and the production and use of the kits.

T.I.S. was first produced in 1983. Production was as follows: 1983: 11,759 kits; 1984: 15,690; 1985: 5,712; 1986: 9,298; 1987: 9,729; 1988: 10,555; 1989: 8,263; 1990: 8,677; 1991: 5,421; 1992: 1,937; 1993: 2,033. The intensification of repressive measures occurred in 1983, 1985, and 1987. Note that the number of kits produced and sold in 1984, 1986, and 1988 increased significantly. At the same time, production resources were sharply limited during the 1980s, meaning that supply could not meet the needs of demand, regardless of the fact that the demand was created by political dictate. Data are from the Commercial Office of the Cantacuzino Institute where these kits were produced.

15. Douches were not made of plastic and rubber. Instead, there was a rubber "irrigator" and a metal bag.

16. See note 13 above. It is a critical point in cross-cultural miscommunication.

17. The practical significance of this point warrants emphasis. In 1990 I spent several days interviewing the medical staff of an enterprise at which some 15,000 women were employed. Even physicians who performed the gynecological exams with a certain sense of political responsibility admitted to their inefficiency. The relationship between the political norm and practical reality was problematic in all do-

mains of life, gynecological exams included. Furthermore, under Ceausescu, doctors performed the gynecological exams in addition to their normal work loads.

18. There are no data supporting a broad generalization of this well-intentioned claim. Undoubtedly there were many men who accepted this sexual practice; there were also many others who didn't. A more recent study done in 1993 does suggest that withdrawal was the method most practiced. Of 4,861 women interviewed, 34 percent claimed to have relied on withdrawal; 8 percent used the calendar; 4 percent used IUDs; 4 percent, condoms. The fact that withdrawal was still widely practiced in 1993 even though contraceptives had become more available implies that withdrawal had been more widely practiced before 1989. (It should be recognized that the continued reliance on withdrawal may be linked to various factors, including the cost of contraceptives.) In this same study, 68 percent of the respondents said that they still used withdrawal because their partners preferred it; 64 percent relied on the calendar method for similar reasons. 62 percent remarked that they had little knowledge of other methods; 24 percent said that doctors recommended that they still use traditional methods. See *Romanian Reproductive Health Survey 1993*, figure 6.2.2, p. 69, "Current Use of Specific Contraceptive Methods," and table 6.5.2, p. 82, "Percent of Women in Union, 15–44 Years of Age Using Traditional Methods of Family Planning."

19. N.G. mentioned related contraceptive methods: "quinine, iodine, oleander leaves, which are toxic, introduced into the vagina."

20. So great were the everyday traumas associated with the pronatalist policies that months after the legalization of abortion, the Ministry of Health still received files of mothers who had died as a result of illegal abortions; some of these were mothers of five children who would have been eligible for legal abortions even during the Ceausescu regime.

21. After the fall of the regime, a private adoption market emerged. Trafficking in children, for humanitarian as well as financial motives, became a similarly lucrative business. This is discussed further in chapter 7.

22. See Sanda Faur, "In numele vietii acuz!" *Femeia*, no. 4, 1974: 28–29: "An engineer was tried for having done 31 illegal abortions. He claimed to have a passion for medicine; he also needed money and had been unable to refuse these women in need. The lawyer queried: 'Out of weakness you broke the law, endangered the lives of women, and extinguished those of children?'" Eventually, 26 of the 31 women were located and brought to trial in shame. One had died. The engineer received an eight-year prison term and three years' interdiction of his civil rights. Others involved in the case received sentences varying in duration from one to five years. The article ended: "Firm punishments in conformity with the law, and with an educational scope: for people to become aware and to know." The intent was that people learn a lesson.

23. After Decree 770 was proclaimed, most illegal abortions were done by doctors. To control this phenomenon, the government began a public, repressive campaign in the early 1970s against doctors who broke the law. Many were arrested. The publicity surrounding these arrests dissuaded colleagues from taking the risk. For example, *Femeia*, no. 1, 1974, contains a column dedicated to "infraction of [the] abortion [law]." Three cases were summarized. The first pertained to a medical

assistant who perforated the uterus and intestines of the woman she was "assisting," a 22-year-old mother. Realizing the gravity of the situation, but frightened, the assistant did not rush the young mother to the hospital where she later died. To set an example, the assistant's trial was held before her entire work collective. The next case was that of a dentist who profited over the course of three years from performing abortions on seventeen women. He was eventually caught and tried along with his accomplices. The third case reported concerned a gynecologist and the 31 women for whom she had induced abortions. The message was clear: sooner or later, abortionists would be caught and punished. Because the medical cadre became more reluctant to perform illegal abortions, a space had been created for others—nonspecialists—to enter the abortion market.

24. All manner of methods were tried by women desperate to rid themselves of unwanted pregnancies without drawing attention to themselves (see chapter 2). One woman reported drinking chemical substances used for developing photographs. On another occasion, a woman who worked for a veterinarian gave her neighbor oxytocin to self-inject; this substance was injected into heifers for similar purposes. Yet another recounted trying to secure a false diagnosis to obtain a legal abortion. To this end, she was hospitalized for two weeks in a psychiatric clinic. After her release she suffered nightmares about her husband taking her daughters from her because he had proof of the mother's insanity. As I pointed out to Henry David, from whose article the information about these additional methods is drawn, a mother's insanity was one of the few grounds available to men to gain custody of children during a divorce proceeding (see Baban and David 1994: 32, 40–41). Again, women often paid exorbitant sums for the assistance of others in their attempts to rid themselves of a pregnancy.

25. See, for example, Order 473, December 9, 1983, "Pentru aprobarea unor norme tehnice privind imbunatatirea asistentei medicale a femeii gravide" (For the approval of technical norms regarding the improvement of medical assistance for pregnant women), annex 2, "Criterii de diagnostic si sistemul de raportare a starii de gestatie, avort si tulburari neuro-hormonale in vederea aplicarii unitare in intreaga retea sanitara" (Criteria for diagnosing and reporting states of gestation, abortion, and neurohormonal disorders for application throughout the entire health system), published in the *Buletin 1*, Ministry of Health, 1987.

26. Ibid.: 45.

27. See, for example, Order 473, December 9, 1983, annex 3, "Norme tehnice privind efectuarea operatiei cezariene" (Technical norms regarding cesareans), pp. 46–58.

28. However, the final decision remained with the doctor "on the basis of his clinical experience" (ibid.: 49). After two cesareans, a woman was eligible for a legal abortion. That raised other problems for meeting the birthrate plan and motivated some doctors not to agree to a second cesarean. Also, since 95 percent of births were expected to be natural, the stakes were raised significantly as to who should receive cesareans.

29. Signs of "violence" seemed to constitute the fine line for most doctors. If any were evident, doctors were less tempted to take the risk of becoming involved in a woman's case history, regardless of the potential financial payoff. The cost-benefit

analysis seemed to suggest that the risk was too great in such cases, whereas in the others, the risk was worth taking.

30. The assumption was that the young doctor had induced her abortion, using her professional training to break the law. Because of these suspicions, she was to be carefully examined for any visible signs.

31. Credibility may be interpreted by some to be synonymous with political reliability. It is important to point out that doctors generally did not admit directly to their own overt complicity with the authorities. The degree of complicity depended on the circumstances. In some instances, doctors' assessments of themselves differ from those of their patients. At the same time, it is equally important to note the consistency of physicians' accounts about the "fine line" mentioned above. There were few clear-cut cases.

32. This statement is self-serving. The physician also stated that she accepted flowers from the poor, nothing more. Many physicians rationalized what otherwise was a functioning system of bribes as "gifts" offered in gratitude for their services. They never directly asked for these "small attentions." That may have been true, but few were so dedicated as to work for the pleasure of working.

33. The image of women as cows came up repeatedly: as if they were cattle being herded by the party authorities, and givers of milk and "calves"; women were treated with the indifference one would accord to animals. I learned of an unsuccessful attempt by the regime to get rural women to sign contracts to produce four children, in the same way that peasants signed contracts with the state for pig production, etc. The analogy of "women as cows" was familiar and repugnant to village women, who questioned what would happen if they were unable to have a third or fourth child. Would they be sent to prison? What if the child died—would they be expected to produce another?

34. Lack of privacy is notorious in Romanian medical practice. However, it is one thing to be exposed before medical personnel and quite another to be viewed by the voyeuristic state.

35. Traditional midwives were early victims of "scientific rationality." They were forbidden to practice unless they were licensed by the state. As the birthrate declined, known traditional midwives were watched by the secret police; they were viewed as prime suspects for performing "traditional" abortions.

36. In 1964 political prisoners were pardoned under the terms of Council of State decrees such as Decree 176 of April 9, 1964; Decree 310 of June 16, 1964; and Decree 411 of June 24, 1964. Prisoners were granted amnesty at different times during the Dej and Ceausescu periods. (I thank Stelian Tanase for the decree numbers pertaining to 1964.)

37. Recall that persons were tried for being "social dangers" to the system.

38. Dr. M. was not the only person to raise the point about divine justice. Unjustly punished deeds were rectified through divine intervention. This is another aspect of Romanian fatalism.

39. I thank Dr. G. and his wife for their willingness to share this material with me and with Smaranda Mezei. I had been given a number of court cases from the Ministry of Justice, among which was this one. Mezei suggested that we attempt to interview the persons named in this case since we had their addresses. At the time,

Dr. G. was in the United States visiting relatives. His wife, still marked by her own experiences with the law, insisted that I speak with him before she would agree to talk with either myself or Mezei. Upon my return to the United States, Dr. G. agreed to talk at length with me about his case. Hours of interviews and discussion ensued. Left to his own devices, his rendition would have been somewhat romanticized. As is, it presents a fascinating portrait of surviving the system and living to tell it.

In the interest of simplifying this complex case history, certain details such as the fines to which he was subjected and his formal requests for financial restitution have been omitted. It must be noted that the official documentation is replete with contradictory "facts." Cases such as Dr. G.'s were decidedly political and must be understood accordingly. Legal documents include court files from the regional level, the Supreme Court, official declarations from the Medical-Legal Institute, witnesses, secret police, and newspaper articles regarding the 1968 case. File numbers are included as feasible. Many were illegible because of the poor quality of the photocopied materials.

I am indebted to Ken Jacobson for his valuable suggestions regarding the final revision of this complex case.

40. This account provides a representative overview of Dr. G.'s experiences during the Ceausescu period; it differs from the other recountings in this chapter in that the complexity of the case does not lend itself to oral history only. The details have been condensed to what appear to be their essence in his rendition of events, as well as that highlighted in the legal documentation.

41. The director's self-defense is illustrative of the lack of professionalism and responsibility and of the petty corruption that were widespread throughout the system, and that in such circumstances as those outlined above, were potentially fatal. The director made contradictory claims: that Dr. G. had not made clear just how urgent the case was, yet he himself was aware of the seriousness of the situation and had wanted to have Dr. I. operate on the woman immediately upon his return. The attempt to blame this misunderstanding on the lack of adequate equipment was, at best, feeble. In similar fashion, Dr. R, who had left her shift early, claimed that she did not know who was supposed to cover for her; she had departed leaving no one on call.

42. See, for example, Titus Andrei, "Dezertori din postul de aparatori ai vietii omenesti," *Scinteia,* June 4, 1968: 1, 4; "La Ministerul Sanatatii s-a pus un diagnostic gresit," *Scinteia,* September 30, 1968: 1–2; Eugen Barbu, "Medici," *Scinteia tineretului,* October 16, 1968: 1, 5; Sergiu Andon, "Sala pasilor pierduti," *Flacara,* no. 37, September 6, 1969: 5; Sergiu Farcasan, "Doctore, fa-ma bine!" *Scinteia,* January 19, 1969: 1–4; "Odiseea ranchiunei sau povestea celor 26 de memorii," *Flacara,* November 15, 1969.

43. See Order of the Ministry of Health 542/1968. The director was demoted from this function for five years, by which time he was scheduled to retire. The physician who had left early was denied the right to practice for three months. Despite the fact that the negligence was gross, the punishments meted out were merely symbolic.

44. This point was contested; the official legal document was not available.

45. A diameter of two centimeters suggests that the instrument used was not a surgical one, a point underscored by Dr. G. in his defense.

46. There is no mention of the operation authorized by Dr. F. in this account.

47. Rumors provided a means for the manipulation of opinion and recollection throughout this case, as in so many others.

48. G.D. was also among the witnesses produced by the prosecution in the case against Dr. G.'s second wife who, as recounted in chapter 4, was tried as an accomplice to his crime.

49. It seems equally suspect that this representative of the tenants' association appeared to know everything that happened in this apartment. His knowledge of the alleged activities in this apartment are all the more perplexing given that apartment buildings in Bucharest did not then have doormen or intercom systems, and that many buildings had scores of apartments in them. This episode points to the manner in which denunciations were institutionalized.

50. Dr. G. was given the following sentences: five years' imprisonment followed by three years' deprivation of civil rights; four years and two years each for two of the illegal abortions; one year for trafficking in narcotics. The number of years Dr. G. was sentenced to spend in prison differed from the number of years meted out for each of the various charges against him. The former—years to be served— was determined by the longest number of years given for any one accusation (i.e., eight years' imprisonment and five years' deprivation of the right to practice), rather than being based on a cumulative calculation of punishments per offense.

51. Health figured prominently in the workings of Romania's communist and immediate postcommunist judicial system. Prison doctors verified the limits of torture that a prisoner could endure. Torture and treatment were closely linked. Health also figured significantly in the serving of sentences. For example, by the spring of 1994, almost all of the former high-ranking party officials who had been imprisoned after the fall of the Ceausescu regime were released on the grounds of poor health.

52. Because of Dr. G.'s multiple hospital stays and continuing health problems, he formally retired from hospital employment in 1981 and became eligible for a pension based on irreversible medical conditions (Department for Labor Problems and Social Protection, Decision 1423/June 27, 1981). I should mention that although Dr. G.'s medical condition was said to have been irreversible then, by 1993 he seemed quite healthy. He had no difficulty mounting the steps of the Lincoln Memorial or of the U.S. Capitol building in 90-degree temperatures and high humidity.

53. See Penal File 814/1981, or 913/1981. The numbers are unclear.

54. The punishment was not figured cumulatively. Dr. G. was to serve the sentence with the most years per charge. For each infraction of Decree 770 he had received five years, meaning that five years was the greatest number of years he would serve. See Rechizitoriul Procuraturii generale-directia I-a, nr. 124/P/October 15, 1988: 4. Also see note 50 above.

55. Despite the constant construction in Bucharest, Romania's capital was plagued by the housing shortages that were characteristic of the entire socialist region. Dr. G.'s acquisition of an apartment in this ideal location made him vulnerable to the interests of others. This was complicated by the fact that he and his wife already had an apartment in one of the apartment complexes on the outskirts of Bucharest.

56. According to Dr. G., a legal disposition applying to persons over the age of

60 stated that for each year of a sentence, the prisoner was to serve three months. With respect to this final case, the sentence was calculated in terms of seven years at three months per year, for a total of 21 months.

57. I have insisted upon characterizing the Ceausescu regime as one that ruled by a culture of fear rather than terror, as was typical of the Stalinist years. In general, I believe this distinction is an important one. However, for women, unwanted pregnancies constituted the basis for terror in the private sphere of their intimate lives.

58. I was unable to confirm L.I.'s year of birth because of her subsequent emigration.

59. Refer to Dr. B.M.'s commentary in this chapter on the same period.

60. Recall that after two cesareans, a woman had the right to a legal abortion; moreover, after a cesarean, it was recommended that she not become pregnant again for two years.

61. Given the precarious conditions in the hospitals during this period, especially in the overcrowded maternity wards, many doctors arranged to treat their patients this way. Women with the financial means could arrange to have a particular doctor follow their pregnancies and then assist at the birth. The price assured women of better care, professional treatment, and perhaps even a room with fewer beds, and, in any case, a single bed for herself. The maternity wards were so crowded that some pregnant women found themselves two to a bed. For the above arrangement to work, it was mandatory that the doctor's on-call duty coincide with the timing of the woman's giving birth. Otherwise, the birth was assisted by the obstetrician on call, who would not have permitted an intruder, even if he or she were a colleague. Yet had this been permitted, one could never know on what occasion an accusation would be made about using the state's medical structure for illicit gain.

62. In popular parlance, all of the children born after the issuance of Decree 770 were referred to as *ceausei*, after Ceausescu who had initiated the law and demographic policy. Initially, to say that a child was a *ceausel* was a euphemistic way of saying the child was among those born in 1967 or 1968. Later, the term came to refer to those children who were unplanned or who were a result of the decree. Some were called *decretei* (little decrees). Children that were born according to a couple's own family planning or who figured among the number of children wanted by a couple were not among those to whom these later meanings applied.

63. Recall that Decree 770 came into effect on November 1, 1966, abrogating the provisions of Decree 463/1957, which had legalized abortion. In October 1966, despite the law's official publication on the first of that month, abortions were still allowed.

64. I thank G.D. for agreeing to tell her story. We had her address but no telephone number, and Smaranda Mezei tracked her down. A meeting between Mezei and G.D. was eventually arranged. Her account is presented here; parts of it have been incorporated into the official version of Dr. G.'s 1974 case file.

65. This interview is excerpted from a reprint of an interview titled "Abortion: A Privilege?" which appeared in *Connexions: An International Women's Quarterly*, no. 5, 1982: 12–13. (It was first translated from *Sozialistisches Osteuropakomitee*, August 1979.) It is an example of how more-privileged women resolved their abortion dilemmas. No information was provided about the person whose story this is, why or

for whom it was written or told, or at what point in her pregnancies she began trying to have an abortion.

66. See appendix, case 1, for a summary of E.M.'s legal case. Smaranda Mezei interviewed her for this chapter on May 29, 1994.

67. Fantastic stories of this kind began to appear in the press after 1990; their veracity is highly questionable.

68. This was usually a euphemistic way of proposing to terminate the pregnancy.

69. Recall the case against Dr. G. in 1974 in which the head of section was increasingly annoyed by Dr. G.'s presence.

70. The reference is to the problem of lowering the infant mortality figures.

71. I thank Katherine Verdery for conducting this interview.

72. The purpose of tying the thread around her thigh was to prevent the root from becoming lodged inside her. The number of hours she left the root inside is considerably longer than that described as necessary by the local midwife.

73. Two children were the norm in this community, regardless of the political demographic policies. As she and others said, many women died as a result of illegal abortions. The reason for their deaths was no secret.

74. This refers to payment for her services. A.T. was a poor woman, and villagers concurred that she did not profit, as others did, from helping a woman in need.

75. Poarta Alba, or the White Gate, was a prison in the Dobrogea region near the Black Sea where prisoners doing forced labor on the canal were incarcerated. Labor conditions were extraordinarily harsh, and many died there. The building of the canal occurred during Gheorghiu-Dej's time. A.T.'s historical confusion does not alter her expressive intention: the prison was "hard."

76. In this case, A.T. informed on Mrs. C. As discussed in chapter 2, pregnancies were registered so that they could be carefully followed to prevent anything untoward from happening.

77. Recall that it was against the law (by decree of the Ministry of Health) for an IUD to be fitted by medical personnel working in any state institution. In the years about which M.P. spoke, imported coffee and cigarettes could only be obtained on the black market. The difficulty of procuring them as well as their high prices transformed these items into viable currencies of exchange.

78. Recall that a sound is a medical instrument introduced into the uterus to cause it to dilate.

79. Refer to the comments of the doctors earlier in this chapter. The hospitalization of women suffering from secondary complications due to illegal abortions is also discussed in chapter 7.

80. To reiterate, it was almost impossible to take the instruments necessary for a curettage out of the hospital. Each kit and instrument was numbered, and each use had to be officially recorded in the registry for kits and instruments used for gynecological surgery. The reason, time, registration number, and name of the person who had signed over the instruments to which doctor, all had to be recorded. Retention of any of these instruments was punished by law.

81. It was essential that the person who introduced the sound did so "cleanly," meaning that no lesions would be left on the cervix, for reasons already made clear.

82. "Each time I ended up in the hospital, I had to stay two or three days. I was

overwrought by the fact that the cost of having an abortion was suddenly increased by the additional informal costs of spending a few days in the hospital, and, of course, of the 'gifts' for those who worked in the ambulance and in the hospital. Complicity had to be compensated. The medical exams and hospitalization were free by law, but as everyone knew, between the law and practice, there was quite a distance. One day in the hospital meant another chunk out of our family budget. And then the small 'gift' for the assistant who treated me, another for the hospital attendant who brought me meals and sheets, and so forth. I didn't mention a gift for the doctor. Under the particular circumstances, it wasn't an issue because we had been colleagues and friends."

## CHAPTER 7. LEGACIES OF POLITICAL DEMOGRAPHY

I am particularly indebted to Jean-Claude Chesnais and Eva Fodor for their generous assistance in the preparation of this chapter. I would also like to thank Nick Andrews, Rebecca Emigh, Michael Heim, Ruth Milkman, Ioan T. Morar, and Katherine Verdery for their contributions.

1. Comrade Zaharescu Barbu in 1967 affirmed the relationship between statistics and lies: "You know, statistics are an instrument with which, if you know how to use them, you can prove anything you want" (Plenary Session of the Central Committee of the Romanian Communist Party, October 5–6, 1967: 158).

2. It is important to note again that "truth" was constituted and officially recognized in the state-controlled public sphere. What was said or known in private—whether at the level of the state or the family—was another matter.

3. The consequences of political demography in a "multilaterally developed socialist" state are, fittingly, multiple in dimension; they are also difficult to evaluate because of the lack of adequate data and studies. The material presented in this chapter offers an overview of what warrants further in-depth analysis.

4. Access to data has been limited. In this chapter I concentrate on the consequences most directly related to the pronatalist policies. Demographic shifts affect the structure and dynamic of the labor force, fluctuations among the school-age cohort, the shape of the age pyramid, etc. (see, for example, Trebici 1991: 27–33; Chesnais 1992). Various studies indicate the differential effects on health resulting from the overall conditions (e.g., shortages of essential foods and medicines, and pollution). See, for example, *Breviarul statistic sanitar 1989*, 1990: 54–55, regarding the rise in female uro-genital ailments; *Starea de sanatate a populatiei din Romania*, Ministry of Health report to the Chamber of Deputies, July 5, 1991, on the incidence of breast and cervical cancer. (I thank Smaranda Mezei for these two references); see also Viorica 1985.

Other studies underscore the changes in age distribution resulting in part from the political demographic policies. The aging of the population combined with a declining birthrate and other factors affected educational and employment patterns, the "marriage market," and the availability of housing. The descriptive demographic meaning of such trends differs importantly, however, from their sociological significance. This latter is beyond the scope of the current discussion. (For example, shifts in available marriage partners can be seen statistically, to be sure; however, this reveals little about marriage patterns per se. With fewer eligible men—historically consistent if variable—women will marry older or younger men. Marriage is a cultural norm in Romania; hence, it is important to know how the change in age distribution has affected marriage choice, and not simply that there has been a change. Regarding housing, the number of persons per family undoubtedly affected living conditions, but how and because of what factors goes beyond the political demographic.) On the age pyramid, see, for example, Muresan 1996, especially figure 6: 833; Trebici 1991: 27–33.

5. See, for example, Chesnais 1983: 1040–47; Watson 1995: 923–34; Eberstadt 1994: 137–52. Also see Hundley 1995: B14.

6. See, for example, Baban, forthcoming; Blayo 1991: 527–46; Hord et al. 1991: 231–40; Serbanescu et al. 1995: 76–87. The literature on family planning in Romania is growing; these are but a few recent studies from which additional sources may be drawn.

7. Generally, poor women are the victims of restricted abortion, a point to be discussed later. For recent reference to illegal abortion as a leading cause of maternal death, see, for example, Lorch 1995: 1, 3. In Kenya, one-third of maternal deaths are due to unsafe abortions.

8. See, for example, Baban and David 1994: 13; Hord et al. 1991: 233; Serbanescu et al. 1995: 77. Note that the baseline figures reported in published studies vary slightly for maternal deaths per 100,000 live births in 1989. Baban and David report 169 maternal deaths per 100,000 live births; Hord et al., 159 per 100,000; Serbanescu et al., 170 per 100,000. All claim Ministry of Health data as their source. While the variation is not statistically significant, it is, nonetheless, sociologically interesting, with respect to accounting for bodies and to statistical reliability. This general problem applies to all other figures cited in this section and the next.

9. Blayo makes this point strongly (1991: 530).

10. Some women that I interviewed over the years recounted that some doctors let women die rather than treat them for post-abortion complications. There are no data available relating such incidents to the tightening of hospital surveillance and other oversight measures.

11. Rochat 1991: 32. I thank Smaranda Mezei for bringing this report to my attention.

12. I am unable to account for the relatively high number of abortions in this column for 1987. The table is highly problematic, but offers a good example of statistical manipulation.

13. Roznatovschi 1989. This document, stamped "secret de serviciu," was not publicly available. The next largest category of women who resorted to abortion (22.8 percent) were women who had five children in their care, thereby being eligible for legal abortions. Only 0.5 percent of women who had had abortions met the legal age requirement.

14. A report regarding abortion-related maternal deaths during the first five months of 1987 cited clandestine abortions, euphemistically referred to as deaths "due to psycho-social factors," as the primary cause of maternal deaths. Of 180 such deaths, 26.6 percent happened somewhere other than medical institutions. Of those

who did make it to the hospital, approximately 24 percent died within 24 hours of admission "as a result of grave toxic-septic conditions." See Sebastian 1987: 8.

15. Stephenson et al. 1992: 1329; also note that data on the "prevalence of postabortion morbidity are not available."

16. Cited in Mezei 1991a: 5. Of the total admitted, 26.6 percent needed intensive treatment for advanced infections, 3.9 percent had hysterectomies, and 1.1 percent died. From Puia et al., n.d. Dr. B. Marinescu also commented that pulmonary and hepato-renal complications resulting from septic shock were especially problematic in the first 24 hours. Gangrene and uterine infection were much more dangerous than peritonitis.

17. Mezei 1991a: 8. She also reports that between 1981 and 1989 the recorded total of motherless children was 8,004. Again, these figures are approximate. According to data given to me by the Center for the Calculation of Health Statistics, the total number of children left motherless between 1982 and 1988 was 7,918 and did not include figures for 1981 or 1989, suggesting that the actual number was higher than 8,004. Whatever the real numbers, many children were left motherless.

18. *Prevenirea mortalitatii materne in Romania. O analiza a asistentei medicale materne si a mortalitatii materne cu recomandari pentru un program de maternitate fara riscuri in Romania, August 1993,* p. 3. In a sample of 1,029 women, 54 percent had one child; 27.5 percent, two children; 8.1 percent, three children; 3.8 percent, four children; 6.5 percent had five or more children. It seems that there were no childless women included. This study confirms the cultural preference for families with one or two children. Smaranda Mezei provided this reference.

The higher death rate among these women was probably also due to their greater age and the number of abortion attempts. Age and number of abortions are related.

19. The ambiguity about the definition of "a mother" is at the heart of abortion concerns: Is a pregnant woman already a mother carrying a child? Does the fetus have individual rights, etc.? In Romania, fetal rights were not at issue; politics, not personhood, shaped abortion concerns. It is noteworthy in the Romanian context that pregnant women without children were not evidently incorporated into the statistical count for maternal deaths—another means of lowering already troublesome figures.

20. I wish to acknowledge my gratitude to the individual who provided me with this information.

21. I am indebted to a former dedicated activist in the domain of obstetrics-gynecology who gave me *Reports on the Measures to be Taken by the Higher Council on Health and the Ministry of Health to Improve the Demographic Indicators.* Many of these reports addressed the demographic situation in specific regions, as well as nationally. The formulaic character of the recommendations becomes clear from reading them at one sitting. I am grateful to this individual for also helping me to interpret the statistical representations.

22. See Blayo 1991: 530. Blayo underscores the unreliability of the Romanian data. The problem of what constituted a declared abortion is critical. Chesnais has suggested that the Romanian rates are higher than assumed. (Smaranda Mezei first provided the reference to Blayo.)

23. Maternal death refers to deaths among women of childbearing age.

24. See Baban, forthcoming: 16. The statistics are drawn from Ministry of Health

data reported to the World Health Organization. The figures reported in the litera-ture differ slightly.

25. Stephenson et al. 1992: 1329. According to Baban, between 1969 and 1989, "there were an average of 341 maternal deaths per year from clandestine proce-dures" (forthcoming: 15). The Ministry of Health has estimated that between 1966 and 1989 an average of 400 women died annually as a result of abortion-related complications. See the report, *Mortalitatea infantila si materna in lume si in Romania,* 1995.

26. The reliability of this sum is questionable and may be an underestimation. This total was quoted in Newman 1991: 16, for the years 1966–1989. However, many maternal deaths due to illegal abortion were not recorded as such at the Medical-Legal Institute, or morgue. According to their records, 7,280 women died from illegal abortions between 1976 and 1989, suggesting that the above total is too low.

27. See *Monitorul oficial al Romaniei,* no.1, December 27, 1989.

28. On the ratio of abortions to live births, see Serbanescu et al. 1995: 78; see table 1, p. 78, for the differentiated urban/rural total fertility rate (TFR). The TFR dropped from 2.3 live births annually per woman between 1987 and 1990 to 1.5 live births annually between 1990 and 1993. The three-to-one ratio (abortions to live births) was also reported in "Abortions in Romania Outpace Births by 3-to-1," *Eugene (Oregon) Register Guard,* May 13, 1991.

29. As above, there is a slight variation in reported figures. See, for example, Hord et al. 1991: 234; Baban reports 84 per 100,000 live births (forthcoming, p. 16).

30. See Serbanescu et al. 1995: 84, and, for example, Hord et al. 1991: 236.

31. A number of studies have been conducted on reproductive health and prac-tices since 1989. The most thorough is the *Reproductive Health Survey, Romania 1993,* 1995. See also Baban and David 1994; Hord et al. 1991; Serbanescu et al. 1995; Stephenson et al. 1992; and the *Romanian National Nutrition Survey, 1991:* 37.

There is widespread gender inequality in taking responsibility for contracep-tion. Given the increase in prostitution and sexually transmitted diseases, the im-portance of overcoming cultural resistance to condom usage cannot be stressed enough. In this regard, the efforts of the Society for Contraceptive and Sexual Edu-cation (SECS, the Romanian International Planned Parenthood Federation affili-ate), should be applauded. The Ministry of Health has been not been as active as it should be; the Ministry of Education has been unwilling to address these issues.

32. See the *Reproductive Health Survey, Romania, 1993:* 167.

33. See, for example, Viorica 1985. Of the 1,870 women who participated in this study, more than three-quarters of them were under 45 years of age. The most se-rious medical problems were gynecological and neuropsychological. On "sex and society," see Baban, forthcoming: 28–30.

34. Stephenson et al. 1992: 1329. See also Baban, forthcoming: 16, for addi-tional references. Regarding birthweight, which is informative with respect to mater-nal and infant and child health, Baban cites the mean birthweight in Romania as "3.2 kg., 0.2 kg. lower than the mean birthweight of infants in Western European countries, indicating a need for improvement of maternal health and nutritional status" (p. 6). Stunting among Romanian children was similar to that of children

318 NOTES TO PAGES 217-219

from low-income families in the United States. See the *Romanian National Nutrition Survey, 1991* (pp. 6, 7). According to this study, low weight-for-height was more characteristic of rural than urban children, although the nutrient intake in general was adequate (p. 13).

35. Serbanescu et al. 1995: 76.

36. This implicitly raises critical questions about what kinds of methodological approaches are appropriate to the study of certain aspects of totalizing regimes. The interdependencies that result from party control and centralized planning severely limit general assumptions about the autonomy of distinct fields of study. On related methodological issues, see Scheper-Hughes, "Demography without Numbers," forthcoming.

Doctors in Romania noted an increase in female uro-genital ailments as well as of breast and cervical cancer during the years of the political demographic policies. (Diagnosis, which might otherwise have remained unknown, may have resulted from the frequency and mandatory nature of gynecological exams.) Increased secondary sterility is also evident. However, there are no longitudinal epidemiological studies to support causal claims about the specific policies. For suggestive but uncorroborated examples of such data, refer to Mezei 1993: 64–67, and 1991a: 5–6.

The effects of Chernobyl have also been associated with an increase in birth defects. The following joke addresses this: "After the Chernobyl accident and news about radiation, Bula put on lead underwear for fear that he wouldn't be able to sire the five children owed to the state" (see Stefanescu 1991: 104).

37. Comisia nationala pentru statistica, *Anuarul statistic al Romaniei*, 1993: 117. Note that the number of infant deaths per 1,000 live births had increased from 25.4 per 1,000 in 1988 to 26.9 in 1989. In 1987 it had climbed back up to 28.9, from which it declined the following year. (Table 7.5 gives the figure as 25.3 per 1,000, pointing to the already mentioned problem with base figures.)

38. Baban, forthcoming: 17. She notes that "in 1968, maternity hospitals were overwhelmed by admissions and a large proportion of the staff were themselves on maternity leave." Albania's infant mortality rate was still higher: in 1965 there were 76.1 infant deaths per 1,000 live births; by 1970 there were 97.9 reported infant deaths per 1,000.

39. The following are comparative infant mortality rates for 1986 or 1987 in selected European countries: Yugoslavia, 27.3; Hungary, 19.0; Poland, 17.5; Bulgaria, 14.7; Portugal (1987), 14.2; Greece, 12.2; Austria (1987), 9.8; Belgium, 9.7; G.D.R. (East Germany), 9.2; Scotland, 8.8; F.R.G. (West Germany), 8.5; France, 8.3; Denmark, 8.1; Norway, 7.9; Italy, 7.8; Switzerland, 6.8; Finland, 5.9; Sweden, 5.9. *Mortalitatea infantila in R. S. Romania in anul 1988*, Centrul de Calcul si Statistica Sanitara, 1989.

The Romanian rate was closer to the Yugoslav and Albanian rates, which remained quite high. Again, under-reporting must be taken into consideration.

40. For the comparative rates, see Trebici 1991: 97, and the *Hungarian Statistical Yearbook, 1990* [*Magyar Statisztikai Évkönyv 1990*, Budapest Központi Statisztikai Hivatal, 1991]. I thank Eva Fodor for the latter.

41. This figure is taken from an oral presentation by Dr. Bogdan Marinescu, then minister of health; it is cited in Hord et al. 1991: 233. Muresan 1996 (Annex 2: 841) gives a figure of 23.3 infant deaths per 1,000 live births for 1993.

42. For comparative caloric intake figures, see Mezei 1993a: 66. She also presents information on infant mortality due to malnutrition and development problems (dystrophy). These data are again questionable, especially since caloric intake in and of itself is not particularly meaningful. On medical causes, see Rosca and Popescu 1989: 3; 1991: 7.

43. Rosca and Popescu 1989: 5. The relationship between low birthweight and high infant mortality in the United States has recently been challenged, positing prematurity as the primary problem rather than weight or size. See Boday 1995: B7.

44. See *Raport cu privire la cauzele care au determinat scaderea sporului natural al populatiei si masurile ce se impun a fi luate de Consiliul Sanitar Superior, Ministerul Sanatatii si Comisia Nationala de Demografie, in vederea imbunatatirii indicatorilor demografici*, March 6, 1984, p. 9. This report is housed in the state archives, under the aegis of the army since 1990.

45. According to data obtained from the Center for the Calculation of Health Statistics, the dynamic of infant deaths did not provide evidence that delaying registration of birth would significantly alter infant mortality statistics, or, rather, their official appearance. For example, in 1973 there were 3,114 infant deaths within the first six days after birth out of a total of 14,444 infant deaths for that year. Of this total, 9,377 occurred between 28 days and 11 months. In 1988, of 9,643 infant deaths, 1,564 happened in the first six days; 6,724 took place between 28 days and 11 months.

Western news sources reported that births were not recorded for one month or even six weeks. There is no supporting evidence for this claim. On unrecorded infant deaths, see also Scheper-Hughes, forthcoming, which notes that poor Brazilians often bury stillborns and premature infants in their backyards. In Romania, persons unable to pay for cemetery burials buried their own in the equivalent of paupers' cemeteries on the outskirts of villages, for example. To what extent this practice pertained to infants is unknown.

46. See Malceolu and Iancu 1989: 2, 16. In his 1991 presentation to the House of Deputies, the minister of health Bogdan Marinescu reported that the mortality rate for this age group remained among the highest in Europe at 2.0 per 1,000. A large number of these deaths were attributed to accidents. Reported in *Monitorul oficial*, no. 168, part II-a, p. 14.

47. I thank the person who provided this typical example of a written report. By the 1980s, the sugar intake problem had been greatly altered by the rationing of sugar. Eva Fodor suggested the carbohydrate distinction. Ruth Milkman underscored the importance of milk for infants and children; milk was difficult to obtain throughout the 1980s.

48. I am grateful to David and Sheila Rothman for sending me the draft version of the Helsinki Watch report they coauthored (Helsinki Watch 1990). All other references may be found in Helsinki Watch 1990. The AIDS paper is by Paun (1988).

49. I was given a copy of this brochure, then displayed in the office of a doctor to whom I had been sent. Medical students claim that in the late 1980s donors' blood was no longer screened. In that the infant AIDS epidemic was largely the result of microtransfusions and reuse of unsterilized syringes, the claims in this brochure must be discounted.

The disinformation about AIDS found its way into jokes: "Question: Why is there no AIDS in Romania? Because it is a twentieth-century disease!" In the black humor of the day, the only person affected was Ceausescu himself: "Did you know that Ceausescu has S.I.D.A.[the acronym for AIDS in Romanian]? What! He has destructive, aggressive, hysterical syndrome (or Sindromul Isteriei Distructive Agresive)" (see Stefanescu 1991: 161 and 125, respectively).

50. Helsinki Watch 1990: 7. They also referred to the blood donation "plan." In return for donating blood, donors received various forms of compensation, such as minimal financial payment, meals, etc. The lack of blood screening contributed to tainted blood supplies.

51. This practice also contributed to an epidemic of hepatitis B in Romania. The incidence of acute hepatitis B in infants increased from 21.5 per 100,000 in 1984 to 192.7 per 100,000 by 1989; it also increased, but to a lesser degree, in children under the age of fourteen. Nonetheless, blood screening was not implemented. See Nicholas 1990: 9.

52. Helsinki Watch 1990: 7. Nicholas (1990: note 47) mentions that transfusions were given to children who had not been abandoned: in maternity hospitals, "transfusions of 10–20 cc. of whole blood," unscreened, had been given to low birthweight babies of undernourished mothers. Blood transfusions were considered to be a "general supportive therapy." See also Beldescu 1990 (I thank Jean-Claude Chesnais for this latter reference).

53. This number is given in the *Anuarul statistic al Romaniei, 1994*: 258, and comes from Ministry of Health data. The figures initially emerging from Romania were lower and undifferentiated with respect to transmission mode. As is true for all of the available statistical evidence, the numbers cited in different studies do not match. For example, see the data compiled by the General Directorate for Preventive Medicine and Health Promotion, December 31, 1994, for the World Health Organization, which gives the total number of AIDS cases among children as 2,715. Ages are not specified.

Social assumptions about the AIDS-afflicted compounded the problems of their treatment and care. Knowing that these children were doomed to death, most people saw no reason to waste scarce resources, including human affection, on them. Poverty and fatalism protected the living at the expense of increased anguish for the sick and dying. On leaving children in God's arms, see Scheper-Hughes 1992.

54. Bohlen 1990a and 1990b; Hilts 1990.

55. Presumably these figures refer to full-blown AIDS cases.

56. This concern is reasonable; at the same time, the involvement of Western organizations may have contributed to short-term amelioration of the immediate crisis. It remains to be seen whether the number of infant/child AIDS cases will continue to increase. According to data reported in the *Romanian National Nutrition Survey, 1991*, the majority of HIV-positive cases were among children over the age of two. These data suggest that the "'birth cohort' of 1988 and 1989 was at greater risk and that the risk has declined for later births" (26). Carefully differentiated data would contribute to a better understanding of the phenomenon. The Ministry of Health report, *Situation de l'infection HIV-SIDA dans le monde et en Roumanie*, 1995, presents a series of proposals to address the HIV-SIDA problem in Romania. (I thank Stelian Tanase for this report, and Andrei Pop for noting the discrepancies in the figures reported.)

57. See *Situation de l'infection HIV-SIDA dans le monde et en Roumanie*, 1995. The proportion of AIDS cases among institutionalized children is not provided.

58. Constanta had the highest incidence of infant AIDS and is believed to have been the entry point of AIDS into Romania.

59. Prostitution has become widespread throughout Eastern Europe since 1989. The farther east, the more visible this historic trade is. Prostitution offers a means for women—married and unmarried—struggling with inflation and unemployment to obtain hard currency. A few nights' work keeps many families afloat, or makes it possible for them to buy goods now readily available but often unaffordable. See also Kligman 1996. Prostitutes were intimidated by my presence and that of a male French colleague when we attempted to speak with them. They feared we were secret police coming to arrest them. Rumor had it that the government wanted to unionize prostitutes as a means of controlling sexually transmitted diseases. The women were not convinced; instead, they believed the authorities wanted to control their wages, as well as continue past surveillance practices under the guise of health control. This way of thinking is not in the least surprising, in view of their past experience with mandatory gynecological exams for "health" reasons.

60. Kertzer 1993. It should be emphasized that the abandoning of infants did not originate in Italy. This practice was well known in France in the mid-eighteenth century. See Donzelot 1979: 26. Kertzer addresses the role of the Catholic Church in the institutionalization of child abandonment.

61. It is perhaps difficult for Westerners to comprehend the facility with which one was able to enter and leave hospitals unnoticed. Some women simply left the hospital of their own accord without informing anyone. Their babies remained wards of the state. The banning of abortion contributed to an increased number of unwanted children who were often then abandoned. On unwanted children, see David et al. 1988.

62. See Kligman 1988. Extended-family relations are no longer contingent on geographical proximity. Recall that urban couples often send their children to grandparents living in rural areas until the children are old enough to go to school (thereby resolving childcare problems for a time). Others rely on material support from relatives living abroad. The variations are complex.

63. Rampant shortages made it difficult for families to raise their children. Poland's orphanages were also full. As is discussed below, some of these children were adopted for hard currency. See "Boom in the Baby Trade," 1988.

64. International media attention focused on this dark human interest story. See, for example, Dobbs 1990a: A1, and 1990b; Breslau 1990: 35; Binder 1990: A8; Sachs 1990; Battiata 1990; Sarler 1991: 18–30; Olszewski 1991: 7–11.

65. Untangling the complexities of the "orphanage system," as some have labeled it, is well beyond the scope of this chapter. A multidisciplinary report by specialists on child welfare was prepared in 1990; I am grateful for the draft copy I received: *Studiu privind optimizarea vietii unor categorii sociale defavorizate si cu precadere a minorilor din institutiile de ocrotire sociala*. It was widely rumored that certain boys had been singled out to be molded into Ceausescu's special guard. As was pointed out in Helsinki Watch 1990, the homes under the direction of the Ministries of Health and of Education were not as grisly as those for the handicapped. On protection of the rights of children, and on the institutional organization of the care of children,

see also *Situatia copilului si a familiei in Romania*, 1995, pp. 75–101 (I am indebted to Ioan T. Morar for obtaining this report for me). It is noted that long-term institutionalization is detrimental to the development of children (p. 79).

66. See *Situatia copilului si a familiei in Romania*, 1995. It was noted that the medicalization of care was not stimulating "for human development, but was extremely traumatic, generating handicaps and chronic illnesses." Moreover, no adequate statistics about institutionalized abandoned children exist; there are still many children without formal identity papers. See also an earlier study conducted *Causes of Institutionalization of Romanian Children in Leagane and Sectii de Distrofici*, 1991.

67. It has recently come to light that some young people over the legal age of eighteen continued to live illegally in these homes. Unprepared for life in postcommunist society, and without other options, their presence has created other problems, such as sexual abuse. See *Situatia copilului si a familiei in Romania*, 1994: 80.

68. See Sachs 1990: 18. C. Sarler has commented that the problem of systematic neglect was widespread. Speaking about the Romanians with whom she came into contact as a British nurse, she observed: "Compassion seems to have died inside them" (Sarler 1991: 22).

69. The available data are unclear on this point. It seems that the age of three delimited the Ministry of Health's responsibilities for the care of institutionalized children, regardless of their circumstances.

70. Here, collusion between parents and state must be noted. Also, as though in anticipation of the events to come, an article appeared in the party newspaper in December 1988 on the unsatisfactory conditions in a children's home (N. Rosca 1988). It had been confirmed that local abuses were the problem: Children were beaten, forced to work against their will during vacations, and not given medical treatment. Appropriate measures were to be taken against those who, through their negligence, had jeopardized the futures of 75 children. The social stigma associated with handicapped persons was reinforced by state policy. Because families with such children did not receive financial support for their care, some parents felt it was necessary to place their children in state institutions. See *Situatia copilului si a familiei in Romania*, 1994: 81.

71. The first quote is from Battiata 1990: A1; the second is from Nachtwey 1990: 28. According to a report about children's rights in Romania, the 1990 total of 100,000 institutionalized children is an estimate; the figures for 1991 and 1992 are stated to be accurate: 92,000 and 91,800 respectively. See the Committee for the Protection of Children, *Conventia O.N.U. cu privire la drepturile copilului—stadiul aplicarii in Romania*, Buletin 4: 18, 1994 (Bucharest: Departamentul Informatiilor Publice), pp. 31–32 (I thank Ioan Morar for providing me with this report). The reliability of any of the above figures must be questioned. Available reports present data that vary widely.

The institutionalized "children" are a large blemish on post-Ceausescu Romania's image.

72. *Engageons-nous pour les enfants roumains; Grija pentru copiii nostri; the Care of Romanian Children*, Bucharest: Romanian Information Clearing House. The Romanian government took legislative steps to address the numerous difficulties associated with the rights and care of children in accordance with the terms set out by the

United Nations. See the governmental report, *Conventia O.N.U. cu privire la drepturile copilului—stadiul aplicarii in Romania,* 1994: 9–15, for a listing of these measures.

73. On the Roma, see Zamfir and Zamfir 1993; Merfea 1991; and *Situatia copilului si a familiei in Romania,* 1994: 89–101.

74. "Protection and Education of Disadvantaged Children," n.d.: 1–2. "Orphans, abandoned children and/or children with physical or mental disabilities" were located in the following types and numbers of institutions: nurseries (60), homes for preschool and school children (214), special training and re-education schools (4), institutions for the protection and special education of disabled children and young people (248), kindergartens and special schools (153), school-homes (16), special re-education schools (2), day centers for education and recovery (212), special vocational schools (39), special high schools and postgraduation schools (10), hospital homes for minors (28). (I thank Ioana Ieronim for supplying me with this information.)

The post-1990 annual adoption figures presented by the Ministry of Foreign Affairs and the Ministry of Justice differ, although not in a statistically significant manner. Nonetheless, it is interesting to ponder on the whereabouts of the missing bodies.

75. As reported in *Situatia copilului si a familiei in Romania,* the increase in the number of institutionalized children has been most marked in the poorest regions of Romania: "Maramures, Iasi, Botosani, Satu Mare, Vaslui" (p. 80).

76. Chatelot: 1995: 14. (The departure of Doctors without Borders was also reported in France and Romania.) The medicalization of the care of the children under the authority of the Ministry of Health (children up to the age of three) has also been criticized in the report *Situatia copilului si a familiei in Romania,* pp. 78–79.

77. The basis for this discussion was published in Kligman 1992.

78. Annually, the number of international adoptions ranged between 18,000 and 20,000 children. *Romania: Infierea de copii romani de catre cetateni straini,* 1991: 10.

79. Law 11/1990 was published in the *Monitorul oficial,* no. 95, August 1, 1990.

80. The first figures are from the Ministry of Justice, March 1, 1995. See also the useful report *Romania: Infierea de copii romani de catre cetateni straini.* During those three months, Americans adopted 240 children; Italians, 197; Germans, 195; French, 151; Canadians, 146; British, 81; Belgians, 76; Swiss, 52; and New Zealanders, 49. Syrians, Cypriots, Austrians, Mexicans, and others also adopted children. See p. 37.

81. Lawson 1991: B1. By comparison, the adoption of South Korean children by U.S. citizens for that period numbered 1,534.

82. On foreign adoptions during the regime years, see "Boom in the Baby Trade," 1988; Dempsey 1989; Galainena 1989: 97–110.

83. Quoted in Galainena 1989: 97. The number of adoptions by the French are given on p. 98.

84. Quoted in Sarler 1991: 26.

85. Just as the postwar Jewish population decreased through emigration, so have Roma left Romania through emigration. It is beyond the focus of this chapter to explore the varied consequences of Roma emigration, especially to Western Europe. When Roma were initially adopted from the orphanages, some Romanians expressed

disdain for foreigners who were saving Roma instead of "Romanian" children in need. Then, Roma were castigated for their willingness to sell their own children. They were not the only ones to do so. There was enough demand to encourage the sellers to increase the supply of their product: children. The development of post-1990 international adoption warrants a monograph of its own.

86. See, for example, Hunt 1991; O'Hanlon 1991; and Sarler 1991, among many such articles. At the same time, adoption presents a potential positive outcome for otherwise unwanted children.

87. See Scheper-Hughes 1990: 57–62.

88. International adoption is part of the global politics of reproduction.

89. Furthermore, I do not mean to gloss over the role of institutional corruption in international adoption.

90. Responding to this questionnaire was voluntary; hence there are no claims to representativeness. Consulate officials indicated that this distribution reflected general trends.

91. Recall the distinction regarding social orphans; the definition used in U.S. immigration law is more narrow and contributed to the ambiguities involved in problematic cases. The discussion about adoption henceforth focuses on American-Romanian cases. Much has been written about U.S. adoptions of Romanian children, which became a focal issue of the debates about granting post-Ceausescu Romania most-favored-nation (MFN) trade status (see below).

92. His was an insightful comment. As the MFN battle over Romania unfolded in Congress, interested parties played the devil more than God and often distorted what was a complex, difficult situation into a sensationalist drama.

93. O'Hanlon 1991: 8.

94. The inability to communicate made it easier to avoid the emotional pain that an explicit knowledge of coercion would have fostered. In the embassy questionnaire, however, many wrote that unfamiliarity with the Romanian language put them at a considerable disadvantage. They were subject to exorbitant fees and ever-changing rules of the game.

95. For a detailed account of these experiences, see Kligman 1992: 405–20. I thank the U.S. consulate employee who gave me the names of villages that had figured prominently as "baby supplier" locales. The mafia-like control of this market quickly became evident. Lest anyone assume that Romanians were the only ones engaged in this business, I was informed that an American parolee had bought a van and gone to the north of the country, where she found children for prospective parents. Once a month, she reported to the embassy, which served as her parole officer. The international dimension of adoption is multifaceted.

96. The mother's one-and-a-half-year-old was then en route to the United States. A Belgian couple had adopted her three-year-old daughter but returned her to her parents after a medical exam revealed that she suffered from hepatitis B. The foreigners did not ask the family to pay back the $400 that had been paid in exchange for the child. Hepatitis B and AIDS became contentious issues for some adoptive parents. The incidence of hepatitis B and AIDS was discussed in the report *Romania: Infierea de copii romani*, especially pp. 39–40; extracts from an article in *The Lancet*, 1990: 1592–93, are reproduced. Consular officials confided that some American adoptive parents, fully aware of the infant AIDS situation in Romania, were

outraged by mandatory HIV testing in keeping with U.S. immigration laws. A TV docudrama on the adoption of institutionalized children registered a symbolic slap at the law in a scene in which an AIDS-infected child was denied entrance into the United States yet was permitted to enter France. The French did not impose regulations that seemed to function against the interests of these children. However, it is beyond the scope of this discussion to explore exactly whose interests were better served. Some children who had been adopted by Americans were later abandoned when they tested positive for HIV.

97. I am grateful to Nancy Scheper-Hughes for alerting me to this rumor before my encounter with it. See Scheper-Hughes 1990. Articles on this subject periodically appear in the *New York Times*.

98. Republished in *Monitorul oficial*, no. 159, July 26, 1991 (initially published in no. 147, July 17, 1991). Similar abuses have occurred elsewhere. Russia also stopped foreign adoptions as the private adoption market and related problems burgeoned. See, for example, Efron 1994. The revised Russian adoption law implements features of the revised Romanian adoption law. Foreigners, for example, are allowed to adopt (including healthy children) only after a six-month search in Russia for prospective parents (see Stanley 1995: A1, 6). Ukraine has also restricted foreign adoptions to curb alleged "incidents of baby-selling" (see entry by C. Lapychak, "Ukrainian Parliament Restricts Child Adoptions by Foreigners," *OMRI Daily Digest* II: 22, January 31, 1996).

99. Some Romanians accused the government of robbing ordinary people of one of the few means by which they could make money so that the government would profit instead. Foreigners also protested this law, criticizing the Romanian government for preventing them from taking Romanian children to a better life. In an update to a guide on how to adopt a Romanian child, the author summarized the consequences of the new law. She concluded, "God Bless You in your efforts to rescue a little one" (see Del Vecchio 1991). It is important to note that some individuals stake their hopes on adoption loopholes because they have been denied approval to adopt in the United States.

100. The increase in infertility has been associated with pollution, malnutrition, and basic deterioration of daily living conditions. Epidemiological studies are unavailable. With respect to intercultural adoption, Roma activists at one point proposed an exception to the law on behalf of Roma children, citing the special circumstances that pertain to them in Romania. In part, it was hoped that foreign Roma seeking to adopt Roma children would be permitted to bypass the waiting period. Non-Roma who have adopted Roma children have formed support groups and are committed to educating their children about their natal culture.

101. Corruption associated with the adoption of Romanian children persists in spite of the law meant to stop trafficking. See, for example, S. Ionescu, "O fetita infiata in Romania este subiectul unui scandal de presa in Italia," *Evenimentul Zilei*, July 24, 1995; C. Stroie, "Cazul unei fetite infiate in Romania este subiect de discutie in parlamentul italian," *Evenimentul Zilei*, August 6, 1995. (I am grateful to Adriana Baban for alerting me to this case.)

102. For example, the U.S. Consulate issued visas for 227 children in 1994 and 334 in 1995. By mid-1997 it had already issued 303.

103. This was noted in the Romanian paper *Adevarul;* see Pepel 1994: 3. See also

Alstein 1992 (op-ed article). A legal limbo has affected the fate of Slovak orphans now in the Czech Republic since the velvet divorce that split Czechoslovakia in two. See Murphy 1995.

104. See, for example, Perlez 1994.

105. The quotation is from the floor statement by U.S. Representative Richard Pombo (R-Calif.) on March 13, 1993. The home in question is in Sighetu-Marmatiei, Maramures. The slanted TV presentation was troubling, for these children would benefit from help. However, the violation of law is not the way to proceed (U.S. Embassy officials also confirmed this distortion by the media) (see ABC News "20/20" transcript #1313, March 1993).

106. This ambiguity was verified by U.S. Embassy officials. As of July 1995, the fate of the children remained shrouded in ambiguities. The one-year treatment period for many of these children has expired, as have their visas. Yet information about their whereabouts has been kept secret. One child has been located living with a Pentecostal family. Her parents' insistence that she be returned has been ignored. Regrettably, it is beyond the scope of this chapter to discuss the manipulation of "medical treatment" as a means of circumventing legal adoption regulations. To be sure, the case in point is fraught with irregularities that call into question the ethics of those involved.

107. I thank Professor Mihai Pop for reminding me that the emergence of street children as an urban problem in Romania is partially the result of the political demographic policies. Regrettably, media and socio-ethnographic accounts of these children's lives has been limited. (Media coverage has also been biased.) Although various governmental and nongovernmental organizations have begun to deal with these children, I was unable to acquire information about their efforts or analyses. My summary discussion of this situation is drawn exclusively from the report *Conventia O.N.U. cu privire la drepturile copilului*, pp. 41–43 (I wish to reiterate my thanks to Ioan T. Morar for obtaining this report for me).

108. *Conventia O.N.U. cu privire la drepturile copilului*, p. 43. The unsolicited washing of auto windows while drivers are stopped at a traffic light is a customary practice among impoverished youth.

109. Supporting data for this claim are unavailable. Racist attitudes toward Gypsies are common throughout Central and Eastern Europe and have played an important ongoing role in post-socialist Romania.

110. Ibid.: 73.

111. See footnote 32 above and Kligman 1992: 402–4. Reliance on abortion as a means of fertility control is prevalent throughout the region. Declining birthrates contribute to population replacement concern; they also serve as fodder for anti-abortion, nationalist rhetoric.

112. This is a problem throughout Eastern Europe. One Hungarian woman (in Hungary) commented that she felt compelled to use condoms with foreigners, but not with Hungarians. See Perlez 1993.

113. In general, the banning of abortion is less consequential for women with resources. Regardless of the law, they are able to support the cost of illegal abortions or of "abortion tourism." The latter has been a long-standing practice in Catholic countries. For example, today women in postsocialist Poland often travel to the Baltics for legal abortions.

114. The statistical rationalization of + or – reliability does not diminish the interpretive issue at hand. This general methodologically based problem has been taken up by Scheper-Hughes (forthcoming). In Romania, the deaths of institutionalized children were undoubtedly under-reported. As nonproductive social(ist) beings, their deaths were perhaps taken to be insignificant. The implications for assessments of genocide and the complexities of complicity with it are not revealed through an analysis of the statistics. Distortions, silences, and omissions point to ethical concerns as well. The relationship between statistics, representation, and political power, and the particular significance of this relationship in modernity are explored by Asad (1994).

## CHAPTER 8.
## COERCION AND REPRODUCTIVE POLITICS

1. Hord et al. 1991: 238.

2. "Abortion: One Romania Is Enough," *The Lancet* 345(8943) (January 21, 1995): 137–38. Norma McCorvey, alias Jane Roe, was the catalyst for abortion reform in the United States in *Roe v. Wade.*

3. The post-1968 "social contracts" between those in power and those subjugated differed throughout the East European bloc. Kadar's well-known "if you are not against us, you are with us" was a far cry from Ceausescu's increasingly neo-Stalinist approach to state-society relations. It is beyond the scope of this work to explore this further.

4. See Ionita 1996.

5. Again, I draw upon Jan Gross's fine characterization of the spoiler state (1988), especially pages 234–38. He points out that totalitarian states were spoiler states in that they spoiled people and their desire to associate with others: "What was new about Soviet totalitarianism was its universal effort to prevent *all* associations. But it is in human nature to associate with others. . . . Have the Soviets not always aspired to forge 'a new man'? Curiously, even though we associate totalitarianism with Organization writ large, its business is with the individual. It can easily enough destroy organizations, but to prevent association it needs to work through individuals to eradicate temptation" (p. 235). What more effective mechanism to meet this end than controlling the body, intimacy, sexuality?

6. The illegalists and communists of the Gheorghiu-Dej era participated out of conviction rather than perceived necessity. Horvath and Szakolczai characterize the basic tension of the communist system as a tension "between fear and faith" rather than "repression and fear." They, like others, note that "communism dissolved itself when its failure, its absurdity, became obvious even to the crucial sections of the party" (Horvath and Szakolczai 1992: 212–13). Their provocative analysis does not apply fully to the Romanian case; anti-Ceausescuism and anticommunism were not equated by many who retained their former positions.

7. Job dissatisfaction did not imply that workers were free to seek other places of work. Internal passports also disciplined the movement and behavior of the work force. Unskilled workers possessed greater freedom of movement. To escape, some workers "dropped out," joining seasonal migrant laborers to earn a living.

8. Kundera 1995: 24.

9. This is part of Vaclav Havel's greengrocer's dilemma mentioned in the introduction: Why place the communist slogan in the shop window? See Havel 1985. On collaboration, see Sampson 1990: 1–10, or the Czech *lustration* case involving Jan Kavan, in Weschler 1992.

10. Kundera 1995: 24.

11. The use of threats is a classic tactic among the annals of torture worldwide; Romanians are not distinctive in this regard. The use of conditional verbs left the listener to battle with the demons of uncertainty.

12. J. Gross 1988: 233–34.

13. It is generally believed that solidarity in the upper ranks of the Securitate had been ruptured and that this played an important role in the events of December 1989.

14. See Scott 1990: 140–54, on gossip, rumors, and the role of anonymity. Although gossip, jokes, and rumors form part of the weaponry of the powerless in regimes with propaganda apparatuses, those very weapons are also wielded by those in power to their own ends. This, in part, complicates any analysis of the arts of resistance that were practiced up, down, and across the political hierarchy. On rumors in Romania, see Sampson 1984b.

15. Some prominent party and secret police members claim that political resistance was also being plotted at that time, although this has not been reliably substantiated.

16. Sayer (1994: 377) emphasizes: "The hegemony of the state is also exactly what is most fragile about the state, precisely because it does depend on people living what they much of the time know to be a lie."

17. The people of Timisoara are surely heroes in the downfall of the Ceausescus. Would those of Bucharest have had the courage to carry on without the fateful shedding of blood in Timisoara? The events of December 16–25, 1989, remain shrouded in unresolved mysteries. Coup, popular uprising, or revolution? See, among others, Ratesh 1993, and Verdery and Kligman 1992.

Twenty-four hours had elapsed from the time Ceausescu faltered in his televised speech to an alienated nation during an official mass gathering to the time the helicopter removed him from the Central Committee Building forever. In a previous article, I noted that Romanians exclaimed that they had accomplished in ten days what had taken the Poles ten years. The ten days began with the spark of bullets in Timisoara and ended with the execution of the Ceausescus by firing squad (see Kligman 1990: 395).

18. Solzhenitsyn 1974. I thank Stelian Tanase who, during a discussion about Havel's related *Power of the Powerless*, recalled this earlier speech.

19. This apt phrase was coined by Jowitt (1992: 269–83).

20. Elena Ceausescu in her final hours ranted to her executioners that she had been a mother to them. The military trial legitimated murder under the guise of justice; the road to democracy was blood-stained.

21. See, for example, Levy-Simon 1988; Goldberg and Kremen 1990; Northrop 1990; Dabelko and Sheak 1992; Mutari, Aslanbeigui, Pressman, and Summerfield 1996.

22. Privilege constitutes the basis for generosity as well as meanness of spirit. Ironically, those who champion the abstract rights of the fetus do so in a socially

and discursively constructed world that simply does not exist. The radical right's failure to accept "empirical reality" (regarding family values and anti-abortion politics) makes them the strange, and undoubtedly reluctant, bedfellows of postmodernism!

23. The Catholic Church historically has attempted to influence fertility behavior, and in this century has utilized its political clout among governments to further its interests.

24. David 1994: 346.

25. Fertility regulation has often been harnessed to nationalism and patriotism. The list of examples is diverse and spans the political spectrum from dictatorships to democracies. For illustrative purposes, see Parker et al. 1992; also see Grossmann 1995.

26. Sen 1994: 71.

27. On the underground provision of illegal abortion in the United States, see, for example, Kaplan 1995; also see Joffe 1995. On birth control practices in general, see Gordon 1977.

28. An analysis of poverty and the poor as signifying practices of the late twentieth century and the dynamics of global economic restructuring would be provocative. It is not accidental that welfare reform is on the political agenda of almost all industrialized (and post-industrialized) states. The concomitant assumptions about women's roles in society reinvigorate classic feminist arguments about patriarchy.

29. The studies on abortion are too numerous to cite. See especially Petchesky 1990: 141–204; Luker 1984; Tribe 1990; Joffe 1995; Kaplan 1995.

30. See, for example, Glenn 1992.

31. These same social conditions are then used to justify the stratification of reproduction, such that poor women who may have been forced into pregnancy are then forced into giving up their babies to wealthier families.

32. I thank Susan Gal for this point.

33. Male homosexuality constrains men's citizenship rights and participation to varying degrees and serves to underscore the basic point about patriarchal control over fertility and sexuality developed in the text.

34. On the latter, see, for example, Pateman 1988 and 1989; Phillips 1991; Eisenstein 1993.

35. Historically, institutionalized practices have protected men. For example, in Italy, the Roman Catholic Church played a crucial role in what was another human tragedy, orchestrated through the involvement of many: "By the beginning of the nineteenth century . . . unmarried women who were pregnant were forced by Church and state officials to deliver their babies to foundling homes established for this purpose. . . . The system was designed by and offered special protections for men—ensuring that they would bear little or no responsibility for the children they sired out of wedlock—but it regulated and punished primarily women" (Kertzer 1993: 2).

36. If the woman carried the pregnancy to term, the man's criminal act would be recognized by virtue of the child's "paternal" history. (Indeed, Speaker of the U.S. House of Representatives Newt Gingrich proposed that pregnancies resulting from rape should be brought to term, but that the man should be criminally punished.) The right to an abortion resulting from rape does not acknowledge the personhood either of the woman violated or of the child.

37. It is only in the late twentieth century that date rape and marital rape have been recognized as unacceptable male behavior.

38. This discussion does not permit a full examination of the complicated relationship between virility and masculinity. For example, Western European and American middle-class notions of virility are linked to issues of male self-control. Self-control, in turn, grants men sexual access to their wives in exchange for socioeconomic protection. Although notions of virility and masculinity are class-differentiated, the general point stands.

39. Patriarchal control of female sexuality in the private sphere is mirrored in the public sphere through the commercialization of sex and sexuality.

40. Attempts to force "deadbeat dads" to support their offspring, for example, have increased, although enforcement is difficult. Policy makers interested in reforming welfare are coming to recognize that teen pregnancies often result from abuse by older men. The age difference is suggestive with respect to relations of power and knowledge. It is yet another example of the lack of male accountability (see Navarro 1996: 1). Lack of male responsibility is also reflected in the realm of modern contraception. Men resist condoms and vasectomies, which can be reversed. The argument that because women get pregnant they must be responsible for contraception turns the rhetoric of sexual and emotional intimacy into a farce of radical individualism that serves male rather than female desire.

41. Clearly, the failure to train physicians to perform abortions, as well as the attempt to violently harass physicians who do perform them, violates these objectives.

42. As Henry David has noted, "public-health-oriented psychologists are realizing that behind all the demographic numbers are people who decide to be sexually active, people who decide to use or not to use contraception, and people who decide to practice responsible reproductive behavior" (David 1994: 348). Also note the discussion of successful educational efforts in Denmark and Holland.

43. I thank Ken Jowitt for reminding me of this point. The unintended consequences of prohibition were varied, among which were increased incidence of death, sickness, and blindness related to the ingredients in moonshine, and the organization of the Mafia with the profits gained from bootleg practices. The war against drugs shares a similar history. However, abortion is not an addiction and should not be treated as such.

44. See especially Madison 1961. The tensions between majorities and minorities, and the privileges of "aristocratic" elites, debated among the Founding Fathers, have come to the fore in the anti-abortion struggle. Women's rights to life and liberty have been increasingly pitted against fetal rights and paternal rights, for example, and independent of factors such as the likelihood of the fetus's and/or mother's survival, infant abandonment, infant addiction, and homelessness.

# SELECT BIBLIOGRAPHY

The citations for articles that appeared in the Romanian press during the Ceausescu regime are given in the notes. Similarly, laws, decrees, and instructions published in the *Buletinul oficial* or the *Monitorul oficial*, for example, are cited in the footnotes. Articles without named authors and diverse Communist Party publications are listed alphabetically at the end of the bibliography.

Abrams, P. 1988. "Notes on the Difficulty of Studying the State (1977)." *Journal of Historical Sociology* 1(1).

Allison, M. 1994. "The Right to Choose: Abortion in France." *Parliamentary Affairs* 47(2).

Alonso, W., and P. Starr. 1987. *The Politics of Numbers*. New York: Russell Sage Foundation.

Alstein, H. 1992. "Rescuing Romania's Orphans." *New York Times*. November 28.

Anderson, B. 1991. *Imagined Communities*. London: Verso.

Asad, T. 1994. "Ethnographic Representation, Statistics, and Modern Power." *Social Research* 61(1): 55–88.

Baban, Adriana. Forthcoming. "Romania." In H. P. David, ed., *Guide to Reproductive Behavior and Public Policies in Central and Eastern Europe: Historical Trends 1945 to the Present*. Westport, Conn.: Greenwood Publishing Group.

Baban, Adriana, and Henry David. 1994. "Voices of Romanian Women: Perceptions of Sexuality, Reproductive Behavior, and Partner Relations during the Ceausescu Era." Washington, D.C., and Bucharest: Transnational Family Research Institute and Centre for Development and Population Activities.

Badea, Iulian. 1987. *Consecintele nefaste ale avortului*. Bucharest: Editura Medicala.

Barbosa, R., and M. Arilha. 1993. "A experiencia brasiliera com o cytotec." *Estudios feministas* 1(2).

Barrett, M. 1988. *Women's Oppression Today*. New York: Verso.

Battiata, M. 1990. "A Ceausescu Legacy: Warehouses for Children." *Washington Post*. June 7.

Behr, E. 1991. *Kiss the Hand You Cannot Bite: The Rise and Fall of the Ceausescus.* London: Hamish Hamilton.

Beldescu, N. 1990. "Nosocomial Transmission of AIDS in Romania." *VI International Conference on AIDS.* San Francisco. Abstract THC 104.

Berelson, Bernard. 1979. "Romania's 1966 Anti-Abortion Decree: The Demographic Experience of the First Decade." *Population Studies* 33(2).

Berelson, Bernard, and Jonathan Lieberson. 1979. "Governmental Efforts to Influence Fertility: The Ethical Issues." *Population and Development Review* 5(4): 581–614.

Berent, Jerzy. 1970. "Causes of Fertility Decline in Eastern Europe and the Soviet Union, Part 1: The Influence of Demographic Factors." *Population Studies* 24(1).

Binder, D. 1990. "Where Fear and Death Went Forth and Multiplied." *New York Times International Edition.* January 24.

Blayo, C. 1991. "Les Modes de Prévention des Naissances en Europe de l'Est." *Population* 3.

Bock, Gisela. 1991. "Antinatalism, Maternity and Paternity in Nationalist Socialist Racism." In Gisela Bock and Pat Thane, eds., *Maternity and Gender Policies: Women and the Rise of the European Welfare States, 1880s–1950s.* London: Routledge.

———. 1989. "Racism and Sexism in Nazi Germany: Motherhood, Compulsory Sterilization, and the State." In R. Bridenthal, A. Grossman, and M. Kaplan, eds., *When Biology Becomes Destiny: Women in Weimar and Nazi Germany.* New York: Monthly Review Press, 271–96.

Boday, J. 1995. "Infant Mortality and Premature Birth." *New York Times.* March 1.

Bohlen, C. 1995. "Catholics Defying an Infallible Church." *New York Times.* November 26.

———. 1990a. "Romania's AIDS Babies: A Legacy of Neglect." *New York Times.* February 8.

———. 1990b. "Fight against AIDS Lags in Romania." *New York Times International,* May 9.

Bourdieu, Pierre. 1992. "Ce que veut dire. L'économie des échanges linguistiques." In P. Bourdieu and L. Wacquant 1992.

———. 1984. *Distinction: A Social Critique of the Judgment of Taste.* Cambridge, Mass.: Harvard University Press.

———. 1977. *Outline of a Theory of Practice.* Cambridge: Cambridge University Press.

Bourdieu, P., and L. Wacquant. 1992. *An Invitation to Reflexive Sociology.* Chicago: University of Chicago Press.

Breslau, K. 1990. "Overplanned Parenthood: Ceausescu's Cruel Law." *Newsweek.* January 22.

Brucan, Silviu. 1992. *Generatia irosita: Memorii.* 2d ed. Bucharest: Universul si Calistrat Hogas.

Bruszt, Laszlo. 1988. "'Without Us but for Us'? Political Orientation in Hungary in the Period of Late Paternalism." *Social Research* 55(1–2).

Buraway, M., and J. Lukacs. 1992. *The Radiant Past: Ideology and Reality in Hungary's Road to Capitalism.* Chicago: University of Chicago Press.

Campeanu, P. 1994. *Romania: Coada Pentru Hrana. Un Mod de Viata.* Bucharest: Litera.

———. 1988. *The Genesis of the Stalinist Social Order.* Armonk, N.Y.: M. E. Sharpe.

Cancea, Paraschiva. 1976. *Miscarea pentru emanciparea femeii in Romania.* Bucharest: Editura Politica.

Cazacu, Honorina. 1991. "Inegalitatea sanselor de acces la invatamant in Romania." *Sociologie romaneasca* 3–4.

———, ed. 1988. *Structura sociala: diversificare, diferentiere, omogenizare.* Bucharest: Editura Academiei Republicii Socialiste Romania.

Ceausescu, Nicolae. 1988. *Rolul familiei in societatea romaneasca.* Bucharest: Editura Politica. Reproduced from: Cuvintare la Plenara largita a Consiliului Sanitar Superior. March 7, 1984.

———. 1986. "Mesajul adresat femeilor din Republica Socialista Romania cu prilejul Zilei internationale a femeii." *Scinteia.* March 8.

———. 1985. "Cuvintare la Conferinta Nationala a Femeilor." March 7.

———. 1984a. Address to the Higher Council on Health, March 7, 1984. Archive no. 495, March 23, 1984.

———. 1984b. "Extrase din cuvintarea tovarasului Nicolae Ceausescu la sedinta Consiliului Sanitar Superior." *Scinteia.* March 8.

———. 1979. *Umanismul socialist.* Bucharest: Editura Politica.

———. 1978. Address to the National Conference of Women. April 21.

———. 1974. "Cuvintare la Conferinta mondiala a populatiei." August 19.

———. 1973a. Address of Comrade Nicolae Ceausescu to the Plenary Session of the Central Committee of the Romanian Communist Party, June 18–19, 1973, with Regard to the Role of Women in the Political, Economic, and Social Life of the Country.

———. 1973b. *Cuvintare cu privire la rolul femeii in viata politica, economica si sociala a tarii.* Bucharest: Editura Politica.

———. 1972a. *Conferinta Nationala a Partidului Comunist Roman.* Bucharest: Editura Politica.

———. 1972b. "Cuvintare la festivitatile organizate la Cluj cu prilejul deschiderii noului an universitar." October 2.

———. 1971. "Largirea orizontului de cunoastere al maselor—conditie a dezvoltarii si perfectionarii continue a democratiei socialiste." *Plenara Comitetului Central al Partidului Comunist Roman,* November 3–5, 1971. Bucharest: Editura Politica.

———. 1969. "Raportul Comitetului Central al Partidului Comunist Roman cu privire la activitatea P.C.R. in perioada dintre Congresul al IX-lea si Congresul al X-lea si sarcinile de viitor ale Partidului." *Congresul al X-lea al Partidului Comunist Roman.* Bucharest: Editura Politica.

———. 1966. "Cuiantarea tovarasului Nicolae Ceausescu la Conferinta Nationala a Femeilor." *Femeia.* 7.

Ceterchi, Ioan, V. D. Zlatescu, and I. M. Copil, eds. 1981. *Drept-Familie-Dezvoltare.* Bucharest.

———. 1974. *Le Droit et la Croissance de la Population en Roumanie.* Bucharest.

Ceterchi, Ioan, V. D. Zlatescu, I. M. Copil, and P. Anca, eds. 1975. *Romanian Legislation on the Population Growth and Its Demographic Effects.* Bucharest: Law and Population Books No. 12.

Chatelot, C. 1995. "Romania's Suffering Children." *Guardian Weekly.* June 25.

Chesnais, Jean-Claude. 1992. *The Demographic Transition: Stages, Patterns and Economic Implications—A Longitudinal Study of 67 Countries Covering the Period 1720–1984.* Oxford: Oxford University Press.

————. 1983. "La durée de la vie dans les pays industrialisés." *La Recherche* 14(147).

Ciobanu, Lina. 1977. "O noua treapta a timpului nostru eroic." *Almanahul Femeia.*

————. 1974a. "Socialist Humanism and the Woman." *Femeia* 11.

————. 1974b. "Prezenta activa a femeilor in efortul creator al poporului." *Femeia* 5.

Ciortoloman, Henriette. 1966. "Consecintele procedurilor abortive." *Sanatatea* 2.

Ciurea Codreanu, Rodica. 1968. *Drama familiei destramate.* Bucharest: Editura Stiintifica.

Clark, Katerina. 1981. *The Soviet Novel: History as Ritual.* Chicago: University of Chicago Press.

Constantinescu, Aurelian, Valentina Negritoiu, and Ecaterina Stativa. 1987. *Pledoarie pentru maternitate.* Bucharest: Editura Medicala.

Costello, C. 1995. "Giving Up My Baby." *New York Times.* November 29.

Croll, E., D. Davin, and P. Kane, eds. 1985. *China's One-Child Family Policy.* New York: St. Martin's Press.

Dabelko, D., and R. Sheak. 1992. "Employment, Subemployment and the Feminization of Poverty." *Sociological Viewpoints* 8: 31–66.

David, H. 1994. "Reproductive Rights and Reproductive Behavior: Clash or Convergence of Private Values and Public Policies?" *American Psychologist* 49(4).

David, H., Z. Dytrych, Z. Matejcek, and V. Schuller, eds. 1988. *Born Unwanted: Developmental Effects of Denied Abortion.* New York: Springer.

David, H., and R. McIntyre. 1981. *Reproductive Behavior: Central and Eastern European Experience.* New York: Springer.

David, H., and N. H. Wright. 1971. "Abortion Legislation: the Romanian Experience." *Studies in Family Planning* 2(10).

de Flers, René. 1984. "Socialism in One Family." *Survey* 28(4).

de Grazia, Victoria. 1992. *How Fascism Ruled Women: Italy, 1922–1945.* Berkeley: University of California Press.

Deliman, Ecaterina. 1977. *Femeia: personalitate politica in societatea noastra socialista.* Bucharest: Editura Politica.

Del Vecchio, A. M. 1991. *How to Adopt from Romania.* Sebastopol, Calif.

Demeny, Paul. 1979. "Population on the World Agenda—1974." In Berelson 1979.

Dempsey, Judy. 1989. "Judy Dempsey Looks at the Problem of Obtaining Exit Documents." *Financial Times.* May 10.

Dikotter, F. 1996. "Throw-away Babies: The Growth of Eugenic Policies and Practices in China." *Times Literary Supplement.* January 12.

Djilas, Milovan. 1958. *Land without Justice.* New York: Harcourt Brace Jovanovich.

Dobbs, Michael. 1990a. "A Ceausescu Legacy: Orphans Abound." *International Herald Tribune.* January 6–7.

————. 1990b. "Children of Tyranny: Ceausescu Raised up a Desperate Generation." *Washington Post National Weekly Edition.* January 15–21.

————. 1990c. "Legacy of Suffering: Ceausescu Ruined Lives with Bizarre Social Planning." *San Jose Mercury News.* January 7.

Donzelot, J. 1979. *The Policing of Families.* New York: Pantheon Books.

Dorobantu, I. 1985. *Educatia pentru sanatate in probleme de demografie.* Bucharest: Editura Medicala.

Durandin, D. 1990. *Nicolae Ceausescu: Verités et Mensonges d'un roi communiste.* Paris: A. Michel.

Eberstadt, N. 1994. "Demographic Shocks after Communism: Eastern Germany, 1989–93." *Population and Development Review* 20(1).

Efron, S. 1994. "Russia Suspends Adoptions by Foreigners." *New York Times.* November 19.

Einhorn, B. 1993. *Cinderella Goes to Market: Citizenship, Gender and Women's Movements in East Central Europe.* London: Verso.

Eisenstein, Zillah. 1993. *The Radical Future of Liberal Feminism.* Boston: Northeastern University Press.

Feher, Ferenc, Agnes Heller, and Gyorgy Markus. 1983. *Dictatorship over Needs.* New York: St. Martin's Press.

Fischer, Mary Ellen. 1989. *Nicolae Ceausescu: A Study in Political Leadership.* Boulder, Colo.: Lynne Rienner.

Foster, George McClelland. 1965. "Peasant Society and the Image of Limited Good." *American Anthropologist* 67: 293–315.

Foucault, Michel. 1991. "Governmentality." In G. Burchell, C. Gordon, and P. Miller, eds., *The Foucault Effect.* Chicago: University of Chicago Press.

———. 1980. *The History of Sexuality.* Vol. 1. New York: Vintage Books.

———. 1979. *Discipline and Punish: The Birth of the Prison.* Translated by Alan Sheridan. New York: Vintage Books.

Gabor, I. 1989. "Second Economy and Socialism: The Hungarian Experience." In E. Feige, ed., *The Underground Economies: Tax Evasion and Information Distortion.* Cambridge: Cambridge University Press.

Gadea, Suzana. 1966. "Raportul Consiliului National al Femeilor din Republica Socialista Romania cu privire la activitatea desfasurata de la ultima conferinta nationala si sarcinile ce revin miscarii de femei in lumina hotaririlor celui de-al IX-lea Congres al Partidului Comunist Roman." *Femeia* 7.

Gal, S. 1994. "Gender in the Post-Socialist Transition: The Abortion Debate in Hungary." *East European Politics and Societies* 8(2).

Galainena, M. 1989. *L'adoption: Voyage au bout d'un désir.* Paris: La découverte.

Georgescu, Vlad. 1985. *Romania: 40 Years (1944–1984).* New York: Praeger.

Ghetau, Vasile. 1991. "Politique pronataliste coercitive, fécondité et avortement en Roumanie." Paper presented at the European Congress of Demography, Paris, October 21–25.

Gillespie, E., and B. Schellhas, eds. 1994. *Contract with America: The Bold Plan by Rep. Newt Gingrich, Rep. Dick Armey and the House Republicans to Change the Nation.* New York: Times Books.

Ginsburg, Faye. 1989. *Contested Lives: The Abortion Debate in an American Community.* Berkeley: University of California Press.

Ginsburg, Faye, and Rayna Rapp. 1991. The Politics of Reproduction. *Annual Review of Anthropology* 20.

———., eds. 1995. *Conceiving the New World Order: The Global Politics of Reproduction.* Berkeley: University of California Press.

Giurescu, Dinu. 1989. *The Razing of Romania's Past.* New York: Preservation Press.

Glenn, Evelyn. 1992. "From Servitude to Service Work: Historical Continuities in the Racial Division of Paid Reproductive Labor." *Signs* 18(1).

Goldberg, G., and E. Kremen, eds. 1990. *The Feminization of Poverty: Only in America?* New York: Praeger.

Goldman, Wendy. 1993. *Women, the State and the Family in the U.S.S.R., 1917–1936.* Cambridge: Cambridge University Press.

Gordon, C., ed. 1980. *Power/Knowledge: Selected Interviews and Other Writings, 1972–1977 by Michel Foucault.* New York: Pantheon.

Gordon, Linda. 1977. *Woman's Body, Woman's Right: Birth Control in America.* New York: Penguin.

Goven, Joanna. 1993. "Gender Politics in Hungary: Autonomy and Antifeminism." In Nanette Funk and Magda Mueller, eds., *Gender Politics and Post Communism: Reflections from Eastern Europe and the Former Soviet Union.* New York: Routledge.

————. 1992. The *Anti-Politics of Anti-Feminism: Gender, State and Civil Society in Hungary, 1949–1992.* Ph.D. diss., University of California at Berkeley.

Graham, L. 1982. *Romania: A Developing Socialist State.* Boulder, Colo.: Westview.

Greenhalgh, S. 1990. "Toward a Political Economy of Fertility: Anthropological Contributions." *Population and Development Review* 16(1).

Greenhalgh, S., and J. Li. 1995. "Engendering Reproductive Policy and Practice in Peasant China: For a Feminist Demography of Reproduction." *Signs* 20(3).

Greenwald, John. 1986. "Mother of the Fatherland: Elena Ceausescu Is a Major Power behind Her Husband's Reign." *Time.* July 14.

Gross, Jan. 1992. "Poland: From Civil Society to Political Nation." In Ivo Banac, ed., *Eastern Europe in Revolution.* Ithaca, N.Y.: Cornell University Press.

————. 1988. *Revolution from Abroad: The Soviet Conquest of Poland's Western Ukraine and Western Belorussia.* Princeton, N.J.: Princeton University Press.

Gross, Peter. 1990. "The Soviet Communist Press Theory—Romanian Style." In Slavko Splichal, John Hochheimer, and Karol Jakubowicz, eds., *Democratization and the Media: An East-West Dialogue.* Ljubljana: Communication and Culture Colloquia.

Grossman, A. 1995. *Reforming Sex: The German Movement for Birth Control and Abortion Reform, 1920–1980.* New York: Oxford University Press.

Hankiss, E. 1990. *East European Alternatives.* Oxford: Clarendon Press.

Haraszti, M. 1978. *A Worker in a Worker's State.* New York: Universe.

Hartmann, B. 1995. *Reproductive Rights and Wrongs: The Global Politics of Population Control.* Boston: South End Press.

Havel, Vaclav. 1990. *The Power of the Powerless: Citizens against the State in Central-Eastern Europe.* Armonk, N.Y.: M. E. Sharpe.

Heinen, Jacqueline, and Anna Matuchniak-Krasuska. 1992. *L'Avortement en Pologne: La croix et la bannière.* Paris: L'Harmattan.

Herman, Edward S., and Noam Chomsky. 1988. *Manufacturing Consent: The Political Economy of the Mass Media.* New York: Pantheon.

Hilts, P. 1990. "W.H.O. Emergency Team Is Sent to Romania to Assess AIDS Cases." *Washington Post.* February 8.

Hodos, G. 1987. *Show Trials: Stalinist Purges in Eastern Europe, 1948–1954.* New York: Praeger.

Hoff, J. 1994. "Comparative Analysis of Abortion in Ireland, Poland, and the United States." *Women's Studies International Forum* 17(6).

Hord, C., H. David, F. Donnay, and M. Wolf. 1991. "Reproductive Health in Romania: Reversing the Ceausescu Legacy." *Studies in Family Planning* 22(4).

Horvath, A., and A. Szakolczai. 1992. *The Dissolution of Communist Power: The Case of Hungary.* London: Routledge.

Huff, D. 1954. *How to Lie with Statistics.* New York: W. W. Norton.

Hundley, T. 1995. "East Europe Death Rate Soars." *San Francisco Examiner.* February 12.

Hunt, K. 1991. "The Romanian Baby Bazaar." *New York Times Magazine.* March 24.

Iliescu, Ion. 1993. *Revolutie si reforma.* Bucharest: Redactia publicatiilor pentru strainatate.

Ioan, Albu. 1988. *Casatoria in dreptul roman.* Cluj-Napoca: Editura Dacia.

Ionescu, Ghita. 1964. *Communism in Rumania, 1944–1962.* Oxford: Oxford University Press.

Ionita, A. 1996. "Those Were the Days." *Romanian Press Review* 1(41). January 29.

Isaacson, Walter. 1992. *Kissinger.* New York: Simon and Schuster.

Istrati, Panait. 1969 [1933]. *Vie d'Adrien Zograffi.* Paris: Gallimard.

Itu, Ion. 1992. *Bancuri din epoca odiosului.* Brasov: Orientul Latin.

Jancar, B. 1978. *Women under Communism.* Baltimore: Johns Hopkins University Press.

Joffe, Carole. 1995. *Doctors of Conscience: The Struggle to Provide Abortion before and after Roe v. Wade.* Boston: Beacon Press.

Jowitt, Kenneth. 1992. *The New World Disorder: The Leninist Extinction.* Berkeley: University of California Press.

———. 1978. *The Leninist Response to National Dependency.* Berkeley: Institute of International Studies.

———. 1971. *Revolutionary Breakthroughs and National Development: The Case of Romania, 1944–1965.* Berkeley: University of California Press.

Kaplan, Laura. 1995. *The Story of Jane: The Legendary Underground Feminist Abortion Service.* New York: Pantheon Books.

Kenez, Peter. 1985. *The Birth of the Propaganda State: Soviet Methods of Mass Mobilization, 1917–1929.* Cambridge: Cambridge University Press.

Kertzer, D. 1993. *Sacrificed for Honor: Italian Infant Abandonment and the Politics of Reproductive Control.* Boston: Beacon Press.

Kertzer, D., and D. Hogan. 1989. *Family, Political Economy, and Demographic Change: The Transformation of Life in Casalecchio, Italy, 1861–1921.* Madison: University of Wisconsin Press.

Kideckel, David. 1993. *The Solitude of Collectivism: Romanian Villagers to the Revolution and Beyond.* Ithaca, N.Y.: Cornell University Press.

Kligman, Gail. 1996. "The Gendering of Identity in Postcommunist Eastern Europe." In V. Bonnell, ed., *Identities in Transition.* Berkeley: Center for Slavic and East European Studies.

———. 1992a. "The Politics of Reproduction in Ceausescu's Romania: A Case Study in Political Culture." *East European Politics and Societies* 6(3).

———. 1992b. "Abortion and International Adoption in Post-Ceausescu Romania." *Feminist Studies* 18(2).

———. 1990. "Reclaiming the Public: A Reflection on Creating Civil Society in Romania." *East European Politics and Societies* 4(3).

———. 1988. *The Wedding of the Dead: Ritual, Poetics, and Popular Culture in Transylvania.* Berkeley: University of California Press.

Klinger, Andras. 1991. "Les politiques familiales en Europe de l'Est." *Population* 3.

Koonz, Claudia. 1987. *Mothers in the Fatherland: Women, the Family, and Nazi Politics.* New York: St. Martin's Press.

Kornai, Janos. 1992. *The Socialist System: The Political Economy of Communism.* Princeton, N.J.: Princeton University Press.

―――. 1986. *Contradictions and Dilemmas: Studies on the Socialist Economy and Society.* Cambridge, Mass.: MIT Press.

Kukutz, Irena, and Katja Havemann. 1990. *Protected Source: Conversations with Monika H. alias Karin Lenz.* Berlin: Basisdruck Verlag.

Kundera, M. 1995. "You're Not in Your Own House, My Dear Fellow." *New York Review of Books.* September 21.

Lampland, Martha. 1995. *The Object of Labor: Commodification in Socialist Hungary.* Chicago: University of Chicago Press.

Lane, C. 1981. *The Rites of Rulers: Ritual in Industrial Society—the Soviet Case.* Cambridge: Cambridge University Press.

Lapidus, Gail. 1978. *Women in Soviet Society.* Berkeley: University of California Press.

―――. 1977. "Sexual Equality in Soviet Policy." In D. Atkinson, A. Dallin, and G. Lapidus, eds., *Women in Russia.* Stanford, Calif.: Stanford University Press.

Lawson, C. 1991. "A Doctor Acts to Heal Romania's Wound of Baby Trafficking." *New York Times.* October 3.

Lazarescu, Dan. 1988. "Etica si deontologia medicala: constiinta profesionala in obiectivul opiniei publice medicale." *Muncitorul Sanitar* 15.

―――. 1987. "Disciplina ca expresie a constiintei profesionale." *Muncitorul Sanitar* 39.

Lefort, Claude. 1986. *The Political Forms of Modern Society: Bureaucracy, Democracy, Totalitarianism.* Cambridge, Mass.: MIT Press.

Lévi-Strauss, C. 1969. *The Elementary Structures of Kinship.* Boston: Beacon Press.

Levy-Simon, B. 1988. "The Feminization of Poverty: A Call for Primary Prevention." *Journal of Primary Prevention* 1 (2).

Lifton, Robert Jay. 1986. *The Nazi Doctors: Medical Killing and the Psychology of Genocide.* New York: Basic Books.

Lippmann, Walter. 1932. *Public Opinion.* London: Allen and Unwin.

Lorch, D. 1995. "Unsafe Abortions Become a Big Problem in Kenya." *New York Times.* June 4.

Luker, K. 1984. *Abortion and the Politics of Motherhood.* Berkeley: University of California Press.

Madison, James. 1961. *The Federalist Papers* No. 10. New York: New American Library.

Magureanu, Virgil. 1979. *Puterea politica: natura si functia sa sociala.* Bucharest: Editura Politica.

Malceolu, E., and D. Iancu. 1989. *Mortalitatea primei copilarii (1–4 ani) 1988.* Bucharest: Centrul de Calcul si Statistica Sanitara.

Marody, M. 1988. "Covert Repressiveness in Polish Society." *Social Research* 55.

Merfea, M. 1991. *Tiganii: Integrarea sociala a romilor.* Brasov: Barsa.

Mezei, Smaranda. 1994. "Régulation politique et comportement démographique en Roumanie." *Les modes de régulation de la réproduction humaine: Incidences sur la fécondité et la santé.* Proceedings of the Colloque international de Delphes, October 6–10, 1992, no. 6. Paris: Presses Universitaires de France.

―――. 1993a. "Policy Regulation and Demographic Behaviour. Romanian Population Policy and Its Consequences." *Referate zum deutsch-französischen Arbeitstreffen auf dem Gebiet der Demographie vom 18. bis 21. Mai 1992 in Bingen.* Wiesbaden: Bundesinstitut für Bevölkerungsforschung.

———. 1993b. "Famille en Roumanie. Bref aperçu historique. Problématique pour une recherche action." *Cahiers de l'institut de l'enfance et de la Famille*, no.1. Paris.

———. 1991a. "Une analyse démosociologique des conséquences de la politique démographique roumaine." Unpublished paper.

———. 1991b. "L'Odysée de la famille roumaine." *Revue française des affaires sociales*, no. 2, April–June.

———. n.d. "Famille roumaine et transition vers un autre système social." Unpublished paper.

Mihailescu, I. 1987. "Consolidarea coeziunii familiale si rata divortialitatii." *Viitorul social* 6.

Mill, John Stuart, and Harriet Taylor. 1870. *The Subjection of Women.* New York: Appleton.

Miller, P. 1993. *The Worst of Times: Illegal Abortion—Survivors, Practitioners, Coroners, Cops, and Children of Women Who Died Talk about Its Horrors.* New York: Harper Perennial.

Milosz, C. 1990. *The Captive Mind.* New York: Vintage.

Mincu, Iulian. 1982. *Notiuni elementare de alimentatie rationala.* Bucharest: Editura Medicala.

———. 1978. *Alimentatia rationala a omului sanatos.* Bucharest: Editura Medicala.

Mincu, Iulian, and Dorina Boboia. 1975. *Alimentatia rationala a omului sanatos si bolnav.* Bucharest: Editura Medicala.

Mincu, Iulian, Natalia Mihalache, and Dan Cheta. 1985. *Elemente de biochimie si fiziologie a nutritiei.* Bucharest: Editura Medicala.

Mincu, Mioara. 1988. *Sfatul premarital.* Bucharest: Editura C.S.A.M.B.

Mitchell, Juliet. 1974. *Psychoanalysis and Feminism.* New York: Vintage Books.

Mitscherlich, Alexander. 1949. *Doctors of Infamy.* New York: H. Schuman.

Moeller, Robert. 1993. *Protecting Motherhood: Women and the Family in the Politics of Postwar West Germany.* Berkeley: University of California Press.

Molyneux, M. 1982. "Socialist Societies Old and New: Progress towards Women's Emancipation?" *Monthly Review* 3: 56–100.

Moskoff, W. 1980. "Pronatalist Policies in Romania." *Economic Development and Cultural Change* 28(3).

Muresan, Cornelia. 1996. "L'évolution démographique en Roumanie: tendances passées (1948–1994) et perspectives d'avenir (1995–2030)." *Population* 4–5: 813–44.

Muresan, Petre, I. Caniola, I. Copil, E. Malceolu, R. Paraschivescu, B. Pascu, C. Prisacaru, L. Roznatovschi, and D. Segal. 1977. *Studiu longitudinal al fertilitatii in R.S. Romania. Rezultatele anchetei din 1974/1975 comparativ cu ancheta din 1967/1968, pe acelasi lot de femei 15–49 ani aflate la prima casatorie.* Bucharest: Ministerul Sanatatii, Centrul de Calcul si Statistica Sanitara.

Murphy, D. 1995. "Children of Border Divorce: Adopt—A Legal Limbo Strands Slovak Orphans." *Los Angeles Times.* May 17.

Mutari, E., N. Aslanbeigui, S. Pressman, and G. Summerfield, eds. 1996. "Women in the Age of Economic Transformation: Gender Impact of Reform in Post-Socialist and Developing Countries." *Review of Social Economy* 54(2): 267–71.

Nachtwey, J. 1990. "Romania's Lost Children: A Photo Essay." *New York Times Magazine.* June 24.

Navarro, Mircya. 1996. "Teen-Age Mothers Viewed as Abused Prey of Older Men." *New York Times.* May 19.

Newman, K. 1991. "Eastern Europe: Update on Reproductive Rights." *MS* II.

Nicholas, S. 1990. *A Special Report: Children in Romania with Human Immunodeficiency Virus Infection.* March 1990. Draft.

Nicolae, Mihai. 1992. *Istorii paralele: bancuri politice 1965–1985.* Los Angeles.

Northrop, E. 1990. "The Feminization of Poverty: The Demographic Factor and the Composition of Economic Growth." *Journal of Economic Issues* 24(1).

Nydon, J. 1984. *Public Policy and Private Fertility Behavior: The Case of Pronatalist Policy in Socialist Romania.* Ph.D. diss., University of Massachusetts, Amherst.

O'Hanlon, L. 1991. "Tragedy and Trauma of the Bucharest Orphan Trade." *Sunday Times.* June 9.

Olszewski, L. 1991. "Rescued from Hell: How Romania's Lost Children Were Brought Back to Life." *San Francisco Chronicle.* August 4.

Parker, A., M. Russo, D. Sommer, and P. Yaeger, eds. 1992. *Nationalisms and Sexuality.* New York: Routledge.

Pateman, Carole. 1989. *The Disorder of Women: Democracy, Feminism, and Political Theory.* Stanford, Calif.: Stanford University Press.

———. 1988. *The Sexual Contract.* Stanford, Calif.: Stanford University Press.

Parvu, Vasile. 1988. "Factorul demografic si cresterea economica." *Revista economica* 17(21).

Paun, L. 1988. *Infectia cu virusul imunodeficientei umane (HIV).* Bucharest: Ministerul Sanatatii.

Pepel, M. 1994. "Daca nu dai ce trebuie, Comitetul roman pentru adoptii trage de timp." *Adevarul.* May 15.

Perlez, J. 1994. "Britons Sentenced in Romania in Baby Case." *New York Times.* October 19.

———. 1993. "AIDS in Hungary: A Threat That Seems Unreal." *New York Times International.* September 14.

Petchesky, R. 1990. *Abortion and Woman's Choice: The State, Sexuality, and Reproductive Freedom.* Boston: Northeastern University Press.

Peter, L. 1993. "Sida: genocid prin imprudenta?" *GM* 1(61).

Phillips, Ann. 1991. *Engendering Democracy.* University Park: Pennsylvania State University Press.

Pietila, H., and J. Vickers. 1994. *Making Women Matter: The Role of the United Nations.* London: Zed Books.

Pollitt, K. 1995. "Subject to Debate." *The Nation* 260(4).

Popescu, Dumitru. 1993. *Am fost si cioplitor de himere.* Bucharest: Expres.

Pressat, Roland. 1979. "Mesures natalistes et relèvement de la fécondité en Europe de l'Est." *Population* 3.

———. 1967. "La suppression de l'avortement légal en Roumanie." *Population* 6.

Puia, S., B. Marinescu, A. Marineanu, and C. Hortopeanu. n.d. *Impactul somatopsihic al mutilarii postavort complicat la femeile histerectomizate.* Ms.

Radcliffe-Brown, A. R. 1940. "Preface." In M. Fortes and E. E. Evans-Pritchard, eds., *African Political Systems.* Oxford: Oxford University Press.

Ratesh, N. 1993. *Romania: The Entangled Revolution.* Washington, D.C., and New York: CSIS and Praeger.

Rev, Istvan. 1987. "The Advantages of Being Atomized." *Dissent* 34(3).

Rochat, R. 1991. *Women's Health, Family Planning, and Institutionalized Children in Romania.* Washington, D.C.: USAID Report.

Rosca, Ecaterina, and A. Popescu. 1991. "Romania: Comparative Social Indicators." *Transition* 2(8).

———. 1989. *Mortalitatea infantila in R. S. Romania in anul 1988.* Bucharest: Centrul de Calcul si Statistica Sanitara.

Rosca, N. 1988. "Raspunsuri ale forurilor de resort." *Scinteia.* December 11.

Rothman, D., and S. Rothman. 1990. *Romania's Orphans: A Legacy of Repression.* Helsinki Watch. Draft.

Roznatovschi, L. 1989. *Aspecte ale intreruperilor de sarcina in R. S. Romania 1988.* Bucharest: Ministerul Sanatatii, Centrul de Calcul si Statistica Sanitara.

Rueschemeyer, M., and S. Szelenyi. 1989. "Socialist Transformation and Gender Inequality: Women in the GDR and in Hungary." In D. Childs, T. Baylis, and M. Rueschemeyer, eds., *East Germany in Comparative Perspective.* London: Routledge, 81–109.

Sachs, S. 1990. "Romania's Lost Children: Nation Sends Its Unwanted to a Cruel Fate in Asylums." *Newsday.* May 22.

Sampson, Steven. 1990. "Dedublarea, diversiunea si conspiratiea." 22. April 4, 1994: 12.

———. 1987. "The Social Contract in Romania," *Cahiers des Études Roumaines,* no. 5.

———. 1984a. "Muddling through in Romania: Why the Mamaliga Does Not Explode." *International Journal of Rumanian Studies* 4:44–58.

———. 1984b. "Rumours in Socialist Romania." *Survey,* 142–64.

———. 1984c. *National Integration through Socialist Planning: An Anthropological Study of a Romanian New Town.* East European Monograph no. 148. New York: Columbia University Press.

Sandu, Dumitru. 1987. *Dezvoltarea socioteritoriala in Romania.* Bucharest: Editura Academiei Republicii Socialiste Romania.

Sarler, C. 1991. "Shame about the Babies: Why Romania Has to Learn to Care." *Sunday Times Magazine.* January 20.

Sawicki, J. 1991. *Disciplining Foucault.* New York: Routledge.

Sayer, D. 1994. "Everyday Forms of State Formation: Some Dissident Remarks on 'Hegemony.'" In G. Joseph and D. Nugent, eds., *Everyday Forms of State Formation: Revolution and the Negotiation of Rule in Modern Mexico.* Durham, N.C.: Duke University Press.

Scheper-Hughes, Nancy. Forthcoming. "Epidemiology and Demography without Numbers." In D. Kertzer and T. Friche, eds., *Anthropological Demography.* Chicago: University of Chicago Press.

———. 1992. *Death without Weeping: The Violence of Everyday Life in Northeast Brazil.* Berkeley: University of California Press.

———. 1990. "The Theft of Life." *Society* 27(6).

Schneider, Jane, and Peter Schneider. 1996. *The Festival of the Poor: Fertility Decline and the Ideology of Class in Sicily, 1860–1980.* Tucson: University of Arizona Press.

Scott, James. 1990. *Domination and the Arts of Resistance: Hidden Transcripts.* New Haven: Yale University Press.

———. 1985. *Weapons of the Weak: Everyday Forms of Peasant Resistance.* New Haven: Yale University Press.

Sebastian, N. 1987. *Informare privind evolutia mortalitatii materne pe primele 5 luni ale anului 1987, comparativ cu perioada corespunzatoare din anul 1986.* Bucharest: Institute for the Welfare of Mothers, Children and Youth. June 15.

Sen, A. 1994. "Population: Delusion and Reality." *New York Review of Books*. January 22.

Serban, R. 1988. "Preocupare constanta pentru o evolutie demografica sanatoasa." *Scinteia*. August 17.

Serbanescu, F., L. Morris, P. Stupp, and A. Stanescu. 1995. "The Impact of Recent Policy Changes on Fertility, Abortion, and Contraceptive Use in Romania." *Studies in Family Planning* 26(2).

Serbulescu, Andrei. 1991. *Monarhia de drept dialectic: A doua versiune a memoriilor lui Belu Zilber*. Bucharest: Humanitas.

Shafir, Michael. 1985. *Romania: Politics, Economics, and Society*. Boulder, Colo.: Lynne Rienner.

Simecka, M. 1982. *The Restoration of Order: Normalization in Czechoslovakia*. London: Verso.

Solzhenitsyn, A. 1974. "Live Not by Lies." *Washington Post*. February 18. In D. Ravitch and A. Thernstrom, eds., *The Democracy Reader*. New York: Harper Perennial, 1992.

Spornic, Aneta. 1975. *Utilizarea eficienta a resurselor de munca feminine in Romania*. Bucharest: Editura Academiei Republicii Socialiste Romania.

Stacey, J. 1983. *Patriarchy and Socialist Revolution in China*. Berkeley: University of California Press.

Stack, Carol. 1975. *All Our Kin: Strategies for Survival in a Black Community*. New York: Harper and Row.

Stanley, A. 1995. "Nationalism Slows Foreign Adoptions in Russia." *New York Times International*. December 8.

Stefanescu, C. B. 1991. *10 ani de umor negru romanesc: jurnal de bancuri politice*. Bucharest: Metropol-Paideia.

Stephenson, P., M. Wagner, M. Badea, and F. Serbanescu. 1992. Commentary: "The Public Health Consequences of Restricted Induced Abortion—Lessons from Romania." *American Journal of Public Health* 82(10).

Tabah, Leon. 1994. "Les Conférences mondiales sur la population." *Population et Sociétés* 290(2).

Teitelbaum, M. S. 1972. "Fertility Effects of the Abolition of Legal Abortion in Romania." *Population Studies* 26(3).

———. 1967. "La suppression de l'avortement légal en Roumanie." *Population* 6.

Teitelbaum, Michael, and Jay Winter. 1985. *The Fear of Population Decline*. New York: Academic Press.

Teodoru, G. C. 1985. *Efectele secundare ale contraceptiei moderne*. Bucharest: Editura Medicala.

Thom, Françoise. 1987. *La Langue de Bois*. Paris: Julliard.

Tien, H. Y. 1991. *China's Strategic Demographic Initiative*. New York: Praeger.

Tismaneanu, Vladimir. Forthcoming. *Stalinism for All Seasons: The Political History of Romanian Communism*. University of California Press.

———. 1992. *Arheologia Terorii*. Bucharest: Eminescu.

Todd, E. 1990. *La chute finale: Essai sur la décomposition de la sphere soviétique*. Paris: Robert Laffont.

Toranska, Teresa. 1987. *Them: Stalin's Polish Puppets*. New York: Harper and Row.

Trebici, Vladimir. 1991. *Genocid si demografie*. Bucharest: Humanitas.

————. 1988. "Demografia intre stiinta si actiune sociala." *Viitorul Social* 81(1).

————. 1981. "La transition démografique dans les pays de l'Europe de l'Est: Le cas de la Roumanie." *Atti del Seminario su La Transizione Demografica. Interrelazioni Tra Sviluppo Demografico e Sviluppo Economico*, nuovo serie.

————. 1979. "Planificarea familiei in perspectiva sociologica." *Viitorul social* VIII(1).

————. 1975. *Mica enciclopedie de demografie*. Bucharest: Editura Stiintifica si Enciclopedica.

————. 1974. "Fertilitatea si statutul social al femeii." *Viitorul social* III(3).

Trebici, Vladimir, and I. Ghinoiu. 1986. *Demografie si etnografie*. Bucharest: Editura Stiintifica si Enciclopedica.

Trebici, Vladimir, and Ilie Hristache. 1986. *Demografia teritoriala a Romaniei*. Bucharest: Editura Academiei Republicii Socialiste Romania.

Trebici, Vladimir, D. Lemnete, and V. Sahleanu. 1977. "La planification de la famille et la contraception en Roumanie." In *Aspects Sociopolitiques et Démographiques de la Planification Familiale en France, en Hongrie et en Roumanie, Dossiers et Recherches*, no. 2.

Tribe, Laurence. 1990. *Abortion: The Clash of Absolutes*. New York: W. W. Norton.

Trotsky, Leon. 1947. *Stalin*. Translated by Charles Malamuth. London: Hollis and Carter.

Turcu, L. 1991. "The Communist Deception Machine in Romania." In L. Bittman and J. Ost, eds., *Propaganda, Disinformation, Persuasion*. Vol. 4: *Thievery, Deception, and Disinformation in International Affairs—Scientific, Technological and Commercial*.

Verdery, Katherine. 1994. "From Parent-State to Family Patriarchs: Gender and Nation in Contemporary Eastern Europe." *East European Politics and Societies* 8(2).

————. 1991a. *National Ideology under Socialism: Identity and Cultural Politics in Ceausescu's Romania*. Berkeley: University of California Press.

————. 1991b. "Theorizing Socialism: A Prologue to the Transition." *American Ethnologist* 18(3).

————. 1983. *Transylvanian Villagers: Three Centuries of Political, Economic, and Ethnic Change*. Berkeley: University of California Press.

Verdery, Katherine, and Gail Kligman. 1992. "Romania after Ceausescu: Post-Communist Communism?" In Ivo Banac, ed., *Eastern Europe in Revolution*. Ithaca, N.Y.: Cornell University Press.

Viorica, C. 1985. *Starea de sanatate a femeilor din sectorul V de productie al Fabricii de confectii si tricotaje Bucuresti*. Ms.

Voicu, George. 1993. "Discursul nationalist." *Sfera Politicii* 11.

Watkins, S. 1986. "Conclusions." In A. Coale, and S. Watkins, eds. *The Decline of Fertility in Europe*. Princeton, N.J.: Princeton University Press.

Watson, P. 1995. "Explaining Rising Mortality among Men in Eastern Europe." *Social Science and Medicine* 41(7): 923–34.

Wedel, J. 1986. *Private Poland*. New York: Facts on File.

Weschler, L. 1992. "The Velvet Purge: The Trials of Jan Kavan." *New Yorker*. October 19.

Winnicott, D. 1965. *The Maturational Processes and the Facilitating Environment*. New York: International Universities Press.

Wright, N. 1975. "Restricting Legal Abortion: Some Maternal and Child Health Effects in Romania." *American Journal of Obstetrics and Gynecology* 121(2).

Zagorin, P. 1990. *Ways of Lying: Dissimulation, Persecution, and Conformity in Early Modern Europe.* Cambridge, Mass.: Harvard University Press.

Zamfir, Elena, and Catalin Zamfir. 1993. *Tiganii intre ignorare si ingrijorare.* Bucharest: Alternative.

Zielinska, E. 1993. "Recent Trends in Abortion Legislation in Eastern Europe, with Particular Reference to Poland." *Criminal Law Forum* 4(1).

Zlatescu, Victor Dan. 1982. "La politique de la population en Roumanie: l'impératif de croissance démographique et ses moyens de réalisation." *Natalité et Politiques de Population en France et en Europe de l'Est,* Institut National d'Études Démographiques, Travaux et Documents, no. 98. Paris: Presses Universitaires de France.

Zlatescu, Victor Dan, and I. M. Copil, eds. 1984. *Population et législation: Modèles et programmes populationnels en Roumanie.* Bucharest: U.N. and National Demographic Commission.


## AUTHORS NOT SPECIFIED

"Abortion: A Privilege?" 1982. *Connexions: An International Women's Quarterly.* 5. Translated from *Sozialistisches Osteuropakomitee,* August 1979.

"Abortion: One Romania Is Enough." 1995. *The Lancet* 345(8943). January 21.

"Abortions in Romania Outpace Births by 3-to-1." 1991. *Register Guard.* May 13.

*Anuarul statistic al Romaniei.* Various Years. Bucharest: Comisia Nationala pentru Statistica.

*Aspects sociopolitiques et démographiques de la planification familiale en France, en Hongrie et en Roumanie.* 1977. *Dossiers et Recherches* No. 2. Paris: Institut National d'Études Démographiques.

"Boom in the Baby Trade." 1988. *Economist.* January 16.

*Breviarul statistic sanitar 1989.* 1990. Bucharest: Centrul de calcul si statistica sanitara.

*Buletinul oficial al Republicii Socialiste Romania.*

*Cartea alba a Securitatii.* 1996. Bucharest: Editura S.R.I.

*Causes of Institutionalization of Romanian Children in Leagane and Sectii de Distrofici.* 1991. Bucharest: Ministry of Health, Institute for Mother and Child Care, and UN Children's Fund.

*Comunicarea Cancelariei C.C. al P.C.R.* 1973. No.1635/1603, April 9, and No. 2810/2762, June 6, Arhiva MAN.

*Conventia O.N.U. cu privire la drepturile copilului-stadiul aplicarii in Romania.* 1994. Bucharest: Departamentul Informatiilor Publice. Buletin 4.

*Decisions of the Commission for Health, Labor, Social Security, and Environmental Protection of the Grand National Assembly.* 1987. Bucharest. Normal session.

*Dictionarul explicativ al limbii romane,* DEX. 1975. Bucharest: Editura Academiei Republicii Socialiste Romania.

*Digest of General Laws of Romania.* 1987. Bucharest: Editura Stiintifica si Enciclopedica.

Directivele Congresului al XI-lea al Partidului Comunist Roman cu privire la planul cincinal 1976–1980 si liniile directoare ale dezvoltarii economico-sociale a Romaniei pentru perioda 1981–1990. 1975. *Congresul al XI-lea al Partidului Comunist Roman.* November 25–28, 1974. Bucharest: Editura Politica.

*Enciclopedia Romaniei.* 1943. Vol. 4. *Economia nationala: circulatie, distributie si consum.* Bucharest: Imprimeria Nationala.

*Engageons-nous pour les enfants roumains; Grija pentru copiii nostri; The Care of Romanian Children.* Bucharest: Romanian Information Clearing House.

Helsinki Watch. 1991. *Since the Revolution: Human Rights in Romania.* New York: Helsinki Watch.

———. 1990. *Romania's Orphans: A Legacy of Repression.* New York: Helsinki Watch, December 27.

"Hotarirea C.C. al P.C.R. cu privire la reabilitarea unor activisti de partid." 1968. *Plenara Comitetului Central al P.C.R. din 22–25 aprilie 1968.* Bucharest: Editura Politica.

Hotarirea Comitetului Politic Executiv al C.C. al P.C.R. cu privire la cresterea raspunderii organelor si organizatiilor de partid, organelor de stat si cadrelor medicosanitare in infaptuirea politicii demografice si asigurarea unui spor corespunzator al populatiei. 1984. *Scinteia.* March 3.

Hotarirea Plenarei C.C. al P.C.R. din 18–19 iunie 1973 cu privire la cresterea rolului femeii in viata economica, politica si sociala a tarii. 1973. Bucharest: Editura Politica.

*Lifting the Last Curtain: A Report on Domestic Violence in Romania.* 1995. Minnesota Advocates for Human Rights Report. February.

*Meeting of the Executive Committee of the Central Committee of the R.C.P.*, 1974. Bucharest: July 3. No. 930. Vol. 1.

*Monitorul oficial al Romaniei.* 1995.

*Mortalitatea infantila in R. S. Romania in anul 1988.* 1989. Bucharest: Centrul de calcul si statistica sanitara.

*Mortalitatea infantila si materna in lume si in Romania.* 1995. Bucharest: Ministerul Sanatatii.

*Normele de organizare si functionare a Consiliului National, a comitetelor si comisiilor femeilor.* 1979. Bucharest.

*Patterns of Fertility in Low Fertility Settings.* 1992. New York: United Nations.

*The Population of Romania.* 1974. Bucharest: National Demographic Commission.

*Prevenirea mortalitatii materne in Romania. O analiza a asistentei medicale materne si a mortalitatii materne cu recomandari pentru un program de maternitate fara riscuri in Romania. August 1993.* 1993. Ministerul Sanatatii din Romania, Directia Generala pentru Programe si Reforme, Directia pentru Asistenta Mamei si Copilului, Institutul pentru Ocrotirea Mamei si Copilului, Fondul Natiunilor Unite pentru Copii, Organizatia Mondiala a Sanatatii.

*Principalele obiective si masuri tehnico-organizatorice de ocrotire a sanatatii in anul 1988.* 1988. Bucharest: Ministerul Sanatatii.

"Protection and Education of Disadvantaged Children." N.d. *Fact Sheet.* Bucharest: Ministry of Foreign Affairs of Romania, Press Division.

*Raport cu privire la cauzele care au determinat scaderea sporului natural al populatiei si masurile ce se impun a fi luate de Consiliul Sanitar Superior, Ministerul Sanatatii si Comisia Nationala de Demografie, in vederea imbunatatirii indicatorilor demografici.* March 6, 1984. Bucharest: Inventory no. 495, March 23, 1984. State archives.

*Recensamantul populatiei si locuintelor din 7 Ianuarie 1992.* 1994. *Vol. 1. Populatiestructura demografica.* Bucharest.

*Record of the Executive Committee Meeting of the National Women's Council.* 1974. Bucharest: April 26. Archival Inventory no. 1047, p. 10.

*Record of the Plenary Session of the Central Committee of the Romanian Communist Party.* 1967. Bucharest: October 5–6.

*Regulament-cadru privind organizarea, functionarea si continutul activitatii cluburilor "Femina."* 1984. Bucharest.

*Rolul femeii in viata economica, politica si sociala a Romaniei socialiste.* 1973. *Documente ale Partidului Comunist Roman.* Bucharest: Editura Politica.

*Romania: Infierea de copii romani de catre cetateni straini.* 1991. Bucharest: Défense des Enfants-International and Service Social International, April.

*Romanian National Nutrition Survey, 1991.* 1993. UNICEF, Romania; Ministry of Health; CDC; and PAMM (Program against Micronutrient Malnutrition). October.

*Reproductive Health Survey, Romania 1993.* 1995. Bucharest: Institute for Mother and Child Health Care; Atlanta: Centers for Disease Control and Prevention.

*Situatia copilului si a familiei in Romania.* 1995. Coordinated by E. Zamfir and prepared by the National Committee for the Protection of Children, the Romanian government, and UNICEF. Bucharest: Editura Alternative.

*Situation de l'infection HIV-SIDA dans le monde et en Roumanie.* 1995. Bucharest: Ministry of Health.

*Starea de sanatate a populatiei din Romania.* 1991. Bucharest: Ministry of Health Report to the Chamber of Deputies. July 5.

*Studi asupra cauzelor care influenteaza fertilitatea populatiei feminine.* 1987. Bucharest: Ministerul Sanatatii.

*Throughout the World—1989.* 1990. Washington, D.C.: U.S. Department of Health and Human Services Research Report No. 62. May.

*Women and Communism: Selections from the Writings of Marx, Engels, Lenin, Stalin.* 1950. London: Lawrence and Wishart.

*Women's Health, Family Planning, and Institutionalized Children in Romania.* 1991. USAID: Trust through Health, Romania Site Visit.

*World Abortion Policies.* 1994. UN Department of Economic and Social Information and Policy Analysis. May 24.

*World Bank Country Study: Romania. Accelerating the Transition: Human Resource Strategies for the 1990s.* 1990. Washington, D.C.: World Bank.

*World Bank Country Study: Romania: Human Resources and the Transition to a Market Economy.* 1992. Washington, D.C.: World Bank.

# INDEX

Abortion: age correlations, 211, 212; age limits, 61, 68, 282n81, 315n13; China, 259–60n1, 288–89n9; importance of legal protection, 245–46; incomplete, 56, 63–64, 208, 211; induced, 46, 56, 63, 157–58, 208–17; international comparative statistics, 209; legal, under political demographic policies, 54–56, 61, 68, 158, 208, 209, 211, 282n81, 308n28, 315n13; post-Ceausescu period, 18, 157, 214–16, 237–38, 243, 307n20; pre-Ceausescu liberalization, 24, 44, 47–49, 52, 120, 268n26; propaganda, 125, 12627, 142, 213; reduced provider availability in United States, 248, 330n41; reliance on, 1, 216–17, 238, 260n2, 326n111, 327; Soviet policies, 47, 48, 53, 277n23, 278n26, 278n31; spontaneous, 56, 101, 149, 163, 180, 186, 192–93, 201, 203, 211; statistics distortion, 95–96, 159, 208, 210–11; therapeutic, 158, 159, 192; tourism, 1–2, 7, 248, 260n3, 262n33; traditional attitudes, 45–46; U.S. policies, 247, 248–49, 279n46, 289n11, 328–29n22, 329n36, 330n44. *See also* Abortion, illegal; Anti-abortion legislation

Abortion, illegal: classification of, 56; complications, 211–12, 316n16; and Decree 770, 56; and economic crisis, 7–8; health professionals on, 157–60; medical problems caused by, 158, 217, 317n33; methods, 56, 66, 196, 280n54, 281n75, 308n24, 313n72, 313n81; and midwives, 46, 309n35; non-health professionals, 157–58, 160–61, 307n22; persistence of, 6–7, 206, 245–46; post-Ceausescu period, 157, 238, 307n20; pre-Ceausescu period, 23, 47; reliance on, 1, 243–44, 260n2; Soviet Union, 48, 53; women's personal stories, 183–88, 189–93, 194–97, 200–201, 202–5, 253–56. *See also* Case histories; Maternal mortality; Political demographic policies; Resistance by health professionals

Adoption, international, 17–18, 229–36, 307n21; during Ceausescu regime, 229–30; and child illness, 324–25n96; and child institutionalization, 233; and class differences, 8, 18, 231, 247, 329n31; coercion in, 232–33, 324nn94–95; and economic crisis, 302n66; former Soviet Union, 325n98; Law 47/1993, 234; Law 48/1991, 233–34, 325nn99–101; media role, 230, 234–36, 326nn105–6; National Adoption Committee, 230–31, 233; and Roma, 230, 323–24n85; statistics, 229, 234, 235, 323n78, 323nn80–81, 325n102

AIDS, 17, 206, 221–24; and adoption, 324–25n96; and blood donation, 221, 222, 320n50; and health/sexual education,

Compositor: Prestige Typography
Text: 10/12 Baskerville
Display: Baskerville

CPSIA information can be obtained
at www.ICGtesting.com
Printed in the USA
LVHW051345060119
602927LV00003B/467/P

9 780520 210752